AF710020

RESEARCH IN
ASIAN ECONOMIC STUDIES

Volume 1 • 1988
Part A

ASIAN INDUSTRIALIZATION:
CHANGING ECONOMIC STRUCTURES

CONSULTING EDITORS

Robert E. Baldwin

H. Peter Gray

Richard Hooley

Richard F. Kosobud

Lawrence B. Krause

John M. Letiche

Kanta Marwah

James Reidel

Kazuo Sato

Gary R. Saxonhouse

Anthony M. Tang

Jang H. Yoo

RESEARCH IN ASIAN ECONOMIC STUDIES

A Research Annual

ASIAN INDUSTRIALIZATION: CHANGING ECONOMIC STRUCTURES

Editor: M. DUTTA
Department of Economics
Rutgers University

VOLUME 1 • 1988
PART A

JAI PRESS INC.

Greenwich, Connecticut *London, England*

Copyright © by JAI PRESS INC.
55 Old Post Road, No. 2
Greenwich, Connecticut 06830

JAI PRESS LTD.
3 Henrietta Street
London WC2E 8LU
England

All rights reserved. No part of this publication may be reproduced, stored on a retrieval system, or transmitted in any form or by any means, electronic, mechanical, photocopying, filming, recording, or otherwise, without prior permission in writing from the publisher.

ISBN: 0-89232-987-4
ISBN: 0-89232-986-6 (set)

Manufactured in the United States of America

TO

Manu/

Pappu/

Basu

CONTENTS

PART A

SECTION IV. ASIAN NIC'S & ASEAN: INVESTMENT PATTERNS/MANUFACTURING PRODUCTIVITY

LIST OF CONTRIBUTORS

Dong-Se Cha	The ILHAE Institute Seoul
Win-Lin Chou	Department of Economics The Chinese University of Hong Kong
Jean-Pierre Dumas	Asian Development Bank Manila
M. Dutta	Department of Economics Rutgers University
Richard Hooley	Department of Economics University of Pittsburgh
Duk-Choong Kim	College of Commerce Sogang University, Seoul
Chung H. Lee	Department of Economics University of Hawaii
Insup Lee	Department of Business Administration University of Delaware
Kuo-shu Liang	Chang Hwa Commercial Bank Ltd. Taipei
Ching-ing Hou Liang	National Chengchi University Taipei

Ching-yuan Lin — International Monetary Fund
Washington, D.C.

Steven A. Y. Lin — Department of Economics
Southern Illinois University

T. B. Lin — New Asia College
The Chinese University of Hong Kong

Kin-Chok Mun — Faculty of Business Administration
The Chinese University of Hong Kong

Seiji Naya — Resources Systems Institute
University of Hawaii

Sukanto Reksohadiprodo — Faculty of Economics
Gadjah Mada University
Bulaksumur, Indonesia

Elbert Y. C. Shih — Department of Accounting and Finance
The Chinese University of Hong Kong

Leonard Silk — The Economics Columnist
The New York Times

Andrew Stern — Department of Economics
California State University, Long Beach

Daniel Tantum — Department of Economics—
Baruch College
The City University of New York

Chyau Tuan — Department of General Business and
Personnel Management
The Chinese University of Hong Kong

PREFACE

Economic development profiles of many Asian countries have recently become increasingly the subject of attention for both academic scholars and economic policymakers in government and corporate sectors in many countries.

Japan is now an acknowledged economic super-power. Will Korea be the second Japan? Taiwan, Hong Kong, and Singapore have made economic histories of their own. If Japan is leading the rest of the world in the present phase of the Industrial Revolution, Korea and India, Walt W. Rostow writes, have been ready with their resources in human capital, especially scientific and engineering skill, for the challenges of historic progression of the industrial revolution. Dwight H. Perkins has referred to China as the new Asian Giant. Staffan B. Linder has written to hail *The Pacific Century*. Is there an Asian economic development paradigm?

In 1981, the United States set a new record in its trade relations with Asia, and crossed "a milestone," when for the first time in its history the United States did more trade on the trans-Pacific routes than on the trans-Atlantic routes, and the trans-Pacific economic exchange continues to grow.

This series, *Research in Asian Economic Studies*, will focus on studies of

Asian economies with special reference to the emerging new pattern of comparative advantages between Asian countries and the United States.

As we progress through the final fifth part of the twentieth century, important changes of parameters have become evident. Ever since World War II, the debates in political forums have centered on the East and the West polarization of the nations of the world. During the same post-war decades, economic discussions generally took place and continue to take place in the context of the North and the South, a bi-polar grouping of the nations of the world—the rich nations in the Northern block and the poor ones in the Southern block. The world in the 1980s and beyond can hardly be viewed in such straightforward polarized divisions. There are strong indicators to point to a progressive development of new regional, multi-polar groupings of nations on the map of the world.

The Northern and the Southern economic groupings resulted in a duopoly-duopsony framework of the world market with the rich nations in one group facing the poor ones in another. Today, the focus appears to be on a new realignment of economic relations among all nations, and economic debates for intra-group cooperation, the North-the North, the South-the South, in the context of an emerging new order of the world economy, is in the offing.

The economies of Asia, especially Japan and East Asian NICs, newly industrializing countries, Korea, Taiwan, Hong Kong and Singapore, have experienced a higher level of industrialization. Members of The Association of South East Asian Nations, (ASEAN), Indonesia, Philippines, Thailand, Malaysia, Singapore (already seen as a member of the NIC group) and Brunei have come to achieve varying degrees of industrial development. India and the nations of South Asia in a recently formed grouping of South Asian Association for Regional Cooperation (SAARC) of India, Bangladesh, Maldives, Nepal, Pakistan, and Sri Lanka, have become a new sub-regional reality, and its industrial potential is well recognized. China's modernization and open economic policy has added a new dimension to the Asian economic reality.

The European Economic Community and its basic oneness, once thought to be only intellectually real, is now very nearly an accomplished fact. The world now watches the unfolding of one unified European Economic Community that began in 1958, and progresses toward 1992. Led by Japan, the Asian economic entity appears to be an approximation to a not-too-distant reality. Each continent on the map of the world has its own regional characteristics, and an economic structure of national economies in each continent of the world may be a more practical approximation to a regional grouping of nations of the world. A continent-based viable group identity for international economic debates may provide an optimal framework for the coming decades.

* * *

In this general context, Asian industrialization is the subject of this present volume. Asian industrialization has resulted in certain structural changes of many Asian economies. This fact has its promises and challenges for the rest of the world. The volume consists of two parts, Part A with 16 chapters in four Sections, and Part B with 17 chapters in its four Sections. In the two parts, it covers a large number of Asian economies—Korea, Taiwan, Hong Kong, the Philippines, Indonesia, Japan, China, India, Bangladesh, Pakistan, Thailand. The volume includes several subject studies with emphasis on economic issues, such as, the role of U.S. multinational corporations, impact of foreign joint ventures on the shareholders' wealth of U.S. corporations, a comparative study of manufacturing productivity in selected Asian economies, Pakistan's agriculture, energy issues and income relationship in Asian NICs, environmental pollution, human capital and international labor migration, comparative financing strategy, interest rate determination pattern in a set of Asian countries, and first family home purchase in Korea explained by the Life-cycle income hypothesis. A general focus on structural changes following industrialization in Asian economies and its impact on United States-Asia economic relations is pervasive.

Section one in Part A consists of three studies on Asian industrialization and its impact on the emerging pattern of the United States-Asia economic relations. In chapter one, Leonard Silk presents an exposition of the changing position of the United States in the world economy. Since World War II, the United States provided the support for the economy of the free world in terms of defense, and monetary and financial stability. Can the United States continue to provide these "international economic public goods" even when the economies of many other nations have vastly grown? Industrialization of Japan and many Asian nations would hardly be possible without these U.S. contributions. The author strongly advocates a new world order of multilateral economic cooperation where all developed nations must work together to provide for all necessary international public goods.

Chapter two presents an investigation of the structural divergence hypothesis following sustained industrialization of Japan and other Asian nations by M. Dutta and Daniel Tantum. The authors argue that the production map of these nations have substantially changed. Changes relate to human and non-human factors that define a well specified production function. The study refers to the comparative roles of management hitherto not emphasized in economic production studies, of government providing for public inputs, of constructive cooperation between the private sector and the government. An attempt, albeit sketchy and preliminary, to construct alternative estimates of incremental human capital output-ratio, paralleling the familiar concept of incremental (physical) capital-output ratio, has also been reported in this paper.

In chapter three, Chung H. Lee and Seiji Naya discuss the process of internationalization of the U.S. service industries and its impact on the economies in the Asian-Pacific basin.

Section II, in chapters 4 through 10, includes seven presentations on the three newly industrializing countries of Asia (Asian NICs)—Korea, Taiwan and Hong

Kong. In chapter four, Duk-choong Kim presents a discourse on Korea's economic development strategy in which the country's government and private business took a very successful collaborative part. In chapter five, Dong-Se Cha's contribution highlights the economic achievements of Korea, and the author argues that Korea is approaching a developed economy regime. In chapter six, Kuo-shu Liang and Ching-ing Hou Liang discuss the state of the economy of Taiwan in the 1980s, and suggest certain policy measures for the future direction of Taiwan's economy. Ching-yuan Lin (since deceased), in chapter seven, analyzes Taiwan's declining investment ratio and the problems its persistent trade surplus with the United States may pose.

In chapter eight, T. B. Lin and Chyau Tuan present a case study of consumer electronics and textile/garment industry in Hong Kong. Mun Kin-chok, in chapter nine, presents an analytic study of American executives' attitude toward the investment climate in Hong Kong. In chapter ten, W. L. Chou and Y. C. Shih analyze the determinants of the Hong Kong-United States trade.

Section III presents two studies on two ASEAN economies, one on the Philippines and another on Indonesia. Jean-Pierre Dumas, in chapter eleven, investigates the role of small and medium level industries in the economic development profile of the Philippines. In chapter twelve, Sukanto Reksohadiprodjo surveys the profile of industrialization in Indonesia.

Section IV includes four studies on investment patterns and manufacturing productivity covering economies in Asian NICs and the ASEAN group. Andrew Stern, in chapter thirteen, presents an economic analysis of U.S. direct investment in manufacturing industries in selected Asian countries. In chapter fourteen, Steven A. Y. Lin discusses the role of U.S. multinationals in the export-led growth of Asian developing economies. In chapter fifteen, Insup Lee reports some interesting research findings regarding the impact of joint ventures in Asian countries on the shareholders' wealth of U.S. corporations. Richard Hooley, in chapter sixteen, presents a comparative study of manufacturing productivity among ASEAN countries and Hong Kong, based on time series data 1970–1980.

Part B, in its four Sections, includes seventeen chapters. Section one has its focus on Japan. In chapter one, Section one, Kazuo Sato and Sheng-yann Lii investigate the market and non-market forces affecting the economic development in the Asia-Pacific arena. The paper takes note of the emerging structural changes in the economies in the region, and argues that the role of non-market factors deserve much closer attention. The authors recommend multilateral/trilateral, certainly not bilateral, cooperation among the trading nations of the region/world. Ken'ichi Odawara, in chapter two, presents a premise that the competition principle in Japanese corporations via-à-vis its labor unions works differently; in Japan, a corporation and its labor union join together in its competition with the rival corporations. The labor union and corporate management relationship in the Western industrial countries is rather antagonistic and it makes the key difference. In chapter three, David Jay Green presents a comparative study of energy and trade policy in Japan and the United States. M. Anne Hill, in chapter four, presents an analytic study of the pattern of investment in human capital in pre-oil shock Japan. In chapter five, Richard Y. P. Joun reports a case study of Japanese investment in Hawaii.

Section two includes two studies on China. In chapter six, Li Jingwen and Fang Hanzhong coauthor a study on China's infrastructure and its role in China's plan for modernization. Chih-Chien Chien, in chapter seven, presents an analysis of China's grain consumption and production, and makes some observations for the future direction in regard to food grain.

Section three consists of two studies on India. In chapter eight, Kanta Marwah and Halldor P. Palsson report an econometric study describing the tracks of the managed exchange rate of the Indian rupee with monetary shocks and external disturbances. Pranab Kumar Chatterjee, in chapter nine, offers a discourse on India's external indebtedness, adding a special discussion on the United States as India's creditor.

Section four consists of five sub-sections: agriculture, environment, energy, human capital/international labor migration, financing mechanisms/interest rate determination.

In chapter ten, Yasmeen Mohiuddin presents a statistical analysis of the employment pattern in the agricultural sector of Pakistan's economy.

In chapter eleven, Richard F. Kosobud, Jnanodoy Bhattacharya, Thomas Daly, Chandan K. Mukhopadyay and Zhang Renze jointly report a study on the global CO_2 environmental problem, and analyze economic pros and cons for Asian cooperation.

Mei-chu W. Hsiao, in chapter twelve, presents an econometric study of the relationship between energy and income in the Asian NICs.

In chapter thirteen, John T. Shieh offers an economic analysis of human capital exchanges between the United States and the Pacific Rim countries.

In chapter fourteen, M. G. Quibria and M. Thant analyze international labor migration with special focus on emigrants' remittances in the context of Asian developing countries.

Masumi Kishi, in chapter fifteen, does a comparative study of strategic financing and market mechanism in the development of the textile industry in Korea and Thailand.

In chapter sixteen, Kanhaya L. Gupta presents a multi-country study relative to interest rate determination in a set of Asian economies.

Bong Joon Yoon, in chapter seventeen, reports an instructive discussion of the life-cycle income approach in the case of the first family home purchase in Korea.

* * *

This volume is based on revised versions of papers [all but one of them] presented at the Third Conference on United States-Asia Economic Relations, sponsored by The American Committee on Asian Economic Studies [ACAES] in cooperation with The Chinese University of Hong Kong, on June 21–25, 1987 in Hong Kong. It is indeed a product of contributions by a large number of individual scholars, and also by many institutions, and we owe them all our sincerest thanks.

- Our very special thanks must go to Dr. Ma Lin, Vice Chancellor of the Chinese University of Hong Kong. Inaugurating the conference, Dr. Ma Lin invited the conferees to take note of the emerging pattern of evergrowing interdependence of the national economies of the world, and face the challenge. In his toast, at a special banquet he hosted in honor of the conferees, Vice Chancellor Ma Lin expressed his hope that in spite of diversities of all sorts—political, cultural, economic—nations of the Asia-Pacific Region will successfully play its common regional role in the world economy.
- Our thanks are also due to Professor Charles Kao, the new Vice Chancellor, and we certainly look forward to a continued programmatic relationship with The Chinese University of Hong Kong, under his leadership.
- The Chinese University of Hong Kong served as the host of the conference, and has earned grateful thanks of all who came to participate in the conference from the United States, from Europe, Canada, and from many Asian countries including Japan, China, India, Korea, Taiwan, Philippines, Indonesia, Bangladesh, and Pakistan.
- The Faculty of Business Administration, The Chinese University of Hong Kong, under the leadership of Dean Y. T. Chung, [now under Dean K. C. Mun] contributed a great deal to the success of the conference, and we record our thankful appreciation for Dean Chung and his distinguished faculty.
- The Conference Host Committee, conisting of Professors Chyau Tuan, (Chairman), Charels F. Steilen (Deputy Chairman), Kam-hon Lee, Victor Mok, Elbert Y. C. Shih (Members), Joseph Law (Secretary) and Yiu-Man Chung (Research Assistant) led the program to be the best that it could be, and they have earned our gratitude.
- Thanks are also due to Rutgers University Council for Asian Economic Research, Department of Economics/Bureau of Economic Research, Rutgers-The State University of New Jersey, for all its helpful cooperation.
- For their generous financial support, we thank Arthur Andersen & Co., Windsor Education Fund of the Winner Co. (Garments) Ltd., Hang Seng Bank Golden Jubilee Education Fund, all in Hong Kong.

We thank

- all our authors whose scholastic contributions made this volume what it is;

- Martha S. Albert, The Chinese University of Hong Kong; Edward Ames, State University of New York-Stony Brook; Peter C. Y. Chow, City University of New York-The City College; Irene H. Chow, The Chinese University of Hong Kong; Edna E. Ehrlich, Federal Reserve Bank of New York; Robert G. Graham, The Chinese University of Hong Kong; Frank T. H. Hsiao, University of Colorado-Boulder; Saleem M. Khan, Bloomsburg University-Pennsylvania; In Kie Kim, Chung Ang University, Korea-Seoul; Woo Bong Lee, Bloomsburg University-Pennsylvania; John M. Letiche, University of California-Berkeley; Reuben Mondejar, Center for Research and Communication, Manila, Philippines; Donald W. Paden, University of Illinois-Urbana; P. K. Rao, Center for Development Research, India-Hyderabad; Rosemary Scanlon, The Port Authority of New York and New Jersey; Michele Schmiegelow and Henrik Schmiegelow, Institute for Asienkunde, University Catholique de Louvair, Belgium; Dean Spinanger, Institute für Weilt-wirtschaft, West Germany-Kiel; Anthony M. Tang, Vanderbilt University, Knoxville-TN; James T. H. Tsao, U.S. International Trade Commission; Dong-Hua Wang, Chung-Hua Institution for Economic Research, Taiwan-Taipei; Jang H. Yoo, Virginia Commonwealth University, Richmond-VA; Kitty Young, The Chinese University of Hong Kong; for their scholastic participation at various sessions of the conference as chairs/discussants/ authors [of papers not completed for inclusion in the present volume].
- Professors Kazuo Sato, Rutgers University; Richard Hooley, University of Pittsburgh; James Riedel, The Johns Hopkins University; Jang H. Yoo, Virginia Commonwealth University; Anthony M. Tang, Vanderbilt University; Edward Lincoln, The Brookings Institution; Richard F. Kosobud, University of Illinois at Chicago; and Chyau Tuan, The Chinese University of Hong Kong, Hong Kong for their distinguished services as members of the Conference Program Committee.
- all members of the Executive Board, The American Committee on Asian Economic Studies [ACAES] for their continuous support for the program.
- Finally, very sincere thanks to Sally Johnson Whelan of JAI Press Inc. who successfully piloted the production/publication of the 1988 volumes.

M. Dutta
Editor

THE AMERICAN COMMITTEE ON ASIAN ECONOMIC STUDIES-EXECUTIVE BOARD

Robert E. Baldwin
University of Wisconsin, Madison

Martin Bronfenbrenner
Duke University

Gregory C. Chow
Princeton University

M. Jan Dutta, *Director*
Rutgers University

H. Peter Gray
Rensselaer Polytechnic Instutite

Richard Hooley, *Associate Director*
University of Pittsburgh

F. Tomasson Januzi
University of Texas, Austin

Lawrence R. Klein
University of Pennsylvania

Richard F. Kosobud
University of Illinois, Chicago

Lawrence B. Krause
University of California, San Diego

Lawrence J. Lau
Stanford University

Chung H. Lee
University of Hawaii, Manoa

Woo Bong Lee
Bloomsburg University

John M. Letiche
University of California, Berkeley

Edward J. Lincoln
The Brookings Institution

Kanta Marwah
Carleton University

James I. Nakamura
Columbia University

Walter C. Neale
University of Tennessee

Gustav F. Papanek
Boston University

Hugh T. Patrick
Columbia University

Dwight H. Perkins
Harvard University

James Riedel, *Treasurer*
The Johns Hopkins University

George Rosen
University of Illinois, Chicago

Vernon W. Ruttan
University of Minnesota

Kazuo Sato, *Associate Director*
Rutgers University

Ryuzo Sato
The New York University

Gary R. Saxonhouse
University of Michigan, Ann Arbor

Joseph J. Stern
Harvard University

Paul P. Streeten
Boston University

Vincent Su
The City University of New York

Anthony M. Tang
Vanderbilt University

James T. H. Tsao
U.S. International Trade Commission

Yien-I Tu
University of Arkansas, Fayetteville

Jang H. Yoo
Virginia Commonwealth University

SECTION I

ASIAN INDUSTRIALIZATION: THE UNITED STATES/ JAPAN AND EAST ASIA

THE UNITED STATES AND THE WORLD ECONOMY: AN ASIAN PERSPECTIVE[1]

Leonard Silk

I. THE CHALLENGE

The development of the Asian economies, spectacular since World War II, has been jeopardized by the severe difficulties experienced by the United States in recent years. The huge deficits in the American trade and balance of payments positions, resulting in a weak and highly volatile dollar, have strained the ability of the United States to prevent a threatened breakdown in the international economic and financial system, in which Japan and the newly industrialized countries of Asia (Asian NICs) now play a crucial role. But their continued economic progress depends on access to the huge American market and to the

Research in Asian Economic Studies.
Asian Industrialization: Changing Economic Structures,
Volume 1, Part A, pages 3–16.
Copyright © 1988 by JAI Press Inc.
All rights of reproduction in any form reserved.
ISBN: 0-89232-987-4

continued growth of the rest of the world. It was the double primacy of the United States in the economic and defense–political spheres that made possible during the post-World War II years the longest spell of economic growth and security that the world has known.

But, after three decades of remarkable prosperity, that phase has now been threatened. Dangers to the system have resulted from the high volatility of exchange rates, huge trade imbalances, and growing protectionism; these have been compounded by the inability of developing countries, particularly in Latin America and Africa, to meet their debt obligations, continuing fears of inflation in the midst of sharp declines in oil and commodity prices, sluggish economic growth in the industrial and developing countries alike, persistent overcapacity and unemployment. Aggravating the strains of clashing national interests are uncertainty and conflict among the major industrial nations over the right policies for solving this complicated set of problems.

If solutions are to be found, the leading industrial nations must reach a common understanding of how to avoid the mistakes that caused the Great Depression and the political disasters that followed from it.

After World War I, and the inflations released by it, the major countries adopted highly restrictive monetary policies, which by the end of the 1920s choked off economic growth. The trend toward deflation was reinforced by countries' mistaken foreign exchange policies. In Britain the pound sterling had fallen to $3.44 in November 1920, but it was restored to its prewar dollar parity of $4.86 when Britain returned to the gold standard in 1925. Britain felt compelled to adopt excessively tight money to hold it there. The results were falling prices, economic slump, rising unemployment, and "the dole." In France, by contrast, the franc was undervalued after the war, and the large inflow of gold and foreign exchange put intense pressure on other countries, including the United States. In the United States restrictive tariff legislation was passed, particularly the 1930 Smoot–Hawley Act, that hurt other countries and forced them to engage in severe deflation to maintain the exchange rates of their respective currencies. The Great Depression stemmed from the post-war boom—and from the deflationary measures some countries adopted to maintain their exchange rates.

Today there are some similarities to that earlier crises, but there are important differences, including exchange-rate flexibility, an awareness of the danger of thrusting the world into a deflationary spiral, a recognition of the destructiveness to the system that unbridled protectionism would bring, and an understanding that the fiscal and monetary policy can be used to stimulate the recovery of a national economy. But, in spite of some intellectual and political progress, divisions persist over how each nation can best pursue its self-interest—whether by holding down inflation and keeping its currency sound or by promoting economic expansions for the system as a whole. After the long post-World War II boom that lasted until the early 1970s and was followed by oil shocks, inflation, and stagnation, the world economy is again suffering from overcapacity and high unemployment. In a closely integrated world it is risky for any single nation, even the largest economy in the world, acting alone, to pursue a strongly stimulative policy without weakening its trade position and its financial structure and without posing a threat to the international economic system.

II. THE U.S. DEBT BURDEN

The threat to the system was intensified by the United States' large and growing "twin" deficits in the federal budget and in foreign trade, and hence by the nation's growing foreign debt and dependence on the massive inflow of capital.

In fiscal year 1986 the U.S. budget deficit reached a record $221 billion, raising the national debt over $2 trillion, double its level in 1981 when President Reagan took office. The reasons for the vast increase in the public debt during the Reagan years are by now all too familiar: (1) the failed theory that so-called supply-side tax cuts would generate such an upsurge of national growth and tax revenues as to provide for expansion in both military and social expenditures, (2) the failed theory (or ideology) that curtailing the growth of federal revenues would force a curtailment of the nonmilitary activities of government (sometimes denominated "the Reagan Revolution"), (3) the rapid military buildup, and (4) the shortfall of revenues resulting from the unexpected and steep recession of 1981–82 and from the overall slow economic growth, with real gross national product increasing at an average rate of only 2.4% per annum during the first 6 years of the Reagan presidency.

Although the budget deficits have been the focus of public and congressional anxiety, the strains on the American economy and the international system have been exacerbated by the less noticed growth of private debt. American business borrowing has grown rapidly, much of it to finance highly leveraged mergers and acquisitions, and so has the borrowing by farmers, real estate investors, and consumers. The total American debt, private and public, has grown to nearly $9 trillion, more than twice its level at the start of the decade. Debt in recent years has grown much faster than the national economy. For two decades before 1982 total debt had held steady at 160% of the rising gross national product (GNP); in the past 4 years the ratio of total debt to GNP has leaped to 200%. This means that large numbers of American business firms and individuals have put themselves in a more difficult position to repay debts if the economy turns down.

The rapid growth in private debts during the 1970s and early 1980s was based on inflationary expectations; borrowers believed that the rising value of the assets they acquired and the declining value of the money they would use to repay their loans would more than justify the high interest rates they had to pay. Lenders and investors took big risks in the belief that inflation would bail out even unsound loans and investments. But the drop in inflation resulting from the sharp recession of 1981–1982, revealed the dangerous overborrowing that had gone on in the inflationary era.

The drop in inflation is doubtless the greatest achievement of the Reagan Administration. It resulted primarily from the restrictive monetary policy pursued by the Federal Reserve under Paul A. Volcker, a policy that the Administration sometimes criticized as the cause of the recession but essentially supported. In 1986 the inflation rate as measured by the rise of consumer prices fell to 1.5%, its lowest rate since 1964, when the Vietnam military buildup was not yet in full sway. But the victory over inflation has been a costly one, and in 1986 the costs of both the inflation and stopping the inflation were still being paid. In the past year many farmers and oil producers were severely hurt or ruined when commodity and oil prices fell. Some 1,500 banks, about 1 out of every 10 in the nation, were on the regulators' list of financially troubled institutions. In 1986 alone, 150 banks failed, more than in any year since the Great Depression. Hundreds of technically insolvent savings and loan institutions were being kept afloat by the regulators who did not want to exhaust the reserves of the Federal Savings and Loan Insurance Corporation.

In spite of anxieties over the weakened financial structure in real estate, agriculture, energy, mining, manufacturing, and banking, the wave of debt creation rolled on in 1986. What kept it rolling were the vast debts incurred, often through so-called junk bonds—high-interest, high-risk bonds—to finance mergers and acquisitions, as well as the debts incurred by corporate managements to fight off hostile mergers or acquisitions. As 1986 drew to a close, the revelation that the well-known arbitrager Ivan F. Boesky had agreed to pay $100 million in settlement of charges in insider trading brought by the Securities and Exchange Commission dealt a shock to Wall Street and the nation.

But "junk bonds" and such defensive devices as "poison pills" and "shark repellants" were only part of the reason total debt in the United States continued to grow rapidly in 1986; the growth was also fed by aggressive lending by financial institutions seeking to achieve a positive spread between their current rate of return and their current cost of money, by the drive of banks and thrift institutions to lend at floating or variable rates, pushing interest-rate risks onto borrowers, and by the interest-rate bargains or "buy downs" offered by auto companies and home builders seeking to make sales in a time of weakening consumer demand. Many businesses, unable to finance repairs, replacements, or current operating costs, increased their debts simply to stay afloat. The drive to expand mortgage credit, much of it on a minimum down-payment basis, brought on a large increase in delinquencies and foreclosures on both homes and commercial properties as real-estate prices declined in many parts of the country, such as Texas and Oklahoma, that were hard hit by the slump in energy and farm prices.

A 1985 study by the New York Stock Exchange concluded that the health of American corporations had been endangered by excessive debt (NY Stock Exchange, 1985). During 1986 nearly 70% of all corporate borrowing was short term; this is an extraordinarily high level. The "quick" ratio (liquid assets as a percentage of short-term corporate liabilities) fell to its lowest postwar level. The "interest coverage" ratio (pretax corporate profits to interest payments) was at a historically low level.

The danger is that if the United States' financial structure has been further weakened by a worsening of the ratio of debt to GNP, the outcome could be an increase in business failures (already at their highest postwar level), particularly if the economy turned down. If, on the other hand, the monetary authorities were to go too far in trying to prevent a downturn, then inflation, high real interest rates, and an overvalued dollar would continue to hurt American competitiveness in world markets.

III. THE INTERDEPENDENT WORLD ECONOMY

The nation's internal and external economic problems are closely connected. The huge and growing public and private borrowing has pushed real interest rates above those in other competing countries. The high interest rates, although essential to attract foreign capital given the inadequacy of saving by Americans, made the U.S. trade deficit worse. The capital inflow, by bidding up the value of the dollar, hurt American exports and import-competing industries, and caused the loss of many American jobs—some estimates run as high as two million—by forcing lay-offs and plant closings at home and shifts of production to foreign locations. The overvaluation of the dollar has not only helped to keep unemployment up but has also augmented the shift of jobs from goods to service industries, and in many cases to lower paid jobs.

There are other factors involved in the job losses and job shifts, including the relatively high level of American wages, the spread of medium- and low-technology industries to other countries (including poor, developing countries), and the failure of American management to modernize as rapidly as their foreign competitors, particularly Japan and the Asian NICs. Added to these problems are the low rate of national savings in the United States, and the high cost and the low return on capital investment in the face of worldwide overcapacity in steel, chemicals, minerals, and other basic industries.

Throughout the world the problems of sluggish economic growth, financial instability, Third World debt, and trade imbalances are interlocked—and lie at the heart of America's problems. As Nobel Laureate Lawrence R. Klein has put it, both the U.S. budget and trade deficits and the related problems of sluggish growth, overcapacity, and unemployment are "endogenous" to the world economic system. It now appears that these problems cannot be solved by the United States alone but must be solved within the context of that wider global system.

The orthodox solution for a nation's problems of insufficient growth, overcapacity, and unemployment—orthodox, that is, since the Keynesian revolution—has been for the government to increase the demand for the goods and services that a nation has the capacity to produce, and hence increase the derived demand for labor (and also for utilization of idle capacity). And the prescription for increasing demand has been to cut taxes, step up government spending, and enlarge the budget deficit. This prescription, crowned by the enormous deficit-financed war effort in World War II, ended the depression of the late 1930s; it has been used, in combination with an accommodative monetary policy, under both Republican and Democratic administrations, in arresting and reversing all the postwar recessions—including the steep recession of 1981–1982. Some economists still consider the Keynesian macroeconomic approach for combating the business cycle the right prescription.

But the huge buildup of budget deficits and total national debt, along with the nation's increased dependence on international capital inflow, makes it difficult and even dangerous, perhaps impossible, for the United States to escape its burden simply by increasing total demand through still greater increases in public or private borrowing. The harvest could be heightened inflationary pressure, a slowing inflow or actual outflow of foreign capital, a decline in investment, a further loss of international competitiveness, more people out of work, and a worsening of protectionism, with ominous implications for the world economy and policy.

What do these new conditions and dangers imply for economic policy? The greatest change required appears to be that the unit of policy thinking must become the world economy rather than the national economy, although this flies in the face of traditional national politics and economic pressures.

National policymakers must be concerned with the wider community of interests, thinking not only about conflicts with adversaries but about mutually supportive relations with allies and trading partners as well. Whether or not the current U.S. Administration is able to tackle the problems facing the world economy, the challenge is of such magnitude that it will be with us for some years.

IV. THE WORLD ECONOMIC LEADERSHIP

Since the end of the Second World War the United States has assumed the leadership of the free world and the primary responsibility for rebuilding and integrating the world economy. But Charles F. Kindleberger (1986), in his presidential address to the American Economic Association in 1985, said the United States has lost its appetite for providing the world with what he called "international economic public goods." These are goods and services that benefit the entire international community but for which individual consumers, businesses, or nations are not necessarily willing or able to pay, such as open markets for the goods of other countries in times of glut, supplies in times of acute shortage, steady flows of capital to developing countries, international money, the coordination of international economic policy, and a willingness to be the lender of last resort in times of financial crisis.

Without a nation strong enough and responsible enough to play the role of leader, the international financial system is in peril. The need for an international lender of last resort, a role played by Great Britian through most of the nineteenth and early twentieth centuries, is greater than ever today with more massive flows of capital and goods, instantaneous communications and shiftability of funds, a plethora of transnational banking and industrial organizations, and the buildup of Third World debt to the trillion dollar level. Unless the United States regains its ability and willingness to sustain nations in danger of default or builds a collective defense with Japan and others (who have continued surpluses in their national accounts with the rest of the world) there could be a financial disaster comparable to those of 1873, 1890, and 1929, or an ever greater one.

One reason for the current danger is that the United States, like Great Britian after 1890, has lost economic power relative to the rest of the world. Although it remains the largest and most important economy in the world, a relative loss of power has been causing the United States to turn inward and focus on its own imperiled interests. "The contraction of concern from the world to the nation," said Kindleberger (1986), "is general, and applies to economists as well as to politicians and the public." Although there had been a recent upsurge of interest in the international dimension, the focus of this interest, he maintained, had been almost exclusively on what the connections mean for U.S. interest rates, trade and industrial policy, growth, and wealth.

Nevertheless, even within these economic constraints and pressures of the American interest groups that feel themselves adversely affected by foreign nations, the Reagan Administration, under the leaderhsip of Treasury Secretary James A. Baker, has been struggling to play the role of leader and (continue to) provide "international economic public goods." The Adminstration has sought open, or at least partially open, markets in a time of gluts; enhanced flows of capital to developing countries in a time of anxiety among banks about their existing overexposure, international money in a time when the dollar is overvalued and the American trade position and balance of payments are extremely weak, and policy coordination among the major industrial countries in a time when other governments, like the United States, are increasingly preoccupied with their own problems and, in some cases, have begun to regard "coordination" as inimical to their national interests. A critical concern for the future is to make sure that the United States, or some groups of nations including the United States, is prepared to play the role of lender of last resort should an international financial crisis develop.

Secretary Baker's difficult task is to advance American interests by pressing other countries to share the responsibilities and burdens of providing international public goods. Since the Plaza meeting of September 11, 1985 of the Group of Five (G-5), at which Japan, West Germany, Great Britian, and France agreed with the United States that the dollar needed to be lowered against their respective currencies, the U.S. Treasury has been pursuing a dollar devaluation policy in order to cut the trade deficit, restrain congressional protectionist pressures, and force monetary support for the United States on Germany and Japan.

The dollar did come down sharply, at least against the German mark and the Japanese yen. But as 1986 wore on, it became less clear whether the U.S. dollar devaluation policy would fit in with the aim of reviving stronger and more stable world economic growth or whether it might even be harmful—particularly if it wound up sending the dollar into a free-fall.

After the middle of the year Japan and West Germany resisted further depreciation of the dollar; Japan feared the loss of export markets and Germany worried about the regeneration of domestic inflation. The United States urged both countries, if they wish to avoid further dollar depreciation against their currencies, to use fiscal and monetary policy, particulary cuts in interest rates, to spur the growth of their domestic economies, to help increase the demand for American exports, and sustain the debt-ridden developing countries.

On the eve of the September 1986 meetings in Washington of the International Monetary Fund (IMF) and the World Bank, a dispute surfaced between Treasury Secretary Baker and Federal Reserve Chairman Volcker over the need for further dollar devaluation. In congressional testimony, Volcker said he thought the dollar had declined enough and that other policy measures were needed to reduce America's trade deficit, but Baker seemed to be threatening further dollar devaluation unless the Japanese, the Germans, and their European partners did more to stimulate their economic growth. Baker's pressure evoked a heated response from the European finance ministers and central bankers, meeting in Gleneagles, Scotland, who warned that, to prevent a further dollar decline, they would intervene in the currency markets. At the IMF meeting in Washington, President Reagan reinforced Treasury Secretary Baker's warning that the dollar would sink further unless the other industrial countries took action to accelerate their growth. But the stalemate continued.

The Europeans insisted that the problem of global imbalance in trade and exchange rates was the United States' fault, a consequence of its huge and continuous budget deficits. They contended that the United States had failed to deliver on its part of the Plaza agreement—bringing down the budget deficit as the Europeans and Japanese accepted the further depreciaiton of the dollar.

President Reagan sought to deflect this criticism by declaring that he would act more strongly than ever to get rid of the budget deficit. "I pledge to you," he declared to the 151 nations assembled at the IMF meeting in Washington, "that I will do all in my power to stop this fiscal death march."

Yet, as the fiscal rhetoric escalated, foreign disbelief that the United States would act to cut its budget deficit deepened; it was believed that the United States was instead trying to put the burden of readjustment on other countries by urging them to reflate their economies and reduce their competitiveness.

The Germans were particularly adamant in refusing to play "locomotive" for the world economy; they maintained that they had taken on that role once before, in response to the blandishments of the Carter Administration, but had weakened their economy in the process and would not do so again.

Chancellor Helmut Kohl and Finance Minister Gerhard Stoltenberg insisted that the German economy was already growing quite fast enough. The president of the Bundesbank, Karl Otto Pohl, resisted American urgings that the German central bank cut its discount rate and step up the growth of money supply, asserting that the money supply was already growing too fast in Germany.

The Japanese were more responsive to Secretary Baker's campaign for greater cooperation in the interests of world economic stability and growth. In late October, Secretary Baker and Finance Minister Kiichi Miyazawa worked out a bilateral agreement stating that action by the key industrial countries was ''critical to promoting world economic growth, reducing imbalances, and resolving international debt problems.'' As part of the accord, the Japanese government agreed to cut the discount rate of its central bank and to submit more stimulative budget to the Diet. But less than 2 months later, on December 25, 1986, the Japanese government approved the smallest spending increase in three decades. ''It is hard to find revenue sources for more public works projects,'' said Miyazawa.

V. MUST THE UNITED STATES LEAD

As the American initiatives vis-à-vis Japan and West Germany demonstrate, the United States in 1986 adopted a policy of ''aggressive bilateralism,'' which was intended to promote its own economic interests, but at the same time to forge coalitions that it hoped would keep the world economy stable and growing. In defending the pressure that the United States was putting on Japan and Germany to expand their economies more rapidly, Secretary Baker insisted that this policy was not aimed primarily at expanding the market for American goods but at preventing a breakdown in the world economy. ''We feel that we are engaged in a life or death struggle here to preserve the world economy,'' he said. And, in the wake of the November congressional elections in which the Democrats gained control of the Senate, Secretary Baker said that the election outcome should prove to the Germans, the Japanese, and America's other trading partners that ''we were not crying wolf'' in warning that a mood of populism, isolationism, and protectionism in the United States posed an increasing danger to the world economy.

The efforts to make bilateral deals with key partners represented a shift from the mutlilateralism that had characterized U.S. international economic policy during the period when it led the way in the construction of the great postwar international economic institutions, including the International Monetary Fund (IMF), the World Bank, and the General Agreement on Tariffs and Trade (GATT). But aggressive bilateralism also marked a shift from the go-it-alone tendencies of the Reagan Administration during its first term, founded on an exaggerated view of America's economic strength. During his first term, President Reagan and his then Treasury Secretary, Donald T. Regan hailed the capital inflow to the United

States as a tremendous vote of confidence in the American economy and regarded the rising dollar as evidence of the nation's vigor and the Administration's successful policies. In the second term, however, with Baker taking over as the Treasury Secretary, dollar machismo gave way to a policy of dollar devaluation. But the policy of dollar devaluation as a means of stabilizing and regenerating world economic growth ran into problems in 1986.

Mainly as a result of the 50% fall in the dollar against the yen, Japan suffered a severe slowdown. Its export industries lost profitability and sales, particularly to its competitors in South Korea. Taiwan, and other newly industrialized countries, which had prevented their currencies from falling significantly against the dollar. (The Asian NICs had their currencies pegged to the U.S. dollar.) The Baker-Miyazawa agreement was achieved because Japan recognized that to safeguard its export markets, it needed to halt further dollar devaluation against the yen. Germany, feeling less threatened by the loss of the American market (a minor part of its export sales) and relatively secure within the European Common Market (in which the bulk of its exports go), rejected the American threat of further dollar devaluation.

Within the U.S. government there were differences of view, particularly between the Federal Reserve on one side and the Treasury and the White House on the other, on how far to push dollar devaluation. The Federal Reserve tended to worry more about inflation and the danger that the dollar would fall out of control and cut off foreign capital inflow, whereas the Treasury and the White House pressed for what were known as "pro-growth" policies, fearing that recession posed a greater danger for the United States and the world economy than inflation. The world could live with inflation, they reasoned—it had done so through the 1970s and early 1980s—but serious recession could trigger a collapse of the world debt structure and bring on deflation and depression.

Another problem troubling policymakers last year was that the U.S. trade deficit continued to worsen in spite of the depreciating dollar and falling oil prices. Most economists thought the widening trade deficit reflected the normal lag in the so-called J-curve. During the initial period after a currency depreciation, according to this theory, import costs rise and export earnings decline as foreign competitors, determined to hold on to market shares, are slow to raise prices. But as their profit margins are squeezed, they do eventually raise prices, causing a drop in their sales as cheaper domestic goods are substituted for imports, and the trade deficit shrinks. Late in 1986 following declines in the trade deficit in August, September, and October, the consensus view of private and official economists was that the J-curve was at the turning point and that 1987 would see a marked improvement in the trade deficit, which would help keep the economy growing. But a huge jump in the trade deficit in November (1986) to a record monthly level of $19.2 billion shook confidence that a more favorable trend had begun.

At best, the improvement in the trade deficit was expected to be slow. Japan and other foreign competitors, in spite of the currency devaluations, were still holding down their export prices in a world suffering from unemployment and overcapacity.

The outlook was for sluggish growth in the world economy to continue, thus limiting the demand for American exports; and other countries had invested heavily in facilities to serve the American market and would not readily give up. Major U.S. trading partners, including Canada, Mexico, and other Latin American countries, had not allowed their currencies to rise much, if at all, against the dollar and were unlikely to increase the demand for American exports. A policy problem facing the United States was whether to press these other countries to accept dollar devaluation against their currencies; but their own unemployment and depressed industries and agriculture implied strong resistence and possibly worse political relations, increasing the risk that further dollar devluation would be counter-productive.

There was further risk that unless the United States moved more decisively to eliminate the budget deficit, the trade deficit would persist anyhow. The United States Trade Representative Clayton K. Yeutter put the problem at the Congressional Summit Conference on World Debt and Trade in New York in early December: "We have contributed mightily to the trade imbalance by allowing our Federal budget deficit to outgrow our total available savings." Warning that Congress might lack the "political patience" to await a trade turnaround, he warned: "We seem poised as a nation to shoot ourselves in the foot just as our trade situation is beginning to improve."

Belief that a more liberal "market-opening" approach might be possible was encouraged by the meeting of the GATT contracting parties at Punta del Este this past fall (1986), launching the Uruguay Round of Multilateral Trade Negotiations. Although the meeting at Punta was more successful than had been expected, it left two major issues unresolved—agriculture and services. Worries remain that it will be a long and hard struggle to contain and reverse protectionist forces.

In the strained world economic environment, many governments will be hesitant to rush into the Uruguay round and commit themselves to an extension of tougher trading rules on agricultural products and other goods and services. The United States itself is in an ambiguous position. In recent years at economic summit conferences and in other forums it has pushed hard for another GATT round; yet it has itself adopted protectionist measures and is resorting to an aggressive bilateralism toward its most important trading partners.

For the world system as a whole, multilateralism offered greater efficiency and equity and the prospect of policy coordination among the industrial countries, and between them and the developing countries. As Sylvia Ostry, Canada's ambassador to multilateral trade negotiations, has argued, coherent development of Secretary Baker's plan for increasing the flow of public and private capital to the developing countries requires not only enhanced cooperation between the IMF and the World Bank but also the contribution of GATT, so that trade in financial services can become a key element in the development process.

During 1986, its first full year in operation, the Baker plan made only slow progress, but enough to show the critical contribution that a coherent multilateral approach can make. A money package supported by the IMF, the World Bank, and commercial banks was quickly put together to help Mexico, which was thrown back into economnic crisis by a severe earthquake, falling oil prices, and government mismanagement.

The most important change introduced by the Baker plan was its stress on growth rather than austerity as the crucial strategy for rescuing the debtor countries. But the Baker plan's critics insisted that whereas this growth strategy represented a significant conceptual advance, it was not supported by enough new money from the industrial countries or by strong enough measures for bringing down interest rates, converting debt to equity and forgiving part of the Third World debt.

The United States, however, is not ready to go much beyond the original Baker plan, feeling strapped for funds to do more and unwilling—perhaps unable—to lean harder on the private banks and international agencies. Some American businessmen, led by James Robinson, chairman of American Express, have been urging Japan to do more to aid the developing countries; indeed, Robinson has proposed that Japan, now the world's largest creditor, launch a "Marshall Plan" for the developing countries. At the start of the new year, Japan, after running a trade surplus in 1986 of nearly $90 billion, announced a multilateral aid program of about $9 billion over 3 years. But neither Japan nor any other country seems ready to shoulder the burden of aid-giver comparable to that which the United States assumed after World War II on behalf of not only its allies but also its wartime enemies, Japan and Germany. Indeed, with memories of the Japanese and German bids for world dominance during World War II still very much alive, there is ambivalence in the United States and other Western countries over how large an international leadership role Japan and Germany should be urged to play. In any case, neither country wants to take on those international responsibilities. Forty years after the war, the United States is still having the leadership role thrust upon it.

VI. THE G-7 AND NEXT

How can the United States best perform that international role?

To do the job in a world in which the line between domestic and international economic policy has been eliminated, the United States must set its own financial affairs in order. This means, first of all, tackling the structural deficit in the federal budget that has aggravated the trade deficit and made the nation so dependent on capital flows from abroad.

How hard and how quickly to hit the budget deficit are both political and economic problems. To hit too hard in the economy's current state, with the economy growing so slowly as to be on the verge of a recession might be to plunge it into the unwanted recession; some economists warn that all-out efforts to reduce the budget deficit would repeat the mistakes of the Hoover Administration and the early Roosevelt Administration, which, in futile efforts to balance the budget, raised tax rates and aggravated the depression.

But to fail to deal with the budget deficit at all might be to worsen foreign and domestic fears about the American debt and the fiscal irresponsibility of its political system, and to heighten the risk that foriegn capital inflow would become a massive capital outflow that would reduce savings available for investment, force up interest rates, and intensify recessionary forces.

The inflow of foreign capital to finance the trade deficit has thus far helped to sustain American living standards by enabling Americans to consume more than they produced. But the cost of amortizing and servicing the growing foreign debt is steadily rising. If the United States is to halt that rise, it must eliminate the deficit in the current account of its balance of payments, and even achieve a surplus that will enable it to repay or at least service its foreign debt.

And how can Japan and the other Asian countries play their role in keeping the international economy stable and growing? In my view, the most important contributions would be these: the trade-surplus countries should open their markets even wider to the goods and services of the deficit countries, including not only the United States but also the developing nations of Latin America, Africa, China, and the rest of Asia; the surplus countries should spur their own domestic economies, as the United States restrains its own, to restore greater balance to the world economy; and those countries that have maintained undervalued currencies against the U.S. dollar should permit them to appreciate. In the case of the richer Asian countries, they should take on more of the burdens of foreign aid loans to the developing world.

Theoretically an overall redesign of the world monetary system might be desirable, but practically the United States is likely to try to work bilaterally or with small groups of countries to solve its own problems and strengthen the international system, much as it has done in the past year and a half, starting with the Plaza agreement among the Group of Five (G-5) in September 1985. This was followed in March 1986 by a G-5 coordinated reduction in central bank discount rates, in April by a second round of discount rate cuts by the G-5 minus Germany, in May at the Tokyo economic summit by an agreement among the G-7 (the United States, Japan, Germany, Great Britain, and France, the original G-5, plus Canada and Italy) on new arrangements for closer policy coordination, in September by an agreement of G-7 finance ministers for a multilateral surveillance exercise, and in October by the Baker–Miyazawa agreement. "These six steps," said Treasury Secretary Baker, "are only a start. We need to build on them while keeping our expectations within reasonable bounds."

All this is certainly "reasonable"; it may even be the best that can be done in the existing circumstances. But the question is whether it is good enough, given the dangers facing the American and world economies, the persistent trade and exchange-rate misaligment, the spreading protectionism, and the precariousness of the debt-ridden developing countries.

VII. CONCLUSION

In sum, there are no "technical" solutions to the economic problems the world is facing. What it most needed is political will—the will of the United States to deal more effectively with its own problems and the will of all the major industrial countries to work together for a common end. It is easy enough to say that with the decrease of American dominance and the diffusion of economic power, Japan and Germany must accept wider international responsibilities and join the United States in efforts to prevent a crack-up after the greatest period of growth the world economy has ever experienced.

But if that cooperative spirit is lacking, a crack-up could indeed come, with severe political as well as economic consequences. The political consequences could include a cut by the United States in its military support for Europe and Asia, if their investors were to start unloading dollar assets and building their own regional redoubts, and that would mean a weakening of the defenses against aggression. In a sense, we have been here before. It is in the knowledge of what could lie ahead if we fail to work together that may be the main reason to hope that we will not let it happen again.

The most important aim of economic cooperation in the year ahead will be to keep the world economy moving foward. For within a pattern of growth the serious problems of world debt, trade, and currency imbalances can be contained, and progress can be made toward their solution.

At the end of the 1920s it was the resort by individual nations to unduly restrictive monetary and fiscal policies and to "beggar-thy-neighbor" protectionism, in the presumed self-interest of each, that caused the Great Depression. That blunder must not be repeated. The greatest change needed to preserve stability and growth is for the world economy, rather than the national economy, to become the *unit* for policy thinking. In spite of the resistance of traditional national policies and interest-group pressures, the development of internationally integrated monetary and fiscal policies has become vital to the economic well-being of every country in every continent.

NOTE

1. Much of the research is based on Leonard Silk, "The United States and the World Economy." *Foreign Affairs 65*(3), 1987, 458–476.

REFERENCES

Kindleberger, Charles F. "International Public Goods without International Government." *American Economic Review* March 1986, 1–13.

New York Stock Exchange Economic Research. *The Financial Health of U.S. Corporations: An Update*. New York Stock Exchange, New York, July 1985.

Silk, Leonard. "The United States and the World Economy." *Foreign Affairs 65*(3), 1987, 458–476.

INDUSTRIALIZATION OF JAPAN AND SELECTED EAST ASIAN COUNTRIES: THE STRUCTURAL DIVERGENCE HYPOTHESIS

M. Dutta and Daniel Tantum

I. INTRODUCTION

Walt Whitman Rostow (1985) continues to call upon his fellow economists to shift their focus of research onto "technology and supply," but the Rostow message must be read with a great deal of care. The "establishment" supply-side economists have indeed been found to be much too dependent on monetary and fiscal policies, such as managing money growth and adjusting tax rate structure, that are within the set of economic control measures that historically grew up in the Keynesian demand-side economics of macroeconomic management. The

Research in Asian Economic Studies.
Asian Industrialization: Changing Economic Structures,
Volume 1, Part A, pages 17–46.
Copyright © 1988 by JAI Press Inc.
All rights of reproduction in any form reserved.
ISBN: 0-89232-987-4

present study addresses the issue of the structural divergences between the two regional markets. Indeed, structural divergences can lead to "leakages" of demand and create serious supply constraints that call for new technology.

The shift of emphasis to research of technology and supply must involve taking into consideration the existing structural differences and divergent changes between the United States on this side of the Pacific, and Japan and selected East Asian economies on the other side of the Pacific. Any continued insistence on ignoring structural differences may prove too costly to all the trading partners of the Pacific economic community. Given structural differences, monetary and fiscal policy mixes are not likely to be adequate measures to correct trade and budget imbalances. They are necessary conditions in managing an economy but they are not necessary *and* sufficient conditions. The point that structural adjustments are necessary for correcting economic imbalances is our maintained hypothesis, and indeed a source of motivation for this study.

II. DIVERGENCE IN ECONOMIC GROWTH AND ACTIVITY

The economic growth of Japan and other East Asian economies, such as Asian NICs (the newly industrializing countries of Asia: South Korea, Taiwan, Hong Kong, and Singapore), has followed a distinctive pattern. The economic performances of the Asian NICs and the ASEAN group (Association of South East Asian Nations: Thailand, Malaysia, Singapore, Brunei, Indonesia, and the Philippines) continue to attract the attention of many contemporary students of economics.[1] These two groups of East Asian countries have experienced economic growth over the last decade, as measured by the trend rate of Gross Domestic Product (GDP) growth, which was significantly greater than that of the United States and the Industrialized Market Economies as a group (Spain, Ireland, Italy, New Zealand, United Kingdom, Belgium, Austria, Netherlands, France, Japan, Finland, West Germany, Denmark, Australia, Sweden, Canada, Norway, United States, and Switzerland). The Asian NICs and the ASEAN group as regions have experienced average annual GDP growth rates of 8.0 and 6.8%, respectively, over the 1973–1984 period, whereas the United States and the Industrial Market Economies as a region have registered average annual growth rates over this same period of 2.3 and 2.2%.[2]

For many of the East Asian countries economic growth over the last 10–15 years can be characterized as export-led. This export-led growth has, for the most part, coincided with a "great" surge of industrialization in the Asian NICs, and in some ASEAN economies. Much has been written about the "virtuous circle" of economic growth in the region, describing the process of industrialization–export–industrialization, and its cumulative impact on economic growth (Shinohara, 1982, 1984, 1987; Findlay, 1986; Kuznets, 1980).

To illustrate the degree to which the growth path of a representative group of East Asian countries—Taiwan, South Korea, Singapore, Japan, and Malaysia—has followed the "virtuous cycle growth path" over the 1973–1984 period, we refer to the movement of industrial production and export volume indices over this period. In comparing indices of industrial production and export volume of these five countries with those of the United States, it is observed (see Tables 1A and 1B) that each country of this East Asian group experienced relatively continuous and significant growth over the above time period.

Over the 1973–1984 period, an index of industrial production for Japan recorded an increase of 37.8%, whereas Korea's index of industrial production increased by 402%. Taiwan, Malaysia, and Singapore all registered growth in their industrial production indices of over 100% during this same period. The United States, on the other hand, exhibited periods of both growth and stagnation as measured by its indicator of industrial production, although for the period as a whole the United States' Industrial Production Index grew by 29%.

For the same five selected East Asian countries as a group, annual export volume growth over the 1973–1984 period averaged 11.80%.[3] Malaysia was low in this group with an average annual growth of export volume of 6.4%, whereas Korea was high with a figure of 18.4%. In contrast, the United States experienced average annual export growth over this period of only 4.25%. The numbers for the five East Asian countries are consistent with the "virtuous circle" description of economic growth that has been cited for many countries of East Asia.

This description of divergence in economic growth, industrial activity, and volume of exports between the two areas of the world leads us to ask the

Table 1A. Index Numbers of Industrial Production: The Selected East Asian Countries and the United States

	1965	*1970*	*1973*	*1975*	*1978*	*1980*	*1982*	*1984*
Japan	32.5	66.8	84.6	72.3	89.0	100	101.3	116.5
Korea	6.5	17.8	31.4	47.6	91.1	100	118.3	157.5
Taiwan	11.9	28.3	49.2	51.4	88.0	100	102.9	131.7
Philippines	47.3	60.1	92.7	79.9	91.9	100	—	—
Indonesia	30.5	54.0	84.7	82.6	103.4	100	84.6	88.1
Singapore	—	33.3	55.0	56.7	77.4	100	103.7	115.4
Malaysia	—	44.4	56.8	63.2	86.9	100	108.9	142.0
Thailand	—	—	—	—	—	—	—	—
United States	60.9	72.3	86.9	78.1	98.0	100	94.9	112.1

Source: Direction of Trade Statistics Yearbook, 1984, IMF, Washington, D.C. For the Philippines and Singapore, the index is of manufacturing production; for Indonesia, it is crude petroleum production. Taiwan data are from *Taiwan Statistical Yearbook, 1986*.

Table 1B. Index Number of Export Volume:
Selected East Asian Countries and the United States

	1972	*1973*	*1974*	*1975*	*1976*	*1977*	*1978*	*1979*	*1980*	*1981*	*1982*
Japan	50.1	53.6	64.6	64.4	78.0	84.6	85.2	85.4	100	110.6	108.1
Korea	24.0	37.0	40.0	49.0	67.0	80.0	91.0	90.0	100	118.0	125.0
Taiwan	32.6	40.1	38.4	38.4	57.8	62.6	77.3	82.4	91.1	100.0	103.0
Philippines	49.7	53.5	47.8	50.6	64.8	78.2	75.8	82.9	100	101.1	106.8
Indonesia	61.0	74.0	76.0	79.0	91.0	103.0	109.0	106.0	100	82.0	78.0
Singapore	38.0	46.0	50.0	46.0	55.0	64.0	71.0	85.0	100	103.0	107.0
Malaysia	58.0	68.0	65.0	64.0	83.0	86.0	92.0	104.0	100	97.0	103.0
Thailand	51.2	47.8	53.5	51.3	71.5	81.6	88.1	96.0	100	111.5	125.3
United States	54.9	68.0	73.9	72.3	74.9	75.2	84.2	93.7	100	96.9	86.6

Source: International Financial Statistics Yearbook, 1985, IMF, Washington, D.C. Data for Taiwan are from *Taiwan Satistical Yearbook, 1985*.

following question: what policy (or policies) are necessary for the United States to adopt that will enable it to emulate the dynamism exhibited by many countries in the East Asian region?

III. POLICY MIX IN THE PRESENCE OF EAST ASIAN INDUSTRIALIZATION AND STRUCTURAL DIVERGENCE

Given the fact of substantial industrialization and the opening up of new markets by East Asian economies, how should the U.S. economy be allowed (or ''steered'') to adjust? Some options are (1) total reliance on the ''invisible hands'' of the free market, (2) monetary policy consistent with the exchange rate management of the G-5 countries (United States, Japan, West Germany, United Kingdom, France, since then, G-7, as Italy and Canada joined the Group) plus fiscal policy inclusive of voluntary export restraints, and (3) study of the patterns of structural differences and sources of divergent change in related economies and adoption of cooperative adjustment measures so that impacts following such structural changes can be mutually absorbed with minimum cost to a given economy in a trading community. The third option would involve a critical review of labor–management relations and of commercial and public policy in the light of the information obtained from such studies.

Two points of note should be made about these options: (1) few seem to share total commitment to the first option, and (2) a mix of monetary–fiscal policies toward adjustment of periodic imbalances in international economic relations among a group of trading nations has already been an accepted practice. We suggest that a much closer study of factors that contribute to basic structural changes within and across a given set of regional economies is now required in an attempt to understand how they come about and the degree to which they are beneficial or not.

Although it is not new, this facet of economic investigation seems to have received little attention, perhaps because it extends the scope of economic analyses beyond the familiar terrain of marginal variations. Schumpeter identified a source of structural change in his analysis of innovation via entrepreneurial decision making. Development economists explain structural differences through analyses of cultural/religious/anthropological differences, and have written about the Protestant ethic or Confucianism. ''Establishment'' econometricians identify structural differences, across time or space with hypothesis testing, using the Chow test or the inclusion of dummy variables. Kornai's treatise on antiequilibrium in economics, and his argument for the adoption of the concept of ''quantum economics,'' has been widely read, and he points to the fact that our peers in physics have studied quantum physics much to the advancement of their discipline. Drucker (1986) invites economists to reread Schumpeter's works in this regard, and Lester Thurow argues for reexamining the production function in terms of the management factor.

IV. THE STRUCTURAL DIVERGENCE HYPOTHESIS AND ECONOMIC ANALYSIS

The "standard" approach taken by an economist to explain divergences in behavior among economic agents across countries is to emphasize an analysis of the agents' behavior given relative prices of commodities, inputs and currencies, and interest rates and incomes, that are faced and received in each country. It is believed that differences between, and interaction among, the countries of concern, with respect to domestic consumption (C), saving (S), production (GDP), and international trade (NX), can be explained by differences in these variables. In addition, it is then maintained that the current states of C, S, GDP, and NX, besides other economic variables, can be "controlled" to some extent by monetary and fiscal policy that will influence prices, interest rates, and expenditures.

In this study it will not be claimed that the "standard" approach is of no value for an analysis of economic relations between the United States and selected East Asian countries. A more modest claim is made. This claim is that, given the relative economic dynamics over the past two decades, there currently exist structural differences and potential for future divergences in structure of such a magnitude that the divergences are too great not to be considered as a significant factor in the determination of relative economic performance. Thus, they should be given more consideration, particulary by the United States, when economic policy is developed concerning the two sets of economies, the United States vis-à-vis Japan and selected East Asian countries. It is suggested that a direct analysis of the structural differences will help us better appreciate the complex workings of the relative growth paths of the two sets of economies under study. Without such analyses, we are afraid that the "standard' approach will lead to unreliable, possibly even misleading, inferences and inadequate policy decisions at the level of macroeconomic management.

An example is the realignment of the dollar, most notably against the yen, and its lack of effect on merchandise trade relative to the expectations of the policy makers. The actions and the "jaw-boning" by the G-5 countries since the Plaza Accord (September 22, 1985 meeting of the G-5 countries), to lower the value of the dollar under the expectation that this would improve the goods–service trade balance, induced a new pattern for the yen–dollar relationship.[4] The threat from Washington is that the dollar shall be allowed to go down until the yen hits the sky and brings Japan to her knees. Students of economics have long memories of such economic war-games. When prices hit the bottom, and then collapse, the economy is in the midst of a Great Depression. In the mid-1980s with growth in prices practically at a halt in the United States, output is far below what it would be at both the level of full capacity utilization and full employment of labor. It has been suggested that in the early 1980s the United States did not exhibit the curious phenomenon of "stag-flation," but has returned to a "new" economic order, involving a slowing down of the economic production with price stability, i.e., creeping rates of real economic growth with a near zero rate of inflation.

What has happened to the yen–dollar exchange rate and trade balance with Japan since the G-5 (later G-7) jaw-boning began? Table 2 reveals that the G-5 finance ministers' objective of lowering the value of the dollar, at least with respect to the yen, was being satisfied. Yet, as of the beginning of the fourth quarter, 1987, the "expected" effect on the bilateral trade balance with Japan had not taken place. The data tell us that the quarterly U.S. trade deficit with Japan from the fourth quarter of 1985 to the third quarter of 1987 has on average *increased* by almost 2.5% whereas the yen–dollar exchange rate over the same period has *decreased* by over 4.5% on average. Economic theory based on "smooth" behavior characterized by lags in quantity adjustment, possibly due to the existence of contracts and adaptive expectations, predicts that an exchange rate and a trade balance will move in opposite directions.[5] Given enough time to elapse, the well-known "J"-curve will supposedly reveal itself. However, we must also consider the possibility of structural differences and continued divergences between the two economies as a factor in explaining this and any persistent trade imbalance.[6]

It has been suggested that for many East Asian economies, management systems are more cost effective and productivity oriented than for the United States. It is "common knowledge" that Japan and several other Asian economies have demonstrated a comparatively high rate of saving. In addition the financial

Table 2. United States–Japan Trade Balance and Yen–Dollar (Y/$) Exchange Rate Since September 22, 1985, G-5 Meeting

Year/Quarter	*Imports*[a]*($)*	*Exports*[a]*($)*	*"Deficit"*[a]*($)*	*Y/$*[b]
85.IV	18,379	5,567	12,812	207.09
86.I	20,888	5,574	15,314	187.88
86.II	20,886	7,499	13,387	170.13
86.III	21,555	7,229	14,326	155.77
86.IV	22,128	6,581	15,547	160.29
87.I	20,331	5,959	14,372	153.17
87.II	21,980	6,615	15,365	142.67
87.III	22,228	7,644	14,584	146.90

[a]*Source:* Taken from or based on data in the *Direction of Trade Statistics*. IMF, Washington, D.C., various months of 1986 and December 1987. The imports are c.i.f. valued and the exports are f.o.b. valued. The "Deficit" here is calculated as the difference between imports (c.i.f.) and exports (f.o.b.).

[b]Quoted from *International Financial Statistics*. IMF, Washington, D.C., March 1987 and October 1987.

and money markets of many of these economies exhibit their own unique features. Some have made references to the relatively significant role governments in many of these economies play in economic decision making, particularly in the area of technology and high-tech industries. Indeed, the current structural divergences have ushered in a new era of economic competition between the two shores of the Pacific, an era in which there is a growing competition in the United States domestic market concerning the share in which goods requiring skilled labor and high-tech production methods will be supplied by the United States or Japan or Asian NIC.

The free market regime remains the basic framework under which these economies can be analyzed and compared. The emerging economic patterns, however, call for analyses beyond marginal variations, which will involve extensive analyses of structural differences within the economic environment of long-run industrialization of Japan and selected East Asian economies. The East Asian industrialization can be characterized in terms of its structural differences relative to the U.S. economy in several areas. To this end, five specific areas of investigation are suggested:[7]

1. comparative divergences in the savings rates and capital formation rates,
2. comparative divergences in labor structures and their associated differences in productivity,
3. comparative divergences in management structures and their associated differences in terms of productivity,
4. comparative divergences in the financial and money markets, and
5. comparative roles of respective governments in educational planning for engineering and technical manpower, policy toward Research and Development (R&D), and contribution to the production process.

These five areas of investigation shall encompass the comprehensive investigation of the production maps of the economies under study. Areas one, two, three, and five shall encompass the real factors in the private sector of a given economy—savings and capital formation, manpower inclusive of management and engineering and science professionals, and the influence and role of government in the production process of the private sector. The fourth area suggested relates to the money and financial sector of an economy, and thus seeks to investigate interactive processes between the money and real sectors of a given economy.

In what follows the present study shall first concentrate its discussion on the three of the above five areas; (2) labor, (3) management, and (5) government/i.e., social/public inputs.

We will then be concerned with discussing, defining, and providing some calculations of ICOR-like measures that have a 2-fold purpose. The two objectives of the measures are (1) to help identify the extent of structural divergence in specific sectors of the respective economies under study, and (2) to provide information on how the selected economies, relative to each other, are progressing toward becoming active participants in the present phase of the industrial revolution.

By becoming an active participant in the process of industrialization, the individual country is observed to have been able to adapt to an innovative use of a given technology, and/or to introduce an innovative new extension of a hitherto known technology. In this regard it has been argued that Japan has already outdistanced the United States in her preparation for the latest phase of the industrial revolution. This current phase of the industrial revolution has been referred to by Rostow (1986) as the "Fourth Industrial Revolution." It has also been observed that several other countries in the region have resolutely geared their manpower planning to the same goal, such as South Korea and India, so that they too can be active participants in the new phase of the industrial revolution.

A. Comparison of Labor Structures

Much has been written by economists about the relative wage levels between most East Asian economies and the United States and how that tends to give the East Asian countries an ("unfair") comparative advantage. Most economists will agree that in the past the relatively higher wage rates in the United States were earned, as it progressively grew, by American Labor because of its relatively higher productivity. Thus, the basic economic issue is not a straightforward comparison of wage rates, rather the substantive issue is instead the investigation of comparative rates of labor productivity. The United States in the last two decades has not compared well with many of its East Asian competitors in this regard, and this is particularly true with respect to Japan. Maddison (1984) reports that the average annual compound growth rate in GDP per man-hour over the 1973–1981 period for the United States was 1.1%, whereas for Japan the same statistic was calculated to be 3.1%. For the 1960–1973 period these rates for the United States and Japan were calculated to be 2.6 and 9.3%, respectively. With respect to labor productivity of the manufacturing sector in the United States vis-à-vis Japan, Norsworthy and Malmquist (1984) report average annual rates of growth over the 1973–1980 period of 1.3 and 6.4%, respectively.

Mo-huan Hsing (1984) reports a comprehensive empirical study that provides some information that may help us explain differences in the growth of labor productivity between selected East Asian economies and the United States. His study compares the United States to the "Asian Growth Belt" (AGB) countries: Japan, Korea, Taiwan, Hong Kong, and Singapore. The two time periods for his study encompass 1963–1970 and 1970–1976. The author concludes:

> "The manufacturing industries in the United States had made quite respectable technological progress relative to output growth over 1963–1970. . . . that the technological progress of manufacturing industries in the U.S. has lagged significantly behind that of Asian Growth Belt

> counterparts (as named above), especially over the second period, 1970–76. . . . This picture looks all the more discomforting if set against that for Japan, Korea, and Taiwan where manufacturing industries have achieved considerably higher technological progress over both periods, accompanied by higher output growth, and except for Taiwan over the first period, also higher capital growth with the efficiency of capital increasing at varying rates (Mo-huan Hsing, 1984: 429, and 434–435).

The same author suggests that in the years after 1976, the discrepancies between the United States and the Asian Growth Belt countries have been further widening in favor of the latter.

Both the relative rates of savings formation, referred to earlier, and the technical progress discrepancy, mentioned above, play a role here in explaining the divergence in labor productivity, since technical progress (at least in the Hick's neutral sense) positively impacts on labor productivity directly, and savings formation positively impacts on labor productivity indirectly through its direct effect on relative rates of capital formation. The relatively poorer U.S. performance in technical progress is to an extent due to the larger relative growth of human resources devoted to R&D in many East Asian countries. Since 1969 the number of engineers and scientists employed in R&D activities in Japan and South Korea has increased 93 and 502%. Relative to 1971 this statistic for the Philippines has grown 335%. For the United States, on the other hand, since 1969 the number of engineers and scientists in R&D has grown 40%. Information on R&D expenditures shares for the United States vis-à-vis Japan, South Korea, and Singapore is also consistent with this view of relative productivity slowdown. For the United States a measure of R&D to GNP marginally increased by 1% over the 1981–1983 period. For Japan and South Korea this same measure increased by 12 and 50%, respectively, whereas Singapore experienced over the 1978–1981 period an increase of 87%.[8]

Some have stated that imported technology was a significant factor in explaining labor productivity gains, particularly in Japan. However, Kosobud reported in his study of Japan: "There is no necessary relationship between the transfer of technology and the total factor productivity shift . . . having yielded some evidence suggesting that imported technology was among the significant progress-inducing inputs that brought about total factor productivity gains during the sample period, 1952–1968" (Kosobud, 1974).

The issue, often mentioned in the literature as technology transfer, has been discussed with respect to the transfer of technology from the United States to Japan and other East Asian economies, but what has occurred is not simply the transfer and straightforward adoption of a given technology. Unlike a typical North–South scenario from the Product Cycle literature, where the "North's" technology is transferred, under an assumed dynamic process, and implemented, as is, in the "South," technology that is accumulated by East Asian countries, such as Korea, Japan, and Taiwan, appears to have been the result of a process of innovative adaptation. For these countries the process of innovative adaptation of transferred technology results in the production of manufactured goods that are differentiated within industries horizontally, and for the United States consumers vertically as well, and produced at a lower cost relative to their American counterparts. The adaptive innovation model seems to have worked as an extension of the Schumpeterian innovation paradigm. Indeed, an adaptive innovation model with a new genre of entrepreneurs has successfully emerged.

It is important when analyzing the relative states of technology to note that behind technology lies the individual who makes actual use of it. The relative supply of skilled manpower in the *real sector* of the East Asian economies is growing significantly while that in the U.S. economy is perhaps lagging, and the issue warrants research. Rostow (1985, 1986) relates this to education policy. He refers to the radical changes in education policy in many Asian countries, and notes its emphasis on programs that will enable rapid absorption of new technologies in production. Emphasis on education is the answer to "a great technological leap" for many Asian economies.

Smith et al. (1985) point out that a key emphasis for many of the East Asian countries is *required* to be education. They suggest that the natural resource-poor Japan, South Korea, and Singapore seem to have no other option than to do this, and that it is no less critical for relatively resource-rich Indonesia. The study points out that the Japanese are fast diverting their economic base from traditional heavy industries into newer areas of "brain technology" that include fifth generation computers, microelectronics, biotechnology, and development of new scientific raw materials. The Koreans have decided to reach out to sources of modern technology in Europe and the United States, from which Japan originally borrowed it, and invested in the initial phase of their "brain intensive" industrialization. To this end, Korea is determined to plan for the education of their children who will make up the workforce for this new high-tech industrial development phase in that country. Policymakers in Singapore refer to their "second industrial revolution, advancing from labor-intensive industries into the knowledge-intensive industries of high technology and business services" (Smith et al., 1985: 73) and realize they must invest massively in higher education. Even if it is less obvious, Indonesia also recognizes that her industrialization program can be successful, if and only if her manpower is appropriately managed and developed.

The basic issue in preparing the labor force is an educational policy that will match the manpower need of an economy as it begins to absorb new frontier technologies into its production system. As history has shown, no nation can plan to be a leader for all time. A nation with a good forward-looking plan, however, can be more successful in maximizing its ability to adapt its production process to new technology, particularly in the continuously innovating manufacturing sector of an economy, and thus minimize costs of adjustment.

The emphasis on education and planned development of manpower remains a key factor for brain-intensive, high-technology industrialization. It is one thing to embody muscle and skill in a given nation's labor force, but it is quite another thing to have "brain" embodied in the human stock available in an economy. Managing the stock of existing human resources and its education in preparation for an incoming set of technological developments must be seen as an issue of *structural* adjustment, not an issue of wage-cut, nor of extracting "givebacks" from the labor union to remain competitive. Economists have done extensive as well as intensive studies into the role of education in economic productivity (Denison, 1984; McMahon, 1984; Psacharopoulos, 1984).

The issue for the United states is not one of concern about the overall education of the American labor force. The issue is the role and availability of technicians, engineers, and scientists (technically trained manpower). A second issue is what should be the degree that the availability of a technically trained manpower is determined by private decentralized market forces vis-à-vis centralized government decisions. Any and all efforts to privatize the American education system, at all levels, directly or indirectly, may not meet the competitive challenge that existing structural differences has presented for the United States. It is well known that governments in Japan and Asian NICs have played, and continue to play, a dominant role in their respective manpower planning. In the United States, public education and land-grant colleges historically came to fill up the then manpower need. Perhaps a parallel public program alone can address itself to the manpower planning need of the challenging high-tech phase of industrialization that is said to be competitively "brain-intensive."

B. Comparison of Management Structures

Recently there has been an outpouring of literature both by academic and nonacademic economists on this subject. The magic of the Japanese management system has been discussed in many different lights (Morita, 1986; Ouchi, 1981).

Notwithstanding the technical difficulties in measuring productivity of management, Peter Drucker (1985) argues that compared with its Japanese peers, American management is far less productive. Ulric Weil (1985) reports that based on a set of confidential data from some American corporations, the relatively poorer performance of American management, in terms of value-added productivity, can be well established.

The general line of argument presented goes as follows: in Japan, the workers participate in decision making and the management remains closely involved with labor in the regular work process. Also a large proportion of managers' *and* laborers' earnings depend on their firm's performance. In the United States, on the other hand, the workers are denied any such participation in decision making, and for the most part labor's wages are not directly tied to their firm's performance. Also unique in the United States, relative to Japan, management uses its managerial prerogative from high-rise corporate headquarters, usually far away from the production work place, and fails to relate itself to the work process. In their participatory role of decision making and self-determination of income, the

Japanese workers enjoy a higher order job security and incentive to perform, and thus share a higher order of commitment to the production process, both in terms of quantity and quality. In the United States, the workers see themselves in a adversary relationship vis-à-vis management, and remain too aware of the pink-slip syndrome. This can lead to a deterioration in the quality and the quantity of the product produced with a given work force.

In addition to the claims of Drucker and Weil that U.S. management has not fared well with respect to productivity, thus contributing to a relatively high unit management cost, it appears that management in the United States relative to selected East Asian countries also experiences a greater degree of labor–management friction. The data in Table 3 indicate that in 1984, for each working age person in the United States, over 5% of a working day was lost due to a labor dispute. For the selected countries in this table the next closest value of this statistic is calculated for Japan, which is many times smaller. In Japan, in 1984, for each working age person, under 0.5% of a working day was lost due to a labor dispute. If this statistic is in any way indicative of the ability of labor and management to cooperate and communicate, it then reflects that the United States is losing out and is at a relative disadvantage.

Historically in economic studies relating to production, little has been done to examine the role of management as an independent, variable input. Indeed, management research has largely been the domain of researchers in the field of management in business school programs. Neither the Cobb–Douglas production function, and its many and varied extensions in economic literature, nor the Leontief input–output analyses (until recent work by Leontief) chose to focus on the role of managment in a production study, even though some economists have written extensively on the complexities of managerial decision making in the modern industrial society (e.g., any managerial economics textbook). Actually, very little analytic research exists on this, even when American management cost

Table 3. Comparative Labor Disputes, 1984

Country	*(1)* *Working age population 15–64*	*(2)* *Working days lost*	*(2)/(1)* *Percentage of working day lost per person of working age*
Japan	81,600	354.05	0.43
Korea	25,670	19.9	0.08
Hong Kong	3,670	3.08	0.08
United States	156,420	8498.8	5.43

Source: Working age population is calculated by mulitplying the percentage of population of working age by mid-year population. Mid-year population data are obtained from the *World Development Report 1986* (The World Bank). Mid-year population and working days lost are in thousands. For working days lost, International Labor Organization *Yearbook of Labor Statistics*, 1985.

per unit of output has been referred to as ''absurdly high,'' and American management–labor relations are said to be quite poor compared with situations in Japan. Indeed, based on the simple line of argument that is consistent with Weil's observation and Druckers view, it can be asserted that the productivity of labor is significantly positively correlated with the productivity of management.

A useful framework for a cross-country comparison of different categories of labor per unit of output is Input–Output (I–O) analysis. Recently, Leontief himself has expanded his I–O Table to include a great deal of disaggregation of labor input in the value-added segment including a row of labor input that is related to management. This continued lack of economic analysis of management and labor productivity on a more disaggregated basis than is now done is a limiting factor in the understanding of the current divergence of growth between the United States–East Asian economies.

C. Comparative Roles of Governments

John Kenneth Galbraith's thesis on ''political power'' in economics and John Kornai's discourse on ''nonmarket information'' in market economies are seminal references concerning the role the government necessarily must take (and they do take) if an economy is to operate effectively.

Robert Wade (1985) writes on the comparatively successful role of government in overcoming market failure in Taiwan, Korea, and Japan, and argues that neither Japan, Taiwan, nor Korea maintained ''a close approximation to a neutral policy regime over the post-war period. They have all actively fostered the development of many new industries, and successfully so, in the sense that many of those industries have become internationally competitive.''

The following government institutions—Japan's MITI, South Korea's Economic Planning Board, and Taiwan's Council for Economic Planning and Development and its Industrial Development Bureau—have played leadership roles in accelerated industrialization of Japan, Korea, and Taiwan. The debate continues, however, as to whether Japan, Taiwan, and Korea would not have grown even faster without the respective governments' observed style of management over their respective economies.

Each modern economy, including that of the United States, produces the gross domestic total of goods and services as it does only with the helpful utilization of government provided inputs (social inputs) of diverse descriptions. Some of these are known to be pure public goods, and others are not pure public goods but provide positive externalities, e.g., infrastructure, such as roads, affirmative action programs, pollution abatement controls, health care, and education. The private sector in a market economy may forego a welfare improving action because it does not have the incentive to provide and/or demand the level of goods and inputs, whose consumption or usage by one does not exclude others from their services. The same problem would occur when the cost of monitoring the usage of what was once social inputs is prohibitive (Musgrave and Musgrave, 1980). A cut in government expenditures will lead to a reduction in the availability of these social inputs, which results in a reduction or stagnation of a given economy's productivity insofar as it depends functionally on the availability of such social inputs.

This possibility can be illustrated with the following analytical example. Let the volume of domestic production (''real'' GDP) be Q and assume I_p and I_s represent vectors of private and social inputs that determine ''real'' GDP, respectively. Also assume that I_p and I_s have some inputs that are common to both. Now if the government were to reduce the amount of those social inputs that are provided also by the private sector, then one could expect that there would be some replacement of these social inputs by the private sector. The overall effect on ''real'' GDP can then be calculated by taking the total differential of the input–output relationship:

$$dQ = (\partial Q/\partial I_s)\, dI_s + (\partial Q/\partial I_p)\, d\mathrm{I}_p$$

If the private sector replaces only those social inputs that were reduced, then it follows that $\partial Q/\partial I_s = \partial Q/\partial I_p$ about the initial point of production. The value of dQ, i.e., whether ''real'' GDP will increase, stay the same, or decrease, then depends on the relationshp between dI_p and dI_s. Given the usual nature of social inputs, the property of externalities, the private sector is not (often cannot be) expected to provide social inputs. Thus, it can be reasonably expected that the absolute value of dI_s will be greater than dI_p, and that the ''real'' GDP will fall, following a reduction in social inputs.

To avoid this result, Rostow has argued that the erosion of social and physical infrastructure of an advanced industrialized economy, as is the United States, should not be allowed to occur. He advocates ''the bringing together of scientists, engineers, entrepreneurs, and the working force to generate and absorb efficiently, and across the board, the technologies of the Fourth Industrial Revolution'' (Rostow 1985: 288).

Education of a populace is an example of a social input, since there is a general consensus that it yields nonexcludable positive externalities to the economy. We can inquire to what degree the government of the United States and selected East Asian governments contributed to the educational process of their respective economies. Table 4 shows that for the countries listed, the importance of central government expenditures on education relative to total expenditures (GNP) is smallest for the United States. Comparing the education financed by central government share in 1972 and 1983 we find that for all the listed East Asian economies it has gone up, in some cases quite substantially, e.g., the Singapore government expenditure share rose from 2.6 to 5.1%, whereas for the United States it fell from an already relatively low level i.e., 0.6 to 0.5%.

Table 4. Central Government Education Expenditure as Percentage of GNP

Country	*1972*	*1983*
Korea	2.9	3.8
Philippines	2.2	3.0
Indonesia	1.2	2.3
Singapore	2.6	5.1
Thailand	3.4	4.1
United States	0.6	0.5

Source: Compiled from data in the *World Development Report*, 1986, The World Bank, Washington, D.C., and for Taiwan, *Taiwan Statistical Yearbook, 1986*.

Of course, the positive aspect of growth of the listed variable in East Asian economies should be emphasized. In a comparison limited to education expenditures by the central government of the United States, however, one can draw only limited conclusions from this set of data.[9]

The optimum degree of direct government cooperation and participation in the management of a given economy, particularly in the areas of new frontier technology and in social investments impacting on the health and education of the country's labor force, shall depend on the specific economy. But the role of government in supplying the necessary social inputs in the absence of which an economy will become internationally noncompetitive cannot be ignored. Indeed, international competitive ability of a given economy depends on its access to both private (I_p) and social (I_s) inputs, and its commitment to ensure their continued and augmented supply.

V. INCREMENTAL I–O RATIOS, DIVERGENCE OF LABOR STRUCTURE/OUTPUT RELATIONS, AND TECHNOLOGICAL INDUSTRIALIZATION

All five areas, as we have identified above, relate to the production map of an economy. The divergences in the above five areas between the United States on the one hand, and Japan and selected East Asian countries on the other hand, therefore impact on the comparative production functions of the two competing economic sets.

Indeed, all the five areas of the proposed research can be related to the value-added and intermediate input segments of the I–O table. In the I–O tables of earlier decades, as we have stated earlier, the value-added segment received rather marginal attention. The heroic assumption of "homogeneity" of labor was continued to be made, and one single row of labor either in man-hour or in money wage payment was the most the first generation I–O tables offered. No mention was made of management and its role. Even though the tables offered extensively meticulous disaggregation of interindustry matrix, they continued to limit their analyses of the value-added segment to the minimum. Recently, Leontief himself has led the expanded study of the hitherto neglected value-added segment of the I–O table. It is in this direction in which fruitful extension of research in production and productivity can be undertaken.

The present study suggests that such an extension of available I–O tables of the economies under study can offer an analytic framework for the comparative study of the production maps of the competing economies. Efforts to add additional rows to the value-added segment of the I–O tables of selected economies will of course be a challenging task.

Pending the massive research task (including collection and compilation of necessary data) of constructing a sufficiently expanded value-added segment of the I–O tables of cross-country economies under investigation, we turn to the literature in development economics in search of tentative answers to the issues raised concerning identification of factors as may contribute to structural divergences of production mapping.

A. A Methodology and Measure of Divergence and Development

The one single parameter in development economics literature that continues to command attention is the incremental capital output ratio (ICOR). Can we then construct two closely parallel ratios, which may not only help us identify to what degree divergence exists in labor and management structures, but will also enable us to identify at what state of the development process, with respect to industrialization, a given country is? We suggest two concepts: (1)Incremental Professional, Technical, and Related Worker/Output Ratio (IPOR), and (2) Incremental Administrator and Management/Output Ratio (IMOR).

Many questions must first be answered. How should they be defined? How should they be measured? What is meant by lower and/or higher IPOR and IMOR ratios in cross-country comparison?

The two concepts stated above, IPOR and IMOR, will be analogous to the hitherto well-established concept, ICOR, or any of its close facsimiles. The textbook definition of ICOR is the amount of new investment necessary to achieve an increase in output of one unit (Herrick and Kindleberger, 1983). The inverse of this ratio measures the increase in output from one unit increase in the capital stock. Thus, the IPOR/IMOR measures parallelling the above parameter, ICOR, will conceptually be the amount of professional and technical workers—administrators and managers required to achieve an increase in output of one unit.

To devise a methodology for the measurement of the ratios proposed here, let us refer to the method of measurement that has been historically applied to ICOR. The estimate for ICOR is in general calculated as the annual gross investment (in constant prices) divided by that year's change in gross domestic product (in constant prices). Calculations are based on sample data for a period longer than 1 year. Measures of ICORs, we report in Table 5, are calculated over an 8-year (1965–1973), then a 9-year (1974–1983) period. In both cases, serious problems in the accuracy of the measure exist, and it may very well be more of a problem the longer the time interval over which the ICOR is calculated. Needless to say, given the similarity of the measures, the criticisms of the ICOR measure will apply to IPOR and IMOR.[10] Given the overall limitation of the concept of ICOR, the present effort to estimate IPOR and IMOR must be viewed with all the critical attention it warrants.

It is also obvious that there exist severe data limitations to construct the proposed measures, IPOR and IMOR. We have used the data from available sources, and we are acutely aware that the sets of data used here are subject to further refinements. We have made use of limited available alternative sets of data in obtaining measures of IPOR and IMOR.

We must also recognize that the ICOR is a measure that allows two economists to take two different views and arrive at two different conclusions with respect to the degree and direction of economic "development" a country is experiencing, and that IMOR and IPOR may be subject to the same critical observation. An attempt to reconcile the two different views by identifying varying stages of development and associating the stage of development with the ICOR is well known and entails constructing a two part argument. If we first consider the early stage of development, Rostow and Lewis (Meier, 1984: 215–216) may be correct in their claim that an increase in ICOR should relate positively to economic growth and hence economic development since at this stage, an economy will have to devote an increasing amount of productive resources to capital stock production. On the other hand, Clark and Liebenstein (Pepelasis et al., 1961: 121–122) refer to the latter stages of economic development process in which a

Table 5. ICOR (Incremental Capital–Output Ratio): Selected East Asian Countries

Country	*1965–1973*	*1973–1983*
Japan	3.1	5.2
Korea	2.4	4.0
Philippines	3.9	5.4
Indonesia	1.6	3.1
Singapore	2.8	4.6
Thailand	3.1	3.7

Source: The World Development Report, 1986, The World Bank, Washington, D.C.

relatively smaller ICOR may be an indicator of economic development. Liebenstein's argument that a smaller ICOR is a sign of relatively more development follows the logic that a declining ICOR is associated with

> (i) an increase in the productivity of labor; (ii) growth of the size of labor force; (iii) increasing ability of the economy to overcome indivisibilities in capital; (iv) relative increase in the demand for services that require less capital goods that characterizes the early phases of industrialization; (v) a rising rate of obsolescence; and (vi) increase in rent per unit of output (Pepelasis et al., 1961: 122).

The debate and the comments that followed then imply that the relationship of the ICOR and the stage of economic development can be expressed by an inverted U-shape. Thus, even when one accepted this measure as providing information of how a country was progressing in its development profile, in relation to industrialization, adequate caution must be exercised when the measure was used to give information on the existing degree of development.

It is suggested that the arguments of Lewis, Rostow, Leibenstein, and Clark can be applied to the IPOR measure, and hence postulate that the diagram of IPOR against stages of development (development meaning becoming an active participant of the current phase of industrial revolution) will also exhibit an inverted U-shape. The path of IMOR, as development proceeds, is more difficult to conjecture.

The argument that IPOR should initially rise for development to take place is based on the observation that those countries that were not active participants in the industrial revolution are presently experiencing a truly relative shortage of the necessary inputs, namely professional and technical workers. Is the situation that the East Asian countries under study and the United States face one of relative manager and administrator "shortage" or "surplus" relative to their respective industrialization profiles? It can be reasonably conjectured that the present phase of industrial revolution is indeed professional and technical labor intensive (relative to manager and administrative labor). To the extent that this decade and the future will be less management and administrator intensive, we should expect to see IMOR decline as development increases, and possibly increase as development moves beyond the present stage of historical progression of the Industrial Revolution.

Figure 1 presents the postulated paths for IPOR and IMOR as development takes place, in the context of a country becoming an active participant in the latest phase of industrial revolution.

With the necessary cautions in mind as were required in the past for economic interpretations of ICOR, measures of IPOR/IMOR, incremental ratios as proposed in this study, will be meaningful for comparative economic analysis. Indeed, in addition to the two ratios, IPOR and IMOR, we may wish to compute additional incremental (and level) input–output ratios with respect to specific inputs, such as research and development, basic science research, public health, education, environment, and child care and development.

Figure 1. IPOR/IMOR: current phase of the industrial revolution and stages of development

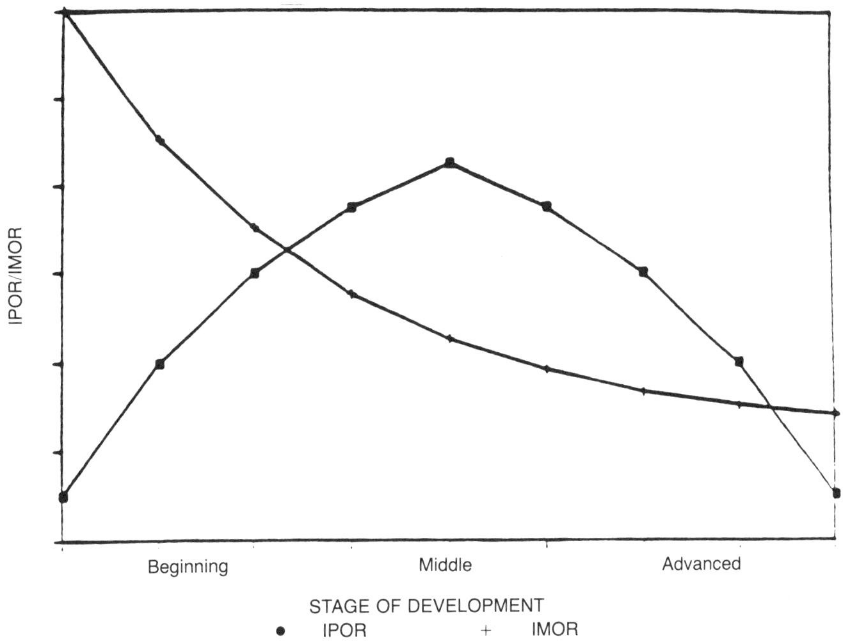

B. Calculations of IPOR and IMOR Measures

Two versions of IPOR and IMOR have been presented. In version 1 the denominators have been converted to constant U.S. dollars by multiplying constant price GDP (GNP) measures by the 1980 U.S. dollar exchange rate with respect to the particular currency of concern (Taiwan constant price GDP was divided by N.T. dollar per U.S. dollar exchange rate). This was done in an attempt to make comparisons across countries depend more on "real" differences rather than nominal differences. It is noted here, however, that the effort to convert the GDPs of the various countries into a common currency value, by using official exchange rates, is deficient to the extent that the official exchange rates do not reflect the purchasing power of the respective countries, relative to the numeraire country (Maddison, 1984). Version 2 is in elasticity form and hence the nominal effects of exchange rates do not exist. Tables 6, 7, 8, and 9 present the estimates we obtain of the IPOR and IMOR ratios.[11] Tables 10 and 11 present the calculations of a level, professional and technical worker/output ratio (PTO), and a level, management and administrative worker/output ratio (MAO), based on the same data sources as Tables 6 though 9.

A comparison of how IPOR-1 and IPOR-2 ranked the selected countries, from highest to lowest, reveals that only one country changed its position by more than two places (Japan by three places). When this comparison is made over IMOR-1 and IMOR-2, the only difference in the rankings is that Philippines and Singapore switch places. Note that in Tables 6 and 8, the estimates are not strictly comparable with the estimates for ICOR, since the values in the numerator of each ratio estimated are in different units, i.e., actual physical quantities vis-à-vis constant dollar values.

A graphical presentation of the calculations from Table 6 and Table 8 are presented in Figures 2 and 3. Figure 2 presents IPOR, version 1, for selected East Asian economies and the United states, and Figure 3 is the graph of IMOR, version 1, for the same countries.

The calculations presented in Tables 6–11 and graphed in Figures 2 and 3 may reveal some interesting aspects with respect to Rostow's observations on the emerging phase of industrialization. In terms of the two incremental ratio measures and their postulated interpretation here, Japan and the three Asian NICs—Taiwan, Singapore, and South Korea—appear relatively more advanced, with respect to the "Fourth Industrial Revolution," than the United States. Under one interpretation of IPOR and development, it can also be conjectured that Thailand and the United States are at a similar stage, and the Philippines and Indonesia are behind.

The IMOR measure is consistent with the observation, based on IPOR alone, that Japan and the three Asian NICs are further along in the competitive industrialization process. Thailand, the most dynamic of the ASEAN countries in terms of income and export growth and industrial activity, and the United States have substantially greater IMOR and IPOR values than the other six countries in our sample. The IMOR value for Indonesia, analyzed in combination with its IPOR, is difficult to interpret in terms of the postulated paths given in Figure 1. It is possible that this economy is uniquely different to the extent that it should not be grouped with the selected countries for the cross-country comparison made here. Indeed, one is justified, by reference to a variety of measures, per capita income, literacy rate, medical services per capita, etc., in concluding that Indonesia is the least economically advanced of the ASEAN countries.

We have also collected data and calculated estimates of the 1982 input–output (level) ratios, PTO and MAO, which are presented in Tables 10 and 11.

The graph of the input–output ratio of scientists and engineers involved in research and development is presented in Figure 4. It reveals that as of 1982, Japan and Korea ranked above the United States in what could be a relevant indicator of economic growth for the near future. Indeed, calculation and interpretation of parallel incremental input–output ratios, relative to inputs such as education, basic research, public health, and other related social inputs from the public (government) sector, would be an appropriate order of research to follow.

Table 6. IPOR Version 1

Country	*(1) Change in constant US$ GDP (GNP) 1978–1982*	*(2) Change of employment in pro., tech., and related occupation 1978–1982*	*(3) (2)/(1) IPOR 1*
United States	43.60	2413	55.34
Japan[a]	186.57	720	3.86
Indonesia	17.91	653	36.46
Korea	9.66	148	15.32
Malaysia	1.88	9.7	5.16
Philippines[a]	5.67	140	24.71
Singapore	8.27	24.5	2.96
Thailand	3.54	198.8	56.16
Taiwan	10.50	68	6.48

[a]GNP.

Table 7. IPOR Version 2

Country	*(1) Percentage change in constant GDP (GNP) 1978–1982*	*(2) Percentage change in employment in pro., tech., and related occupation 1978–1982*	*(3) (2)/(1) IPOR 2*
United States	1.63	16.60	10.18
Japan[a]	17.33	18.04	1.04
Indonesia	28.83	61.72	2.14
Korea	17.53	30.83	1.76
Malaysia	9.16	4.10	0.45
Philippines[a]	18.26	14.71	0.81
Singapore	41.13	29.96	0.73
Thailand	10.65	35.52	3.34
Taiwan	26.61	21.25	0.80

[a]GNP.

Table 8. IMOR Version 1

Country	*(1) Change in constant US$ GDP (GNP) 1978–1982*	*(2) Change in manager and adm. employment 1978–1982*	*(3) (2)/(1) IMOR 1*
United States	43.60	1207	27.63
Japan[a]	186.57	160	0.86
Indonesia	17.91	–8	–0.45
Korea	9.66	18	1.86
Malaysia	1.88	–0.2	–0.11
Philippines[a]	5.67	37	6.53
Singapore	8.27	31.9	3.86
Thailand	3.54	112.1	31.66
Taiwan	10.50	–2	–0.19

[a]GNP.

Table 9. IMOR Version 2

Country	*(1) Percentage change in constant US$ GDP (GNP) 1978–1982*	*(2) Percentage change in manager and adm. employment 1978–1982*	*(3) (2)/(1) (PTO)*
United States	1.63	11.73	7.20
Japan[a]	17.33	7.84	0.45
Indonesia	28.83	–17.02	–0.59
Korea	17.53	12.33	0.70
Malaysia	9.16	–.35	–0.04
Philippines[a]	18.26	21.51	1.18
Singapore	41.13	120.83	2.94
Thailand	10.65	38.05	3.57
Taiwan	26.61	–3.64	–0.14

[a]GNP.

Table 10. PTO Ratio 1982

Country	*(1) Pro., tech., and related workers*	*(2) Constant US$ GDP or GNP*	*(3) (1)/(2) PTO*
United States	16951	2713.80	6.25
Japan[a]	4710	1263.03	3.73
Indonesia	1711	80.05	21.38
Korea	628	64.78	9.7
Singapore	106.3	13.26	8.02
Philippines[a]	1092	36.69	29.76
Thailand	758.5	36.74	20.65
Taiwan	388	49.94	7.77

[a]GNP.

Table 11. MAO Ratio 1982

Country	*(1) Manager and adm. workers*	*(2) Constant US$ GDP or GNP*	*(3) (1)/(2) MAO*
United States	11493	2713.80	4.24
Japan[a]	2200	1263.03	1.74
Indonesia	39	80.05	0.49
Korea	164	64.78	2.53
Singapore	58.3	13.26	4.40
Philippines[a]	209	36.69	5.70
Thailand	406.7	36.74	11.07
Taiwan	53	49.94	1.06

[a]GNP.

Figure 2. IPOR for selected East-Asian countries and the United States, 1978–1982.

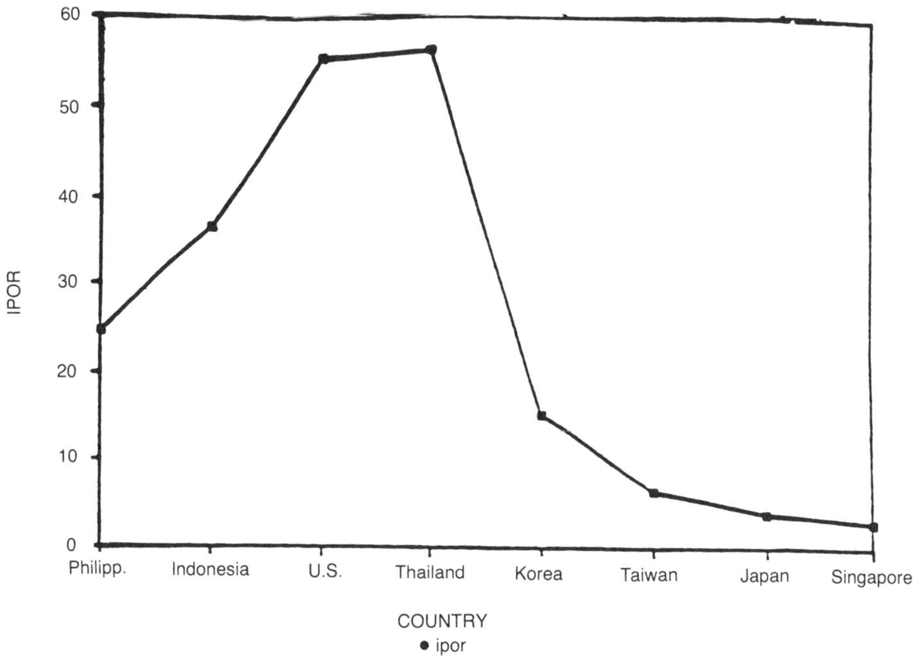

Figure 3. IMOR for selected East-Asian countries and the United States, 1978–1982.

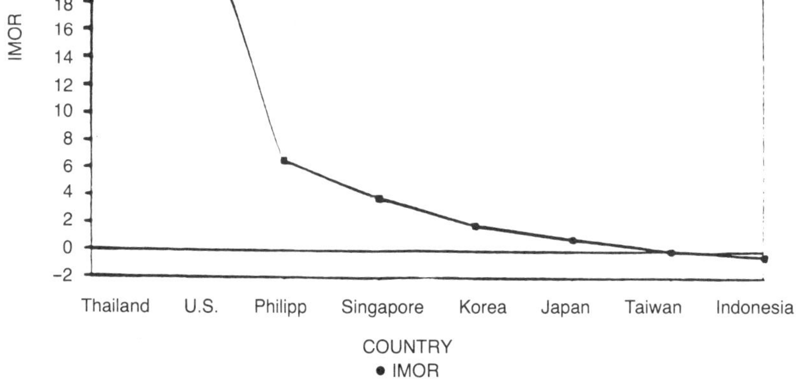

Figure 4. RDO for selected East-Asian countries and the United States, 1982.

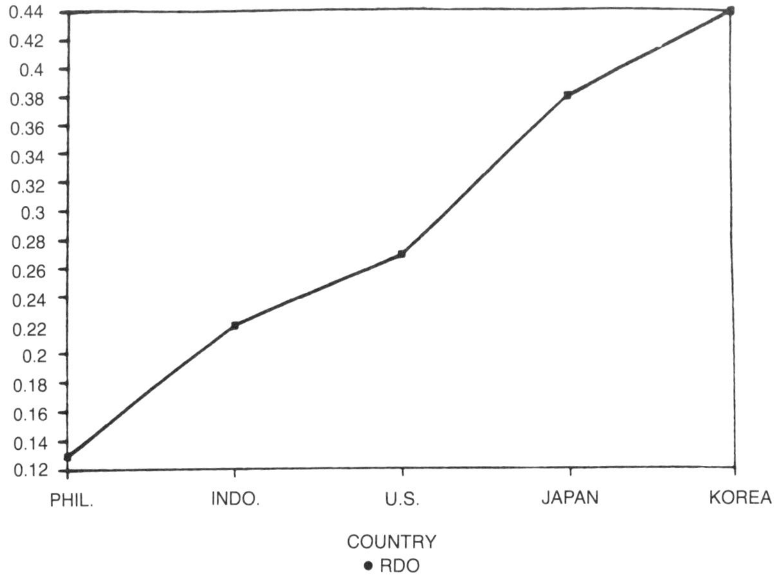

(*Source:* see footnote 11.)

VI. CONCLUSION

Economic research concerning comparative cross-country competitiveness will benefit significantly from studies of production maps of competing economies, wherein input definitions have not remained narrowly understood. In this study it has been emphasized that in doing this research not only must the nonhomogeneity of labor inputs within economies be considered, but also the degree of divergence in labor structure across economies.

This study has suggested five areas for investigation to contribute toward an understanding of the relative economic performance between Japan and other selected East Asian economies vis-à-vis the United States. In this context three of the five areas of comparative divergence have been further analyzed: (1) labor structures and their associated differences in productivity, (2) management structures and their associated differences in productivity, and (3) the roles of respective governments in educational planning for engineering and technical manpower, policy toward Research and Development (R&D), and contribution to the production process.

Structural differences and the possibility of continued divergence in these areas have been underscored. What emerges from the study is a pattern of structural divergence between Japan and other selected Asian economies on one side and the United States on the other. Findings thus indicate that the countries in the former group are more effectively prepared for interregional competition in the present phase of the industrial revolution.

Thus, given the structural differences and continued divergence of the production maps of the respective economies, it follows that trade restrictions and/or fiscal–monetary restrictive (expansion) measures to improve the current U.S. trade and budget imbalances will not prove sufficient for any economy in the group, including the United States. Indeed, such measures may produce counterproductive results, since it may protect the United States from competition that eventually would induce rational and appropriate economic adjustments. The efforts to maintain and/or recapture cross-country economic competitiveness must be sought in adequate studies of the production maps of economies in competition in the world market. The next step would then be to take effective measures to maintain or increase the ability of a country to compete, thus expanding the production/consumption possibilities, not only for an individual country, but for all countries in the world economic community.

ACKNOWLEDGMENTS

Acknowledgment is due to Edward Ames, Richard F. Kosobud, Kazuo Sato, Sidney I. Simon, and Anthony M. Tang for their helpful comments and critiques, and also to the Department of Economics, Faculty of Arts and Sciences, Rutgers–The State University of New Jersey, New Brunswick, New Jersey for all its helpful cooperation. Youngjun Yoon collected data for this study and we thank him. Our special thanks to Janine Matton for her editorial assistance.

NOTES

1. For an example of a recent study of this area of the world see Bradford and Branson (1987). Of particular interest with respect to the present study is the chapter by Silk (this volume) that discusses some issues that are analyzed here. Also, See Dutta (1984, 1987); and, Linder (1986).

2. The Asian NICs and ASEAN Group growth rates are arithmetic averages of the individual country's growth rates within the respectively defined regions. For sources of data used for calculation or presentation of these GDP growth rates see *The World Development Report, 1986* and *Taiwan Statistical Yearbook, 1986*.

3. Export volume annual growth over the 1973–1984 period is calculated as an arithmetic average.

4. The time at which an active policy to lower the value of the dollar against "key" currencies, including the yen, was initiated has been identified to be even earlier than this date, in particular, the January 19, 1985 meeting of the G-5 countries (United States, Japan, England, West Germany, France) in Washington, D.C. (Subsequently, Italy and Canada have joined the group and hence it is referred to as G-7.)

5. For a heuristic discussion as well as theoretical and empirical analysis of two scenarios that result in a "J"-curve pattern of adjustment see Magee (1973) and Wilson and Takacs (1980).

6. Baldwin and Krugman have taken a step in this direction by considering the possibility that it is a divergence in growth of average labor productivity between the United States and Japan in the

tradeable goods sectors, which is not reflected in total productivity measures, that results in a consistent loss in competitiveness and persistent manufactured goods trade imbalance. For further details see Paul R. Krugman and Richard E. Baldwin (1987).

7. Shinichi Ichimura (1986) has discussed "ten factors" in this regard. Paul W. Kuznets (1986) has defined five areas for investigation. Vernon W. Ruttan (1986) has advocated that investigations should be extended beyond standard economic variables, and include anthropological factors.

8. Calculations given here are based on figures from *Statistical Yearbook 1986* (UNESCO, V102–V104, Tables 7–11) and various pages of the *International Financial Statistical Yearbook 1987* (IMF). The numerator of the calculations are current R&D expenditures, which do not include capital expenditures.

9. Note that for the United States, significant expenditures on education are made at the state and local government levels. However, to the extent that the total state and local expenditure shares have not increased between 1972 and 1983, one can argue that the relative importance of education in government budgets for the United States is declining. Even if the state and local shares have increased, it can be argued that the federal expenditures on education may be the most critical component for the United States insofar as competitive technological innovation is concerned.

10. Some of the problems that apply to these incremental I–O ratios are discussed in Bruce Herrick and Charles F. Kindleberger (1983: 171–175).

11. For Tables 6 through 9, Malaysia GDP and employment are over 1978–1979, whereas Thailand's GDP and employment are over 1980–1982.

For Tables 6, 8, 10, and 11, GDP (GNP) is in billions, and workers are in thousands.

Sources of data used for the calculation of variables in Tables 6 through 11 are as follows:

For GDP, International Monetary Fund (IMF), *International Financial Statistics Yearbook, 1986*. For Exchange Rate, United Nations Organization (UNO), *United Nations Statistical Yearbook, 1982*; for Taiwan, *Taiwan Statistical Yearbook, 1986*; and for Singapore, *Pacific Basin Economic Indicators*, Vol. 9, September 1984.

For labor inputs, personnel engaged in R&D, labor structure by occupation, "Professional, Technical, and Related Workers Employed," "Administrators and Managerial Workers," International Labor Organization (ILO), *Yearbook of Labor Statistics, 1986*; for Taiwan, *Taiwan Statistical Yearbook, 1985*.

The occupation titles used in above data sources are major group titles for the Internation Standard Classification of Occupations. "Professional, Technical, and Related Workers Employed" include the following categories: physical scientists and related technicians, architects, engineers, aircraft and ships officers, life scientists, medical, dental, and veterinary workers, statisticians, mathematicians, system analysts, economists, accountants, jurists, teachers, workers in religion, authors, journalists, sculptors, painters, photographers, creative artists, composers, performing artists, athletes, sportpersons. "Administrators and Managerial Workers" include administrators, managers, legislative officials, and government administrators. For the most part, the data from the *Yearbook of Labor Statistics* (ILO) follow the classification system of the International Standard Classification of Occupations.

REFERENCES

Bradford, Colin I., Jr. and William H. Branson (eds.) *Trade and Structural Change in Pacific Asia* (National Bureau of Economic Research). Chicago: The University of Chicago Press, 1987.

Denison, Edward F. "Accounting for Slower Economic Growth: An Update." In John W. Kendrick (ed.) *International Comparisons of Productivity and Causes of the Slowdown*, 1–46. Cambridge, MA: Ballinger Publishing Company, 1984.

Drucker, Peter F. "How to Measure White Collar Productivity." *The Wall Street Journal* November 26, 1985, 30.

———. *The Frontiers Of Management*. New York: Truman Talley Books/E.P. Dutton, 1986.

Dutta, M. (ed) *Studies in United States–Asia Economic Relations*. Durham, NC: The Acorn Press, 1984.

———. (ed.) *Asia-Pacific Economics: Promises and Challenges*, Vol. 6, Parts A and B, Greenwich, CT: JAI Press, 1987.

Findlay, Ronald "Trade and Development: Theory and Asian Experience." *Asian Development Review*, 1986, 23–44.

Herrick, Bruce, and Charles F. Kindleberger. *Economic Development*, 4th ed. New York: McGraw-Hill, 1983.

Hsing, Mo-huan. "A Comparative Study of Technological Progress of Manufacturing Industries in the United States and the Asian Growth Belt." In M. Dutta (ed.) *Studies in United States–Asia Economic Relations*, 417–437. Durham, NC: The Acorn Press, 1984.

Ichimura, Shinichi. "Ten Factors in Asian Economic Growth" (mimeo). Paper presented at the Vanderbilt University Special Economic Development Conference, October 16–19, 1986.

Kosobud, Richard F. "Measured Productivity Growth in Japan, 1952–1968." *Japan Economic Studies* 1974 (Spring Number).

Krugman, Paul R. and Richard E. Baldwin. "The Persistence of the U.S. Trade Deficit." *Brookings Papers on Economic Activity 1*, 1987, 1–55.

Kuznets, Paul W. "Korea and Taiwan: Implications of Rapid Growth in the Pacific," In Kermit Hanson and Thomas Roehl (eds.) *The United States and The Pacific Economy in the 1980s*, 51–78. Indianapolis: Bobbs-Merrill, 1980.

———. "An East Asian Model of Economic Development: Japan, Taiwan and South Korea" (mimeo). Paper presented at the Vanderbilt University Economic Development Conference, October 16–19, 1986.

Linder, Staffan Burenstam *The Pacific Century*, CA, Stanford: Stanford University Press, 1986.

Maddison, Angus. "Comparative Analysis of the Productivity Situation in the Advanced Capitalist Countries," In John W. Kendrick, (ed.) *International Comparisons of Productivity and Causes of Slowdown*, 59–92. Cambridge, MA: Ballinger Publishing Company, 1984.

Magee, Stephen P. "Currency Contracts, Pass-through and Devaluation." *Brookings Papers on Economic Activity 1*, 1973, 303–323.

McMahon, Walter W. "Comments" on "Comparative Analysis of the Productivity Situation in the Advanced Capitalist Countries." In John W. Kendrick (ed.) *International Comparisons of Productivity and Causes of Slowdown*, 93–108. Cambridge, MA: Ballinger Publishing Company, 1984.

Meier, Gerald M. *Leading Issues in Economic Development*, 4th ed., 215–216. New York: Oxford University Press, 1984.

Morita, Okio. *Made in Japan*. New York: E. P. Dutton, 1986.

Musgrave Richard A. and Peggy B. Musgrave. *Public Finance in Theory and Practice*, 3d ed. New York: McGraw-Hill, 1980.

Norsworth, J. R. and David H. Malmquist. "Recent Productivity Growth in Japanese and U.S. Manufacturing." In William J. Baumol and Kenneth McLennan, (eds.) *Productivity Growth and U.S. Competitiveness*, 58–69. New York: Oxford University Press, 1984.

Ouchi, William. *Theory Z: How American Business Can Meet the Japanese Challenge*. Philippines: Addison-Wesley Publishing Company, 1981.

Pepelasis, Adamantios, Leon Mears, and Irma Adelman. *Economic Development: Analysis and Case Studies* 121–122 and 445–446. New York: Harper and Brothers, 1961.

Psacharopoulos, George. "The Contribution of Education to Economic Growth: International Comparisons." In John W. Kendrick (ed.) *International Comparisons of Productivity and Causes of The Slowdown*, 335–356. Cambridge, MA: Ballinger Publishing Company 1984.

Rostow, Walt W. "Is There Need for Economic Leadership? Japanese or the United States?" *American Economic Review* Proceedings Volume *75*(2), 1985, 285–291.

———. "Economics: Revolution Is Ahead." *International Herald Tribune* August 16–17, 1986, adapted from *The Newsday*.

Ruttan, Vernon W. ''Cultural Endowments and Economic Development: What Can We Learn from Anthropology?'' (mimeo). Paper presented at The Vanderbilt University Economic Development Conference, October 16–19, 1986.

Shinohara, Miyohei. *Industrial Growth, Trade, and Dynamic Patterns in the Japanese Economy.* Tokyo: University of Tokyo Press, 1982.

———. ''Trade and Industrial Adjustments in the Asia–Pacific Region and Japan.'' In M. Dutta (ed.) *Studies in United States–Asia Economic Relations*, 51–72. Durham, NC: The Acorn Press, 1984.

———. ''Patterns and Backgrounds of Dynamics in the Asia–Pacific Economies.'' In M. Dutta (ed.) *Asia–Pacific Economies: Promises and Challenges*, 23–48. Greenwich, CT: JAI Press, 1987.

Smith, Michael, Jane McLoughlin, Peter Large, and Rod Chapman. *Asia's New Industrial World.* London/New York: Methuen, 1985.

Wade, Robert. ''The Role of Government in Overcoming Market Failure: Taiwan, South Korea, and Japan'' (mimeo). In Helen Hughes et al. (eds.) *Explaining The Success of East Asian Industrialization*, 1985.

Weil, Ulric. Presentation made on the performance of American Management at American Economic Association annual meetings, December 28–30, 1985, New York.

Wilson, John E. and Wendy E. Takacs. ''Expectations and the Adjustment of Trade Flows under Floating Exchange Rates: Leads, Lags, and the J-Curve.'' *International Finance Discussion Papers No. 160* (Board of Governors of The Federal Reserve System, Washington, D.C., April 1980).

THE INTERNATIONALIZATION OF UNITED STATES SERVICE INDUSTRIES AND THE ECONOMIES IN THE ASIA–PACIFIC REGION

Chung H. Lee and Seiji Naya

I. INTRODUCTION

In recent years the United States has experienced a significant increase in international "trade in services."[1] Although during the 1971–1985 period it ran an increasing deficit in its balance on the merchandise account, the United States experienced a surplus in its balance of private services (travel, passenger fares, transportation, royalties and fees, and other miscellaneous private services).

Statistics on trade in services do not, however, reveal the full extent of U.S. international transactions in services and their contribution to the balance of

Research in Asian Economic Studies.
Asian Industrialization: Changing Economic Structures,
Volume 1, Part A, pages 47–68.
Copyright © 1988 by JAI Press Inc.
All rights of reproduction in any form reserved.
ISBN: 0-89232-987-4

payments. In recent years U.S. service industries have increased direct foreign investment, and this means that U.S. service firms now carry out a significant portion of overseas sales through their foreign affiliates and that a large share of the growing income on U.S. foreign investment should be attributed to direct foreign investment in service industries (Table 1).

What are the implications of these changes in U.S. international transactions in services for United States–Asia economic relations? This is a question of some importance to the Asia–Pacific region, as it contains some of the most rapidly developing countries in the world and thus may provide a potentially significant market for U.S. service industries. The United States is, of course, the largest economy in the region, and, hence, whatever happens there warrants careful scrutiny for its effect on the other economies.

Table 1. U.S. Transactions in Private Services and Income on Assets, 1971–1985 (Millions of Dollars)

	Private services[a]			*Income on assets*[b]		
Year	*Credit*	*Debit*	*Balance*	*Credit*	*Debit*	*Balance*
1971	10,539	9,990	549	11,801	3,592	8,209
1972	11,629	11,495	134	13,898	3,888	10,010
1973	14,062	13,575	487	20,872	5,819	15,053
1974	16,975	15,625	1,350	26,513	7,822	18,691
1975	18,796	16,412	2,384	24,239	8,022	16,217
1976	21,655	18,764	2,891	27,954	8,791	19,163
1977	23,374	20,866	2,508	30,554	8,675	21,879
1978	27,103	23,738	3,365	40,402	13,006	27,396
1979	31,155	27,157	3,998	61,837	21,838	39,999
1980	37,040	29,428	7,612	69,944	29,528	40,416
1981	41,724	32,093	9,631	82,731	35,451	47,280
1982	41,398	32,634	8,764	79,431	36,598	42,833
1983	41,336	34,915	6,421	72,419	34,585	37,834
1984	43,258	41,068	2,190	80,992	47,700	33,292
1985	44,208	43,870	338	84,500	43,497	41,003

Source: Anthony J. DiLullo, "Service Transactions in the U.S. International Accounts, 1977–80," *Survey of Current Business* November 1981, 29–46; and various other issues.

[a] Private services are travel, passenger fares, transportation, royalties and fees, and miscellaneous private services.

[b] Excludes U.S goverment receipts and payments.

II. THE INTERNATIONALIZATION OF U.S. SERVICE INDUSTRIES[2]

There are two ways in which a foreign market may be served—by exporting a goods or service to the foreign market or by establishing a foreign affiliate.[3] Since these are alternative ways of serving a foreign market, trade statistics as conventionally reported tend to underestimate the extent of the internationalization of an industry. A better measure of internationalization should therefore be based on the exports of the industry and the sales of its foreign affiliates.[4] However, due to the paucity of data and the incompatibility of classification systems used for reporting balance of payments and direct investment statiscs, the necessary pooling of data is not possible. Here, trade in services and investment in services are reported separately, and no attempt is made at a precise measurement of the extent of the internationalization of U.S. service industries.

A. Trade in Services

Service transactions that are reported in the balance of payments and regarded as traded in the conventional sense of the word are travel, passenger fares, transportation, royalties and fees, and other miscellaneous private services.[5] These are transactions that generally do not require the establishment of a foreign affiliate. Reported figures on these, however, overestimate trade in services, since some of the royalties and fees belong to other sectors in the economy, and since miscellaneous private services include expenditures on goods by foreign diplomatic entities and international organizations.

Trade in services takes place when resident firms or individuals provide services to nonresident firms or individuals either across national boundaries or within national boundaries. In this case either providers or receivers of services move physically across national boundaries. Alternatively, some services, i.e., the use of intangible properties, are transmitted across national boundaries through contractual arrangements unaccompanied by either providers or receivers of services. An example of the latter is an intangible property telematically transmitted across national boundaries. The transmission of such a property, which is stored on magnetic tape upon receipt, is a case of what Bhagwati (1984) calls "disembodiment" of services from providers or what Sampson and Snape (1985) call "separated" services. Both conceptually and analytically, such transmission of an intangible property is not different from the export of a book containing valuable information. The fact is, however, that the latter is regarded as trade in goods and the former as trade in services. What this example demonstrates is the difficulty involved in defining trade in services and in finding data that correspond to the correct definition of the term.

In 1971 the total value of U.S. private services exports was in excess of $10 billion. It then increased almost every year, reaching a sum in excess of $44 billion in 1985. U.S. imports of private services also increased during this period, from about $10 billion in 1971 to nearly $44 billion in 1985 (Table 1).

We have noted that some of the fees, royalties, and other private services properly belong to other sectors. It is possible their inclusion in the category of private services accounts for the surplus on the services account. Since there is no way of separating fees, royalties, and other private services that belong to the service sector from those that belong to other sectors, it is impossible to carry out a conclusive test of this speculation. It is possible, however, to shed some light on this by separating travel, passenger fares, and other transportation (TPOT) from fees, royalties, and other services (FROS). If the latter can be shown to account for surpluses on the services account, there are grounds for skepticism of the argument that the U.S. comparative advantage has been shifting toward service industries.

Table 2 shows that the United States experienced a deficit every year during the 1971–1985 period on the TPOT account (except for 1981) but a surplus on the FROS account. There is no clear trend in the deficit, but there is a definite upward trend in the surplus. The increasing surplus in the balance of private services must thus be attributed to the increasing surplus on the FROS account. Since the FROS account contains items that may belong to nonservice sectors, caution is needed in inferring changes in the U.S. comparative advantage from aggregate statistics on private services.

B. Direct Foreign Investment by Service Industries and Sales of Foreign Affiliates

Trade is not the only channel through which firms make sales abroad—this is also accomplished through foreign affiliates. In fact, since services are nonstorable and thus nontransportable, much of their international sales is carried out through foreign affiliates. Therefore, the full extent of the internationalization of U.S. service industries cannot be comprehended without an examination of U.S. multinational enterprises (MNEs) in service industries and their overseas activities.

In 1977 there were 3,425 MNEs based in the United States, and of these 1,213 were in service industries (excluding banking). In that year the worldwide sales of U.S. MNEs amounted to more than $2 trillion, and the service industries (excluding banking) accounted for 20% of the total sales, or $403 billion (Barker, 1981).

These figures seem to indicate that service industries (excluding banking), which are the predominant sector in the U.S. economy, are not yet as global in their reach for markets as other industries. The number of MNEs in service industries and their share of all MNEs' sales do not correspond to the importance of the service sector in GNP and employment. Furthermore, the 1977 data show that foreign affiliates of the service industries accounted for 19% of their 1977 worldwide sales, whereas those of the manufacturing industries and of mining and

Table 2. U.S. Balance on Private Services, 1971–1985 (Millions of Dollars)

Balance	*1971*	*1972*	*1973*	*1974*	*1975*	*1976*	*1977*	*1978*	*1979*	*1980*	*1981*	*1982*	*1983*	*1984*	*1985*
Travel, passenger fares, and other transportation	−2,345	−3,063	−3,158	−3,184	−2,814	−2,558	−3,565	−3,573	−2,935	−997	144	−992	−4,227	−8,593	−11,128
Fees, royalties, and other services	2,894	3,197	3,645	4,534	5,196	5,449	6,073	6,938	6,933	8,609	9,487	9,756	10,648	10,783	11,466

Source: Anthony J. DiLullo, "Service Transactions in the U.S. International Accounts, 1977–80," *Survey of Current Business* November 1981, 29–46; and various other issues.

petroleum accounted for 29 and 53% respectively. These figures indicate that as of 1977 the service industries were not as internationalized as other industries and that service MNEs were not as extensive in their international transactions as those in other industries.

Table 3 reports sales by foreign affiliates of U.S. MNEs for 1977 and 1982, two benchmark survey years. Between the two years sales for all industries increased by 44%, but those for service industries increased by 126%. What is more striking is that sales by other services—hotels, business services, motion pictures, health services, etc.—increased by 240%. The share of total sales by affiliates accounted for by service industries thus increased from 12% in 1977 to 18% in 1982.

Between 1977 and 1985 the U.S. investment position (the net value of investors' equity and outstanding loans to foreign affiliates) increased for each and all of the three major industry groups and the four subgroups in service (Table 4). However, services' share of the total investment position decreased slightly. The decrease

Table 3. Sales by Foreign Affiliates of U.S. Multinational Enterprises (Millions of Dollars)

Industry/Sector	*1977*	*1982*
All industries	647,969 (100%)	935,780 (100%)
Manufacturing	297,697 (46%)	359,269 (38%)
Services	76,072 (12%)	171,605 (18%)
Trade[a]	45,044 (7%)	122,664 (13%)
Finance (excluding banking), insurance, and real estate	25,054 (4%)	28,651 (3%)
Other services	5,974 (1%)	20,290 (2%)
Other industries	274,200 (42%)	404,906 (43%)

Sources: Betty L. Barker, "A Profile of U.S. Multinational Corporations in 1977," *Survey of Current Business* October 1981, 38–57. U.S. Department of Commerce, Bureau of Economic Analysis, *U.S. Direct Investment Abroad*, December 1985.

[a] The figure for 1977 is for both wholesale and retail trade, but that for 1982 is for whosesale trade only.

Table 4. U.S. Direct Investment Position[a] Abroad, Yearend (Millions of Dollars)

Industry/sector	*1977*[b]	*1978*[b]	*1979*[b]	*1980*[b]	*1981*[b]	*1982*[c]	*1983*[c]	*1984*[c]	*1985*[c]
All industries	145,990 (100%)	162,727 (100%)	187,858 (100%)	215,375 (100%)	228,348 (100%)	207,752 (100%)	207,203 (100%)	212,994 (100%)	232,667 (100%)
Manufacturing	62,019 (43%)	69,669 (43%)	79,023 (42%)	89,290 (41%)	92,388 (40%)	83,452 (40%)	82,907 (40%)	85,253 (40%)	95,586 (41%)
Services	42,454 (29%)	48,478 (30%)	54,300 (29%)	60,683 (28%)	63,410 (28%)	53,738 (26%)	53,410 (26%)	55,489 (26%)	65,724 (28%)
Trade	16,836 (12%)	19,517 (12%)	22,670 (12%)	25,913 (12%)	28,336 (12%)	20,788 (10%)	21,278 (10%)	21,790 (10%)	23,822 (10%)
Banking	4,370 (3%)	5,622 (3%)	6,501 (3.5%)	7,264 (3%)	8,513 (4%)	10,317 (5%)	12,387 (6%)	13,246 (6%)	14,728 (6%)
Finance (excluding banking), insurance, and real estate	21,248 (15%)	23,339 (14%)	25,129 (13%)	27,506 (13%)	26,561 (12%)	18,018 (9%)	15,075 (7%)	15,828 (7%)	21,914 (9%)
Other services	—	—	—	—	—	4,615 (2%)	4,670 (2%)	4,625 (2%)	5,260 (2%)
Other industries	41,517 (29%)	44,580 (30%)	54,535 (32%)	65,402 (34%)	72,550 (34%)	70,562 (34%)	70,886 (31%)	72,252 (34%)	71,357 (31%)

Sources: U.S. Department of Commerce, Bureau of Economic Analysis, *U.S. Direct Investment Abroad*, 1977 and 1981; BEA mimeos (11/21/86); and *Survey of Current Business* *65*(8), August 1985 and *66*(8), August 1986.

[a] Investment position is the net value of direct investors' equity and outstanding loans to foreign officials.

[b] Data based on the 1977 benchmark survey.

[c] Data based on the 1982 benchmark survey of U.S. direct investment abroad.

could be a statistical artifact due to the updating of the benchmark survey year from 1977 to 1981: the data for 1977–1981 are based on the 1977 benchmark survey, whereas the data for 1982–1985 are based on the 1982 benchmark survey. Nevertheless, a salient point that seems to emerge from Table 4 is that the service sector has not been any more active in investing abroad in recent years than the other sectors in the economy.

Among the four subgroups of the service sector banking was more active, increasing its share of the total investment position from 3% in 1977 to 6% in 1985, whereas trade and FIRE (finance, excluding banking, insurance, and real estate) were less so, decreasing their share from 12 to 10% and 15 to 9%, respectively. Clearly, there is a large variation in the extent of internationalization among individual service industries and there is little evidence to support the contention that the U.S. comparative advantage has shifted toward *the* service sector.

The figures in Tables 3 and 4 thus indicate that in recent years the service sector has increased its international activities but has not increased its internationalization relative to the other sectors in the economy. This may be due to the fact that certain services such as those that are government provided are inherently untradable, but it is also possible that only recently certain U.S. service industries have gained a comparative advantage and they have yet to take full advantage of their competitive strength in the world market. Furthermore, it may be that many foreign countries have restricted trade and investment in services, and consequently U.S. service industries have not been able to expand their international activities as much as they otherwise could.

III. U.S. TRADE AND INVESTMENT IN SERVICES IN THE ASIA–PACIFIC REGION

A. Trade in Services

Information on the bilateral trade in services between the United States and any of the other countries in the Asia–Pacific region is difficult to obtain as there are few published data on the bilateral trade in services. Data are, however, available for trade in services with the rest of the world for each of these countries, thus providing some information on the upper limit to the bilateral trade in services.

The figures in Table 5 represent the share of services exported and the share of merchandise exported for the countries in the region, and they can be taken as measures of the openness of the respective sectors. The figures indicate the service sector is less open than the other sectors, but the large variation in the share of services exported suggests diversity in services and varying degrees of tradability of services.

Table 5. The Share of Services[a] and Merchandise Exported, 1983

Country	*Share of services exported (%)*	*Share of merchandise exported (%)*
Indonesia	2	37
Japan	4	29
Korea	17	57
Malaysia	14	86
Philippines	10	24
Singapore	87	216
Taiwan	12	86
Thailand	8	38
United States	2	18

Sources: International Monetary Fund, *Balance of Payments Statistics*, Vol. 35, Part I, 1984. Taiwan Directorate-General of Budget, Accounting and Statistics, *Statistical Yearbook of Taiwan 1985*. The World Bank, *World Development Report 1985*.

[a] Services are all branches of economic activities excluding the agriculture sector (agriculture, forestry, hunting, and fishing) and the industrial sector (mining, manufacturing, construction, and electricity, water, and gas).

Although the United States and Japan have a small share of services exported, they are nevertheless the region's two largest exporters of services. As can be seen in Table 6, the sum of services exported from all the other countries during the 1976–1983 period does not match the sum of exports from these two giants. The same can also be said for merchandise exports.

The next largest exporters of services are three of the newly industrializing countries of the region—Singapore, South Korea, and Taiwan (no data are available on Hong Kong's services exports). It is well known that these countries have achieved rapid economic development by heavily exporting labor-intensive manufactured goods. What is perhaps less well known is that these countries are also relatively large exporters of services. Why the countries that are relatively large exporters of merchandise are also relatively large exporters of services is a question yet to be answered fully, although a complementary relationship has been suggested by Balassa (1983) and Praet (1985) for certain industries such as shipping (with trade) and software (with computer hardware).

Table 6. Exports of Merchandise and Services of Asia-Pacific Countries, 1976–1983 (Billions of SDRs)[a]

Merchandise		*Services*[b]	
United States	1,210.80 (100)	United States	171.61[c] (100)
Japan	765.09 (63)	Japan	106.83[d] (62)
Taiwan	114.39 (9)	Singapore	39.91 (23)
Indonesia	109.14 (9)	Korea	28.50[e] (17)
Korea	108.34 (9)	Taiwan	13.27 (8)
Malaysia	67.84 (6)	Thailand	7.51 (4)
Singapore	58.27 (5)	Philippines	7.00 (4)
Thailand	35.69 (3)	Malaysia	6.93 (4)
Philippines	29.63 (2)	Indonesia	2.25 (1)

Sources: See Table 5.

[a] Figures in parentheses are percentages, with figures for the United States used as a base.

[b] Includes shipment, passenger services, other transportation, travel, and other goods, services, and income.

[c] Other goods, services, and income consist of communications, technical services of construction and related industries, nonmerchandise insurance, and other.

[d] Other goods, services, and income consist of agents' fees, management fees, merchandise transactions abroad (net), nonmerchandise insurance, and other.

[e] Other goods, services, and income consist of construction services, management services, nonmerchandise insurance, and other.

Table 7 shows the same relationship between merchandise imports and services imports: The countries that are relatively large importers of merchandise are also relatively large importers of services.

Table 8 presents data on trade in services for the individual years of 1976 through 1983 and cumulatively for the entire 1976–1983 period. All of the countries experienced a high rate of growth both in exports and imports of services. The rate of growth in exports ranged from 31% for Indonesia to 10% for the United States, whereas the rate of growth in imports ranged from 26% for Malaysia to 11% for the United States. It is interesting to note that the developing

Table 7. Imports of Merchandise and Services of Asia–Pacific Countries, 1976–1983 (Billions of SDRs)[a]

Merchandise			
United States	1,428.25 (100)	United States	180.29 (100)
Japan	654.97 (46)	Japan	176.12 (98)
Korea	124.46 (9)	Korea	21.71 (12)
Taiwan	99.57 (7)	Taiwan	18.20 (10)
Singapore	97.61 (7)	Indonesia	17.81 (10)
Indonesia	82.65 (6)	Singapore	16.18 (9)
Malaysia	59.84 (4)	Malaysia	15.17 (8)
Thailand	44.94 (3)	Thailand	8.84 (5)
Philippines	41.66 (3)	Philippines[b]	7.60 (4)

Sources: See Table 4.

[a] Figures in parentheses are percentages, with figures for the United States used as a base.

[b] 1977–1983.

countries in the region all had a higher rate of growth in both the exports and imports of services than did the United States and Japan.

During the 1976–1983 period all but South Korea and Singapore had deficits on the services account. Singapore's surpluses may be explained by the fact that it is an entrêpot economy. The case of South Korea is different, however. Its surpluses were largely due to its export of construction services; during this period South Korea had a surplus of 9,068 million Special Drawing Rights (SDRs) on the construction service account.

To demonstrate whether the importance of services trade relative to merchandise trade has changed over time, the ratio of services trade to merchandise trade has been calculated. Calculations show that there was some increase in the ratio of exports for Indonesia, Malaysia, the Philippines, and Thailand; there was a slight decrease for Taiwan. For Japan, South Korea, Singapore, and the United States—the top four exporters of services in the region—there was no change, indicating that their exports of services and merchandise had increased at the

Table 8. Trade in Services.[a] 1976–1983 (Millions of SDRs)

Country/group	Year									Average annual growth rate (%)
	1976	1977	1978	1979	1980	1981	1982	1983	1976–1983	
Indonesia										
Credit	96	98	186	144	251	382	558	539	2,254	31
Debit	–1,414	–1,426	–1,839	–2,172	–2,588	–4,134	–4,282	–4,021	–17,806	18
(Net)	(–1,318)	(–1,328)	(–1,653)	(–1,928)	(–2,337)	(–3,752)	(–3,724)	(–3,482)	(–15,552)	
Japan										
Credit (x10^3)	8.70	9.71	9.40	11.11	14.15	18.16	17.81	17.79	106.83	11
Debit (x10^3)	–13.64	–14.92	–16.06	–20.00	–23.64	–29.37	–28.94	–29.55	–176.12	12
(Net) (x10^3)	(–4.94)	(–5.21)	(–6.66)	(–8.89)	(–9.49)	(–11.21)	(–11.13)	(–11.76)	(–69.29)	
Korea										
Credit	1,138	2,162	2,989	3,063	3,375	4,568	5,630	5,572	28,497	28
Debit	–978	–1,666	–2,473	–2,616	–3,002	–3,556	–3,603	–3,813	–21,707	23
(Net)	(160)	(496)	(516)	(447)	(373)	(1,012)	(2,027)	(1,759)	(6,790)	
Malaysia										
Credit	335	413	497	609	876	1,119	1,412	1,667	6,928	26
Debit	–707	–879	–1,061	–1,604	–2,255	–2,366	–2,799	–3,494	–15,165	26
(Net)	(–372)	(–466)	(–564)	(–995)	(–1,379)	(–1,247)	(–1,387)	(–1,827)	(–8,237)	
Philippines										
Credit	467	465	600	622	852	1,198	1,379	1,417	7,000	19
Debit	–579	–674	–701	–856	–1,112	–1,285	–1,535	–1,436	–8,178	15
(Net)	(–112)	(–209)	(–101)	(–234)	(–260)	(–87)	(–156)	(–19)	(–1,178)	

Singapore										
Credit	2,391	2,615	2,890	3,401	4,563	7,141	8,612	8,408	39,911	21
Debit	–907	–1,086	–1,230	–1,577	–2,157	–2,653	–3,144	–3,425	–16,179	21
(Net)	(1,484)	(1,529)	(1,660)	(1,824)	(2,406)	(4,488)	(5,468)	(4,983)	(23,732)	
Taiwan										
Credit	869	992	1,450	1,443	1,639	2,158	2,286	2,431	13,268	17
Debit	–1,083	–1,050	–1,464	–2,142	–2,276	–2,941	–3,392	–3,854	–18,202	21
(Net)	(–214)	(–58)	(–14)	(–699)	(–637)	(–783)	(–1,106)	(–1,423)	(–4,934)	
Thailand										
Credit	352	408	600	735	1,051	1,278	1,461	1,623	7,508	25
Debit	–618	–691	–765	–1,007	–1,212	–1,451	–1,406	–1,687	–8,837	16
(Net)	(–266)	(–283)	(–165)	(–272)	(–161)	(–173)	(55)	(–64)	(–1,329)	
United States										
Credit ($x10^3$)	14.96	14.89	16.01	18.27	21.64	27.45	29.17	29.22	171.61	10
Debit ($x10^3$)	–15.84	–17.09	–18.02	–19.99	–21.64	–26.28	–28.82	–32.61	–180.29	11
(Net) ($x10^3$)	(–0.88)	(–2.20)	(–2.01)	(–1.72)	(0)	(1.17)	(0.35)	(–3.39)	(–8.68)	

Sources: See Table 5.

[a] Includes shipment, passenger services, other transportation, travel, and other private goods, services, and income.

same rate. In the ratio for imports there was a slight increase for Malaysia, but by and large there was no change in the ratio for the other countries.

These findings seem inconsistent with the argument that U.S. comparative advantage has shifted in recent years to service industries. If it had, there would have been an increase in the ratio for exports and a decrease in the ratio for imports for the United States, and the converse would have been true for some of the other countries. This inconsistency may, however, be due to the fact that there is a complementary relationship between services and goods transactions. According to Balassa, growth in services such as data processing, engineering design, and construction abroad is often linked with transactions in goods, with one or the other being the leading transaction or the two being jointly carried out. Given this relationship, the observed patterns of trade would not reflect a shift in comparative advantage from manufacturing to service industries.

To further shed light on this issue in the context of the Asia–Pacific region we classified the countries in the region in terms of the balance of trade in merchandise and the balance of trade in services for the 1976–1983 period. South Korea and Singapore had a surplus in the services account but a deficit in the merchandise account. Indonesia, Japan, Malaysia, and Taiwan had a deficit in the services account but a surplus in the merchandise account. The Philippines, Thailand, and the United States had a deficit in both accounts. Given the numerous barriers to trade, the pattern of comparative advantage in the region can hardly be inferred from this pattern of trade balance. Nevertheless, it casts doubt on the contention that the United States now has a comparative advantage in services vis-à-vis the other countries in the Asia–Pacific region.

B. Direct Foreign Investment in Services

Since data on the U.S. direct investment position in services are not available for some individual countries in the region, it is impossible to find a direct measure of the importance of the region as a host for U.S. multinational service enterprises. The figures in Table 9 are for the U.S. direct investment position in all industries for the region as well as for individual countries during 1976–1983. They thus provide some information on the upper limit to U.S. direct investment position in services for the region.

Throughout these years Japan was the most important host country, followed by Hong Kong. The Philippines was more important than Indonesia and Singapore in the earlier years, but its position later reversed as the U.S. direct investment position decreased absolutely in the Philippines but increased rapidly in Indonesia and Singapore. South Korea, Taiwan, and Thailand were the least important countries in the region in terms of U.S. direct foreign investment.

Table 9 also shows that the U.S. investment position in the Asia–Pacific region increased from $13 billion in 1979 to about $21 billion in 1983, but it was only 7% of the total in 1979 and 9% in 1983. It is clear from these figures that

Table 9. U.S. Direct Investment Position (All Industries) in Asia–Pacific Countries and Its Share in Total Investment Position, Yearend (Millions of Dollars)

	Year				
Country/group	*1979*	*1980*	*1981*	*1982*	*1983*
Hong Kong	1,770	2,078	2,729	3,015	3,310
Indonesia	1,191	1,314	1,847	2,615	3,042
Japan	6,208	6,243	6,755	6,928	8,059
Korea	689	575	779	829	650
Malaysia	561	632	847	1,030	1,118
Philippines	1,254	1,259	1,320	1,297	1,102
Singapore	860	1,204	1,835	1,822	1,965
Taiwan	393	498	562	622	695
Thailand	200	361	551	585	729
Total Asia–Pacific countries[a]	13,126 (7)	14,164 (7)	17,225 (8)	18,743 (8)	20,670 (9)
Total all countries	186,760	215,578	226,359	221,512	226,117

Source: U.S. Department of Commerce, *Survey of Current Business*, various issues.

[a] Figures in parentheses are percentages.

although its share has increased over time the U.S. investment position in the Asia–Pacific region is still only a small fraction of the total U.S. direct investment position.

The data so far presented provide a very rough picture of the importance of U.S. direct investment in services in the Asia–Pacific region; however, they say little about how important it is in comparison with services exports from the United States. For this, comparison of services exports with the sales of foreign affiliates in services is needed.

Table 10 shows sales made in 1982 by the majority-owned U.S. foreign affiliates located in the Asia–Pacific region and in all countries. These are for both goods and services and for sales made to markets outside as well as inside the United States. Obviously, the sales of foreign affiliates, whether in goods or in services, were primarily to markets outside the United States: For all affiliates combined the share of sales going to these markets was 90% for goods and 89% for services, whereas for the affiliates located in the Asia–Pacific region it was 83 and 96% respectively.

In 1982 the sales of services made by the majority-owned U.S. foreign affiliates to the rest of the world was 53 billion SDRs, whereas U.S. export of services was 29 billion SDRs. (Sales by those located in the Asia–Pacific region to the rest of the world were a little over 3 billion SDRs.) These figures demonstrate that direct foreign investment, not trade, is the major vehicle for the internationalization of U.S. service industries.

Table 10. Sales of Majority-Owned U.S. Foreign Affiliates, Country of Affiliate by Destination, 1982 (Millions of SDRs)[a]

Country of affiliate	*Goods*			*Services*[b]		
	Total	*Sales to the United States*	*Sales to the rest of world*	*Total*	*Sales to the United States*	*Sales to the rest of world*
Asia–Pacific countries[c]	63,563 (100)	10,614 (17)	52,949 (83)	3,533 (100)	149 (4)	3,384 (96)
All countries	601,375 (100)	62,800 (10)	538,575 (90)	60,070 (100)	6,747 (11)	53,322 (89)

Source: Obie G. Whichard and Michael A. Shea, ''1982 Benchmark Survey of U.S. Direct Investment Abroad,'' *Survey of Current Business 65*(12), December 1985.

[a] Figures in parentheses are percentages.
[b] Services include sales in the following industries: oil and gas field services, petroleum tanker operations, petroleum and natural gas pipelines, and petroluem storage for hire, finance (except banking), insurance, and real estate, services (as narrowly defined in the SIC), agricultural services, metal mining services, transportation, communication, and public utilities. For a more detailed discussion of services included see source article.
[c] Hong Kong, Indonesia, Japan, Malaysia, Philippines, Singapore, Korea, Taiwan, Thailand, and ''other'' (excluding Australia and New Zealand).

IV. BARRIERS TO TRADE AND INVESTMENT IN SERVICES

In most countries of the world service industries are regulated to an extent unmatched in other industries. Some of the regulations are explicitly protectionist in intent, acting as barriers to trade and investment in services. Others are not, although they may function as such. In fact a regulation does not have to be overtly protectionist to be an obstacle to trade and investment in services, as Alexander and Tan (1984) clearly demonstrated in their study of barriers to U.S. service trade in Japan. Consequently, it is not an easy task to determine whether a law or regulation governing a service industry is a barrier or not.

One way of coping with the difficulty of defining what constitutes a barrier to trade and investment in services is to establish basic principles and procedures as criteria for identifying a measure as a barrier. The following principles and procedures proposed in *U.S. Study on Trade in Services* (Office of the U.S. Trade Representative, 1983) may be used as criteria:

1. *National treatment.* This is the principle that "foreign services and their suppliers should be treated on the same basis as domestic firms supplying these services." In other words, this principle requires that laws and regulations should be applied nondiscriminatorily to domestic and foreign firms.
2. *Least restrictive regulations.* This is the premise that if regulation of an industry is justified, it should be regulated in the least restrictive manner possible.
3. *Nondiscrimation.* This is the most-favored-nation principle extended to services.
4. *Right to sell.* This principle would prohibit the practice of denying market access to foreign service firms, provided that access does not conflict with "sovereign goals and interests."
5. *Transparency.* "Regulations that hamper or distort trade in services should be transparent, i.e., open and unambiguous."

What follows is a list of barriers encountered by U.S. service industries in the Asia–Pacific region. (It has been compiled by the Office of the U.S. Trade Representative.) Given the previous discussion of the principles and procedures proposed by the United States, it is clear why they are listed as barriers. The list is not comprehensive but it nevertheless provides a general picture of the barriers encountered by U.S. service industries.

- *Insurance*: Market access is denied; foreign insurers are not permitted to establish branches or subsidiaries.
- *Leasing*: The application process to obtain authorization for new leasing operations is not transparent, lacking specified criteria; there are percentage

limitations on foreign ownership and expatriate employment; leasing of imported goods is not permitted.

- *Motion pictures*: There are quotas on film imports; market access is denied to foreign film distributors; use of foreign technical exports is restricted; quotas on film imports.
- *Franchising*: There is a lack of protection of trademark; trademark litigation involves costly court proceedings; cessions to unauthorized foreign reinsurers are limited.
- *Maritime transportation*: There is a percentage requirement for national-flag carriers.
- *Advertising*: All broadcasting materials are required to be produced locally using local labor; market access is limited; the establishment of wholly-owned or majority-owned branches or subsidiaries is not permitted.
- *Banking*: Foreign ownership is limited; establishment of foreign bank branches is prohibited.
- *Air transportation*: The national carrier receives preferential treatment in charter flight operations and pays lower taxes than foreign carriers; there is a monopoly on ground handling services by the national carrier.

The preceding list indicates that most of the barriers are investment-related in the sense that they constitute obstacles or difficulties in establishing and operating affiliates abroad. Some, such as those in motion pictures, are certainly trade related but they constitute a small minority. It follows that various issues relating to barriers to international commerce in services and their removal have to do primarily with direct foreign investment in services and not with trade in services.

V. THE LIBERALIZATION OF INTERNATIONAL SERVICE TRANSACTIONS AND IMPLICATIONS FOR DEVELOPING COUNTRIES

In recent years much has been written about barriers to trade and investment in services and on how to reduce or eliminate these barriers. Arguments for the liberalization of trade and investment in services cannot be persuasive, however, unless they are supported with firm theoretical and empirical analysis of the effects on the liberalizing country.

Perhaps the strongest argument made in favor of liberalization in terms of its effect on the importing country is that of Hindley and Smith (1984), that is, that the theory of comparative cost applies to both goods and services. However, trade in services is small relative to transactions carried out by foreign affiliates, and consequently the theory of comparative cost explains only a small segment of the phenomenon. Furthermore, trade in services runs into fewer barriers than investment in services. Thus, what must be demonstrated is a case in favor of liberalizing direct foreign investment (DFI) in services.

As argued elsewhere (Lee and Naya, 1988), DFI in services is socially efficient because it saves on transaction costs. What matters to the host country however, is its share of the gains resulting from this economization. The modern theory of the MNE does little to explain how the gains will be distributed between the host and the investing countries. There is a broad range of views on this—from the extreme position that with minor exceptions the developing host country has received no gains from international services transactions to the neoclassical position of shared gains.

One approach that might be used to settle this controversy would be to delineate conditions under which the host country can gain from DFI in services and then demonstrate that such conditions do exist. One of these conditions is that DFI increases competition in the industry affected, the presumption being that the more competitive the industry becomes the greater the improvements in allocative efficiency and x-efficiency. Furthermore, increased competition would tend to force foreign affiliates to pass on to consumers more of the quasi-rents on their technological superiority in the form of lower prices. The difficulty with this approach of demonstrating gains from DFI in services to the host country is that few countries have had DFI in services long enough to accumulate adequate data for such a project. An alternative approach, adopted in this study, is to examine critically various arguments made in favor of maintaining barriers to DFI in services.

Perhaps the harshest criticism of DFI in services has been voiced by Clairmonte and Cavanagh (1984). In their view, the entry of the MNE into the host country's industry has insidious effects on the values of the society, and they are not merely limited to economic effects such as those on income and employment. The MNE may in fact have undesirable effects on social values and the cultural identity of the host country. Although such arguments against the MNE should not be lightly dismissed, they lie outside the realm of economic analysis and are thus beyond the scope of this study. This analysis is confined to various arguments for restricting the entry of the MNE on economic grounds.

An UNCTAD study (1985) states that many services such as railways and electricity generation (i.e., public utilities) are major employers, and governments sometimes regard employment as a more important issue than economic efficiency.

For some governments employment may undeniably be more important than economic efficiency, especially in the short run. But the question then is why the same argument does not also apply to manufacturing industries. The answer may be found in the fact that the output of a service affiliate is entirely for the local market, whereas that of a manufacturing affiliate is usually exported. The government of a developing host country may thus regard a manufacturing affiliate as contributing to the employment of its citizens but a service affiliate as displacing its local competitors and not adding any net employment.

A fallacy of this view is that it does not take into account indirect effects of DFI in services. These are the favorable effects on employment in other industries, which are brought about by increased efficiency in service industries. These effects may more than offset the possible negative effect on employment. Thus, protecting service industries for the purpose of creating employment may have a negative employment effect on other industries and on the economy as a whole.

In most countries many service industries are highly regulated in terms of rates charged and entry conditions. Arguments in favor of regulations are that competition leads to the disruption of services, that buyers have only imperfect information on services provided, and that foreign entry increases dependency on foreign countries.

In the context of this study there are two issues relating to regulation of service industries. The first is whether there should be such regulation; the second is whether there should be discrimination against the entry of the MNE. These are separate issues, since service industries may be regulated either without discrimination against the entry of the MNE or with restriction on its entry. This distinction becomes important when negotiations are carried out to reduce or eliminate barriers to foreign entry. If regulations are bona fide and are not set up to restrict foreign entry, then demanding deregulation, however it may be justified in terms of economic reasoning and evidence, could be construed as an attack on national sovereignty over policy matters. If regulations are discriminatory, however, demands for ''national treatment'' of foreign affiliates are less likely to be viewed as an incursion into national sovereignty. The problem with this distinction between nondiscriminatory and discriminatory regulations is that it is difficult in practice to make the distinction. As pointed out by Alexander and Tan in their study of barriers to U.S. service trade in Japan, even if protectionist goals are the basis of regulation, they do not have to be overt to be effective. To make the necessary distinction in such a situation and to make the true objective for regulation transparent are formidable tasks.

An argument may be made against liberalizing service industries on the ground that it has a negative effect on the balance of payments. However, the liberalization may have a positive effect. Since it leads to improved efficiency in service industries, there will be a decrease in the relative prices of service-intensive commodities. If service-intensive commodities are exportables, the liberalization will bring about an increase in the country's exports, whereas if they are importables, it will lead to a decrease in imports. The liberalization will thus improve the country's trade balance, although it may have an adverse effect on the services account. This link between the liberalization of service industries and trade in goods needs to be further elaborated and empirically estimated. Empirical demonstration of the link may help allay the fear on the part of the developing countries that liberalizing service industries will lead to balance-of-payment difficulties.

VI. CONCLUSIONS

This study has addressed the extent of the internationalization of U.S. service industries, barriers to trade, and investment in services, and some of the possible effects of liberalizing international service transactions on the developing countries in the Asia–Pacific region. Knowledge of these is still meager, as research on trade and investment in services has just recently begun, and data necessary for rigorous empirical research have yet to be collected and become widely available for scrutiny.

In spite of this lack of knowledge one thing seems to be reasonably clear—the continuing industrialization of the region's developing countries and continuing technological innovations in certain U.S. service industries will eventually shift U.S. comparative advantage away from manufacturing industries with standardized technologies toward these service industries. Furthermore, as pointed out by Lipsey and Kravis (1985), technological innovations in these service industries will improve the competitiveness of U.S. service enterprises vis-à-vis their counterparts in the rest of the world, whether the United States has a comparative advantage in these industries or not. These changes will require structural adjustment in the U.S. economy, with resources moving from manufacturing industries to service industries. For this structural adjustment to be carried out smoothly it is necessary that the other countries undertake policies that will accommodate the adjustment. These countries cannot expect to continue to expand exports of manufactured goods to the United States without making it possible for U.S. service industries to expand their trade and investment abroad at the same time. Without such accommodating policies structural adjustment in the U.S. economy will be much more difficult, and this difficulty will only increase political pressure for protectionist measures against imports of many manufactured goods. In other words, the politicoeconomic effect of restricting further internationalization of U.S. service industries may be limited expansion of U.S. import of manufactured goods.

Liberalization of international service transactions may thus lead to expansion of international trade in manufactured goods in two ways: First, it is likely to improve comparative advantage in the manufacturing industries of services-importing countries as their service industries become more efficient and as services become less costly as inputs for manufactured output. Second, liberalization would lessen political pressure for protectionist measures in the United States against imports from newly industrializing countries. This linkage between international service transactions and trade in manufactured goods certainly requires further study. However, whatever meager knowledge there is on this linkage is sufficient enough to warn against regarding international transactions in services as a matter affecting only the service sector.

NOTES

1. The term "trade in services" refers here to transborder transactions in services between residents and nonresidents. In the literature, it sometimes refers to both trade and investment in services or invisibles in the balance of payments, which include factor services such as investment income and workers' remittances.

2. Internationalization refers to the process of producing and distributing a goods or service, whether carried out at home or abroad, for a foreign market.

3. Here "affiliate" denotes any establishment created abroad with direct foreign investment.

4. This method may lead to double counting, as sales by an affiliate may be nothing more than commodities distributed by the affiliate, which imported them from its parent company.

5. The term "services" refers to the output of service industries and not to the services provided within a firm, for instance, in a manufacturing industry. The latter cannot be included in trade in services for the same reason the value of an intermediate product contained in other exported goods is not added to the export of the intermediate product.

REFERENCES

Alexander, Arthur J. and Hong W. Tan. *Barriers to U.S. Service Trade in Japan*. Rand Corporation, September 1984.

Balassa, B. "Comments." In W. R. Cline (ed.), *Trade Policies in the 1980s*. Cambridge: MIT Press, 1983.

Barker, Betty L. "A Profile of U.S. Multinational Corporations in 1977." *Survey of Current Business* October 1981, 38–57.

Bhagwati, Jagdish N. "Splintering and Disembodiment of Services and Developing Nations." *The World Economy* June 1984, 133–143.

Clairmonte, Frederick F. and John H. Cavanagh. "Transnational Corporations and Services: The Final Frontier." *Trade and Development* No. 5, 1984, 215–273.

Hindley, Brian and Adasdair Smith. "Comparative Advantage and Trade in Services." *The World Economy* 1984, 369–389.

Lee, Chung H. and Seiji Naya (eds.) *Trade and Investment in Services in the Asia-Pacific Region: An Emerging Issue*. Boulder: Westview Press, 1988.

Lipsey, R. E. and I. B. Kravis. "The Competitive Position of U.S. Manufacturing Firms." *Banca Nazionale del Lavoro Quarterly Review* June 1985, 127–154.

Office of U.S. Trade Representative. "Selected Problems Encountered by U.S. Service Industries in Trade in Services," 1985.

——— *U.S. National Study on Trade in Services*, 1983.

Praet, P. "EC and ASEAN in the International Exchange of Services: A European Perspective." In J. Welbroek, P. Praet, and H.C. Reiger (eds.), *ASEAN-EEC Trade in Services*. Singapore: Institute of Southeast Asian Affairs, 1985.

Sampson, Gary P. and Richard H. Snape. "Identifying the Issues in Trade in Services." *The World Economy* June 1985, 171–182.

UN Conference on Trade and Development. *Services and the Development* (TD/B/1008/Rev. 1), 1985.

SECTION II

ASIAN NICs:
KOREA / TAIWAN / HONG KONG

KOREA'S ECONOMIC STRATEGY:
BUSINESS, GOVERNMENT, AND ECONOMIC DEVELOPMENT

Duk-Choong Kim

I. INTRODUCTION

It is now generally accepted that Korea's economic development over the last two decades has been rather remarkable and in many ways unique. So it will be highly relevant, and hopefully insightful, to identify the actors in this enterprise and to examine the leadership of this rapid change in economic activities and industrial structures in Korea.

First, we begin by offering an appreciation of the new approaches to analyzing interrelationships among political, social, and economic factors affecting the

Research in Asian Economic Studies.
Asian Industrialization: Changing Economic Structures,
Volume 1, Part A, pages 71–81.
Copyright © 1988 by JAI Press Inc.
All rights of reproduction in any form reserved.
ISBN: 0-89232-987-4

Korean Peninsula. For Korea, interdependence between national security and economic growth has been a historic reality.

II. RELATIONSHIPS AMONG ECONOMIC, POLITICAL, AND SOCIAL FACTORS IN KOREA

Once thought to be impossible, Korea's achievements in economic development now appear to be taken for granted. This is due, in large part, to the extensive coverage given to Korea in recent years by the media throughout the world, and to the increased attention paid to Korea's postwar development by Western academics. Also, almost as remarkable as the economic growth itself is the fact that this growth has been accompanied by an increasingly equalitarian income distribution, a pattern that many economists once considered beyond the reach of any noncommunist nation.

Indeed, we may find in Korean experience several factors that contradict or defy generally accepted theories of economic growth. The first is Korea's human resources. Like the other equally successful Newly Industrializing Countries (NICs) of Asia, Korea almost totally lacks natural resources. With manpower for all practical purposes its only real resource, Korea was forced to make efficient use of this asset, which very fortunately, it has successfully done. Second, the continuous threat to physical survival posed by North Korea has helped motivate the people of South Korea to achieve rapid economic growth. Consequently, the existence of the external threat is important in understanding Korea's progress over the last two decades. Third, in conventional literature, noneconomic factors are regarded as exogenous variables. In Korea, however, these factors are at least partially interdependent, and usually integral/endogenous variables.

Finally, another major factor why Korea is an exception and does not quite fit into generally accepted existing theories on economic growth is the importance of the role of government. In other developing countries, government's economic planning role has been indicative rather than allocative. Governments have provided infrastructure vital to industrial progress, and an overall stable and supportive fiscal and monetary framework as incentives for the private sector. In Korea, the government played a more direct and dominant role setting a business environment itself in the form of a business–government partnership. The role of government in the economic development of Korea involved more than offering directives to the private sector (Jones et al., 1980).

In analyzing Korea's economic development, it is therefore important to examine seemingly noneconomic factors in order to show how the external threat affected the nation's economic growth profile. Korea's national security has greatly influenced, and has at the same time been considerably influenced by, a complex interweaving of social, political, and economic factors. The external threat from the North is of course the clearest single factor affecting national security policy.

But both the immediate and the less immediate threats from abroad to Korea's national security fit into a broader international economic and politial map. These interrelationships are described in Figure 1.

The robustness of the health of the society requires some degrees of consistency between aspirations and accomplishments, and between feelings of entitlement and its fulfillment. These depend on the nature of the relationships between the people at various levels of the social strata, which in turn are modeled by people's perceptions of what is right, desirable, and just. Political institutions in Korea are judged on how successfully they are able to direct the resource flows and to regulate the above interrelationships. Such considerations are clearly reflected in the nature of the nation's political governance system.

Historical precedents show that the availability of natural resources is not an absolute conditions for economic development. Nations such as Japan and Switzerland have amply demonstrated that the proper combination of will and skills can make up for an absence of such resources. Korea has now reinforced this point. To some degree, the experience of other developing nations also

Figure 1. A flow diagram of interrelationships between external threats and economic growth of Korea.

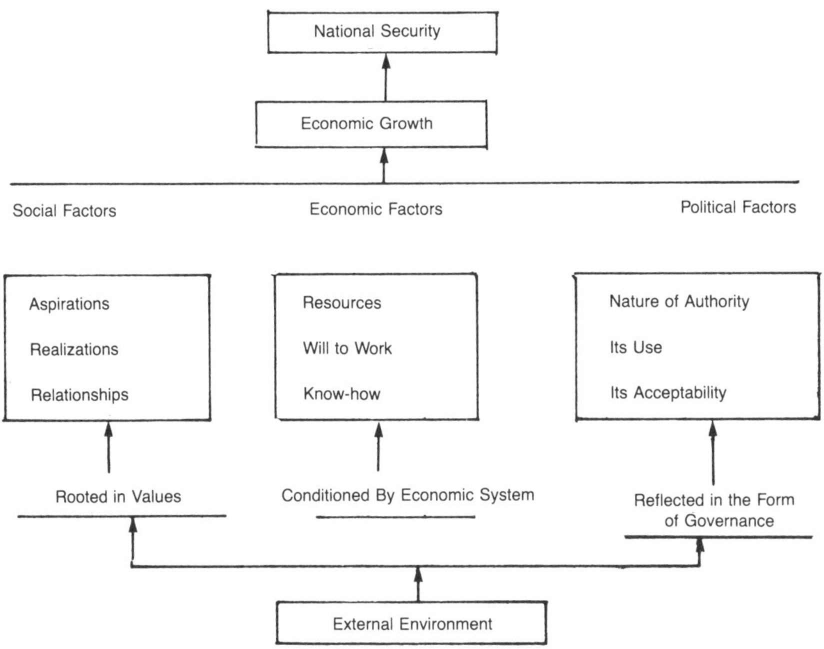

supports this contention. What distinguishes the Korean experience from others, however, is the degree to which noneconomic factors have had a direct effect on economic factors. This phenomenon is ignored in most existing theories of ries of economic growth (Kim and Park, 1985).

III. NATIONAL SECURITY AND HIGHER RATE OF ECONOMIC GROWTH

Korea's consistently high economic growth rates averaging 8.2% between 1962 and 1985 were in large part achieved by setting seemingly impossible goals. A "sensible" target, given the domestic resources then available, particularly the low level of domestic savings, would have been annual growth rates of about 3%. But the decisions to set targets were made largely on political grounds, which, in turn, were largely based on security considerations. First, rapid growth was absolutely essential to bear a heavy defense burden resulting from the constant threat from North Korea. Second, a high growth rate was needed to keep the unemployment rate below 6%, which Korean policymakers believe is the maximum level tolerable for economic and social stability.

Perkins has argued that political stability is a key prerequisite for continued economic growth of developing nations. Social stability has been essential to political stability, which in turn has been a precondition for sustained economic growth and also for national security (Mason et al., 1980). Conversely, national security has been needed to maintain political and social stability and economic growth. National security needs, having been given top priority, have been a powerful stabilizing force in Korea. In other words, setting a high economic growth rate as a national goal was indeed a political decision based on critical national security considerations.

This political decision has been dramatically successful. Even during the early 1980s when both domestic and international conditions were relatively more unstable than in earlier years, Korea was able, after negative growth in 1980, to maintain an overall growth rate of 7%.

The impact of a politically motivated commitment to economic growth on savings and investment in Korea is illustrated in Table 1. Domestic savings were insufficient to finance the high rates of economic growth discussed above. Consequently, Korea had to rely for many years on foreign capital. During the first Five-Year Economic Development Plan (1962–1966), domestic savings were 8% of GNP, and some 60% of investment came from foreign sources (by 1985, the latter had declined to 10%). However, because of Korea's earlier large dependence on external sources for growth financing, its total foreign debt reached approximately US$ 46.8 billion in 1985 (Table 2).

In view of Korea's low domestic savings rate, this high foreign debt level has been unavoidable. Korea's debt/service ratio is currently about 18.5%, and this

Table 1. Economic Growth and Financing the Growth

	1962–66 (%)	*1967–71 (%)*	*1972–76 (%)*	*1977–81 (%)*	*1982–85 (%)*
Growth rate	7.9	9.7	10.2	5.6	7.7
Gross investment	16.3	25.7	26.6	30.7	30.4
Domestic savings	8.0	15.6	20.3	23.5	25.6
Foreign savings	8.6	10.1	7.9	5.9	4.7
Statistical discrepency	–0.3	—	–1.6	1.3	0.1
Foreign savings/ Gross investment	54.3	39.5	24.8	19.2	15.5

Source: The Bank of Korea, Seoul, Korea: *Economic Statistics Yearbook, 1986.*

Table 2. Debt Profile (Billion $US)

	1970	*1975*	*1980*	*1985*
Debt outstanding	2.2	8.5	27.3	46.8
Foreign assets	—	—	7.5	11.2
Net debt	—	—	19.8	35.6
Debt service ratio	18.2	12.0	13.1	18.5
	(—)[a]	(14.4)	(18.7)	(20.1)[b]

Source: Economic Planning Board, Government of Korea, Seoul, Korea: *Major Statistics of Korean Economy, 1986.*

[a] Including short-term interest payment.

[b] 1984 figure.

rate is expected to fall steadily over the remainder of this decade. However, including short-term interest payments, the debt/service ratio was 20.1% in 1984. In the prevailing uncertain international economic environment, foreign debt is an obstacle to the conduct of an effective economic policy.

A growth model with fewer and lesser amounts of foreign loans might have been technically feasible, but it would have resulted in lower rates of growth, and brought about adverse consequences for national security. Thus, Korea's high foreign debt as well as its high growth rates have been directly related to national security considerations. This debt has of course been a burden, but the price of not having incurred it would have been even greater than the debt burden itself.

A comparison of savings rates, including household savings, among the three countries—South Korea, Taiwan, and Japan—illustrates the unique relationship between economic development and national security as it has prevailed in Korea during the last two decades. Table 3 shows that the domestic savings rate and the household savings rate in Japan in 1984 were 30.6 and 15.8%, respectively. Those rates in Taiwan, for the same year, were 33.7 and 15.1%, respectively. However, in the same year in Korea, the corresponding rates were lower at 27.9 and 9.9%, respectively. Nevertheless, government and corporate savings rates were similar in all three countries.

The reason for this discrepancy lies in the consideration of national security. As early as the 1960s, some South Korean economists realized that a high growth strategy would invite a certain degree of inflation; yet national security considerations made rapid growth a necessity, even at the price of higher inflation. But when the "oil shock" hit in 1973, Korea, as an oil-importing nation, was unable to avoid a steep rise in inflation in the short term. The second oil shock in 1979–1980 further handicapped its efforts to curtail inflation. In addition, as a direct result of the continuing threat from North Korea, South Korea incurred very considerable defense costs. Although inflation has subsided greatly in the last few years, the decades of high growth were, however, marked by high inflation that undermined household savings. In short, Koreans have had to pay a price to protect their national security, and the country's economy has largely responded to the premise that national security should receive the first priority over all other goals (Kim, 1985a).

Table 3. Intercountry Comparison of Savings Rates in 1984

	Korea (%)	*Taiwan (%)*	*Japan (%)*
Domestic savings rate	27.9	33.7	30.6
Household savings rate	9.9	15.1	15.8

Source: The Bank of Korea, Seoul, Korea: *Economic Statistics Yearbook, 1986.*

IV. THE ROLE OF THE PRIVATE SECTOR IN KOREA'S ECONOMIC DEVELOPMENT

Let us now focus on Korean entrepreneurs who are the principal actors in Korea's economic development. The occupation of Korea by Japan from 1910 through 1945 stifled any potential entrepreneurial class in Korea. Furthermore, the Korean War of 1950–1953 had devastating effects on all sectors of the Korean economy. When South Korea began its industrial development efforts in the early 1960s, entrepreneurial power first emerged in Korea. Korea's industrial and economic take-off was due largely to joint government–entrepreneurial efforts. In the later stages of this process, a genre of genuine entrepreneurs emerged and gradually played a more crucial role in Korea's economic development.

In order to understand the growth of entrepreneurship and the role of entrepreneurs in Korea's economic development, various stages of the development profile must be fully appreciated. To that end, it is important to review the economic situation that prevailed in Korea before the beginning of the present development process. The short-lived ecstasy of liberation in 1945 was followed by a division of the nation, and then by a war that left the country and its economy and the national psyche traumatized. In addition, millions of refugees from North Korea exacerbated the unemployment problem. The nation was stunned, and the economy was isolated and stagnant after the war that ended in 1953. The annual average rate of inflation between 1945 and 1955 was 108%, and capital resources were nonexistent.

In 1961, per capita income was US$ 85, and the domestic savings rate was as low as 3%. Korea launched its ambitious first Five-Year Economic Development Plan in 1962, when total exports were a meager US$ 55 million. In 1986, per capita income had reached US$ 2,271, the wholesale price index was down 2.2% from 1985, and the consumer price index registered a 2.3% increase. The domestic savings rate climbed to 33%. Exports were US$ 35.7 billion and imports US$ 31.6 billion, with a total of US$ 67.3 billion of international trade. Over a period of some 25 years, the Korean economy had been transformed from a state of stagnant isolation into an open dynamism. Table 4 indicates the roles that the government, the entrepreneurship, and others played during this period of Korea's economic and industrial development (Sakong and Jones, 1980).

In the 1950s, the only major domestic industries were food and clothing. With social conditions uncertain due to the aftermath of the Korean War, entrepreneurs were making no industrial investments; the focus was on speculative short-term investments in the commercial sector. In short, entrepreneurs hardly existed, but merchants were quite numerous and influential. The primary concern of the government, the merchants, and the populace at large was its basic survival amid the ruins of the war.

Things began to change in the 1960s. For the first time, the government (Table 4, section A) made capital available to entrepreneurs, who eagerly grasped the

Table 4. Government Effects on Economic Factors, Noneconomic Factors, and Entrepreneurs

(A) Economic factors	(B) Noneconomic factors	(C) Entrepreneurs
Labor	*Legitimacy*	*Planning*
Education—general	Export awards	Areas
Training schools	Public acceptance	Risk-taking
Regulation promoting foreign construction	Tax awards	Exports
		Heavy industries
Mobility—rural to urban	*Social Mobility*	
Capital	"SAEMAUL" factories	
Money market development	*Ideology*	
Guarantees for international projects	National identity	
Funds for specific projects	Companies open to public	
Exports, heavy industries, small-medium companies	Foundation	
R & D	*Psychology*	
Establishment of institutions	Achievement orientation	
Cooperative programs	General Trading Companies (GTCs)	
Market Abroad	*Motivation*	
Information (KOTPA, KIET)	Confrontation with North Korea	
Government to government negotiations		

opportunity to initiate western-style enterprises. At the same time, the government's policies were affecting such noneconomic factors (Table 4 section B) as the continued confrontation with North Korea and the increased social mobility brought about by expanding economic opportunities. All these policies were affecting entrepreneurs directly or indirectly as is indicated in Table 4, section C. The government's planning resulted in increased entrepreneurial risk-taking in such areas as exports and development of heavy industries. As the heavy and chemical industries began to expand, export emphasis still continued to be geared to such light industrial products as textiles.

During the 1970s, change became more pronounced again as a result of government policy; particularly during the latter half of the decade, various industries moved toward accelerated industrialization. But during this period, the government had its greatest impact on noneconomic factors. In the economic sector (Table 4, section A) the government began to establish technical schools and training programs for more rapid development of heavy industry. These technical institutions were established by, and in some cases run by, the government, when industries were unable to establish their own programs. Simultaneously, through government regulations, the larger companies were required to set up their own schools and institutes to train manpower for activities in such increasingly important fields as heavy industries and overseas construction. Also during this period, the government began to target more funds for certain specific areas. General Trading Companies (GTCs) were established primarily as the government policy initiatives in order to expand markets abroad and to help make Korean enterprises more credible in the world market. As planned, Korean GTCs played an important role in promoting exports. The share of exports by heavy chemical industries accounted for by GTCs became close to three quarters of the total national exports of all industries in 1984. It increased from 23% in 1976 to 74% in 1984. That the Korean GTCs played a positive role in economic growth became all too evident. Exports have constituted about half of total economic growth during the last two decades (Kim, 1985b; Westphal, 1978; Krueger, 1979). In Research and Development (R&D), the government began to establish various research institutions in cooperation with the private sector.

In the noneconomic section (Table 4, section B) during the 1970s, government was favorably affecting the legitimacy of entrepreneurs, by giving them more recognition and respectability. As a result, the social status of entrepreneurs rapidly improved. The government, for example, established an annual National Export Day, and awarded decorations to corporations for making outstanding contributions to Korea's export drive. The traditional Korean custom of looking down upon businessmen rapidly disappeared. With a view to broadening of ideological acceptability, the government was beginning to force businessmen to go public, which led to the gradual replacement of "family" firms by publicly incorporated corporations. The government also began to encourage the establishment, by expanding companies and business conglomerates, of foundations dedicated to the general welfare of the Korean people. In this way, corporations were guided toward bearing greater social responsibility.

The government's greatest success during the 1970s was in the noneconomic realm, and the most far-reaching program was the Saemaul (New Community) Movement in both rural and urban factories. This highly successful program interlinked important factors, such as national identity, motivation, and achievement orientation. The program continues to operate with success.

V. PROSPECTS FOR THE ROLE OF ENTREPRENEURS IN KOREA

There is no question that economic development in Korea has been government led. But, at the same time, development has largely been driven by private corporations in a "concerted free enterprise system." This system differs from the "purer" form of free enterprise in that harmonization among various economic objectives within the business community was achieved by close and continued consultations among business, government, and, in some cases, labor leaders. In this way, the country could set the national economic priorities and pursue national objectives without resorting to direct government fiat or the administrative allocation of resources. In Korea, government policies have made their weight felt, but what has emerged over the years is a highly cooperative system between government and the private sector.

In the early stage of economic development of Korea, government administrators were an elite group that, because of the anticommercial bias of traditional Confucianism, tended to denigrate business activity. They were also inclined toward centralized government. Yet the fundamental logic of achieving a higher rate of economic growth in the face of the external threat eventually led to a successful modification of the old attitude. As the private sector became larger, government officials were in fact forced to adjust their attitudes toward the business leadership. For those in political power it became important to take note of the fact that the annual sales of one large corporate group grew to be nearly equal to the entire government budget.

The aforementioned changes in Korea in the recent past have made an uncertain world even more uncertain. In view of recent changes in Korea's political structure and the rapid evolution of the world economic environment, one may ask whether the Korean economy is still characterized as one dominated by government leadership. The question merits response.

First, economic efficiency must have been the highest priority in contemporary Korea, if it is to overcome unfavorable internal and external economic conditions and maintian a high rate of economic growth. This means that, to some extent, the basic thrust of economic policymaking has shifted gears: a progressively gradual transition from a government-managed economy to a system led by the private sector with initiatives based on the free market mechanism has taken place. Otherwise Korea's competitive economic efficiency in the world market will be adversely affected.

Government cannot lead the way in international marketing simply because it does not have the related entrepreneurial know-how. The high degree of openness of the Korean economy during the Fifth Five-Year Plan implies that internationalization of Korean enterprises is of paramount importance. This also means that international marketing has enhanced the importance of the open economic status of Korea, and the private sector alone can lead Korea's role in the world market.

Second, the old policy of direct financial support by the Korean government for exports is at a critical juncture. Korea's total exports reached US$ 35 billion in 1986. Korean firms have become too large to merit consideration for continued export subsidies. If subsidies were at 10% of total exports, the sum would be as high as US$ 3.5 billion. Deficit spending on this scale is to be ruled out simply because of its inflationary consequences.

Furthermore, it is becoming increasingly obvious that Korea has graduated from the traditional class of developing countries: economically developed countries of the world have awarded Korea a diploma in recognition of its economic development. Indeed, Korea is a newly industrialized country, and has earned its membership of the community of Asian NICs. Any kind of continued export subsidies will very likely bring retaliation by Korea's trading partners in the world market.

Third, the life cycle of commercial products is becoming shorter (normally 5–10 years) due to the very rapid pace of recent technological change. Indeed, the life expectancy of electronic products is now only 3–5 years, as some experts state. Only the private sector is equipped to effectively deal with this new challenge of the present phase of industrialization.

Fourth, Korea's political evolution calls for new approaches in economic policy. Regardless of the form of government, presidential or parliamentary, the size of its constituency is going to be vastly larger over time. The government will have to be more responsive to the popular political will, and the private market system alone can be responsive to the nation's fast growing economic needs.

VI. CONCLUSION

To sum up, the specifics of emerging Korean reality add up to a solid argument for a smaller government role, and for an increasingly greater emphasis on the marketplace in directing the future course of its economy. Fortunately, Korea is already endowed with a new genre of entrepreneurs whose dynamic and efficient leadership will provide the engine of Korea's continued economic growth.

REFERENCES

Kim, Duk-Choong. "Security and Economic Development." *Korea and World Affairs* 9(1), Spring 1985a, 77–90.

———"The Role of Korean General Trading Companies in Economic Development." Symposium on General Trading Firms, Bangkok, Thailand, August 1985b.

Kim, Kwang-suk and Joon-Kyung Park. *Sources of Economic Growth in Korea: 1963–1982*. Seoul, Korea: The Korea Development Institute, 1985.

Kruger, Anne O. *The Developmental Role of the Foreign Sector and Aid*. Cambridge, MA: Harvard University Press, 1979.

Mason, Edward S., Mahn-Je Kim, Dwight H. Perkins, Kwang-Suk Kim, and David C. Cole. *The Economic and Social Modernization of the Republic of Korea*. Cambridge, MA: Harvard University Press, 1980.

Sakong, Il and LeRoy P. Jones. *Government, Business, and Entrepreneurship in Economic Development: The Korean Case*. Seoul, Korea: The Korea Development Institute, 1980.

Westphal, L. "The Republic of Korea Experience with Export-led Industrial Development." *World Development* 6, 1978.

KOREA APPROACHING A DEVELOPED ECONOMY REGIME

Dong-Se Cha

I. INTRODUCTION

The Korean economy has undergone rapid economic development over the last 25 years. Within a generation it has grown from a poor war-devastated country into a leading newly industrialized country.

Today, the Korean economy is a showcase of development in a market-oriented economy. Thirty years ago, no one believed that Korea could achieve so much in such a short period of time. This is why the Korean economy is sometimes called "the miracle."

It is not easy to identify precisely the elements that have led to Korea's present success. However, one factor that is mentioned very often as the critical determinant of Korea's success is human resources.[1] Since Koreans have culturally valued education, the nation's literacy rate has been one of the highest in the

Research in Asian Economic Studies.
Asian Industrialization: Changing Economic Structures,
Volume 1, Part A, pages 83–108.
Copyright © 1988 by JAI Press Inc.
All rights of reproduction in any form reserved.
ISBN: 0-89232-987-4

world for many years. As a consequence, Korea was endowed with abundant human capital already in 1962 when the First Five-Year Economic Development Plan was inaugerated. Through efficient mobilization of human resoures and effective exploitation of a favorable world economic environment, Korea has succeeded in achieving a sustained high growth.[2]

Currently, Korea is certainly in a period of transition. Among others, Korea's per capita GNP passed $2,000 a few years ago and is expected to reach $4,000 within 5 years. Its industries are also expected to undergo rapid structural changes. During this transition period, however, Korea will face many new challenges and opportunities. If Korea succeeds in meeting the new challenges and in exploiting the new opportunities effectively, then it will be able to join the ranks of the advanced countries within the next generation.

This study will focus on, first, how Korea has been preparing for the transition; second, the challenges and opportunities that Korea is facing; and third, the medium- and long-term prospects for the Korean economy to the year 2000.

II. ECONOMIC PERFORMANCE IN THE PAST 25 YEARS

A. Macroeconomic Performance

Korea's economic achievement is best illustrated by the growth of income. In 1962, per capita income was only $87, but 25 years later, by 1986, it had grown to $2,300. The average annual growth rate of real income during this period exceeded 8% whereas in the advanced countries it has been 2.5%. Also, as a result of the sustained growth in income the percentage of the population suffering from absolute poverty has drastically declined. In 1965, 41% of the total population earned lower than minimum living costs, but by 1980, this ratio fell below 10%. In addition, the unemployment rate has fallen substantially. In 1986, it was 3.8% compared to 8.2% in 1963. Even if there is still considerable underutilization of the potential labor force, the fall in the unemployment rate implies a significant improvement in economic welfare.

Until 1981, however, Korea had suffered from high rates of inflation. During the period 1962–1980, the rate of increase in the average annual consumer price exceeded 16%. In 1981, the consumer price rose as high as 21%. A strong stabilization policy had been launched in 1979, but it did not succeed in bringing inflation under control until 1982, when the consumer price rise was finally reduced to a single digit. Since then, Korea's inflation rate has been in the range of a 3–4% annual rise in consumer prices.

In the meantime, Korea's export-oriented development strategy has been increasingly successful, as recent trends demonstrate. In 1962, Korea's exports amounted to only about $54 million; in 1986 exports expanded to $35 billion. Even more impressive than the increase in export volume has been the change in the composition of export commodities. In the 1960s, Korea's major export items included raw materials such as minerals, agricultural products, and plywoods. In the 1980s, the major export items have become electronic products such as color TVS and microwave ovens and high-technology goods, such as, automobiles, ships and computers.

In terms of the current account balance, Korea's performance had not been very successful until 1985. Having sustained sizable current account deficits, Korea accumulated an external debt of $44.5 billion by the end of 1986. In 1986, however, there was a dramatic shift in the current account balance, with a surplus of $4.6 billion posted. The current account surplus is expectd to reach around $8 billion in 1987 and to prevail for a considerable period of time.[3]

The domestic savings rate continued to be lower than the domestic investment rate until 1985. As a result, a substantial portion of total domestic investment had to be financed by foreign capital inflow. But in 1986, the domestic savings rate, having reached 32.8%, exceeded the domestic investment rate of 30.2% for the first time (see Table 1).

Table 1. Major Economic Indicators

	1962	*1981*	*1986*
GNP per capita (current prices in $US)	87	1,719	2,268
GNP growth rate (%)	3.1	6.6	12.5
Consumer price increase (%)	6.5	21.3	2.3
Unemployment rate (%)	8.2[a]	4.5	3.8
Exports (billion current $US)	0.054	21.3	34.7
Imports (billion current $US)	0.422	26.1	31.6
Current account balance (billion $US)	−0.054	−4.6	4.6
Domestic savings rate (%)	3.2	20.5	32.8
Investment rate (%)	12.8	28.7	30.2
External debt (billion $US)	0.16	32.4	44.5

Sources: The Bank of Korea, *Economic Statistics Yearbook; also Monthly Bulletin*, April 1987. Economic Planning Board, *Major Statistics of Korean Economy*. Korea Development Institute, *Quarterly Economic Outlook*, April 1987.

[a] In 1963.

B. Structural and Qualitative Changes

The Korean economy has undergone substantial structural and qualitative changes in line with its quantitative expansion. Significant changes have been made in the economy's industrial structure, trade structure, and financial structure, and advances have come in technology and income distribution.

1. Industrial Structure

What Korea has been pursuing in the last 25 years has been rapid industrialization rather than mere growth in income. Thus, substantial changes in industrial structure have naturally accompanied Korea's economic development. In 1961, manufacuring production accounted for 13.6% of the total GNP, whereas agricultural production and services accounted for 39.1 and 45.4% of the GNP, respectively. In 1986, however, manufacturing and services were responsible for up to 30.1 and 57.0% of the GNP, respectively, whereas the contribution of agricultural production to the GNP fell to 12.8%.

The distribution of employment among industries has demonstrated a similar change. Both the manufacuring industry and the service industry have been absorbing the labor force released from the agricultural sector, as seen in Table 2.

When compared to advanced countries, however, Korea still maintains a relatively large proportion of its labor force in the agricultural and fishery industry. The percentages of total employment involved in primary industry in Japan and the United States were 12 and 2% in 1981, respectively, whereas 23.4% of the labor force remains in that sector in Korea in 1986 (see Table 3).

Table 2. Structure of Production

	Share in GDP (%)		*Share in employment (%)*	
	1961	*1986*	*1964*	*1986*
Agriculture, forestry and fishery	39.1	12.8	61.9	23.4
Mining and Manufacturing	13.6	30.1	8.8	25.9
SOC. and other services	45.4	57.0	29.3	50.7

Sources: Economic Planning Board, *Major Statistics of Korean Economy*. The Republic of Korea, *The Sixth Five-Year Economic and Social Development Plan, 1986.*

Table 3. Structure of Production and Employment in Selected Countries

	Structure of production (1984)			*Structure of employment (1981)*		
	Agriculture, forestry, and fishery (%)	*Mining and manufacturing (%)*	*SOC, and other services (%)*	*Agriculture, forestry, and fishery (%)*	*Mining and manufacturing (%)*	*SOC, and other services (%)*
Singapore	1	39	60	2	39	59
U.K.	2	36	62	2	42	56
Japan	3	41	56	12	39	49
West Germany	2	46	52	4	46	50
United States	2	32	66	2	32	66
Korea (1986)	12.8	30.1	57.0	23.4	25.9	50.7

Sources: The World Bank, *World Development Report*, 1986. Economic Planning Board, *Major Statistics of Korean Economy*.

2. *Trade Structure*

Korea's export commodity structure has changed in line with its production structure. In the early 1960s, the primary industry products such as agricultural, marine, and mining products were the major export items. As shown in Table 4, however, manufacturing products accounted for 95.4% of the total exports in 1985. Therefore, in terms of composition of exports Korea can be viewed as being as industrialized as any advanced country.

Table 5 shows a comparison of major export items in Korea, Japan, and West Germany. Textiles represented the greatest proportion of exports for Korea (23.1% in 1985), steel for Japan (19.4% in 1974), and machinery for Germany (22.0% in 1972). The total export volume of Japan and Germany amounted to about $50 billion in 1974 and in 1972, respectively. The export commodity structures of Japan in 1974 and Germany in 1972 were different from that of Korea in 1985 in that they exported more machinery and automobiles. Korea, on the other hand, exported more ships and electronic products.

As indicated in Table 6, Korea is now a typical importer of raw materials. In 1985, raw materials and capital goods accounted for 91.6% of total imports, with consumer goods and food accounting for the remaining 8.4%.

Table 4. Exports by Products

	1961	*1980*	*1984*	*1985*
Agricultural products (%)	19.1	2.6	1.7	1.4
Marine products (%)	17.0	4.3	3.0	2.9
Mining products (%)	42.0	0.8	0.3	0.3
Manufactured goods (%)	21.9	92.3	95.0	95.4

Source: Economic Planning Board, *Major Statistics of Korean Economy*, 1981, 1986.

Table 5. Exports by Commodity Group of Korea, Japan, and West Germany

	Korea (1985)	*Japan (1974)*	*West Germany (1972)*
Total exports (Billion $US)	30.3	55.5	46.7
Machinery (%)	3.3	10.7	22.0
Automobiles (%)	2.6	9.4	15.2
Ships and boats (%)	16.6	10.1	—
Electronics (%)	16.1	12.1	9.6
Iron and steel (%)	8.5	19.4	6.5
Textiles and clothing (%)	23.1	7.3	4.3
Chemicals (%)	7.3	7.3	11.7

Source: The Republic of Korea, *The Sixth Five-Year Economic and Social Development Plan*, 1986.

Table 6. Imports by Commodity Group (Million $US)

	1981		*1982*		*1983*		*1984*		*1985*	
	Amount	*%*	*Amount*	*%*	*Amount*	*%*	*Amount*	*%*	*Amount*	*%*
Raw materials	16,215		15,516		15,564		17,625		17,429	
(Crude oil)	6,317		6,097		5,572		5,771		5,572	
Capital goods	6,158		6,223		7,815		10,109		11,093	
Consumer goods	1,620	6.20	1,509	6.22	1,525	5.82	1,581	5.16	1,410	4.53
Food	2,139	8.19	1,093	4.51	1,288	4.92	1,315	4.29	1,203	3.86
Total Imports	26,132		24,251		26,196		30,631		31,136	

Source: Korean Traders Association, *The Trend of Foreign Trade*, 1986.

3. *Financial Structure*

Korea's financial market has been gradually developing over the last 25 years. The development of a country's financial sector is often measured by the Financial Interrelation Ratio,[4] which is the ratio of financial assets to national wealth or gross national product. For Korea this ratio grew from 0.62 in the 1960s to 1.20 in the 1970s, and to 2.16 in 1983. However, this is still low compared to a 4.56 for Japan and 3.12 for Taiwan in 1982.[5]

From Table 7, it can be seen that indirect financing by issuing commercial papers and stocks is still an important source of external financing for businesses in Korea. An important reason for this is that the development of banks and other financial intermediaries has been delayed by government intervention in the financial sector. Table 7 reveals that the banks have been moving backward compared to nonbank financial institutions. The development of Korea's capital markets has not matched the development of other sectors in the Korean economy.

4. *Technology*

Technology, which is an essential factor in economic development, is often used as a gauge in measuring a nation's economic potential. Korea, driven by its historic emphasis on education, has been making steady efforts to develop technology and to increase the numbers of high quality engineers. The ratio of R&D expenditure to GNP grew from 0.47% in 1967 to 2% in 1986. This level is still far behind the 2.7% of the United States and the 2.37% of Japan in 1985. However, it should be noted that the ratio was about 2% in both West Germany and Japan, when they had about $2,000 per capita income.

In addition, the number of R&D personnel in Korea has been steadily growing, although it still remains relatively low compared to the advanced countries. About 1 out of every 1,000 people in the Korean population is involved in R&D, whereas more than 3 out of every 1,000 work in R&D in the United States and Japan. On the other hand, Korea shares 1% of the total patent applications in the world whereas Japan shares 33%.This reveals that Korea is still far behind the advanced countries in technological development.

5. *Income Distribution*

The income distribution of Korea has periodically alternated between improvement and deterioration over the last 25 years. As demonstrated in Table 8, the income distribution measured by the Deciles Distribution Ratio, which is the ratio of the income share of the lowest 40% to that of the highest 20%,[6] was deteriorating until 1980. Since 1980, it has improved slightly. The income distribution measured by Gini's coefficient shows similar results. The lower Gini's coefficient is, the better the income distribution. By international standards, Korea's income distribution is relatively equitable. Compared to other developing countries on a similar development level, Korea's income distribution appears favorable, as Table 9 indicates.

Table 7. Financing Sources of Businesses in Korea[a]

	Indirect financial market[b]							Direct financial market (Corporate Bill market) (%)		Misceli-aneous (%)	Total (%)
	Bank and Nonbank Total	Bank			Nonbank						
	(%)	Subtotal	Loan	Stock and bond	Subtotal	Loan	Stock and bond				
1971–75	81.7	60.7	58.5	2.2	21.0	17.9	3.1	14.1	(1.3)	4.2	100.0
1976–80	77.8	48.1	42.8	5.3	29.7	23.5	6.2	17.4	(3.1)	4.8	100.0
1981–83	77.4	42.4	37.3	5.1	34.9	25.6	9.3	18.3	(6.2)	4.3	100.0
1983	72.6	36.7	33.2	3.6	35.6	27.4	8.2	22.4	(6.8)	5.0	100.0

Source: The Bank of Korea, *Flow of Funds Account*, 1985.

[a] Exlcuding financial transactions with foreign countries and intercompany credit.

[b] Including government loan and private loan market.

Table 8. Distribution of Income and Index of Concentration

	1965	*1970*	*1976*	*1980*	*1982*	*1985*
Lowest 20% (%)	5.7	7.4	5.7	5.1	6.9	6.1
Second quintile (%)	13.6	12.3	11.1	11.0	12.0	11.6
Third quintile (%)	15.5	16.3	15.4	15.9	16.2	16.3
Fourth quintile (%)	23.3	22.4	22.4	22.6	21.9	22.3
Highest 20% (%)	41.8	41.6	45.3	45.5	43.0	43.7
Highest 10% (%)	25.8	25.4	27.5	29.5	28.1	28.3
Deciles distribution ratio (%)	0.46	0.47	0.371	0.354	0.44	0.405
Coefficient of concentration (Gini's coefficient) (%)	0.344	0.332	0.391	0.389	0.357	0.363

Source: Economic Planning Board, *Social Indicators in Korea*, 1981, 1986.

Table 9. Income Distribution of Selected Countries

	Korea (1985)	*Japan (1979)*	*United States (1980)*	*Taiwan (1981)*	*Brazil (1972)*	*Mexico (1977)*
Lowest 20% (%)	4.08	8.7	5.3	8.8	2.0	2.9
Second quintile (%)	11.63	13.2	11.9	13.8	5.0	7.0
Third quintile (%)	16.23	17.5	17.9	17.6	9.4	12.0
Fourth quintile (%)	22.35	23.1	25.0	22.8	17.0	20.4
Highest 20% (%)	43.71	37.5	39.9	37.0	66.6	57.7
Highest 10% (%)	28.29	22.4	23.3	—	50.6	40.6
Deciles distribution ratio (%)	0.36	0.58	0.43	0.61	0.11	0.17

Source: The World Bank, *World Development Report*, 1986. Economic Planning Board, *Social Indicators in Korea*, 1986. Executive Yuan, *Taiwan Statistical Data Book*, Taiwan 1985.

III. CHANGES IN THE ECONOMIC POLICY REGIME

The years between 1979 and 1982 marked a period of change in Korea, economically as well as politically. The change of government in late 1979 and 1980 made possible a thorough reexamination of past policies and current issues. The new government was able to take a more objective stance in evaluating past performances and in planning new policy directions.

The most important change during this period was that of philosophy rather than of specific policy measures. From 1962 to 1980, the government had the most control over economic decision making. Since 1980, however, such control has been gradually turned over to the market. The power of the market mechanism and competition have been recognized as the ultimate guiding forces in the decision-making process of the economy.

The salient features of Korea's economic policy since 1980 have been liberalization, internationalization, and the promotion of competition. All of these characteristics are well reflected in the Fifth Five-Year Economic and Social Development Plan started in 1982 and the Sixth Five-Year Economic and Social Development Plan beginning from 1987. In conjunction with this new direction Korea's financial policy, trade policy, and other policy measures have been undergoing fundamental reforms.

A. Financial Policy

The traditional role of financial policy in Korea was quite different from that in the advanced countries, in which financial policy is nothing more than monetary policy, the primary objective of which is income and price stability. In Korea, however, financial policy was an instrument for industrial policy. Thus, the primary objective of the financial policy was industrial development rather than income and price stability.[7]

Financial policy was implemented through government intervention in the financial sector. Throughout the 1960s and the 1970s, the government moved back and forth between direct and indirect control of monetary and credit management. Even when the government did not exercise direct control over credits and loans, the financial institutions were allowed no real autonomy. The government exercised great influence on the financial institutions' normal operations and management.

Furthermore, the Bank of Korea never had a central bank's independence, which is the necessary condition for its normal operation. Due to excessive government intervention in the allocation of financial resources, the development of the financial market was severely suppressed. As a result, during most of the last two decades, the real interest rates of the banking institutions were negative, while a complicated system of preferential loans created a segmentation of the financial markets and a distortion in the allocation of financial resources.[8] After realizing that the social cost of financial distortion became a heavy burden for the national economy, the government began pursuing financial liberalization in the 1980s.

The financial liberalization has focused on the liberalization of interest rates, the denationalization of commercial banks, and the reduction of control over credit allocation. The liberalization of interest rates begin with the simplification of the interest rate structure. The government abolished the complicated preferential lending rate system in 1982 and unified the bank lending rates to the single figure of 10%. Since 1984, the government has widened the interest rate spreads, and commercial banks have gradually been permitted to lend at wider margins as seen in Table 10. Also in 1981, in an effort to liberalize interest rates, the government established a commercial paper market that is not subject to government control.

The five national commercial banks were privatized by 1983, and the government's control over the operation of the commercial banks has been gradually reduced. Various measures were taken to promote the managerial autonomy of the banks. Among others, reserve requirements were substantially reduced. In November 1979, the average required reserve ratio stood at 23% of the deposits of the commercial banks. This ratio was gradually reduced to 3.5% in November 1981; it currently stands at 4.5%. The government's intervention in the bank's credit allocation has also been gradually reduced. The size of the National Investment Fund, which is one of the major sources for policy directed loans, was also reduced and finally abolished in 1987. However, the government introduced another intervention in credit allocation in an effort to correct the undesirable consequences of past policies. In order to reduce the concentration of bank loans toward business conglomerates, the government has stipulated that 55% of the increase in local banks' credit and 35% of the national commercial banks' credit must go to small and medium-sized firms. In addition, the government has been intermittently freezing at certain levels the percentage of total bank credit that can be extended to the 30 largest conglomerates.[9]

Another important facet of the financial liberalization has been the internationalization of the domestic financial market. The government has relaxed the entry of foreign banks into the Korean domestic market, presently allowing 53 branches of 46 foreign banks to operate (Table 11). The foreign banks now account for about 18.44% of total lending by the banking system, compared with 8.9% in 1978. It should be noted that in Japan the foreign banks' share stands at 2.1% as of February 1987.

Table 10. Selected Interest Rates on Loans

	1980	*1982*	*1984*	*1985*	*1986*
Commercial banks (%)					
Discounts on bills	19.5	10.0	10.0–11.5	10.0–13.5	10.0–11.5
Loans for exports	12.0	10.0	10.0	10.0	10.0
Overdrafts	21.5	10.0	10.0–11.5	10.0–11.5	10.0–11.5
Loans on install. savings deposits	17.5	10.0	10.0–11.5	10.0–11.5	10.0–11.5
Term loans					
Up to 1 year	19.5–20.0	13.5–16.0	10.0–11.5	10.0–12.5	10.0–11.5
3–8 years	20.5	10.0	10.0–11.5	10.0–13.5	—
8–10 years	21.5	10.0	10.0–11.5	10.0–13.5	—
Other financial institutions (%)					
Korea Development Bank					
Equipment for key industries	18.5	10.0	10.0–11.5	10.0–13.0	10.0–13.0
Using government funds	13.0	10.0	10.0	10.0	10.0
Using foreign funds	7.5–10.75	7.5–10.75	7.5–10.75	7.5–10.75	10.0–11.0
Korea Housing Bank					
Private	10.8	10.0	10.0	10.0	—
Public	8.0	8.0	8.0	8.0	—
Mutual savings and finance companies	—	20.0	18.5	18.5	18.0
Mutual credit cooperatives	23.5	13.0	13.5	14.5	14.5
Agricultural cooperatives	15.0	10.0	10.0	10.0	10.0
National Investment Fund (NIF)	18.5–19.5	10.0	10.0–11.5	10.0–13.5	—
National Housing Fund U4 (NHF)	15.0–18.0	10.0	10.0	10.0	—
Curb market rate	45.0	30.6	24.7	—	—

Sources: The Bank of Korea, *Economic Statistics Yearbook*, 1986; *Monthly Bulletin*, April 1987.

Table 11. Foreign Banks' Share in Selected Countries

	Japan *(1987.2)*	*Taiwan* *(1982)*	*West Germany* *(1982)*	*Singapore* *(1981)*	*United States* *(1982)*	*Korea* *(1987.2)*
Deposits (%)	0.6	2.6	2.6	84.9	6.4	2.35
Loans (%)	2.1	7.8	2.2	76.5	12.0	18.44
Total assets (%)	2.0	6.7	2.1	83.4	10.8	18.8

Sources: The Bank of Korea, *Economic Statistics Yearbook*, 1986; *Monthly Bulletin*, April 1987. The Bank of Japan, *Economic Statistics Monthly*, April 1987.

B. Trade Policy

Korea's trade policies in the 1960s and the 1970s were characterized by export incentives and protection of the domestic market.[10] Export incentives included tariff exemptions, preferential credit allowances, and tax advantages. The domestic market was protected by direct and indirect controls on imports and high tariffs, although some liberalization measures were taken in the late 1970s. However, in the 1980s, export incentives have been substantially reduced, and import liberalization has been accelerated. Moreover, the government has been steadily reducing the amount of export credit, which is automatically extended to exporters, by reducing the credit proportion per dollar of exports from 94.8 percent in 1979 to 82.5 percent in 1982, and to 69.9% in 1987, as Table 12 shows. In addition, the interest rate differential between export credits and other loans was removed in 1982.[11]

At the same time, the government has been drastically liberalizing imports. The import liberalization ratio, which stood at 68.6% in 1980, rose to 80.4% in 1983, and to 91.5% in 1986. This ratio will rise to 95.4% in 1988, which is the level in advanced countries. Tariffs have also been significantly reduced, as the average tariff rate was reduced from 36% in 1978 to 19.9% in 1986. It should be noted that the government has been pursuing the rapid import liberalization policy inspite of strong criticism from the public.

Table 12. Trends of per Dollar Export Credit and Interest Rate Differential (in Won)

	1974		*1979*	*1980*	*1982*	*1983*	*1985*		*1986*	*1987*
	11.2 (%)	*12.7* (%)	*7.2* (%)	*10.1* (%)	*11.18* (%)	*11.17* (%)	*3.4* (%)	*10* (%)	*10* (%)	*5.30* (%)
Nominal exchange rate (A)	397.5	484	484	652.2	745.2	795.5	835.9	892.2	873.2	822.6
Amount of dollar credit per dollar export (B)	383	430	459	542	615	655	690	740	670[a] 700[b]	575[a] 680[b]
Loan ratio (B/A)	96.4	88.8	94.8	86.7	82.5	82.3	82.5	82.9	76.7 80.2	69.9 82.7
Differential between interest rates on general loans and export loans	6.5	6.5	10.0	7.0	—	—	0–1.5	0–1.5	0–1.5	0–1.5

Source: The Bank of Korea, *Economic Statistics Yearbook.*

[a] Credit to large industries.

[b] Credit to small and medium industries.

C. Regulation on International Capital Movement and Foreign Exchange

Korea has maintained tight control over foreign exchange transactions and international capital movement. Regulations on capital outflow have been more restrictive than on inflow, since a foreign exchange shortage was a serious problem at the early stages of development. However, the control on capital inflow has also been fairly restrictive.

The policy on foreign direct investment was somewhat ambivalent until 1984. Korea wanted to attract more foreign direct investment in certain industries by providing a tax haven and guaranteeing principal and interest payments. On the other hand, foreign direct investment over $100 million was strictly regulated, and many other restrictions effectively discouraged foreign direct investment into Korea. But in 1984, the door to foreign investment in most industries except for defense-related industries, was opened more widely. Foreign investment of less than $300 million and joint ventures of less than 50% foreign ownership are now approved automatically. However, foreign direct investment into foreign countries by Koreans still remains under tight control.

Foreign investment into the Korean stock market was not allowed until 1980, except in a few cases such as the foreign bond issues floated by the government-owned Korea Development Bank. In 1981, however, the government adopted a long-term plan for securities market internationalization. In accordance with this plan, the government has allowed foreigners to invest in the Korean securities market to a limited extent through investment trust companies. The "Korea Fund," a U.S. investment trust, is allowed to invest up to $100 million in Korean securities. As of 1987, the "Korea Euro Fund," a British investment trust, is allowed to invest up to $30 million. Also, a number of Korean business firms has sold convertible bonds on the Euro-market. Finally, many foreign securities companies have set up branch offices in Seoul, and some of them are participating in the securities business through joint ventures with Korean securities companies.

IV. CHALLENGES AND OPPORTUNITES

In the next phase of Korea's development, there are both new challenges and opportunities ahead. If Korea meets these challenges successfully while making effective use of new opportunities, the nation's goal of becoming an advanced country will most likely be achieved in the coming generation. If not, however, the goal might remain unrealized, perhaps forever.

A. Challenges Ahead

Korea has sustained high growth for the last 25 years and is now coping with the challenges that its very success has brought. The political and social tension, the conflict between market-oriented policy and concentration of economic power, the interindustrial and interregional disequilibrium, and the need for policy adjustment to the balance of payments surplus are the new challenges that have resulted from the process of development.

1. Political and Social Tension

Political and social tensions have recently been on the rise in Korea with the first peaceful transfer of power in its history occurring in early 1988. The fundamental causes of the recent tension and unrest are rooted in the Korean people's new-found desires and frustrations, which have come from the process of economic development.

In the last 25 years, Koreans tacitly agreed to temporarily put political freedom aside to concentrate the nation's energies on economic development, the foremost objective of the nation. Yet, as economic achievement has not only fulfilled the basic needs of Koreans but also made it possible for the Korean people to enjoy some material comfort, the social welfare function of Korean people has changed, and therefore democracy and political freedom have come to command a high priority. The Korean people can now only be satisfied with more political freedom and democratization.

It is true to say that Koreans are now seven times better off than they were 25 years ago, as far as real income is concerned. This does not necessarily mean, however, that they are now seven times happier. Happiness does not, of course, have a one-to-one relationship with income. The feeling of relative poverty generated by the unequal distribution of the fruits of the growth may have made many Koreans feel even more dissatisfied than before, even if they are now much better off on the average. Some 30 years ago, most Koreans had to worry about "Barley Hills," which meant painful hunger before the harvest of barley in the spring. They were all absolutely poor then, without much relative poverty to speak of. Now, most Korean people no longer even remember experiences such as absolute poverty. Moreover, current statistics show that Korea's income distribution is relatively equitable. Yet, the problem has to do with the Korean people's perception of income distribution. Koreans are one of the most homogeneous people in the world and are thus very sensitive to the income levels of their neighbors. Therefore, many Korean people who consider themselves members of the middle-income group resent the living standards of the rich few in Korea. This sensitivity tends to breed discontent among Koreans toward big business and government.

2. Conflict between Equity and Sustained Growth

Korea's current economic policy gives high priority to equity and social welfare in order to ease the social tension generated by the perception of relative poverty. This policy direction is well reflected in the Sixth Five-Year Economic and Social Development Plan, which sets economic advancement and welfare improvement based on efficiency and equity as the primary targets. However, close attention must be paid to the possibility of conflict between the two seemingly complementary targets. At this point, it is economic advancement that the Korean people are most eager to achieve. But the question is whether Korea has accumulated enough wealth to pursue those two goals at the same time. Korea's per capita income is merely $2,300. It was just last year that for the first time in its history Korea experienced a trade surplus and its domestic savings rate exceeding the domestic investment rate. Korea still has more than $40 billion of foreign debt, which is equal to about 40% of its GNP. Thus, in the near future, it is doubtful whether Korea will be able to sustain a high rate of growth while pursuing a full-fledged social welfare and income distribution policy at the same time.

In a similar vein, the Korean government has taken measures to regulate the activities of the big businesses or *chaebul*. This can be interpreted as the government's efforts to encourage the growth of small- and medium-sized business and, at the same time, to relieve the people's distress arising from the feeling of relative poverty. However, it is yet to be seen whether discouraging big businesses will be helpful in encouraging small- and medium-sized businesses to grow faster. One worrisome possibility is that big businesses, which played such an important role in the growth in the 1960s and the 1970s, may lose some of their force.

3. *Interindustrial and Interregional Disequilibrum*

Korea has adopted a kind of unbalanced growth strategy. So far, high priority has been given to the assembly industry by the big businsses, which contributed substantially to the expansion of export volume and employment opportunities. This unbalanced growth strategy has succeeded in achieving the rapid industrialization of Korea in spite of its weak foundations in basic technology. The shipbuilding and automobile industries are models for such success stories. While contributing to the growth of big businesses, however, the unbalanced growth strategy has inevitably led to disequilibrium between big businesses and small- and medium-sized businesses. The development of small- and medium-sized businesses that can supply the parts and raw materials to the big businesses has been lagging behind. This unbalance between the big assembly industries and the small- and medium-sized parts and raw materials industries is now a serious handicap in the second phase of Korea's economic development.

Another form of disequilibrium that has prevailed in Korea's development is interregional disequilibrium. Interregional disequilbrium is not entirely unrelated to interindustrial disequilibrium. Seoul, the capital city of Korea, and its suburbs are the center of the Korean economy. This region produces about 30% of Korea's GNP. The southeastern region is second to Seoul in its development, whereas the southwestern and northeastern regions still remain relatively underdeveloped. The interregional disequilibrium raises serious political as well as economic issues for Korea. Economically, it results in underutilization of resources. Politically, it breeds regional antagonism.

4. Policy Adjustment to the Balance of Payments Surplus

Korea's current account surplus, which stood at $4.6 billion in 1986, is expected to reach $8 billion in 1987 and be even higher thereafter.[12] This is definitely a great boon for the Korean economy, which still has a large amount of external debt. Yet, this favorable trend brings a new challenge. Since Korea has been financing the current account deficits through capital inflows during the entire period of its economic development, the monetary policy of the government as well as the financial management of businesses and banks have all been accustomed to the balance of payment deficits. With the reversal of the trend in the balance of payments, however, the government, the businesses, and the banks must adjust monetary policy and financial management accordingly. For instance, the government should find appropriate policy instruments to absorb the excessive money supply created by the surplus and effectively divert a certain proportion of resources from the export sector to the domestic sector. If the surplus continues, the government will then have to decide whether the present export-oriented growth strategy should be continued or changed.

Korean businesses and banks have never experienced currency appreciation. However, the won has been appreciating continuously since 1986 when the first balance of payment surplus was recorded. Most Korean businesses are astonished by this unexpectd phenomenon, although Japanese businesses have somehow been managing to survive a 70% appreciation of the yen in the last 2 years. Thus, the balance of payment surplus is creating a number of challenges for Korean businessmen and policymakers, although it is a blessing for the Korean economy.

B. The Erosion of Growth Factors

Some challenges have resulted from the gradual erosion of certain factors that have substantially contributed to economic growth in the past. The favorable world trade environment and cheap labor costs were important factors of growth in the Korean economy in the last 25 years. However, these factors are now eroding fast, and it behooves Korea to revise its traditional development strategy.

1. Deteriorating World Trade Environment

The favorable world trade environment in the 1960s and the 1970s was a critical element in the rapid growth of Korea's exports. In the 1980s, however, the new protectionism triggered by the deterioration of the U.S. trade balance has become a serious bottleneck to the continued expansion of world trade. The new protectionism of the advanced countries is a very serious threat to Korea, a country pursuing an export-oriented growth strategy. It is almost impossible for the Korean economy, 40% of whose GNP is made up by exports, to maintain high growth without the continued expansion of exports. Moreover, Korea is particularly vulnerable to the protectionist pressure from the United States since the United States, the largest market for Korea's exports, absorbs 40% of the country's total exports.

The pressures from the advanced countries are three-fold. On the one hand, the advanced countries have tended to raise import barriers, invoking the Voluntary Export Restraint, Orderly Marketing Agreement, or Safeguard Clause. On the other hand, they have increasingly narrowed the GSP treatment for Korean exports. Thus, Korean businesses now face great difficulties in using price competitiveness as an edge to expand the market, and thus have to develop high-quality products to maintain a market share in the advanced countries. The advanced countries are also increasing their pressure on Korea to open its market. As Korea's import liberalization is expected to accelerate in coming years, Korean businesses will have to compete fiercely with foreign competitors in the domestic market. They will then have to give up their traditional price discrimination policy. In the past, Korean export industries were able to enjoy much higher mark-ups in the protected domestic market while selling cheaper in the foreign markets. In the future, however, they will have to lower prices in the domestic market because of competition from abroad.

2. *Rising Labor Cost*

Cheap labor costs have been an important factor contributing to Korea's international competitiveness. Korea's wage level is still very low compared to that of the advanced countries. However, the wage level has been rising at a rate of 10% in the last 5 years and is expected to rise more rapidly. This will undermine the competitive edge of Korean products against those of other developing countries. This raises the issue of industrial adjustment, which has far-reaching implications for the future of many of Korea's traditional industries. The plywood industry, for instance, which was leading the export sector in the 1960s, has given way to its competitors in Southeast Asian countries. It seems very difficult for the textile and shoe industries to maintain their competitiveness much longer unless they introduce a new technology to save labor. Therefore, Korea will have to place a high priority on technology-intensive industries in the future, and this direction is already reflected in the Sixth Five-Year Plan. However, it will take a considerable amount of time for the Korean economy to upgrade its overall technology level. The task is how to face the challenges of impending wage increases, the resulting industrial adjustment, and the inevitable need for technological advancement.

C. New Opportunities

1. Widening Scope for Industrial Cooperation with the Advanced Countries

A large number of businesses in the advanced countries are seeking some form of cooperation with Korean businesses for various reasons. American businesses need to face Japanese competition, Japanese businesses need to overcome the effects of the appreciation of the yen, and Europen businesses need to bring in a new dynamism from the growth center of the world economy to increase their competitiveness. They promise new opportunities for Korean businesses that have never had such an enthusiastic response from abroad. Yet, this is not unique to Korea, since Hong Kong, Taiwan, and Singaporc are all being welcomed in such a manner. Therefore, Korean businesses will have to fully exploit these new opportunities to speed up their internationalization and thus should utilize them as a stepping stone for the ''second take-off.''

2. Japan and China as Potential New Markets

Geographically, Korea is located in a unique position because it stands closer to both China and Japan than any other country. Historically, its geographical location brought many hardships to Korea. At this point in time, however, this particular geographical feature provides Korea with numerous opportunities. Through historical and cultural relationship, Korea is definitely in the best position to understand both China and Japan. For example, Japanese is the easiest foreign language for many Koreans to learn. Thus, in every respect, Korea has an advantage in approaching both countries.

Japan has been known for the impenetrability of its domestic market. But Japan cannot remain closed forever. It will be forced to open its market by pressures from the outside world. The tremendous appreciation of the yen is a strong force speeding up the opening of the Japanese market. If the Japanese market fully opens up, the accessibility to the second largest market in the world will be indeed a great advantage for Korea.

China has already been expanding its exposure to the West. Without a formal diplomatic relationship, however, Korea still has many problems doing business with China. But if the big powers including the United States, the Soviet Union, Japan, and China initiate and conclude an agreement that eases tensions in the Korean peninsula, Korea's trade with China will be dramatically increased. The potential for trade expansion with a country that has a population of one billion certainly poses a great opportunity for Korea.

3. Room for More Efficiency

The government has played an important role in the economic development of Korea.[13] Yet, as the size of the economy grows and its structure becomes more complicated, it is evident that there is a limit to the role of government. If the government retains the old habit of intervention, it will result in an enormous waste of resources through inefficiency. Thus, with the substantial growth in the size of the economy, the Korean government has been pursuing extensive deregulation, which is expected to promote efficiency by fostering competition and allowing the market mechanism to reign.

Deregulation has a double edge. To some businesses, it will mean reduction in costs. To other businesses, it will mean the withdrawal of government support. Overall, however, deregulation will contribute to sharpening the competitive edge of the Korean business.

Another source of efficiency is the internationalization of small- and medium-sized businesses, most of which have been domestic market oriented. But recently, they are turning outward, as they are facing more severe competition with foreign goods even in the domestic market. The logical conclusion for small- and medium-sized businesses is to enhance efficiency and competitiveness.

V. PROSPECTS TO THE YEAR 2000

A. Long-Term Goals

Between now and the year 2000 will be a critical period for Korea, because the transition from a newly industrialized country to an advanced economy will have to be made, if at all, during this period. (Table 13). Thus, Korea's goal in the next

*Table 13.*Prospects for the Korean Economy in 1991 and 2000

	1991	*2000*
GNP per capita (current prices in $US)	4,000	6,900[a]
GNP deflator (%) (1980 = 100)	3.5	3.9
Exports (billion current $US)	56	173
Imports (billion current $US)	53	168
Current Account Balance (billion $US)	5	5
External Debt (billion $US)	33	—
Unemployment rate (%)	3.7	—
Savings rate (%)	33.5	36.5
Investment rate (%)	31.3	35.3

Sources: The Republic of Korea, *The Sixth Five-Year Economic and Social Development Plan*, 1986. Korea Development Institute, *Korea Year 2000: Prospects and Issues for Long-Term Development*.

[a] In 1991 prices. Calculated under the assumption that GNP will grow by 7.2% and population by 1.0% annually during 1990–2000.

decade or so is to accomplish this transition as smoothly as possible. In achieving this goal, the Sixth Five-Year Economic and Social Development Plan is calling for (1) institutional adjustment to fit the advanced economy and cooperation between the government and the leaders of the society, (2) industrial adjustment and technological improvement through cooperation between management and labor for the acceleration of economic growth, and (3) welfare improvement through regionally balanced development.[14]

B. Prospects to the Year 2000

1. Economic Growth

The Korean economy is expected to grow at an annual rate of 7–8% in real terms for the next 5 years. In 1991, according to the Sixth Five-Year Economic and Social Development Plan, Korea's per capita income will reach $4,000. The population is assumed to increase 1.18% annually. A report by the Korea Development Institute (1986) projects that the Korean economy will maintain its potential growth rate of 7.2% per annum during 1991–2000. By extrapolation, Korea's per capita income in the year 2000 is estimated to grow to $6,900 under the assumption that population growth will be reduced to 1.0% per annum. This means that, in terms of per capita income, Korea can reach the level of today's Italy, which recorded a per capita income of $6,400 in 1984.

2. Trade

According to the Sixth Five-Year Economic and Social Development Plan, exports will increase at an annual rate of 10% in the next 5 years. Exports are expected to reach $56 billion and imports $53 billion by 1991. The Sixth Five-Year Economic and Social Development Plan seems quite conservative in its projection for exports. Therefore, in 1991, total trade volume may far exceed $109 billion, which is the prediction of the Sixth Five-Year Plan.

The increase in exports will be led by technology-intensive items such as automobiles, electronic products, and machinery. For the next 5 years the balance of payments surplus is projected to be $5 billion per annum, thus lowering Korea's external debt to $33 billion in 1991. The study by the Korea Development Institute (1986) projects that both exports and imports will grow at an annual rate of 12.5% in 1991–2000, and thus the trade volume will exceed $300 billion by 2000.

3. Industry and Technology

The electronics, machinery, and automobile industries will be the leading industries until 2000. The productivity increase of these industries will be backed by the development of service sectors such as construction engineering, machine design, marketing, and consulting. The manufacturing sector is expected to grow at an annual rate of 9.5% until 1991 and 8.0% thereafter until 2000. The share of GNP contributed by the mining and manufacturing sector will increase to 32.7% in 1991 from 30.1% in 1986, whereas the share of the agriculture and fisheries sector will drop to 10.6% from 12.8%. By 2000, it is expected that the share of the agriculture and fisheries sector will fall further to 7.5% whereas the share of the mining and manufacturing sector will increase to 33%.

In the period of 1991–2000, the service industry will be the fastest growing sector, and thus its share of GNP will increase to 40.4% in 2000. To support the changes in industrial structure, investment in technology and human resources will rapidly increase. The ratio of R&D expenditure to GNP will grow to 2.5% in 1991 from 2% in 1986. The government has an ambitious plan to raise this ratio to 5% by 2001.

4. Social Welfare and Living Standards

The unemployment rate will remain at 3.7%, and the rate of inflation in consumer prices will stay at 3% until 1991. Living standards will steadily improve in line with income growth. For example, 1.7 million new houses will be built in the next 5 years. Therefore, the housing diffusion ratio will grow to 71.5% in 1991 from 69.9% in 1986. This ratio will continue to rise to 82% in 2000. A substantial improvement in living standards will be made in terms of water supply, sewage treatment, roads, and telephone services. The gap between rural and urban development will be narrowed. With improving living standards, the average life expectancy will rise to 72 years in 2000 from the current 69 years.

VI. CONCLUSION

In economics, nothing is absolutely free: "There is no such thing as a free lunch." Indeed, Koreans have paid for their economic development with a heavy investment in education and a lot of sweat. It seems clear that Koreans will now have to work even harder to reach and realize their goal of becoming an advanced economic regime. As pointed out earlier, many new challenges and opportunities are lying ahead, waiting for Koreans to meet and to exploit.

In order to meet the challenges for entrance into an advanced society, Korea will have to carefully analyze the current issues concerning the domestic and world economy in order to plan an effective strategy. It is essential that the strategy be made in a global context. First, political stability is a *sine qua non* for sustained development. Even in a brief period of political instability, the whole basis of economic development could be destroyed. Second, human resources, the primary source of growth in the Korean economy, should be continuously developed to maintain the momentum of development into the future. A social atmosphere that encourages and rewards hard work and a sound work ethic should be established. Third, competition and the market mechanism, which inevitably increase efficiency, should be promoted through further deregulation, liberalization, and internationalization.

With all these efforts, is it certain that Korea will achieve the status of an advanced economy in the next generation? Last, but not least, is the element of luck, which could certainly facilitate the road to a higher future ahead.

NOTES

1. On the sources of growth in the Korean Economy, see Kim, Kwang-Suk and Park, Joon-Kyung (1985); also, Song, Byung-Nak (1984).
2. On the role of education in the developmet of Korean economy, see McGinn et al. (1980); also Mason et al. (1981).
3. The government prediction is $5 billion, however. See, *The Sixth Five-Year Economic and Social Development Plan, 1986*.
4. For more details on this, see Goldsmith (1969).
5. Because of statistical difficulties, GNP was used as a substitute for national wealth.
6. For more details on this, see Adelman and Morris (1967, 1973); also Kim, Chul Whan (1987).
7. See Suh, Dong-Suk (1987).
8. See Kim, Dong-Won (1986); also Kim, Joong Woong, (1986).
9. See The World Bank Report, *Korea Managing the Industrial Transition, 1986*.
10. See Kim, Soo-Yong (1980).
11. See Park, Yung-Chul (1985).
12. The Korean government is more conservative on this. See *the Sixth Five-Year Economic and Social Development Plan, 1986*.
13. See Sakong and Jones (1980).
14. Korea Development Institute (1986); also, Kim, Kihwan (1987a,b).

REFERENCES

Adelman, I. and C. T. Morris, *Society, Politics and Economic Development: A Quantitative Approach*, Baltimore: Johns Hopkins Press, 1967.

——— *Economic Growth and Social Equity in Developing Countries*. Stanford: Stanford University Press, 1973.

Goldsmith, R. W. *Financial Structure and Development*. New Haven, 1969.

Kim, Chul Whan. "The Current Conditions and Reasons for the Income Inequality." *The Korean Economy*. Kyung Se Won, Seoul, 1987.

Kim, Dong Won. "Monetary Policy and Price." *The Korean Economy*. Chung Sa, Seoul, 1986.

Kim, Joong Woong. "Economic Development and Financial Liberalization in Korea: Policy Reforms and Future Prospects." *Financial Development Policies and Issues*. Seoul: The Korea Development Institute, 1986.

Kim, Kihwan. *The Korean Economy: Past Performance, Current Reforms, and Future Prospects*. Seoul: The Korea Development Institute, 1987a.

——— "Korea in the 1990s: Making the Transition to a Developed Economy," mimeo. May 1987b.

Kim, Kwang Suk and Joon Kyung Park. *Sources of Economic Growth in Korea: 1963–1982*. Seoul: The Korea Development Institute, 1985.

Kim, Soo Yong. *The Korea's Trade Policy and Price Fluctuation*. Seoul: Korea Institute for Economics and Technology, 1980.

The Korea Development Institute. *Korea Year 2000: Prospects and Issues for Long-Term Development*. Seoul: The Korea Development Institute, 1986.

Mason, E. S. et al. *The Economic and Social Modernization of the Republic of Korea*. Seoul: The Korea Development Institute, 1981.

McGinn, N. F. et al. *Education and Development in Korea, Studies in the Modernization of the Republic of Korea: 1945–1975*. Cambridge, MA: Council on East Asian Studies, Havard University, 1980.

Park, Yung Chul. "Economic Stabilization and Liberalization in Korea, 1980–1984." *Monetary Policy in Changing Financial Environment*. The Bank of Korea, September 1985.

Sakong, Il and L. P. Jones. *Government, Business, and Entrepreneurship in Economic Development: The Korean Case*. Seoul: The Korea Development Institute, 1980.

Song, Byung Nak. *The Korean Economy*. Park Young Sa, Seoul, 1984.

Suh, Dong Suk. "The Financial Industry and the Direction of Financial Liberalization in Korea." *The Korean Economy*. Kyung Se Won, Seoul, 1987.

The World Bank. *Managing the Industrial Transition*, 1986.

Statistics

The Bank of Korea. *Economic Statistics Yearbook*, various issues.

——— *Monthly Bulletin*, various issues.

——— *Flow of Funds Account*, 1985.

Economic Planning Board. *Social Indicators in Korea*, 1986.

——— *Major Statistics of Korean Economy*, 1981 and 1986.

Executive Yuan. *Taiwan Statistic Data Book*. Taiwan, 1985.

The Korea Development Institute. *Quarterly Economic Outlook*.

Korean Traders Association. *The Trend of Foreign Trade*, 1985.

Ministry of Finance. *Fiscal and Financial Statistics*, 1986.

Republic of Korea. *The Sixth Five-Year Economic and Social Development Plan*, 1986.

The World Bank. *World Development Report*, various issues.

The Bank of Japan. *Economic Statistics Monthly*, April 1987.

TAIWAN IN THE 1980S:
POLICIES AND PROSPECTS

Kuo-shu Liang and Ching-ing Hou Liang

I. INTRODUCTION

The economic conditions of Taiwan, during the early postwar period, were similar to those in many resource-poor, low-income developing countries. It was overpopulated, and the natural rate of growth of its population exceeded 3% per annum. The domestic market was small, and the inordinate military needs competed with development projects for scarce resources. The economy suffered from chronic balance-of-payments deficits and a violent inflation (Jacoby, 1966: 118; Lin, 1973: 30–31). Manufacturing activity accounted for 11% of NDP (Net Domestic Product) in 1952, whereas 38% of NDP originated in the primary sector. Exports accounted for 8% of GNP (Gross National Product) and the percentage share of manufactured exports in total exports was only 7.6 in 1955. In such an environment, the commitment to development by the government was a matter

Research in Asian Economic Studies.
Asian Industrialization: Changing Economic Structures,
Volume 1, Part A, pages 109–137.
Copyright © 1988 by JAI Press Inc.
All rights of reproduction in any form reserved.
ISBN: 0-89232-987-4

of necessity. It was the history of poverty and war that made the government and the people establish economic development as its first priority.

A broad base for economic development was laid by land reform, which was carried out during 1949–1953 (Tang and Liang, 1973: 116–117), and the government policies pursued until the late 1950s were those typically associated with a strategy of import substitution. The multiple exchange rate system and strict import controls that were adopted by the government during this period favored industrial expansion oriented toward the domestic market. In addition, the government extended loans on favorable terms, allocated imported materials directly to manufactures, and assisted the sales of products.

The relatively easy phase of import substitution appeared to have reached its limit in a relatively short period in the protected, narrow domestic market. In response to underutilization of existing capacity and poor growth prospects associated with inward orientation, the government introduced a series of major policy reforms during the period 1958–1961. The overvalued currency was devalued, and the complicated exchange rate structure was simplified and finally unified in June 1961. Laws and regulations governing investment and imports were liberalized. The emphasis of trade and industrial policies shifted from strict import controls to export promotion. Marked changes in commodity composition of Taiwan's exports over time provide positive evidence of a successful export-led industrialization.

From the beginning of the export drive in the early 1960s until the middle of the 1970s, the outward-looking policies for industry and trade were essential for the rapid growth and remarkable structural transformation of the Taiwan economy. Taiwan provides a classic example of an economy following its comparative advantage and reaping the gains from trade illustrated by the traditional theory of international trade. The rapid expansion of labor-intensive manufactured export contributed to efficient industrialization, by permitting specialization according to comparative advantage and stimulating technological improvement. It also improved living standards as well as income distribution through the creation of new productive employment and a rapid increase in real wage rates (Lee and Liang, 1982: 310–383).

The prospects for sustaining economic growth became less favorable in the turbulent years of the 1970s and the 1980s. The domestic and international environments of the economy have been changing at an accelerated pace in recent years. This study attempts to analyze recent economic development in Taiwan by reference to the policies applied and policy recommendation being made that may be pursued to exploit the growth potential of the Taiwan economy in the 1980s. Section II briefly discusses economic development in the turbulent years of the 1970s and the early 1980s. Section III examines the future policy priorities for achieving growth and productivity gains in rapidly changing economic environments. A brief conclusion follows.

II. ECONOMIC DEVELOPMENT IN THE 1970s AND THE 1980s

From the beginning of the export drive in the early 1960s until the middle of the 1970s, the outward-looking policies for industry and trade were essential for the steady growth and remarkable structural transformation of the Taiwan economy. In addition to the outward-looking development strategy, the climate conducive to Taiwan's rapid economic growth was created by factors such as a strong and stable government leadership, the commitment of the pragmatic bureaucracy to accelerate economic development, a reasonably well-educated and hardworking labor force, a weak labor organization, and the right incentives. The general economic climate became favorable for the entrepreneurs to seize opportunities. The compound annual rate of growth in the index of manufactured output, rising at 11% during the period 1955–1960, accelerated to 21% during the period 1965–1970. As the growth of manufactured output accelerated, the share of manufactured products in total exports rose from 28% in 1960 to 77% in 1970. Moreover, the rapid development of labor-intensive export industries permitted economic growth to be more labor absorptive and equitable. Employment and real wages in manufacturing revealed a clear trend of accelerated increase in the 1960s and the early 1970s. Manufacturing employment rose 9% a year during the period 1965–1970, whereas real wages increased at a rate of 6.6%. Taiwan is also one of the few developing economies that achieved an impressive growth record with relative price stability in the 1960s.

The turbulent decade of the 1970s witnessed, however, two oil shocks, first in late 1973 and then in 1979. The recovery of the economy after the first oil shock was rapid and could be primarily attributed to the timely implementation of the economic stabilization program in early 1974, the continuous growth of manufactured exports with increased proportion of exports being directed to the oil producing countries, and the high rate of gross domestic capital formation through major government investment projects in infrastructure and heavy and petrochemical industries.

The second oil shock unfortunately aggravated the widespread adverse effects. The growth rate of GNP and the volume of exports declined sharply. The slow growth in the industrial countries reduced the demand for manufactured goods. The export competitiveness eroded as the value of the U.S. dollar, to which NT dollar was tied, appreciated. Protectionist sentiment resulted in higher and widespread trade barriers. Rising real wages threatened Taiwan's ability to compete with new exporters of labor-intensive products. Meanwhile, the prices of many products produced by the domestic heavy and petrochemical industries remained high relative to world market prices. Stagnant demand for exports, high real interest rates, lower profits, low capacity utilization in many industries, and uncertainties eroded business confidence. As a consequence, the real growth rate of gross fixed capital formation fell sharply from 15.7% in 1980 to 3.7% in 1981, and even became negative in 1982 and 1983.

The Taiwan economy in 1984 experienced once again simultaneous rapid economic growth and price stability as a result of a booming export trade. The growth rate of real GNP rose from 7.9% in 1983 to 10.5% in 1984. The wholesale price index rose only 0.48% over the previous year and the consumer price index even slipped 0.03%. However, the growth rates showed a clearly decreasing trend after the latter half of 1984, because the U.S. demand was flattening. The growth rate of real GNP fell to 5.1%, and export value in NT dollars increased only 2.7% in 1985. The year 1985 was somewhat disappointing from the viewpoint of economic growth.

Following slow growth in 1985, Taiwan was back on the path of rapid export-led growth in 1986, helped by the appreciation of the yen and major European currencies, depressed prices of oil and other primary products, and falling interest rates. 1986 growth of 10.8% more than doubled over 1985. Taiwan's major macroeconomic indicators remained fairly impressive in 1987. Real GNP registered an annual rate of 10.5% growth. Per capita GNP reached $4,991. Wholesale price index declined 4.4% and consumer price index only rose 0.4%. The rate of unemployment was 2.0%, i.e., the lowest level since 1982. However, at the microeconomic level, a pressing question is how well the exporters can compete and survive with the NT dollar appreciating 41.8% against the U.S. dollar during the period September 20, 1985 to December 31, 1987, and the NT dollar still remains strong.

One of the most important economic issues in Taiwan today is the huge trade imbalance with the United States. Taiwan exported 44.2% of its exports to the United States; its trade surplus amounted to $16 billion in 1987 inspite of the rapid appreciation of the NT dollar. Since Taiwan is heavily dependent on the U.S. market and its economic power is relatively weak, it lacks retaliatory leverage. In addition, it is a relatively healthy economy being widely supposed to be capable of absorbing the detrimental effects of the protectionist measures. These characteristics make Taiwan a likely target of U.S. protectionist measures.

Table 1 shows percentage annual contribution of each component to the growth rate of GDP at 1981 prices.[1] It can be observed that percentage annual contribution of each component to the growth rate of GDP fluctuated a great deal. However, it is clear that the contribution of gross domestic capital formation dropped drastically during the period 1981–1986, its contribution even became negative in 1982 and 1985. In contrast, the contribution attributable to external components $(X - M)$ far exceeded that attributable to domestic absorption $(C + G + I)$ in most years during the period. Taiwan has run too great a trade surplus, while investing too little in the industrial modernization and economic infrastructure.

The economy of Taiwan is presently at a crossroad, and current structural problems are basically the result of the very success of past development efforts.

Table 1. Taiwan's Economic Growth: Percentage Annual Contribution by Each Component to the Rate of Growth of GDP at 1981 Prices: 1955–1985[a]

	C	*G*	*I*	*X*	*M*
1955	63.82	27.24	2.15	4.00	-2.79
1960	51.40	30.51	28.92	14.90	25.72
1965	62.28	15.97	23.67	27.90	29.82
1970	52.39	20.89	34.89	48.60	56.76
1975	58.47	8.79	38.06	58.82	64.14
1980	42.76	14.66	36.53	69.78	63.72
1981	30.03	9.87	1.12	71.03	12.06
1982	85.50	37.60	-121.69	26.04	-72.54
1983	34.88	9.86	0.67	121.25	66.66
1984	49.01	10.82	7.44	92.87	60.14
1985	61.10	19.56	-67.47	37.33	-49.47
1986	30.19	5.66	4.72	155.66	96.23

Source: DGBAS: *National Income of Taiwan* (Taipei: various years).

[a] Due to statistical discrepancy, the sum of each component may not add up to 100.00%.

The era of relatively stable real wage rates and unit labor cost appears to have come to an end, and indeed real wage rates have risen considerably since the 1970s (Table 2).

After the second oil shock, higher labor cost, slow growth, and low inflation made it difficult for business to make profits. Companies that took on heavy debts to invest in real estate in the hopes of making quick and easy profits were in trouble. The shift to slower growth and stable prices demanded that entrepreneurs reexamine and reshape their production, financing, investment, and marketing strategies. Drastic measures are needed to cut costs, control quality, diversify products, and manage debts to stay competitive. Capital spending plans need to be geared to increase productivity and quality rather than to expand capacity.

In addition, the rising costs of pollution and environmental degradation and the poverty of public services and welfare activities can no longer be ignored. The government must restructure its policy to give greater priority to pollution control, consumer protection, and social welfare improvement. Government--business relations in the 1980s will certainly be less advantageous for business compared to previous decades.

Table 2. Average Annual Percentage Changes in Wages, Labor Productivity, and Unit Labor Costs in Manufacturing, 1952–1986

	1952–1955	*1955–1960*	*1960–1965*	*1965–1970*	*1970–1975*	*1975–1980*	*1980–1986*	*1952–1986*
Money wages	16.11	9.42	8.04	11.19	21.01	17.95	9.5	12.5
Consumer prices	9.90	9.52	2.39	4.36	12.20	8.67	3.7	6.9
Real wages[a]	5.65	-0.07	5.52	6.54	7.85	8.54	5.7	5.2
Labor productivity	11.51	6.26	9.89	10.37	2.73	8.25	4.7	7.1
Unit Labor costs[b]	4.60	3.16	−1.85	0.82	18.28	9.70	4.7	5.4

Source: Council for Economic Planning and Development, *Taiwan Statistical Data Book* (Taipei: various years); *Adjusted Statistics of Manufacturing in Taiwan Area* (Taipei: 1st Quarter 1952 – 4th Quarter 1976); *Adjustment of Labor Force, Unemployment and Employment by Sector's in Taiwan Area* (Taipei: 1952–77); Ministry of Economic Affairs, *Taiwan Industrial Production Statistics Monthly* (Taipei: various issues); DGBAS, *Commodity-Price Statistics Monthly* (Taipei: various issues); *Monthly Bulletin of Labor Statistics* (Taipei: various issues).

[a] Money wages divided by the index of urban consumer prices.

[b] Difference between rate of change of money wage and rate of change of labor productivity. Labor productivity is calculated by dividing output index by employment index.

III. POLICY PRIORITIES IN THE 1980s

Although the increasing complexity of the economy demands greater decentralization of economic decision making, industry has not always been in a position to effect adjustments unaided. Many firms have been unsure about how to move to improve their technological base. The role of industrial policy is to provide information on the direction of changes in industrial structure, help remove structural rigidities, coordinate with macroeconomic policies to assist industry adapt to new conditions and perform more efficiently, and promote the flow of resources to activities where they can be most productively employed (Jaffe, 1984: 11–13).

The Taiwan government has recognized that new directions are imperative. In May 1985 it created the Economic Reform Committee to undertake a review of the economy, identify existing constraints on new growth opportunities, and make proposals within 6 months to modernize the legal and institutional framework of the entire economic system and restructure the economy. Whether the Taiwan economy can successfully restructure its industry and attain the high rate of economic expansion that it experienced in the past will depend to a great extent on ensuring technology transfers, reforming financial systems, diversifying export markets, and liberalizing imports and foreign exchange control to reduce the risks of protectionism.

A. The Significance of Technology Transfers in Export-Led Industrialiation

Table 3 shows the sources of growth in Taiwan's manufacturing sector during the period 1962–1981. Even though the growth rate of exogenous technical progress dropped from 9.4% per annum during the period 1962–1973 to 1.6% during the period 1974–1981, the contribution of the increase in capital stock appeared to be very significant.

By far the most important determinant of technical progress is the continuous inflow of foreign technology through imported capital goods. Modern technology is embodied in machinery and equipment imported from abroad. Export-led industrialization encourages a more rapid rate of capital formation and technical progress by financing the imports of capital goods through rapid export expansion. It also produces learning effects to local entrepreneurs in developing marketing and design capabilities. The pace of export-led industrialization will, in turn, be facilitated by technical progress (Lee, 1981: 12–13, 128). From this standpoint, the government and industry leaders have felt uneasy about the recent decreases in the investment and in import of machinery and equipment.

Table 4 shows overseas Chinese and foreign investment during the period 1978–1986. The contribution of direct foreign investment to exports has not been important in Taiwan apart from a few manufacturing sectors such as electronics

Table 3. Sources of Growth in Taiwan's Manufacturing Sector: 1962–1981[a]

Annual growth rate	*1962–1973*	*1974–1981*	*1962–1981*
Valued added (%)	17.04	9.15	13.88
Labor (%)	8.76	5.29	7.37
Capital stock (%)	6.46	10.57	8.10
Technical progress (%)	9.40	1.59	6.27

Sources: Derived from Council for Economic Planning and Development, *Taiwan District Industry-Level Fixed Capital Stock Survey in 1975* (Taipei); DGBAS, *National Income of Taiwan* (Taipai: various years); DGBAS, *Taiwan Labor Statistics Monthly* (Taipei: various issues).

[a] Sources of growth in the manufacturing sector are decomposed by applying the following formula:

Growth rate of value added = (share of labor income in value added) x (growth rate of labor force) + (share of capital income in value added) + (growth rate of capital stock) + residual (technical progress).

Capital income = rents + interests + profits + depreciation

Labor income = compensation of employees.

Table 4. Overseas Chinese and Foreign Investment in Taiwan 1978–1986 (in US$ Millions)

Year	*Investment in arrival*	*Reinvestment of profits*	*Total*
1978	68	23	91
1979	69	51	120
1980	109	62	171
1981	87	60	147
1982	79	46	125
1983	112	50	162
1984	121	88	209
1985	254	67	321
1986	273	54	327

Source: Investment Commission, Ministry of Economic Affairs, *Statistics on Overseas Chinese and Foreign Investment, Technical Cooperation, Outward Investment, and Outward Technical Cooperation, Taiwan* (Taipei: various years).

and electrical appliances, and to a lesser extent chemicals (Ranis and Schive, 1985: 106).

Export-oriented foreign firms appeared to use more labor-intensive techniques than their local counterparts in the same industry (Schive and Yeh, 1982). Given the footloose nature of export-oriented direct foreign investment, investing firms adapt their techniques to local circumstances to take full advantage of low labor costs. The transfers of technology normally focus on training within the firm as well as outside, extending to the suppliers of inputs and users of final products. Taiwan Singer showed how direct foreign investment helped local firms improve the quality of parts supplied and the sewing machine industry in general (Ranis and Schive, 1985: 124–129).

Increasing emphasis on technology transfers is both an opportunity and a necessity. The interesting feature of the figures in Table 2 is the discontinuation of past trends in the changes in real wages and labor productivity. The rise in labor productivity accelerated and unit labor costs remained unchanged or even declined in the 1960s. This undoubtedly strengthened the competitive edge of Taiwan's labor-intensive manufactures in the world market. However, the absolute size of the agricultural labor force began to decline in 1969 as outflow rate accelerated in the late 1960s. The era of relatively stable real wage rates and unit labor costs came to an end. Failure to recognize the dynamic nature of comparative advantage would freeze capital, labor, and other scarce resources in industries in which opportunities are declining and lead to the neglect of advantageous new export opportunities.

The government cannot avoid serious adjustment problems when some major industries lose international competitiveness. For instance, the textile and clothing industries have exemplified many of the issues involved in trade between the industrial countries and the newly industrializing countries. Quantitative restrictions on imports have encouraged producers to move into higher value added fashionable products to maintain export earnings in spite of restrictions on import volume. However, the continued viability of the existing industries has been at stake. Outdated technology and skill have hindered progress in bleaching and dyeing. Success in producing fashionable textiles requires a sensitive response to shifts in consumer preferences, ability to produce in small lots with very tight delivery schedules, and precise quality controls. The recent adjustment problems have intensified because structural rigidities have been reinforced by trade frictions.

Some of the defensive measures taken in the past during the recession years to provide special assistance to the companies in trouble resulted in the perpetuation of an inefficient allocation of productive resources and aggravated problems of overcapacity.[2] Policies that try to reverse or significantly delay market adjustment processes will be extremely costly and counterproductive. The government policy must be more adjustment oriented and encourage industry to be more responsive to new challenges and opportunities. A number of traditional labor-intensive industries, such as cotton textiles, footwear, toys, and canned foods, have to improve competitiveness through modernization and shifting to new product lines.

Although traditional industries in trouble can pose significant policy problems, perhaps the most important and difficult task is to develop the climate in which new industries can prosper. The present industrial policy has been striving to restructure the economy by switching the focus of industrial development from unskilled and labor-intensive manufactures and capital-and-energy-intensive heavy and chemical industries to high-technology areas. Strategic industries include machinery manufacturing, and information and electronics industries. These industries are skill intensive, relatively low capital intensive, and energy saving. In addition, they support the automation of other industries and accelerate the economy's rate of increase in productivity. They will be next in line for the achievement of a high rate of export expansion as the growth of experience and capacity in manufacturing permits the economy to move beyond simple labor-intensive types of production.

The characteristics of structural change are shown in Table 5. While the share of the primary sector in the economy has declined, the manufacturing sector has grown rapidly. Within manufacturing, the share of output in the traditional labor-intensive industries, such as textiles, wearing apparel, and food, has declined. By contrast, output and employment in strategic industries have grown very rapidly. Nevertheless, it should be noted that to foster the growth of machinery and electronics industries and expand their share of world trade are not easy tasks. Unlike process industries such as cement, steel, and chemicals, in which production is machine paced and the technology is embodied mainly in imported equipments, machinery is skill intensive and requires a longer learning period. Moreover, the operation scales of most firms in Taiwan are small. Most firms produce a wide spectrum of products instead of concentrating on a few parts and components. As a result, they are poorly suited for efficient production of machinery. Productivity has also been hampered by a high turnover of labor. In most cases, products are imitated due to the lack of R&D capability. Supplies of materials such as special steels, ceramics, and electronics still lag behind. Machinery produced by small companies is being sold without credit, and the after-sales services are inadequate.

The electronics industry is tightly ruled by technological change. Taiwan has scores of entrepreneurial personal computer makers, working their way up through the basic stages of computer technology, progressing from printed circuit boards to home computers to IBM-compatible systems. But most local producers are still very much in the business of assembling components and computer peripherals, with high-technology inputs being imported. Some producers may not be able to survive unless they enter into close subcontracting or depend on OEM sales with the major international corporations. Only a handful of the companies have sufficient technical and financial resources to make the successful transition from clonemaker to system integrators.

Concerted efforts should be made to promote a successul development of the strategic industries. Incentives to the strategic industries take the form of extending

Table 5. Structural Change: 1970–1985[a]

	Shares of GDP (current prices) (%)		*Shares of employment (%)*	
	1970	*1985*	*1970*	*1985*
Primary sector	16.89	6.50	38.31	17.46
Manufacturing sector	33.53	40.92	20.94	33.49
Electrical machinery and appliances	3.13	5.16	1.40	4.55
Machinery, transport equipment, and metal products	3.36	5.52	3.30	4.59
Heavy industries	7.50	10.75	2.34	2.54
Textiles, wearing apparel, and food	10.17	8.72	7.41	8.72
Other	9.38	10.79	6.49	13.09
Construction	3.90	4.32	5.05	7.01
Electricity and gas	2.52	4.25	0.37	0.46
Service sector	32.13	33.99	28.13	31.32
Retail and wholesale trade	14.84	13.89	13.61	17.99
Financial and real estate	2.61	3.55	1.42	1.67
Transport and communication	6.04	6.12	5.42	5.22
Other service	8.64	10.42	7.67	6.44
Government	11.02	10.03	7.21	9.79

Sources: Directorate-General of Budget, Accounting and Statistics, *National Income of Taiwan* (Taipei: various years); *Report on the Manpower Utilization Survey in Taiwan Area, Taiwan Government*(Taipei: various years).

[a] Heavy industries include petroleum and coal products, chemicals, and basic metals. Employment of government sector does not include servicemen.

low-interest loans, the right to retain earnings of up to 200% of paid-up capital, and the right to delay the start of its 5-year income tax holiday by up to 4 years. The government is also encouraging the establishment of venture capital firms to help promote high-technology ventures and technical upgrading. However, adequate financial mechanisms, such as adding the share of unlisted ventures in the over-the-counter securities market, are needed to stimulate the provisions of risk capital for new ventures.

Table 6 indicates a generally increasing trend in approvals of technical cooperation projects and royalty payments in recent years. Technical cooperation provides an important channel for the transfer of technology. In order to move faster

Table 6. Approved Technical Cooperation Projects and Royalty Payment 1978–1986

Year	*Approved technical cooperation projects*	*Royalty payments (US$ million)*
1978	110	52
1979	133	69
1980	143	86
1981	124	95
1982	144	99
1983	141	95
1984	168	122
1985	197	151
1986	192	172

Sources: Investment Commission, Ministry of Economic Affairs, *Statistics on Overseas Chinese and Foreign Investment, Technical Cooperation, Outward Investment, and Outward Technical Cooperation. Taiwan* (Taipei: various years); The Central Bank of China, *Balance of Payments, Taiwan District, Taiwan* (Taipei: various years).

in capturing a share of the world market for high-technology products in the 1980s, the government has set the target for R&D spending by the government and public and private enterprises at 1.2% of GNP by 1985, and 2% by 1989. However, national R&D expenditures still remained at a low level as is shown in Table 7.

Technology transfers in high-tech areas involve high risk. A system of ''socializing'' the risk must be developed, with the government assuming a part of it by providing government-financed training, some R&D funds, and start-up capital as well as by encouraging collaboration among university research centers and businesses. The expanded technological research cooperation will optimize the use of scarce skilled personnel and facilities, and reduce the costs both financially and intellectually by providing a mechanism for pooling research efforts.[3] At the same time, macroeconomic measures must complement industrial policy that takes into account the important microeconomic differences among different sectors. The Economic Reform Committee has recommended that business and personal income taxes be cut, that interest rates be reduced, and that the central bank conduct foreign exchange market intervention to avoid unduly affecting international price competitiveness and dampen seasonality. It also recommended tax simplification, relaxation of foreign exchange controls, reduction of the average nominal tariff rates to 15–20% by 1991, replacement of the positive list with a negative list of commodities subject to import controls as well as of activities eligible for overseas Chinese and foreign investment, abolishment of such performance requirements as exporting a minimum portion of a foreign company's output or using a certain amount of local components, financial deregulation, and a fundamental reform of the financial system. The major objective of these recommendations is to achieve a better functioning market economy.

Table 7. National R&D Expenditures as Percentage of GNP: 1978–1985.

Year	*National R&D expenditures as percentage of GNP*
1978	0.30
1979	0.42
1980	0.55
1981	0.76
1982	0.70
1983	0.73
1984	0.99
1985	1.06

Source: National Science Council, *Survey of R&D Activities, Taiwan* (Taipei: various years).

B. Recommendations for Financial Reform

The experience of Taiwan confirms that the industry and trade sectors have to be dynamic and government policies have to be flexible to deal with the internal and external challenges. The success of outward-oriented industrialization has resulted in the growing export surplus. The trade surplus widened from $77 million in 1980 to $16.9 billion in 1986 and $16.4 billion during January–September, 1987. Taiwan's trade and current surpluses expanded substantially. As is shown in Table 8, export surplus as percentage of GNP widened from −1.2 in 1980 to 20.3 in 1986.

Table 8. Key Indicators of the Significance of Export Surplus 1980–1986[a]

	1980	*1981*	*1982*	*1983*	*1984*	*1985*	*1986*
Export surplus/ GNP (%)	−1.21	2.08	5.26	8.98	11.44	14.23	20.30
Export surplus/ exports (%)	−2.28	3.97	10.39	16.66	20.06	25.80	34.36
Foreign assets of the central bank/ imports (%)	12.63	24.48	44.42	54.95	66.97	99.12	139.48

Sources: DGBAS: *National Income of Taiwan* (Taipei: various years); Department of Statistics, Ministry of Finance, *Monthly Statistics of Exports and Imports, Taiwan* (Taipei: various years); The Central Bank of China, *Balance of Payments, Taiwan District, Taiwan* (Taipei: various years).

[a] Exports surplus, GNP, and exports are based on the data of national income statisticss, and imports on the Customs data. Foreign assets of the Central Bank are the 12 month averages.

Although new outflow of long-term capital amounted to US$1.4 billion in 1986 compared with an inflow of US$1.2 billion in 1980, capital outflows were swamped by the massive current surplus. Short-term capital inflow in 1986 increased five times compared with 1985 mainly due to the crawling appreciation of NT dollars. The size of Taiwan's foreign exchange holding has become remarkable by any standards. Taiwan's foreign reserves amounted to 1 year and 5 months of its imports in 1986 (Table 8).

An export surplus represents more domestic savings than domestic investment or a positive net foreign investment, which is unusual for a newly industrializing country. In fact, Taiwan exports its savings in very large amounts to the United States to help finance the U.S. budget deficits offsetting much of the U.S.–Taiwan trade imbalance.

Savings and investment balances for the period 1980–1986 are shown in Table 9. From 1980 to 1986, nominal GNP expanded by NT$1,304.3 billion, of which consumption increased by NT$716.6 billion and gross savings by NT$587.8 billion, implying an aggregate marginal propensity to save of more than 40%. Domestic uses of the increased savings even decreased by NT$5.5 billion, whereas the net acquisition of foreign assets rose significantly by NT$553.1 billion.

The gross domestic investment was only 18.0% of GNP whereas gross national savings amounted to 38.7% in 1986, generating a huge export surplus. The difference between domestic savings and investment has been accumulated mainly in the form of short-term foreign financial assets. Taiwan is still a newly industrializing economy that has to maximize the static and dynamic allocative efficiency, and yet as much as 19.1% of GNP was transferred abroad, and thus was not utilized for domestic economic activities in 1986.

One reason for transferring huge domestic savings abroad may be an inadequate and out-of-date financial regime that has failed to function as an efficient intermediary between savers and investors. Because the processes of market restructuring and regulatory reform have remained incomplete, financial deregulation and a fundamental reform of the financial system become imperative. The Economic Reform Committee that functioned during the period of May–November 1985 made the following recommendations for financial reform.

1. The public interest considerations associated with banking and finance include concerns about concentration, conflicts of interest, depositor or investor protection, and unfair competition. The financial system must be reformed in such a way that discipline operates through prior restraints and situations do not exist in which restraint and discipline are achieved only as a by-product of instability and failure. Short-term liquidity support operations that enable time to fashion permanent solutions to problems must not slip into long-term bailouts for those who have acted in an irresponsible or undisciplined fashion (Corrigan, 1987: 50-51). The Economic Reform Committee recommends improving the

Table 9. Savings and Investment Balances 1980–1986 (NT$ Billion)

	1980	*1981*	*1982*	*1983*	*1984*	*1985*	*1986*
GNP at current prices	1,468.1	1,739.8	1,859.0	2,044.1	2,277.8	2,398.4	2,772.4
less:							
Consumption (public + private)	984.0	1,183.4	1,293.9	1,388.4	1,510.2	1,594.6	1,700.6
equals:							
Gross national savings (= A)	484.1	556.4	565.1	655.7	767.6	803.8	1,071.8
of which:							
Households	170.9	227.9	246.7	298.6	338.9	356.3	479.5
Corporate	83.9	71.6	65.1	71.7	103.0	94.9	182.7
Depreciation	108.9	137.6	154.1	170.6	188.9	210.8	225.8
Government (current savings)	116.8	115.9	94.0	113.1	130.0	131.8	140.3
Domestic uses of savings (= B)	504.0	529.8	468.0	469.4	484.4	449.1	498.5
Housing	64.7	72.8	67.5	62.8	68.6	67.3	65.0
Gross fixed nonresidential investment	324.8	345.7	336.8	331.3	333.9	324.0	387.3
Government investment	67.0	75.5	84.3	78.2	81.9	85.8	98.2
Stockbuilding	47.5	35.8	–20.6	–2.9	–0	–28.0	–52.0
Residual savings for foreign investment [= (A) – (B) approximately]	–23.3	23.2	91.8	184.6	276.6	344.7	529.8

Source: DGBAS: *National Income of Taiwan* (Taipei: various years)

bank examination process, streamlining the regulatory structure, strengthening capital requirements, improving disclosure, and reinforcing reporting requirements.

2. The Banking Law and the Central Bank Law stipulate that the Central Bank prescribes the ceiling of bank deposit rates and approves the range of lending rates as proposed by the Banker's Association. Not surprisingly, controls spawned evasions and innovations. Corporations circumvented lending rate floors by issuing commercial papers and bankers acceptances to fund large sums in the money market at rates lower than the bank deposit rates under the current situation of excess liquidity caused by a huge export surplus, high domestic savings, and underinvestment. The bank's role on extending credit to high-quality borrowers was significantly undercut. The rate of profitability in traditional intermediation activities became relatively low and was put under pressure. Financial disintermediation created pressure for interest rate deregulation. The Banking Law and the Central Bank Law have to be revised to completely deregulate bank rates in due course. In addition, the banks cannot continue to rely mainly on collaterals and customer relationships to assess risks. If a more market-oriented financial system is the ultimate goal of financial reform, then an improved system of financial disclosure together with the emergence of a reliable credit rating system should become a part of the reform.

3. Other than progress in interest rate deregulation, foreign banks have been strongly pressing the government to allow them to attain national treatment. Facing a more competitive market, the government authorities should pay more attention on the economies of scope in banking activities. Legislation and administrative orders that limit the ability of banks to grow and diversify will raise the operation costs of the banks. The government authorities should allow banks to take full advantage of cost complementarity of economies of scale. In addition, commercial banking has to become more international by establishing an extensive network of foreign branches.

4. Most of the domestic banks are state owned and subject to the onerous regulations of numerous government agencies. The most troublesome regulations are very difficult standards and procedures for writing off bad loans. Small mistakes can cost a loan officer an administrative penalty in the civil service appraisal system; he or she also may be liable to repay bad loans. It has to be stressed that an effective credit apparatus must entail risk and must provide room for the extension of credit to borrowers in the face of adversity. Some losses are an inevitable part of risk taking, which is part of the process of economic development. The Economic Reform Committee recommends enacting a special law governing state-owned banks with minimum state interference so that banks avoid resembling a government bureaucracy. Bank regulation should be based on the Banking Law applied to both government banks and private banks. It has to provide the bank sufficient scope to take initiative and operate efficiently. The government should exercise its authority only in the capacity of shareholders. The Economic Reform Committee also recommends privatizing major commercial banks and allowing the entry of new private banks to promote competition.

5. In order to equip the financial system to meet the challenges of financial deregulation and international competition, the Financial Subcommittee recommends enacting a law governing mergers and conversions of financial institutions that will restructure the financial system. Financial institutions should be allowed to apply for mergers or conversions, if these changes (a) improve efficiencies and strengthen sound banking, (b) exploit economies in providing financial services but avoid interrupting an adequate supply of credit facilities for the medium and small business sectors as well as excessive concentration of financial powers, and (c) provide adequate protection of the interests of shareholders.

6. Because the gains to the economy as a whole from the development of money and capital markets are considerable, the Economic Reform Committee recommends diversifying high credit-standing instruments in the money market, establishing prudent criteria to evaluate the credit rating of the issuing companies of commercial papers and bankers acceptances, allowing the new entry of bills finance companies, improving the interbank market functions, making clearer the definition of the responsibilities of the Securities Exchange Commission and the Stock Exchange, adopting rules to clearly define fair trading practices, strengthening the supervision of brokers and traders and monitoring market behavior for irregularities, and improving accounting and disclosure requirements for listed companies.

These financial reforms have been phased in slowly. Delaying inevitable reforms will be too costly.

C. Foreign Exchange Liberalization

It appears that the NT dollar appreciation is a critical element in the corrective policies pursued to reduce huge export surplus. The new protectionism in the United States also takes the forms of aggressive protectionism to press market opening, macroeconomic policy coordination, and substantial exchange rate adjustments.

In order to avoid having the NT dollar appreciate too fast against the U.S. dollar, the Central Bank has been discretely intervening to moderate exchange rate fluctuations. However, a policy of "leaning against the wind" designed simply to slow down exchange rate changes allows an internal objective of maintaining competitiveness to override an exchange rate target of reducing export surplus (Williamson, 1983: 64–70). In addition, the adoption of a controlled crawling appreciation strategy reduces uncertainty for short-term financial speculation and introduces destabilizing short-term capital movements that make monetary management progressively difficult.

The annual rate of increase in money supply measured by M_{1B} that consists of net currency issued, checking accounts, passbook deposits, and passbook savings deposits was 41.5% in December 1987. The Central Bank has been issuing huge amounts of treasury bills, central bank certificates of deposit, and savings bonds to sterilize the excess liquidity to alleviate the inflationary pressure it could have. The outstanding balance of treasury bills, certificates of deposits, and savings bonds amounted to NT$1,172 billion, i.e., 1.9 times as much as reserve currency in December 1987.

Taiwan has to follow policies that allow its currency to better reflect economic fundamentals, and a controlled crawling should not follow a simple rule. It has to add a random element to avoid speculation. It also has to be noted that the appropriate exchange rate will be influenced by the mix of policies aimed at expanding domestic demand to reduce excess savings, dismantling existing export incentives to reduce distortions in resource allocation, opening the domestic market to more imported goods, and lifting foreign exchange controls, even though the purchasing-power-parity effective exchange rate index will serve as a base to identify the direction of the change in the appropriate exchange rate.

Purchasing-power-parity effective exchange rate on exports is defined as the nominal exchange rate of NT dollars per U.S. dollar of exports adjusted for changes in wholesale prices in Taiwan and abroad as well as for changes in the exchange rates of Taiwan's major trade partners. As is shown in Table 10, the nominal exchange rates were fairly stable during the period 1982–1985. The slightly undervalued nominal exchange rates as compared with the purchasing-power-parity effective exchange rates during the period 1980–1986 undoubtedly maintained exporters' competitiveness on an export-weighted, inflation-adjusted basis inspite of wide fluctuations in currency values of major industrial countries and a crawling appreciation of the NT dollar. On a purchasing-power-parity effective basis, the NT dollar in 1987 was just as competitive as it was at the end of the last decade.

The NT dollar appreciated against the U.S. dollar by 41.8% during September 20, 1985 (a day before the G-5 New York meeting) to December 31, 1987. However, the recent rapid NT$ appreciation has not as yet greatly affected Taiwan's trade performance. The postponement of adverse J-curve effects could be explained by numerous factors:

1. The Japanese yen and the deutsche mark have appreciated much more than the NT dollar, which has allowed Taiwan's exportables to remain competitive against Japanese and German goods. Table 10 shows that the purchasing-power-parity effective exchange rate rose 8.4% in 1987, in spite of the fact that the nominal rate appreciated 19.0% against the U.S. dollar

2. The U.S. domestic demand growth has been running distinctly high, averaging over 3% in the first two quarters of 1987, rising to 4% in the third (Morgan Guaranty Trust Company of New York, 1987: 11). Increased demand in the United States has delayed the progress in reducing trade imbalance.

3. Protection, notably by voluntary export restraints of labor-intensive manufactures, provides an assured sales outlet and, depending on the relevant

Table 10. Purchasing-Power-Parity Effective Exchange Rates on Exports: 1979–1987[a]

	1979	*1980*	*1981*	*1982*	*1983*	*1984*	*1985*	*1986*	*1987*
I. Average nominal exchange rate for exports	36.02	36.00	36.84	39.11	40.06	39.60	39.85	37.82	31.77
II. Purchasing-power-parity index on exports	100.00	93.98	95.10	99.04	102.36	104.52	108.13	109.89	115.57
III. Effective exchange rate index on exports	100.00	100.44	101.34	99.01	98.64	101.05	102.23	101.09	115.27
IV. Purchasing-power-parity effective exchange rate index on exports (II/III)	100.00	93.57	93.84	100.02	103.77	103.43	105.77	108.70	100.26
V. Purchasing-power-parity effective exchange rate on exports (I/IV)	36.02	38.47	39.26	39.10	38.60	38.29	37.68	34.79	31.69

Sources: The Central Bank of China, *Financial Statistics Monthly, Taiwan District, Taiwan* (Taipei: various years); DGBAS, *Commodity Price Statistics Monthly, Taiwan District, Taiwan* (Taipei: various years); IMF, *International Financial Statistics* (Washington D.C.: various years).

[a] Purchsing-power parity index and effective exchange rate index are weighted by Taiwan's annual export value with 11 major trading partners (the United States, Japan, Korea, etc.).

price elasticities, enables the exporters to capture the rents arising from the ability to raise the export price to the extent of the difference between the international price and the higher domestic price in the importing country. At the microeconomic level, bilateral export restraint arrangements have paradoxically offered greater security in trade flows than would an unrestricted trade regime.

4. The exporters appeared to refrain from "passing through" to U.S. purchasers virtually the full effect of the NT dollar appreciation so as to avoid losing much of their U.S. market share. In spite of the rapid appreciation of the NT dollar, Taiwan's net terms of trade improved only 17.0% during the period September 1985 to October 1987.

5. The NT dollar appreciation and import liberalization measures lowered oil and raw material costs, enabling selling prices not to change much in spite of rapid appreciation. The unit value index of imports declined 25.9% from September 1985 to October 1987.

6. To hedge exchange rate risks on sales contracts denominated in the U.S. dollar, exporters have been borrowing U.S. dollar preexport loans and selling forward dollars. For instance, on October 30, 1987, the spot rate was US$1 = NT$29.91, but 6 months before exporters sold their forward dollars at the rate of NT$32.31. The difference between forward rate and spot rate amounted to NT$2.4 or 8.0% of the spot rate. The forward cover provided by the Central Bank and the authorized commercial banks has provided exporters facing considerable delay with a cushion against the full impact of the rapid NT dollar appreciation.

7. The shift to slower growth and stable prices after the second oil shock forced many entrepreneurs to reexamine and reshape their production, financing, investment, and marketing strategies. Many efforts were made to cut costs, improve quality, diversify products, and manage debt to stay competitive. Many firms have become more resilient.

The sizes of Taiwan's trade surplus and foreign exchange holdings have now reached a level high enough to cause anxieties and frustration. Foreign exchange holdings of $75 billion far exceeded the level required for prudent and virtual provision against future adversity. By the end of 1987, the fall in the value of the U.S. dollar cut the NT dollar value of the reserves that Taiwan's Central Bank had accumulated by NT$372 billion. This sum was the result of not spending the money in better ways and also could be regarded as a gift from the taxpayers of Taiwan to the U.S. government. It was only in recent years that the government and the people began to recognize that an excessively export-biased economy, tight foreign exchange control, and extremely low import propensity, and, consequently, accumulating huge foreign reserves could cause serious trade frictions, huge exchange-rate losses, and threaten economic stability.

The government revised related laws and regulations and lifted most of the foreign exchange controls on July 15, 1987. The foreign exchange controls that remain in effect and still need Central Bank approvals are confined to non-trade-related inward remittances of more than US$50,000 and outward remittances of more than US$5 million by any individuals and firms within a year. The government still restricts capital inflow to bring short-term financial speculation under control. The Central Bank also decided not to provide any hedges against forward exchange transactions by cancelling the forward contract buy-back ratio on July 15, 1987. However, the reforms aimed at increasing the role of the market and reducing existing barriers to capital movements need to relate to the dynamics of the liberalization and the relationship between liberalization and exchange rate exchange rate stabilization. It has to be stressed that the credibility of the reform is critical to its success. The internal consistency of the policies and the simplification of formalities being pursued are fundamental and critical to establish credibility. It is particularly important to stabilize the local currency's exchange rate so as to induce substantial capital outflow as expected by the policy reform.

With a huge trade surplus and excess savings, the government has to expand public investments in educational facilities, environmental preservation, and transportation infrastructure. At the same time, Taiwan has to make better use of its foreign exchange earnings for foreign investment abroad rather than simply accumulating more and more foreign reserves. A number of businesses in Taiwan have made overseas investments and run multinational businesses. Local business activities in outward investment have gradually expanded since the late 1970s. A company undertakes foreign investment to extend foreign markets due to limited local markets, to maintain competitiveness in the international marketplace in the face of constantly rising local wage rates and appreciating local currency that make the manufacturing of standardized products at home less competitive, and to avoid tariff and nontariff barriers proliferating in the current environment of heightened international trade protectionism. Outward investment is mainly in electric appliances, chemicals, textiles, plastic shoes, and handbags in the United States and Southeast Asian countries. The emergence of the multinationals in Taiwan is a recent phenomenon. Foreign investments in manufacturing appear to be an effective method of heading off protectionist action in the United States and other markets.

D. The Needs for Revising Mercantilist-Oriented Trade Regime and Diversifying Export Markets

In addition to accelerating technology transfers, reforming financial systems, and liberalizing foreign exchange control, Taiwan has to revise its mercantilist-oriented trade regime and diversify export markets. With a huge trade surplus, Taiwan must dismantle existing export incentives by reviewing the tax laws and the functions of export-processing zones, the export–import bank, and the External Trade Development Council. At the same time, if Taiwan does not open its market for imports, it will be vulnerable to charges of "unfair trade." Trade liberalization will make imported goods available at lower prices and have a beneficial impact on consumers, provide a spur for improvements in productivity by reducing prices of imported machinery, trigger accelerated adjustment among industries that compete with imports, and lead to better treatment for exports in foreign markets through bilateral negotiations to obtain mutual concessions under the current world trade environments with selective protectionism often being applied arbitrarily. Moreover, from a political standpoint, the increased stake of foreign exporters in the domestic market would act as a political counterweight to protectionist sentiment abroad. Foreign exporters would behave as an antiprotectionist pressure group in their home countries, fearing loss of exports due to retaliation.

Import restrictions have been relaxed considerably in recent years. The government has made wide-ranging tariff cuts targeted by the United States and eliminated a controversial duty-paying scheme. However, the government has the tendency to overstate the steps that it has taken to liberalize imports. In spite of the trade liberalization process, the ratio of Taiwan's manufactured imports to nominal GNP has generally shown a downward trend. The import ratios of all other categories of commodities have also declined during the period 1980–1986 as is shown in Table 11. The elasticities of imports with respect to GNP were in the range of 1.4–1.9 during the period 1956–1980. It dropped sharply to 0.8 during the period 1980–1986. The expansion of the domestic heavy and petrochemical industry base, the more efficient uses of imported inputs for export processing, and depressed prices of oil and other primary products may explain some of the reasons for this sharp drop. In addition, restrictions apply to particu-

Table 11. Import Ratios to GNP: 1980–1986

	1980	*1981*	*1982*	*1983*	*1984*	*1985*	*1986*
Finished manufactures (SITC 7+8)/GNP (%)	15.55	14.96	13.65	12.90	12.94	11.42	12.79
Semifinished manufactures (SITC 5+6)/GNP (%)	10.51	9.19	8.15	9.19	9.10	7.87	9.49
Energy (SITC 3)/GNP (%)	12.35	11.57	9.64	9.55	8.22	7.20	4.30
Raw materials excluding energy (SITC 2+4)/GNP (%)	6.75	5.67	5.20	5.21	5.26	4.43	4.44
Food (SITC 0+1)/GNP (%)	3.21	3.22	2.85	2.86	2.62	2.43	1.96

Sources: Department of Statistics, Ministry of Finance, *Monthly Statistics of Exports and Imports, Taiwan (Taiwan District)* (Taipei various years); DGBAS, *National Income of Taiwan* (Taipei: various years).

lar sources of origin, and the status of applicants. There is also the reluctance of the lower ranks of bureaucracy to give up discretionary powers and make unjustifiable reinterpretations of the policies that they are charged with enacting.

Tariff structure should not be adjusted fragmentarily under renewed foreign pressure. The government should make serious attempts to revise and simplify the entire tariff structure with a clear conception of the economic rationale in view (Lee and Liang, 1982: 322–332). In addition, the liberalization of import restrictions and the reform of the tariff structure should be carried out on the basis of a program made public in advance to minimize the adjustment costs to firms.

Finally, Taiwan has been facing twin trade imbalances, one with the United States and another with Japan. The relative importance of Japan both as a market for Taiwan's exports and as a source of Taiwan's imports has not changed very much during the period 1980–1986. The leading components of imports from Japan have been machinery and equipment, metal products, and chemicals. These three categories of commodities accounted for 83.6% of the total imports from Japan in 1986. Japan has supplied capital goods and intermediate products for the manufactured goods Taiwan exports to the United States and elsewhere. In addition, Japan has benefited more than the United States from the steps being taken to lower trade barriers under U.S. pressure. As a result, Taiwan's trade with Japan has been persistently in deficits. Trade deficits with Japan amounted to $4.9 billion in 1987. Taiwan has to take advantage of the yen's appreciation to launch a sustained effort to increase its exports to Japan.

In contrast, Taiwan's merchandise trade surplus with the United States increased by $11.5 billion to $16.0 billion from 1980 to 1987. Taiwan's exports to the United States amounted to 44.2% of its total exports in 1987. Table 12 shows the changes in Taiwan's export structure with the United States during the period 1965–1985. In 1965, forest products and tropical agricultural products were the two largest export commodities. By 1973, specialized machinery had replaced forest products as the largest export commodity, and many labor-intensive manufactures such as clothing and apparel, miscellaneous manufactured articles, footwear, and travel goods had become the leading export commodities. During the post-1973 period, the export base continued to broaden. Although the importance of labor-intensive commodities has remained unchanged, telecommunications equipment, electrical machinery, office machines, and data processing equipment have emerged as the major exportables. It has to be noted that more than half of these exportables were shipped to the United States in 1985. The U.S. market accounted for more than 70% of the exports of furniture and footwear. In addition, exporting large quantities of labor-intensive products to the United States tended to compete with those industries that were important sources of employment, usually the least competitive and prosperous, and, consequently, the most protectionist in the United States. Because of the danger of U.S. protectionism, Taiwan has to change the composition of its exports and diversify its markets by seeking other important trade partners.

Table 12. Taiwan's Ten Major Commodity Exports to the United States: 1965–1985 (NT$ Million)

SITC	Commodity	Value	Percentage of total exports of the commodity
	1965		
63	Wood and cork manufactures	834	71.8
05	Vegetables and fruit	726	16.0
84	Clothing and apparel	519	66.1
06	Sugar, honey	346	14.3
65	Textile yarn and fabrics	328	15.4
89	Miscellaneous manufactured articles	320	56.6
72	Specialized machinery	222	47.3
55	Essential oils	114	39.5
24	Wood, lumber, cork	97	19.4
29	Animal and vegetable materials	92	56.8
	1973		
72	Specialized machinery	19,275	67.9
84	Clothing and apparel	13,260	52.2
89	Miscellaneous manufactured articles	8,891	57.0
85	Footwear	5,298	61.5
63	Wood and cork manufactures	4,518	34.5
73	Metalworking machinery	1,787	44.9
69	Metal manufactures	1,768	51.4
05	Vegetables and fruit	1,681	17.0
71	Nonelectrical machinery	1,145	20.6
83	Travel goods, handbags	1,066	49.6
	1985		
89	Miscellaneous manufactured articles	86,260	56.8
84	Clothing and apparel	85,158	60.9
85	Footwear	63,457	71.0
76	Telecommunications equipment	60,205	64.2
77	Electrical machinery	46,074	49.3
69	Metal manufactures	38,458	63.5
75	Office machines and data processing equipment	28,391	56.8
78	Road vehicles	22,575	56.4
82	Furniture and parts	22,364	73.2
83	Travel goods, handbags	19,740	60.5

Sources: Inspectorate General of Customs, *The Trade of Taiwan* (Taipei: various years); Research, Development, and Evaluation Commission, *Commodity Trade Statistics of Taiwan (SITC Revised), 1954–74* (Taipei: August 1976).

Broadly speaking, the relative importance of domestic supply and foreign demand in determining the rate of growth of a country's exports will vary according to its share in the export market. The greater the country's share the more probable that its exports will grow more or less in line with the growth in foreign import demand for the product it exports. The smaller its share, the more important is its ability to produce for export at prevailing world prices (Maizels, 1968: 168). The need to expedite the diversification of its markets and product composition is evident if Taiwan is to sustain its export growth.

Market diversification, the state of the world economic environment, and prevailing limitations on trade by the industrial countries, all are arguments in favor of a trade and industrial development strategy that supports a more balanced and widespread expansion of exports from a broad array of manufacturing subsectors instead of a sudden large spurt in a few traditional exportables. Participation in the international division of the production process can be enhanced by repealing domestic content regulations that raise the cost of domestic production and limit a firm's choice among inputs. Sectoral diversification of exports could proceed with a substantial increase in intraindustry trade. For instance, firms can specialize in certain kinds of machinery and equipment and import others, produce cars and particular varieties of electronic consumer appliances, and import parts and components for assembling (World Bank, 1984: xii; Balassa, 1985: 250). Emphasis on intraindustry trade through increased import liberalization and an expansion of exports on a broad front would diffuse the tensions that spring up when trade is one-sided, and resources would be used more efficiently according to the nation's comparative advantage.

Index of intraindustry trade (B_i) is defined as

$$\mathrm{B_i} = \left[1 - \frac{|X_i - M_i|}{X_i - M_i} \right] \mathrm{x}\ 100$$

where X_i and M_i are the value of the exports and imports of industry i. B_i varies between 0 and 100. When the exports are exactly equal to imports of an industry, B_i is 100. When there are exports but no imports, or vice versa, the measure is 0 (Grubel and Lloyd, 1975; 21).

Table 13 shows that labor-intensive products other than miscellaneous manufactures are characterized by very low intraindustry trade levels or very high degrees of national specialization, whereas the intraindustry trade levels of transport equipment and machinery are very high. Transport equipment in particular showed a clearly increasing trend of intraindustry trade.

High-quality manpower with basic academic training in science and technology is Taiwan's most important and most abundant resource. The continued process of financial resource accumulation also allows the economy to move toward the development of more capital-intensive manufactures. Machinery and transport equipment will be next in line for the achievement of a high rate of

Table 13. Changes in the Indices of Intraindustry Trade by Industry 1965–1985

SITC	*Industry*	*1965*	*1973*	*1985*
84	Clothing and apparel	0.3	0.6	0.5
85	Footwear	0.0	0.0	0.3
83	Travel goods, handbags	3.9	0.9	0.5
89	Miscellaneous manufactures	60.6	43.1	32.2
65	Textile yarn and fabrics	65.4	49.5	27.1
69	Metal manufactures	79.6	70.2	23.3
75, 76 77	Electrical machinery, telecommunications equipment, office machines, and data processing equipment	49.1	90.2	62.2
71, 72 73, 74	Power generating, specialized and general industrial machinery	21.8	46.2	88.6
78, 79	Transport equipment	18.3	74.6	98.5

Sources: Department of Statistics, Ministry of Finance, *Monthly Statistics of Exports and Imports, Taiwan (Taiwan District)* (Taipei: various issues); Research, Development, and Evaluation Commission, *Commodity Trade Statistics of Taiwan* (Taipei: August 1976).

export expansion as the growth of experience and capacity in manufacturing permits the economy to move beyond traditionally labor-intensive types of production. With higher intraindustry trade levels and through greater opportunities for product differentiation, the development of these industries will make the industrial structure more balanced, and thus enable it to more actively participate in the international division of the production process. Substantial increase in intraindustry trade through sectoral diversification of exports will consequently contribute to diffuse the tensions of trade frictions.

IV. SUMMARY AND CONCLUSIONS

The major findings of this study may be summarized as follows:

1. From the beginning of the export drive in the early 1960s, outward-looking policies for industry and trade have been essential for the rapid growth

and the remarkable achievement in the structural transformation of the Taiwan economy. Taiwan provides an example of an economy following its comparative advantage and reaping the gains from trade illustrated by the traditional theory of international trade. The rapid expansion of labor-intensive manufactured exports contributed to efficient industrialization by permitting specialization according to comparative advantage and stimulating technological improvement. It also improved living standards as well as income distribution through the creation of new productive employment and a rapid increase in real wage rates.

2. The Taiwan economy is presently at a crossroad, and the current problems of structural adjustments and huge trade imbalance with the United States are the result of the success of past development efforts. Whether the economy can successfully restructure its industry and attain the high rate of economic expansion that it experienced in the past will depend to a great extent on ensuring technology transfers, reforming financial systems, liberalizing foreign exchange control, revising mercantilist-oriented trade regimes, and diversifying export markets. Taiwan also now has the ability to boost domestic demand through major investment projects in the economic and social infrastructure, reform its tax system with a view to achieving a better balance among savings, consumption, and investment. Investment in the economic and social infrastructure has to encourage private sector participation wherever possible.

3. There are numerous cases of conflicts among ministries as evidenced in many policy debates due to the differences in policy priorities in different agencies of the government. The Central Bank places priority on price stability and an orderly foreign exchange market. The Ministry of Finance seeks a balanced budget and adequate aggregate demand. The Ministry of Economic Affairs is the champion of industry and trade development and perhaps the most actively interventionist. The Council for Economic Planning and Development is concerned with growth, efficient resource allocation, and, recently, social welfare. Some inevitable economic reforms have been phased in only slowly. Slow decision making, distortions in policy, and reluctance in initiating high-risk investment projects due to conflicts among bureaucrats have to be avoided.

4. The most important lesson that appears to emerge from this study is that trade strategy and industrial policy have to be adjustment oriented and coordinated with macroeconomic policies to help improve the efficiency and flexibility of the industry and trade sectors to meet internal and external challenges. The industrial policy has to look to the future and should not simply react to situations that have gotten out of hand. It is necessary to create an open domestic economy to make its manufacures competitive and to expedite restructuring of the industry, with a view to maintaining the country's comparative advantage, its continued growth, and world market competitive edge. It also has to be noted that some policy measures that would prove effective in restructuring the economy and reducing trade imbalance are unpopular and will face resistance from interested groups, since these measures are certain to require sacrifice from some sectors

of the economy. However, the slower the restructuring of the economy and the wider and deeper the trade frictions become, the longer the time and the larger the sacrifice necessary for a solution shall be.

NOTES

1. By definition

$$Y = C + G + I + X - M \tag{1}$$

where Y = GDP, C = private consumption expenditures, G = government consumption expenditures, I = gross domestic capital formation, i.e., gross investment, X = exports of goods and services, and M = imports of goods and services. We can therefore derive the following formula:

$$dY/Y = dC/C \bullet C/Y + dG/G \bullet G/Y + dI/I \bullet I/Y + dX/X \bullet X/Y - dM/M \bullet M/Y \tag{2}$$

All components are expressed at constant prices. Equation (2) shows that the growth rate of GDP equals the sum total of the rates of increases of its components multiplied by their respective weights, i.e., the ratios of the components to GDP. And these weighted rates of increase can be regarded as the separate contributions (in absolute point shares) to the observed rate of growth of GDP attributable to each of its components.

2. The defensive measures took the form of tax incentives, special loan facilities, and deferred repayment of outstanding bank loans.

3. The greatest government help to local computer makers has been its sponsoring the collaboration of a technology research institute and business center to develop a basic IBM PC clone design that does not violate IBM patent rights.

REFERENCES

Balassa, Bela. *Change and Challenge in the World Economy*. London: Macmillan Press, 1985.

Corrigan, E. G. "Financial Market Structure: A Longer View." *Seventy-Second Annual Report, Federal Reserve Bank of New York*, 3–54. New York, 1987.

Grubel, H. G. and P. J. Lloyd. *Intra-industry Trade*. London: Macmillan Company, 1975.

Jacoby, N. H. *U.S. Aid to Taiwan: A Study of Foreign Aid, Self-Help and Development*. New York: Praeger, 1966.

Jaffe, I. "Industrial Policies: Responses to a Common Core of Problems." *The OECD Observer* No. 130, September 1984, 11–13.

Lee, Eddy (ed.) *Export-Led Industrialization and Development*. Singapore: Maruzen Asia, 1981.

Lee, T. H. and Kuo-shu Liang. "Development Strategies in Taiwan." In Bela Balassa (ed.) *Development Strategies in Semi-Industrial Economies*, 310–383. Baltimore, MD: The Johns Hopkins University Press, 1982.

Lin, Ching-yuan. *Industrialization in Taiwan, 1946–1972: Trade and Import-Substitution Policies for Developing Countries*. New York: Praeger, 1973.

Maizels, A. *Exports and Economic Growth of Developing Countries*. London: Cambridge University Press, 1968.

Morgan Guaranty Trust Company of New York. "Global Growth and Adjustment at Risk." *World Financial Markets* September/October 1987, 1–14.

Ranis, G. and C. Schive. ''Direct Foreign Investment in Taiwan's Development.'' In W. Galenson (ed.) *Foreign Trade and Investment: Economic Development in the Newly Industrializing Asian Countries*, 85–137, Madison, WI: Wisconsin University Press, 1985.

Schive, C. and R. S. Yeh. ''Multinational Corporations and Host Country Technology: A Factor Proportion Approach in Taiwan.'' Discussion Paper Series No. 82-01, Council for Asian Manpower Studies (mimeo), 1982.

Tang, Anthony M. and Kuo-shu Liang. ''Agricultural Trade in the Economic Development of Taiwan.'' In G. S. Tolley and P. A. Zadrozny, (eds.) *Trade, Agriculture and Development* 115–146. Cambridge, MA: Ballinger, 1973.

Williamson, J. *The Exchange Rate System*. Washington, D.C.: Institute for International Economics, 1983.

The World Bank. *Korea: Development in Global Context*. Washington, D.C., 1984.

TAIWAN'S DECLINING INVESTMENT RATIO AND ITS PERSISTENT TRADE SURPLUS WITH THE UNITED STATES

Ching-yuan Lin

I. INTRODUCTION

In the years following the second oil shock (1979–1980), Taiwan's investment ratio continued to decline whereas its high savings ratio remained largely unchanged. Meanwhile, Taiwan's import demand remained stagnant, whereas its exports expanded along with the recovery of U.S. import demand in 1983. The resulting growth in Taiwan's trade surplus contributed to the United States' growing external deficit, adding fuel to the protectionist pressure (Figures 1 and 2, and Appendix Tables A1 and A2).

Research in Asian Economic Studies.
Asian Industrialization: Changing Economic Structures,
Volume 1, Part A, pages 139–158.
Copyright © 1988 by JAI Press Inc.
All rights of reproduction in any form reserved.
ISBN: 0-89232-987-4

Figure 1. Evolution of Taiwan's Current Account Balance, and Savings and Investment Ratios, 1972–85

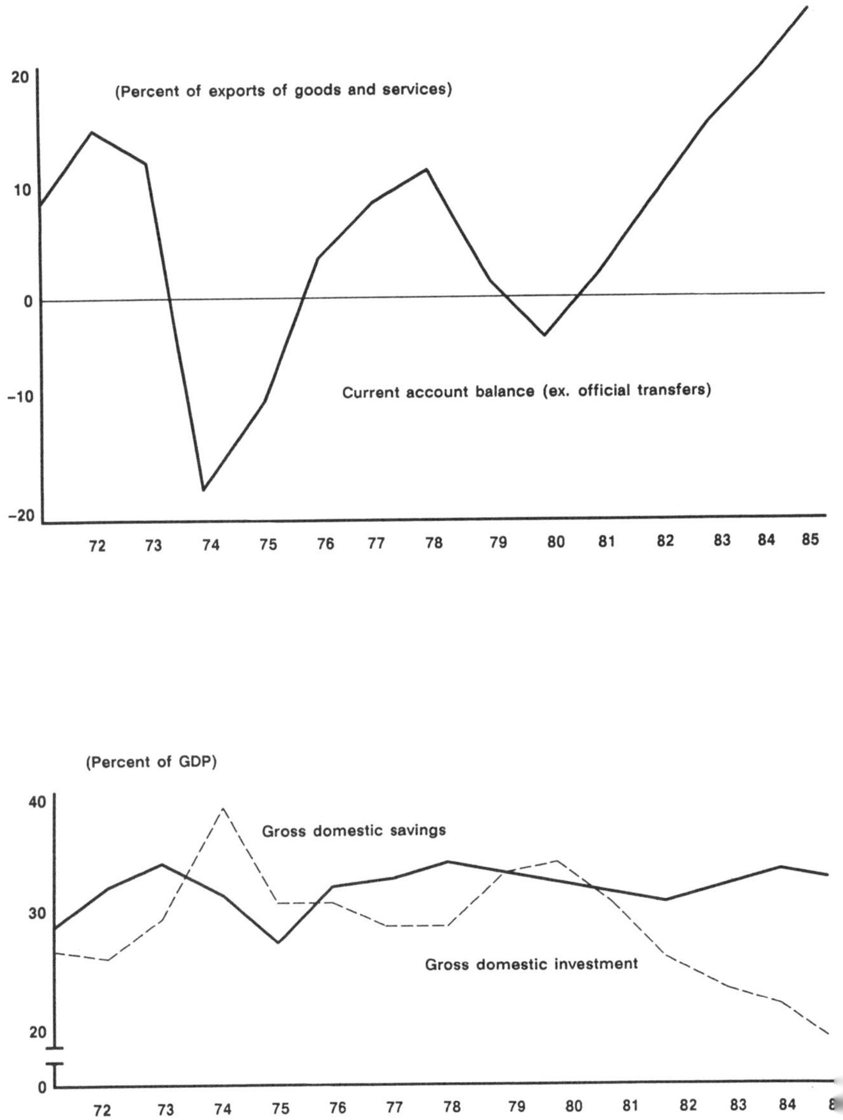

Figure 2. Evolution of Taiwan's Overall Trade Balance and Trade Balance with the United States, 1972–1985 (in billions of dollars)

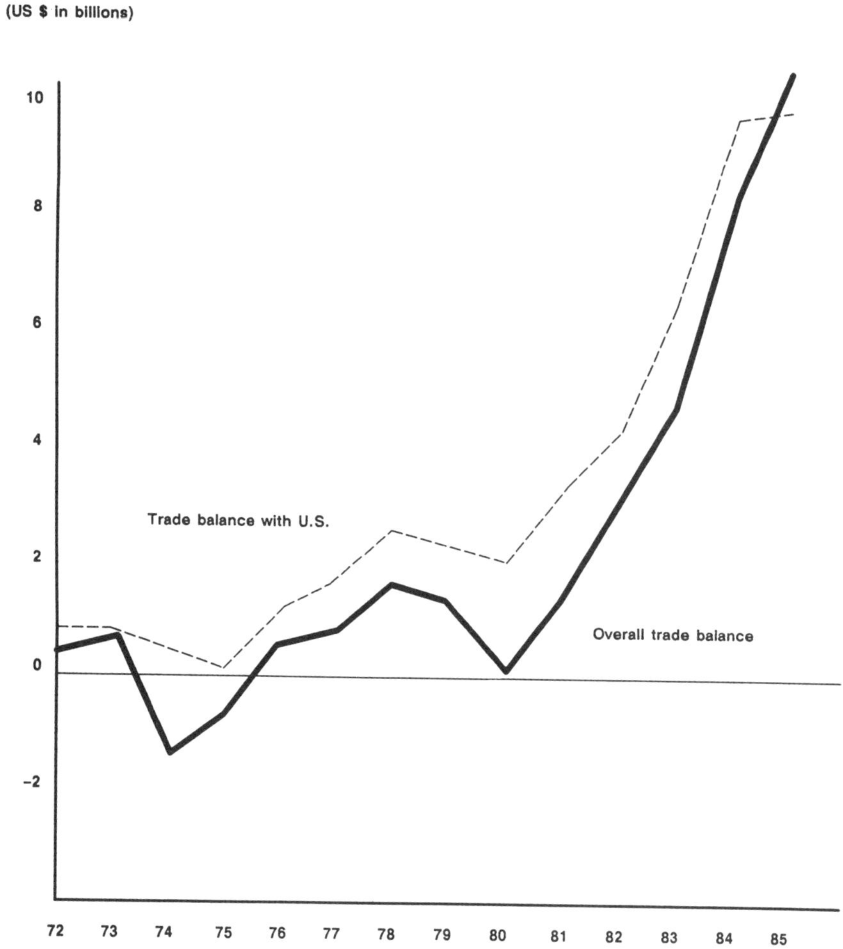

Why did Taiwan's investment and import demand remain stagnant while its high savings ratio was sustained? What could Taiwan do to stimulate investment and reduce trade surplus with the United States?

II. MAJOR FACTORS BEHIND THE DECLINING INVESTMENT RATIO

Taiwan's gross investment ratio has declined steadily over the last several years, from over 33% of GDP in 1979–1980 to less than 20% in 1985. (Figure 1). Meanwhile, the gross savings ratio was maintained at more than 32% of GDP, only slightly lower than the previous peak of 35% in 1978. Part of the decline in the investment ratio was accounted for by the decline in the import cost of oil and other primary commodities, which diminished the firms' incentives for additional stock accumulation. Even excluding stock changes, however, the decline in the investment ratio was quite significant, with gross fixed investment declining from 28–31% of GDP in 1979–1981 to 19% in 1985 (Appendix Table A1).

Why did the investment ratio decline so sharply? Two major factors can be considered: (1) the decline in the private corporate sector's profit margins, and (2) an increase in political uncertainty, as explained briefly below.

A. The Decline in the Private Manufacturing Sector's Profit Margins

As percentage of revenue, private manufacturing corporations' profits declined from around 7.0% in 1977–1979 to slightly above 5% in 1981–1983 and to 4.0% in 1984 (Table 1).[1] This decline resulted initially from the sharp rise in import costs occasioned by the second big jump in oil prices during 1979–1980 and the subsequent decline in export demand, but it continued through 1983–1984 in spite of the recovery of export demand. In terms of U.S. dollars, the rise of import costs accelerated from 6.6% per annum in 1965–1973 to 12.0% in 1973–1978 and 7.6% in 1978–1985. By contrast, the growth of export volume continued to decline, from 26.3% per annum to 14.0%, and then to 9.8% (Table 2). The

Table 1. Taiwan: Profit Margins in Manufacturing, 1977–1984 (as Percentage of Revenues)

	Total manufacturing	*Public enterprise*	*Private corporations*[a]
1977	9.6	21.1	7.3
1978	—	—	—
1979	7.4	10.8	6.8
1980	—	—	—
1981	4.5	2.0	5.2
1982	—	—	—
1983	6.0	10.4	5.2
1984	6.0	17.3	4.1

Source: *Ministry of Economic Affairs, Report on Industrial and Commercial Surveys: Taiwan Area.* Taiwan (various issues).

[a] Excluding noncorporate manufacturing.

Table 2. Taiwan: Growth of Exports and Imports and Changes in Terms of Trade before and after the Oil Shocks (in Annual Compound Rate of Change)

	1965–1973	*1973–1978*	*1978–1985*
Value in U.S. Dollars			
Exports	33.3	23.1	13.4
Imports	27.1	23.8	9.0
Volume			
Exports	26.3	14.0	9.8
Imports	19.2	10.5	1.3
Unit value in U.S. dollars			
Exports	5.5	8.0	3.3
Imports	6.6	12.0	7.6
Terms of trade	1.0	–3.6	–4.0
Import purchasing power of export earnings[a]	12.5	9.9	5.4

Source: Council for Economic Planning and Development. *Taiwan Statistical Data Book*, 1986, Taipei.

[a] Index of export value deflated by index of import unit value.

slowdown in export growth, in turn, caused a slowdown in the growth of real domestic demand, particularly in the investment for capital equipment and inventories. Gross fixed investment, which increased by more than 18% per annum in the 8 years before the first oil shock, declined to 10.7% in the subsequent 5 years, and further to 5.0% in the 7 years after the second oil shock. Furthermore, stock accumulation expanded sharply during 1973–1974 in conjunction with the world commodity boom and oil shocks, then declined sharply in response to the stagnation in world commodity markets and the slowdown in economic activity (Table 3).

Another contributing factor to the worsening of profit margins was the sharp rise in the manufacturing unit labor costs, which rose from 2.1% per annum in 1965–1973 to 6.7% in 1973–1978, and then to 10.2% in 1978–1985. The labor cost acceleration resulted from both a sharp decline in the growth of labor productivity and a continued rapid growth of money wages. In the 7 years after the second oil shock, manufacturing output per employee increased by only 2.7% per annum, at only half the rate in the preceding 5 years (1973–1978), and only a quarter of the rate in the 8 years before the first oil shock (1965–1973), whereas money wages continued to rise at 11–13% per annum throughout the whole period. The latter represented a real wage growth of 5.6% per annum, in spite of a sharp slowdown in the growth of real GDP and a severe worsening in terms of trade (Table 4).

Table 3. Taiwan: Growth of Real Output and Real Domestic Demand, before and after the Oil Shocks (in Annual Compound Rate of Change)

	1965–1973	*1973–1978*	*1978–1985*
Real GDP	11.0	8.5	6.5
Real domestic demand[a]	10.0	7.0	4.8
Real consumption	8.7	6.9	6.3
Real gross investment	16.5	9.3	1.3
Fixed investment	18.1	10.7	5.0
Increase in stock[b]	3.6	4.5	1.3
Population	2.6	1.9	1.7
Per capita GDP	8.2	6.5	4.7

Source: Council for Economic Planning and Development, *Taiwan Statistical Data Book*, 1986, Taipei.

[a] Real output plus imports minus exports, weighted by base year values.

[b] Increases in stock as percentage of GDP for each period.

Table 4. Taiwan: Manufacturing Labor Productivity and Unit Labor Costs before and after the Oil Shocks (in Annual Compound Rate of Change)

	1965–1973	*1973–1978*	*1978–1985*
Output	22.2	12.3	6.5
Employment	11.9	5.9	4.0
Labor productivity	9.2	6.0	2.4
Nominal wages	11.5	13.1	12.8
Unit labor costs[a]	2.1	6.7	10.2
Cost of living	4.5	7.2	6.8
Real wages	6.7	5.5	5.6
Product wages[b]	5.4	5.4	8.1
Share of employee compensation in national income	53.0	58.2	61.6
Paid employees as percentage of total employment		59.2	64.1

Sources: Council for Economic Planning and Development. *Taiwan Statistical Data Book*, 1986 (Taipei); Directorate-General of Budget, Accounting, and Statistics, *Yearbook of Labor Statistics* (various issues).

[a] Index of nominal wages deflated by index of labor productivity.

[b] Index of nominal wages deflated by index of export unit value of goods and services, both in local currency.

As a consequence of the unfavorable developments in both costs and demand, the private manufacturing corporations' financial situation worsened. Not only were their profit margins squeezed, but their net saving also declined sharply, from 2.3% of GDP in 1976–1980 to a mere 1.3% in 1981–1984 (Appendix Table A1). These situations caused financial difficulties for many weaker firms in 1985. The latter was exacerbated by the weak financial structure of firms and the tendency for their bank and nonbank creditors to reduce their loan exposure at a time when these firms were encountering cash-flow problems.

B. The Increased Political Uncertainty

The increased political uncertainty stemmed from the authorities' failure to respond adequately to the changing political environment in East Asia, involving the Peoples Republic of China and Taiwan. In spite of its geographical proximity to mainland China, Taiwan's economic development in the past three decades was built on increasing trade with the United States, Japan, and many other countries across the ocean, whereas there was little trade with nearby mainland China. This peculiar geographic pattern of trade and economic development came into being partly because of China's political and economic seclusion from the Western world after the Korean War, This situation has changed dramatically with China's decision since late 1978 to introduce market-oriented economic policies and establish closer political and economic relations with the Western countries. This put China in direct competition with Hong Kong, Taiwan, and other East Asian developing countries with regard to the development of export markets and the acquisition of trading partners, technology, and foreign capital. This new situation called for certain political and economic adjustment on the part of Taiwan in order to establish a new political base for stable long-term economic development. This reestablishment of a new political base continues to be delayed. The situation was complicated by the impending, yet untested political succession in Taiwan and the atmosphere of political unrest in neighboring South Korea and the Philippines. These problems, combined with the eruption of political and financial scandals, cast a long shadow over Taiwan's long-term investment climate.[2]

III. COST–PRICE RELATIONSHIP

Why did manufacturing wages continue to rise strongly in 1982–1984, in spite of the stabilization of domestic prices and the sluggish labor demand? Was this a temporary phenomenon, or did this represent a major change in labor supply conditions, which may ultimately affect Taiwan's export competitiveness?

Until the first oil shock in 1973–1974, rapid rises in money wages were accompanied by rapid rises in labor productivity, so that the increase in unit labor costs was quite moderate, at only 2.1% per annum from 1965 to 1973. This favorable trend was interrupted by the onslaught of the oil shocks, which sharply increased the rate of wage increase while reducing labor productivity. Fortunately, the rapid control of inflation in 1974–1975 and the subsequent recovery of export demand enabled a sharp recovery in the growth of manufacturing output and labor productivity in 1976–1978. Thus, for nearly two decades from 1960 to 1978, strong export and labor demands enabled the average wages of the labor-intensive, export-oriented manufacturing industries to rise in relation to the rest of manufacturing, which was more capital intensive or more domestically oriented in the source of demand (Table 5).

This trend toward wage convergence was interrupted in the period after the second oil shock (1978–1985), when the growth of labor productivity slowed down sharply, owing to sluggish export growth and weak domestic demand. The latter caused a dampening influence on labor and wage demands in the labor-intensive, export-oriented industries. In fact, the unemployment rate, which declined to the postwar low of 1.2% in 1980, increased to an average of 2.7% in 1983–1985, higher than the last peak in 1975 (Table 6). In spite of the sluggish labor market, money wages in these sectors increased by 12–15% per annum, with a real gain of 4–8% per annum. In several of these industries (textiles and apparel, food processing, plastics, and wood products), moreover, the growth of real wages exceeded the growth of labor productivity, thus exacerbating the rise in unit labor cost (Appendix Table A3).

Part of the strong wage growth must be attributed to the decline in the growth of labor supply for the urban sectors relative to the growth of labor demand. For one thing, the growth of population 15 years and older declined from 3.5% per annum in 1973–1975 to 2.6% in 1978–1985, with a corresponding decline in the growth of the labor force. Second, the share of the labor force engaged in agriculture, forestry, and fishery declined from 36.7% in 1970 to 19.5% in 1980, thus increasingly restricting the number of the rural workers who could easily be transferred to the nonagricultural sectors without extensive reorganization in agricultural operations to raise productivity.

Another factor that may have influenced the private sector wage growth has been the stronger wage growth in the public sector, which averaged 18–20% per annum in such industries as sugar, liquor, tobacco, and petroleum, which far exceeded the rate of productivity growth in these respective sectors (Appendix Table A3). Because of differences in fringe benefits, particularly those related to retirement, there was not much direct inflow of career workers between the public and private sectors in the short-run; the two sectors drew their new recruits and noncareer workers from the same pool of new graduates and other sources of labor supply.

Table 5. Taiwan: Relative Wages in Manufacturing, 1960, 1973, 1978, and 1985 (as Ratio to the Manufacturing Average)

	1960		*1973*		*1978*		*1985*	
	Total employees	*Blue collar*	*Total employees*	*Blue collar*	*Total employees*	*Blue collar*	*Total employees*	*Blue collar*
1. Nine sectors with below average wages in 1960[a]								
a. Range	0.52–0.97	0.55–0.96	0.69–1.00	0.72–0.96	0.71–0.99	0.76–1.02	0.85–1.01	0.83–1.05
b. Average	0.86	0.66	0.88	0.87	0.88	0.89	0.91	0.91
2. Eleven sectors with above average wages[b]								
a. Range	1.13–1.67	1.12–2.05	0.95–1.79	1.00–1.75	0.90–1.55	0.92–1.50	0.90–1.75	0.99–1.78
b. Average	1.36	1.31	1.27	1.28	1.25	1.26	1.23	1.21
3. Ratio (1b)/(2b)	0.63	0.50	0.69	0.68	0.70	0.71	0.74	0.75

Source: Computed from Directorate-General of Budget, Accounting, and Statistics, *Yearbook of Labor Statistics*, 1986 (Taipei).

[a] Includes textiles, apparel, wood products, food products, rubber products, leather products, miscellaneous instruments, and electric and electronic products.

[b] Includes beverage and tobacco, plastics, chemicals, chemical products, nonmetallic mineral products, basic metals, metal products, machinery, transport equipment, paper and printing, and petroleum and coal products.

Table 6. Taiwan: Developments in Employment and Unemployment, 1970–1985

	Share of labor force in		*Female labor force participation ratio*	*Share of female in manufacturing*	*Unemployment rate*	
	Agriculture	*Industry*			*Total*	*Female*
1970	36.7	27.9	35.5	29.4	1.70	2.18
1971	35.1	29.9	35.4	33.4	1.66	2.10
1972	33.0	31.8	37.1	38.7	1.49	1.99
1973	30.5	33.7	41.5	41.4	1.26	1.66
1974	30.9	34.3	40.2	39.6	1.53	2.00
1975	30.5	34.9	38.6	40.8–47.9	2.40	3.07
1976	29.0	36.4	37.6	42.2–48.6	1.78	2.14
1977	26.7	37.6	39.3	41.9–49.4	1.72	1.98
1978	24.9	39.3	39.2	43.4–50.7	1.67	1.87
1979	21.5	41.8	39.2	44.2–50.0	1.28	1.53
1980	19.5	42.4	39.3	43.3–49.7	1.23	1.48
1981	18.8	42.2	38.8	49.7–48.6	1.36	1.63
1982	18.9	42.2	39.3	49.6	2.14	2.25
1983	18.6	41.1	42.1	50.0	2.71	2.75
1984	17.6	42.3	43.3	49.7	2.44	2.47
1985	17.5	41.4	43.5	49.6	2.91	2.99

Source: Directorate-General of Budget, Accounting and Statistics, *Yearbook of Labor Statistics*, 1986 (Taipei).

IV. THE ROLE OF ECONOMIC POLICIES[3]

Taiwan, as well as Japan, was very successful in controlling the resurgence of inflation in 1974, which resulted from the 1972–1973 export boom and subsequent cost-push caused by the quantum jumps in oil prices that occurred at the end of 1973. This was accomplished mainly by monetary restraints, both through restricting credit expansion and by sharply raising the officially controlled interest rates.

In the aftermath of the second oil shock (1979–1980), Taiwan's monetary policy was cautious, but not as tight as in 1974. In fact, real domestic credit increased by a moderate, but steady rate [5% per annum in 1979–1980, compared with a slight decline in 1974 (Table 7)]. Nevertheless, in addition to monetary restraints, the authorities undertook a significant reduction in the tariff rates and in the taxable value of imports. These measures helped to contain the resurgent inflationary pressure.

However, during 1981–1982, the growth of Taiwan's exports continued to slow down because of prolonged recession in the world economy and the decline in the competitiveness of Taiwan's exports. Between 1978 and 1982, the unit labor costs of Taiwan's manufacuring industries increased by almost 15% per annum, because wage adjustments far outran the growth of labor productivity (Table 4). The worsening of Taiwan's relative cost position was exacerbated by the effective appreciation of its currency brought about by the continued appreciation of the U.S. dollar (to which the Taiwan currency was tied) against major currencies; a 4.8% devaluation in the Taiwan currency against the U.S. dollar in August, 1981 was not enough of a correction. As a consequence, during 1981 and 1982, capacity utilization continued to decline, inventory liquidation became widespread, and private investment dropped off sharply. During 1981–1982, real domestic demand increased by only 1% per annum (Table 3). Faced with the deepening recession in the economy, the authorities took various measures during late 1982 to relax credit expansion, and to improve investment incentives. During 1983–1984, supported by a resurgence in exports and expansionary fiscal and monetary policies, Taiwan's economic growth recovered strongly.

However, the recovery in Taiwan's economic growth was based primarily on the resurgence of export demand, whereas domestic investment continued to decline in relation to GNP. This led to a sharp expansion of both excess saving and current account surplus, the latter particularly vis-à-vis the United States (Figures 1 and 2). This situation, in view of the latter's large external deficit, subjected Taiwan to increasing protectionist pressures from the United States.

Table 7. Taiwan: Exports, Import Unit Value, Money Supply and Domestic Credit in Both Nominal and Real Terms, and Real Domestic Demand, Selected Periods from 1966 to 1983 (in Percentage Changes)

	1966–1971	*1972–1973*	*1974*	*1975*	*1976–1978*	*1979–1980*	*1981–1983*
Exports (US$)	28.9	47.5	25.8	–5.9	33.7	22.6	12.2
Imports ($US)	2.3	20.7	47.6	–4.2	7.7	22.8	2.5
Money supply (M2)	21.4	31.1	24.7	28.0	29.6	15.6	22.8
Domestic credit	19.7	31.9	42.2	30.3	21.8	22.8	17.0
Inflation[a]	2.9	9.6	44.1	—	4.1	16.0	4.5
Real money supply[b]	18.0	19.6	–13.5	28.0	24.5	–0.3	17.5
Real domestic credit[b]	16.3	20.3	–1.3	30.3	17.0	5.9	12.0
Real domestic demand[c]	10.2	10.9	10.2	1.0	8.5	9.7	1.8

Source: IMF International Financial Statistics, national publications, and author's estimates.

[a] Average rate of change in the CPI (Consumer Price Index) and WPI (Wholesale Price Index).

[b] Deflated by an average rate of changes in the CPI and WPI.

[c] Estimated by using the relation: domestic demand equals GNP (Gross National Product) minus exports plus imports, in volume terms.

V. PERSISTENT AND GROWING TRADE SURPLUS WITH THE UNITED STATES

From 1981 to 1985, merchandise trade surplus (exports, FOB and imports, CIF) jumped from $1.4 billion to $10.6 billion (Figure 2). This resulted primarily from (1) the stagnation of imports of capital goods, because of the sharp decline in investment demand, (2) the slackened imports of fuels and raw materials, due to the marked decline in world market prices caused by diminished global demand, and (3) the stagnation in the imports of consumer goods caused partly by the delay in expanding import liberalization.

Another factor was the sharp increase in exports to the United States, dominated by electronic products. However, the net value of electronics exports was much smaller than its gross value, because such an operation required sizable imports of electronic base products from Japan, the United States, and Europe.

Because the sharp expansion in exports to the United States was not accompanied by a commensurate growth of imports, trade surplus with the United States expanded sharply from $3.1 billion in 1981 to $10.0 billion in 1985 (Figure 2). Part of the sluggishness in imports can be attributed to the declining trend of agricultural prices, but this sluggishness also exposed the contradiction between Taiwan's trade policy and its agricultural policy.

VI. POLICY IMPLICATIONS

The growing trade surplus, under the government's conservative attitude toward private investment abroad and the prohibition of private holding of foreign currency at home,[4] resulted in the tripling of the authorities' foreign exchange reserves from $7.2 billion in 1981 to $22.6 billion in 1985. This exerted strong pressure for the appreciation of the Taiwan currency, inviting speculative capital inflow, and caused excessively rapid expansion of domestic currency. In fact, by the end of 1986, the foreign exchange reserve more than doubled again to $46 billion, twice the size of annual imports, whereas the money supply (M1B) quadrupled, thus posing strong inflationary pressure.

This situation naturally invited strong pressures from the United States to speed up liberalization of Taiwan's import restrictions and to appreciate Taiwan's currency against the U.S. dollar. Although extensive tariff reductions and import liberalization are indeed overdue, it is more difficult to decide the equilibrium exchange rate for various reasons:

(1) The Taiwan currency is undervalued partly because of the extensive tariffs and import restrictions now in place. Until these are reduced or removed, the Taiwan currency will remain undervalued even if the exchange rate is determined by market forces alone.

(2) More basically, the present strength of Taiwan's export products still includes some subsidiary elements, not only in such explicit items as special low

interest rates for export and special income tax treatment, but also in the preferential use of industrial plant sites, the soft government regulation of environmental pollution, and the undercompensation of labor due to the government's prohibition of labor union activity. This undercompensation involves not only low basic wage rates, but also the lack of fringe benefits such as adequate medical facilities and housing facilities for young female workers, and financial provisions for retirement.[5] Only after most of these subsidiary elements for export activity are eliminated, and the pricing of Taiwan's export is placed on a real cost basis, can we expect the exchange rate to adjust to its long-term equilibrium rate.

Thus, the authorities in Taiwan currently face an important policy choice: should they maintain the present system largely unchanged, thus benefiting foreign consumers at the cost of domestic workers and the population in general, while inviting incessant pressures from its largest trading partner, the United States? It is true that as an island economy of less than 20 million in population, Taiwan must continue to look outward in order for its population to have a rapid growth of per capita income and enjoy a high standard of living. However, after two and a half decades of export expansion under government support, the export industry should be able to forsake this support and stand on its own.[6]

In the final analysis, the competitiveness of Taiwan's manufactured exports depends on its peoples' diligence, its Confucian tradition for learning, and its capacity to absorb and adapt new knowledge, technology, and skills, which was strengthened during the last three quarters of a century of modernization process. This was helped by the authorities' pragmatic policy management in the control of inflation and in changing the incentive system to meet the needs of the changing economy during the postwar decades. What is now needed is stronger emphasis on the acquisition of technology and skills. The latter includes not only "high-tech" industries, such as semiconductors, which have so far been emphasized, but "mid-tech" industries, such as the manufacturing of cost-competitive, high-quality automobiles. On this last item, Taiwan apparently lags behind South Korea, inspite of its initial experience in starting import-substituting industries, and in promoting manufactured exports. Other than the detrimental effects of prolonged protection, it appears that the Chinese industrialists in Taiwan were less aggressive than their Korean counterparts in paying for and acquiring the necessary technology for manufacturing automobiles that were internationally competitive.[7]

The increasing tensions created by the concentration of Taiwan's exports to, and its trade surplus with, the United States are part of the global problem that involves not only Taiwan, but also Japan and many European countries. Because of its size and abundance of natural resources, U.S. trade with the rest of the world is based not only on differences in factor cost (manufacturing), but also on differences in natural resource endowment. If the rest of the world wishes to export manufactured goods to the United States, it simply must accept as much agricultural goods in return. The trade problem caused by the contradiction between trade policy and agricultural policy is an internal problem, which has to be resolved before entering the international arena.[8]

Until 1895, Taiwan's trade was oriented toward the mainland, and then until 1945, toward Japan. Its orientation since 1945 has been determined by two major factors: Mainland China's seclusion from the Western world and Taiwan's capacity to exploit the vast U.S. market. The latter factor is based on principles beneficial to both parties: namely, differences in relative factor cost. This has facilitated the release of Taiwan's traditional oceanic orientation and its people's sea-going adventurous characteristic, like the old Athens millennia ago, which forsook the rocky Greek interior and instead looked outward toward the Mediterranean to create a Hellenistic world. This glorious achievement can be repeated by modern Taiwan, because historically, it was very much isolated from mainland China until 400 years ago (Ch'ing dynasty). Since then, however, the political reality has not allowed seclusion from mainland China, except under special conditions created by wars.

Until this political dilemma is resolved, and a new political framework between Taiwan and the mainland is created (which does not conflict with the interests of the United States and Japan), market participants may hesitate in making long term commitments. Thus, although Taiwan's economic fortune may rise and ebb according to business cycles in the industrial economies, a more fundamental solution must be found.

APPENDIX

Table A1. Taiwan: Evolution of Savings and Investment Ratios, 1971–1985 (Percentage of GDP)

	1971	*1972*	*1973*	*1974*	*1975*	*1976*	*1977*	*1978*	*1979*	*1980*	*1981*	*1982*	*1983*	*1984*	*1985*
Savings	28.9	32.4	34.7	31.7	27.5	32.5	32.8	34.8	33.8	32.7	31.5	30.4	32.0	33.2	32.1
Households	13.2	13.8	16.2	13.6	11.0	11.8	13.3	13.6	13.1	11.6	13.0	13.3	14.6	15.0	14.1
Corporate	4.8	5.0	5.2	3.1	2.5	5.1	4.2	4.7	3.5	5.7	4.0	3.7	3.5	4.0	4.8
Public	2.1	1.9	1.3	1.8	2.1	2.4	2.2	2.1	2.0	2.8	2.9	2.9	2.4	2.4	—
Private	2.7	3.1	3.9	1.3	0.4	2.7	2.0	2.6	1.5	2.9	1.1	0.8	1.1	1.6	—
Depreciation provisions	6.9	7.2	7.1	6.7	7.0	7.4	7.6	7.9	7.8	7.4	7.9	8.3	8.4	8.3	8.8
Government	4.0	6.4	6.2	8.3	7.0	8.2	7.7	8.6	9.4	8.0	6.6	5.1	5.5	5.9	4.4
Investment	26.7	25.8	29.3	39.5	30.6	30.8	28.4	28.6	33.3	34.3	30.3	25.2	23.0	21.5	18.2
Gross fixed capital formation	23.4	23.9	25.1	28.7	31.3	27.9	25.9	26.1	28.4	31.1	28.2	26.3	23.1	21.8	19.3
Stocks	3.0	1.9	4.2	10.8	–0.7	2.9	2.5	2.5	4.9	3.2	2.1	–1.1	–0.1	–0.3	–1.1
Savings minus investment	2.2	6.6	5.4	–7.8	–3.1	1.7	4.4	1.5	0.5	–1.6	1.2	5.2	9.0	11.7	14.4
Growth of real fixed investment	22.7	16.6	10.9	13.9	21.2	2.1	4.6	12.8	14.2	15.7	3.7	–0.5	–3.5	–4.4	

Source: Computed from Council for Economic Planning and Development (Taipei), *Taiwan Statistical Data Book* (various issues).

Table A2. Taiwan's Trade Balance with Major Trading Partners (Exports, FOB, and Imports, CIF, in Billion Dollars)

	1960	*1970*	*1974*	*1978*	*1981*	*1982*	*1983*	*1984*	*1985*
Total trade	–0.1	–0.04	–1.3	1.7	1.4	3.3	4.8	8.5	10.6
With Japan	–0.4	–0.4	–1.4	–2.1	–3.5	–2.4	–3.1	–3.3	–2.1
With United States	–0.9	0.2	0.4	2.6	3.4	4.2	6.7	9.8	10.0
Exports	0.02	0.2	2.1	5.0	8.2	8.8	11.3	14.9	14.8
Imports	0.1	0.4	2.4	4.8	4.8	4.6	4.6	5.1	4.7
All other countries	1.3	0.2	–0.3	1.2	1.5	1.5	1.2	2.0	3.7
Crude oil	–0.02	–0.05	–0.6	–1.6	–4.5	–3.9	–4.1	–3.8	–3.3
Other	1.3	1.9	1.7	2.8	6.0	5.4	5.3	5.8	7.0

Source: Taiwan Statistical Data Book.

Table A3. Wage Growth in Private and Public Enterprises, 1978–1985 (Percentage per Annum)

	Relative wage 1978					
	All employees	*Blue collar*	*Wage Growth 1978–1985 all employees*	*Real wage growth*	*Labor productivity*	*Unit labor cost*
Sectors with below average wages						
Apparel	0.72	0.76	14.4	7.2	1.5	12.7
Leather products	0.77	0.81	14.1	6.8	10.7	3.1
Textiles	0.86	0.87	15.2	7.9	4.7	10.0
Miscellaneous	0.89	0.89	12.1	5.0	3.4	8.4
Plastic products	0.80	0.82	12.8	5.6	4.9	7.5
Food	0.91	0.88	14.4	7.1	4.6	9.1
Instruments	0.91	0.92	12.4	5.2	5.6	6.4
Electric and electronics	0.93	0.87	13.2	6.0	8.9	3.9
Rubber products	0.99	1.02	13.1	5.9	6.0	6.7
Wood products	0.96	1.01	11.5	4.0	3.3	7.9
Sectors with above average wages						
Metal products	1.00	1.12	11.5	4.4	1.2	10.2
Nonmetallic mineral products	1.02	1.03	12.6	5.4	1.8	10.6
Chemical products	1.13	1.03	11.0	3.9	2.4	8.4
Paper and printing	1.26	1.29	11.5	4.4	3.6	7.6
Machinery	1.27	1.30	10.4	3.4	6.5	3.7
Beverage/tobacco	1.33	1.31	15.5	8.1	4.1	11.0
Transport equipment	1.40	1.44	11.0	—	4.1	6.6
Basic metals	1.43	1.52	11.4	4.3	6.4	4.7

Petroleum and coal products	1.50	1.42	15.4	8.1	0.8	14.5
Chemicals	1.55	1.50	13.1	5.9	2.4	10.4
Public sector, above average wages						
Sugar	1.39	1.29	18.2	10.7		
Liquor	1.41	1.48	15.7	8.3		
Tobacco	1.20	1.22	19.8	12.2		
Fertilizers	1.85	1.84	13.0	5.8		
Petroleum	1.50	1.42	16.2	8.8		

Source: Directorate-General Budget, Accounting and Statistics, *Yearbook of Labor Statistics*, 1986.

NOTES

1. In contrast to the declining trend in the private sector, the public manufacturing corporations' profit margins fluctuated sharply, largely reflecting changes in the oil import cost and the status of its passthrough. Other than its fluctuation, the financial situation of the public manufacturing sector was dominated by the Tobacco and Liquor Bureau, whose profit margins amounted to as high as 58–65% because of its monopoly status.

2. Including the assassination of a Chinese-American writer, Chiang-nan (Henry Liu) in Dale City, California in October, 1984, and the irregularity in dealing with the insolvency of the large Cathay Group in Taipei in the winter of 1985.

3. This section is based on the author's "Policy Responses to External Shocks: Brazil versus Taiwan and South Korea," International Monetary Fund, Washington, D.C. (mimeo).

4. The authorities are actively considering removing the archaic prohibition of private holding of foreign currency.

5. A Basic Labor Law requiring employers to provide for retirement pensions was enacted in July 1984, but its implementation has been resisted by powerful employers.

6. Thus, Taiwan enters a third stage in its trade-policy orientation. The first stage was inward oriented, and the second and third stages are outward oriented. The third stage, however, must be based on Taiwan's technological excellence instead of relying on both policy and nonpolicy related subsidies.

7. It was reported in the *Wall Street Journal* that the Korean industrialists often invited Japanese technicians over on long weekends, by providing all the transportation and lodging costs, in addition to paying high per diems.

8. Years ago, the author ventured to suggest that at some point in the future, it might be better for Taiwan to abolish tariff and import restrictions, and function as a mega-Hong Kong, but such a stage is still far off. (see Lin, 1973: 160).

REFERENCES

Lin, Ching-yuan. "Policy Response to External shocks: Brazil versus Taiwan and South Korea." Washington, D.C. International Monetary Fund (mimeo), 1984.

———*Industrialization in Taiwan, 1946–1972*. New York: Praeger, 1973.

INDUSTRIAL EVOLUTION AND CHANGES IN TRADE ENVIRONMENT: A CASE STUDY OF CONSUMER ELECTRONICS AND TEXTILE/GARMENT INDUSTRIES IN HONG KONG

T. B. Lin and Chyau Tuan

I. INTRODUCTION

Consumer electronics and textile/garment are the most important export-oriented industries in Hong Kong. The long-term development and short-run adjustment strategies of these industries have been greatly influenced by the changing envi-

Research in Asian Economic Studies.
Asian Industrialization: Changing Economic Structures,
Volume 1, Part A, pages 159–186.
Copyright © 1988 by JAI Press Inc.
All rights of reproduction in any form reserved.
ISBN: 0-89232-987-4

ronments of international trade. The major concern of these industries is always how to respond and adjust to changes in overseas market as is the case with the other newly industrialized countries in the Pacific Basin.

More specifically, since trading environment is deteriorating due to rising protectionism in the major importing markets, particularly in the United States and E.E.C., it has become a *must* for the Asian newly industrialized countries (NICs) to restructure their economy and to adopt new strategies to upgrade their vital industries in general and their textile and garment industries (T/G) in particular. Besides, as the Asian NICs generally share similar experience of industrial development, the difference between the T/G and electronics industries in these nations is basically quantitative rather than qualitative in nature, at least up to the early 1980s. As a result, the competition among them has been very keen in the major western markets. Although the threat of nontariff barriers is not yet too serious to consumer electronics, the adjustment to the changing trade environment is a pressing issue for them.

The situation for Hong Kong is more delicate. Under the government's policy of "positive noninterventionism," the electronics and T/G industries in Hong Kong have to meet the external challenge by themselves. But it may provide a unique background for analysis at the same time. Therefore, the major purpose of the study is first to trace the evolution of the T/G industry and consumer electronics in Hong Kong during the last two decades, and second, to analyze its experiences and responses to changes in external demand in the setting of a "free economy" regime. The lessons learned from the past should be useful for devising effective strategies for the industries' future development.

Specifically, the objectives of the study are (1) to review development and export performance of the consumer electronics and T/G industries in Hong Kong since the 1960s, (2) to compare the path of evolution and industrial adjustments under different external pressures for the two industries, (3) to conduct an investigation at the firm level in order to observe individual firm's behaviors, responses, and strategies in the face of external changes, and (4) to draw implications for new industrial policy in the future.

Definition of Product Groups

In this study, commodities manufactured and classified as group 383 by the United Nations International Standard Industrial Classification of All Economic Activities (ISIC, 1968 edition) are operationally defined as consumer electronics. Electronic toys, transistorized radios, electrical appliances and housewares, television receivers and communication equipments, sound reproducing and recording equipments and apparatus, computing machinery and equipments, and consumer electrical and electronic products n.e.s. are seven subgroups within this category. In addition, subgroup ISIC 3854 (manufacture of watches and clocks—electronic) is also discussed along with the 383 group as it is important for Hong Kong exports and is usually treated as a consumer electronic product.

For the textile and garment industry, it comprises ISIC groups 320, 322 (manufacturing of wearing apparel), and 325–329 (manufacture of textiles including knitting).

However, as far as detailed export statistics are concerned, consumer electronic products will include 21 of the United Nations Standard International Trade Classification, Revision 2 (SITC, Rev. 2) three-digit groups in this study. Although ISIC and SITC groups are not exactly compatible, the two operational definitions have been adopted alternatively for the sake of convenience in utilizing available official statistics.

II. EVOLUTION OF THE INDUSTRIES AND THEIR EXPORT PERFORMANCE

A. Background

During the last 20 years, Hong Kong has experienced a rapid economic growth. Its GDP has grown at an average compound annual rate of 16.8% in nominal terms and 10.0% in constant prices over the period 1961–1981. On a per capita basis, the corresponding growth rates were 14 and 7.3%, respectively. To compare the two subperiods, 1961–1971 and 1971–1981, the latter seems to have fared even better. These growth rates exceeded the average for all other developing countries as well as that for the developed nations during the said time span. By 1986, the per capita GDP had reached HK$50,000 or approximately US$6,400. which was second only to Japan and roughly on par with Singapore.

This rapid growth could be attributed to the remarkable performance of export activities in the manufacturing sector (Table 1). During the period 1961–1971, Hong Kong's domestically produced exports grew at an average annual rate of 16.7%. The performance during 1971–1981 was even better, with an average compound rate of 19.3%, and reached its recent high in 1984. A higher rate of

Table 1. Growth of International Trade in Hong Kong, 1961–1985 (Percentage per Annum)

	1961–1971	*1971–1981*	*1981–1985*	*1961 level (HK$ in millions)*	*1985 level (HK$ in millions)*
Domestic exports	16.68	19.32	10.06	2,939	129,882
Reexports	13.17	28.45	20.32	991	105,270
Imports	13.00	21.19	10.95	5,970	232,617
Total trade	14.22	21.42	12.42	9,900	467,769

Source: Calculated from *Hong Kong Review of Overseas Trade in 1985* (Census and Statistics Department, Hong Kong, 1986).

growth in the reexport trade was observed in the last decade, mainly due to the more liberal trade policy of the People's Republic of China since 1978. The annual (compound) growth rate of reexport averaged 28.5% during 1971–1981. This factor certainly contributed to the further development of the service sectors in Hong Kong (Lin et al., 1980; Lin and Tuan, 1985).

In the same period, total per capita exports have risen more than 37-fold from HK$1,104 in 1959 to HK$41,283 in 1984.

The textiles and garment (T/G) industry has firmly held the top position among all industries in terms of production, employment, and exports since the early 1950s. It constituted 53% of the total manufacturing output in 1973. The share has become smaller recently, but its top rank remains unchanged. The industry played an even more important role in job creation, providing 40–45% of manufacturing positions during 1960–1984. Textiles and garment firms contributed nearly half of the domestic exports from 1960 to 1970, and some 40% in the mid-1980s.

Even if garment and textiles firms are counted separately, the former sector is still considered the most important industry in all respects in the Hong Kong economy (Table 2).

Table 2. General Conditions of Textile and Garment Industry in Hong Kong, 1960–1984

	Establishment				*Persons engaged: share in manufacturing employment*		*Domestic exports: share in merchandise exports*	
	Number		*Share in manufacturing*					
Year	*T*[a]	*G*[b]	*T*	*G*	*T*[c]	*G*[c]	*T*	*G*
1960	815	753	14.6	13.4	26.5	19.2	—	—
1970	2540	2299	14.7	13.3	21.6	18.8	10.7	36.4
1978	4540	7905	11.7	20.4	15.3	30.7	7.0	38.6
1979	4677	8616	11.1	20.4	14.5	29.0	7.3	36.0
1980	5013	8991	11.0	19.8	14.0	28.7	6.7	34.1
1981	4985	9266	10.7	19.8	13.6	28.6	6.6	35.2
1982	4991	9128	10.6	19.4	13.0	29.4	6.1	34.7
1983	4912	9129	10.5	19.5	12.9	29.4	6.8	32.9
1984	5068	9602	10.3	19.6	12.8	29.3	6.3	33.8

Source: Hong Kong Annual Report and *Hong Kong Trade Statistics* (December), various issues (Census and Statistics Department, Hong Kong).

[a] ISIC 325–329, Manufacture of Textiles (including knitting).

[b] ISIC 320 and 322, Manufacture of Wearing Apparel, except knitwear, leather products, and footwear.

[c] Textiles and garments employment in 1984 were 115,429 and 265,353, respectively. Total manufacturing employment for the year was 904,709.

In terms of earnings from domestic export, the electronic industry [including consumer electronics (CE) and non-CE sectors] overrode textile industry in the early 1970s and became the second largest contributor, next only to the garment industry. It is noted that with less than 2% of establishments, the electronics industry created some 9% of employment opportunities, accounted for more than 15% of the total export value in 1978, and also attracted most of the investment from overseas during the period 1972–1978.

As far as consumer electronics is concerned, the disaggregated industrial data released since 1978 have also shed light on its configuration. The contribution in terms of domestic export earning and employment was significant during 1978–1984, even without counting the parts of electronic watches and clocks (Table 3). Consumer electronics ranked fifth and second in employment and domestic exports, respectively, since 1978, and strongly held its second position in export and the third place in employment since 1983, again without counting electronic watches and clocks. Otherwise this achievement would have been realized as early as 1978.

B. A Brief History of Hong Kong's T/G and Consumer Electronics Industries

On the demand side, textile products are important necessities. As to the supply side, the T/G industry can be built up mainly with unskilled labor and relatively small amounts of capital. These facts cause the industry to be considered a strategic or leading industry in most LDCs. To Hong Kong, development of the T/G industry was a natural result of the influx of refugees and capital following the political change in China in 1949. Some of the refugees were entrepreneurs running textile firms in China and continued their operations within the familiar industry. As Hong Kong was the first to industrialize its economy in this region, the T/G industry in Hong Kong could take advantage of the booming western markets for exports since the late 1950s, and drive more and more local entrepreneurs to form their own firms. As a result, Hong Kong has built a relatively stronger basis to cope with environmental change, particularly the rising trade barriers since the 1970s.

Because the basic technology of the T/G industry is mature, and the life span of the major product categories is generally long, only changes in manufacturing methods (as knitted vs nonknitted) or in materials (cotton, wool man-made fibers, silk, etc.) can be discerned during the last 30 years. To overcome various trade restrictions, measures, such as undertaking overseas investment or upgrading products, have also been taken (Lin and Tuan, 1987).

As in the case of the T/G industry, the local CE industry generally does not need a large capital investment. Historically, intensive labor utilization in the assembling process of the CE products contributed to its rise in Hong Kong. However, since the nature of basic technology is totally different, the process of its development is distinguishable.

Table 3. General Conditions of Consumer Electronics[a] in Hong Kong, 1970–1984

Year	Establishment				Persons engaged				Domestic exports[b]	
	Number		Share in manufacturing		Size		Share in manufacturing		Share in Merchandise exports	
1970	110		—		26,284		—		4.4	(1.1)
1978	360	(76)[c]	0.80	(0.17)	57,694	(7,862)	6.55	(0.89)	7.9	(6.7)
1979	756	(256)	1.54	(0.52)	81,345	(13,267)	8.03	(1.31)	8.3	(7.8)
1980	966	(612)	1.84	(1.17)	94,312	(18,748)	8.97	(1.78)	8.1	(9.2)
1981	1096	(702)	2.27	(1.45)	92,086	(22,746)	9.24	(2.28)	7.4	(8.8)
1982	898	(722)	1.99	(1.60)	82,189	(23,996)	8.94	(2.61)	7.2	(8.6)
1983	1008	(927)	2.18	(2.00)	90,168	(23,654)	9.63	(2.37)	8.5	(7.9)
1984	1106	(860)	2.21	(1.72)	95,948	(21,616)	10.04	(2.26)	9.0	(6.4)

Sources: Industry Survey Report: The Electronic Industry (Commerce and Indsutry Department, Hong Kong, 1970); *Survey of Industrial Production; Hong Kong Review of Overseas Trade* (Census and Statistics Department, Hong Kong, various years).

[a] ISIC 383 (1978–1984). Transistorized/main radio sets, television, amplifier units, flash units, and other finished products (1970).

[b] The sum of communications and sound recording and reproducing apparatus equipment, and electronic calculating machines.

[c] The figures in parentheses are ISIC 3854, manufacture of electric watches and clocks (for establishment and persons engaged); as to domestic exports, 45% (1978) to 77% (1983) of watches/clocks exported were electronic in nature.

The electronics industry in Hong Kong started in 1959 when a local Chinese firm began to assemble transistorized radios. The modest beginning was the result of a decision by Japan to freely export electronic components for radio receivers. Since the birth of the industry, most of its products have been exported. The growth of the industry depended entirely on overseas demand.[1]

The radio receivers industry, the oldest branch of Hong Kong's electronics industry, grew continuously since the mid-1960s and firmly held the leading position within the electronics industry in terms of export value until 1981 when it was overtaken by electronic watches and clocks. However, with a relatively stable performance, this item, together with other audio equipment, such as cassettes and tape recorders, still accounts for a major part of consumer electronics exports.

On the other hand, just as the transistorized radio was first initiated by a local Chinese firm in 1959, manufacturing and assembling consumer electronic products have continuously attracted local entrepreneurs. Electronic calculators (1968) and electronic watches (1973) were first assembled by local firms and both were responsible for the rapid growth of consumer electronics in Hong Kong thereafter. The progress in electronics technology greatly enchanced the ability of local entrepreneurs to find a market niche and quickly respond to demand changes. The rise and fall of firms manufacturing different kinds of electronic watches, TV and electronic games, and telephone sets during the first half of the 1980s have been amazing. The facts indicate how local consumer electronics firms are able to adapt to changes in market conditions.

C. Export Performance of T/G and the Consumer Electronics

Because of the saturation in the market of T/G products and the quota constraints, the growth of Hong Kong T/G exports is very stable in terms of product composition and market concentration.

From Table 4 it is noted that there was not much change in export shares of major material categories (cotton, MMF) or in the shares of major method categories (knit, nonknit) during the period 1975–1984.

In terms of overseas market, the United States, West Germany, and U.K. are the top three for Hong Kong garment export since the beginning of 1970s (Table 5). However, the U.S. market share of total Hong Kong export consistenly increased from 30.5% in 1973 to 55.1% in 1985. Regardless of the imposed restrictive quota constraint on most of the Hong Kong T/G exports, the production of high value added (and hence high priced) commodities has contributed to the concentration of its exports in the U.S. market.

In the textile segment, China, followed by the United States and the United Kingdom, has been the largest market for Hong Kong's exports since 1982.

Table 4. Export Shares of Major Product Categories of Clothing by User, Materials, and Methods of Manufacture, Selected Years (Percentage of Value)

Year	*User: women/girls*	*Materials* Cotton	Man-made fiber	*Methods* Knit	Nonknit
1975	46	46	28	36	54
1976	44	49	34	34	57
1978	48	47	32	34	58
1980	48	48	31	34	59
1982	52	47	30	34	61
1984	57	46	23	39	57

Source: Complied from *Hong Kong Review of Overseas Trade*, various years (Census and Statistics Department, Hong Kong).

Table 5. Domestic Exports of T/G by Market, Comparative Share (Percentage of Value)

	Garments			*Textiles*		
Year	*U.S.*	*W. Germany*	*U.K.*	*U.S.*	*U.K.*	*P.R.C.*
1973	30.5	18.8	19.1	21.1	18.8	—
1975	30.9	19.6	15.6	18.5	20.8	—
1976	32.0	18.7	12.6	19.3	16.8	—
1977	39.0	15.8	11.0	19.2	16.9	—
1978	39.9	16.6	12.1	15.6	19.9	1.1
1979	35.8	17.9	14.0	11.5	18.5	4.2
1980	34.7	18.3	13.7	13.2	12.5	7.5
1981	38.7	15.3	12.7	13.8	11.8	10.8
1982	40.2	15.0	11.7	11.4	12.0	15.2
1983	47.0	13.3	10.1	14.8	10.5	18.2
1984	50.6	11.9	9.5	14.0	8.4	20.1
1985	55.1	10.2	8.6	13.1	8.2	25.0

Source: Same as Table 4.

In relative terms, consumer electronic products can be classified into two groups: matured and fad (or fashion) products. All kinds of radio-broadcast receivers and electronic calculators (electronic calculating machines) are typical examples for the former; in addition, electronic watches and clocks, particularly after 1980, can also be considered matured products.

The main characteristics of the matured products group are relatively longer life span and stable demand. However, the relative share of this group, or the above mentioned three product categories together, in terms of total electronics exports (products and parts) has been steadily declining since the mid-1970s from some 60% to less than 40% in 1984.

On the other hand, fad products such as TV games, electronic games, and electrical line telephone apparatus, are characterized by a shorter life cycle and fluctuating demand. This group contributed 5–10% of the total electronics export earnings for Hong Kong during the first half of the 1980s. In response to variations of external demand and competition, a few standardized and matured technologies and products developed in the industrialized nations have been channeled in recently. Around 1984 the local electronic manufacturers started manufacturing microwave ovens, private automatic branch exchange (PABX) systems, cellular mobile telephones, stereo television, satellite television receivers, and video cassette recorders. However, the pattern has remained unchanged. As most local CE firms are relatively small in size and lack capital for accommodating any significant change, the new products to be manufactured locally should be low risk, less capital intensive, and not time consuming in changing the existing production lines.

In addition to the significant variation in product composition of the CE exports, the relative share in the overseas markets of the matured products also fluctuated during the last decade (Table 6). Although the United States has held its position as the largest importer of most Hong Kong CE products (e.g., radios, watches, and clocks) since the 1970s, the irregular alternation of the figures in the table may well indicate the keen competition in the world market.

To investigate the comparative advantage of the T/G and CE industries, the relative export performance of nine SITC three-digit commodity groups since 1977 has been calculated (Table 7). It is easily seen that the values of all these groups are larger than 1.25 since 1980. Eight of them even have a value larger than 2.5 since 1977. This implies that almost all major exported commodity groups in Hong Kong's T/G and consumer electronics industries can be defined as "goods with strong comparative advantage" according to *JETRO's* standard. The rest is still qualified as "goods with rather strong comparative advantage."[2] Relatively speaking, the T/G products have enjoyed a better position than those of the CE as a whole in the world market.

Table 6. Domestic Exports of Consumer Electronics, Comparative Share (Percentage of Value)

	Radio-broadcast receivers			*Watches and clocks*	
Year	*U.S.*	*W. Germany*	*U.K.*	*U.S.*	*W. Germany*
1973	51.9	10.2	12.4	18.4	2.0
1975	43.0	18.2	5.1	24.4	3.7
1976	43.0	17.2	5.1	29.7	6.3
1977	42.9	15.3	4.6	31.8	5.4
1978	36.8	17.8	8.5	29.1	7.6
1979	26.3	18.6	13.6	24.7	11.3
1980	29.6	15.1	10.1	25.8	9.9
1981	33.8	10.7	10.3	27.4	7.3
1982	40.7	8.9	6.6	35.0	6.5
1983	44.5	9.9	6.2	37.3	7.1
1984	52.7	6.5	5.0	39.1	6.7
1985	46.9	5.5	4.7	40.4	6.2

Source: Compiled and calculated from *Hong Kong Review of Overseas Trade*, 1973–1984; *Hong Kong Statistics*, 1984 (Census and Statistics Department, various years).

Table 7. Relative Export Performance[a] of the Major Commodity Groups in Consumer Electronics, Hong Kong, 1977–1981

Commodity group	*1977*	*1978*	*1979*	*1980*	*1981*
762: Radio-broadcast receivers	14.03	11.83	14.13	13.87	11.49
764: Telecommunications equipment	0.62	0.90	1.11	1.26	1.45
775: Household equipment	3.01	3.10	3.67	5.08	5.91
885: Watches and clocks	14.70	15.54	19.64	22.84	20.59
894: Toys, games, sporting goods	18.74	16.78	18.68	17.23	16.89
652: Cotton fabrics	8.56	8.56	8.67	9.06	9.52
842: Outgarments, men	17.94	16.10	15.71	15.12	15.29
843: Outgarments, women	20.49	19.25	17.83	18.14	21.22
844: Underwear	33.11	27.50	26.12	26.26	26.48

[a] For a definition refer to note 2.

III. SALIENT FEATURES OF THE INDUSTRIES

A. Product Coverage

The diversification of consumer electronics is obvious when one looks at its product coverage. There were 110 firms and 26,284 employees in 1970 producing six categories of finished products: transistorized radio sets (100), TV sets (2), phonograph units (1), alarm units (1), flash units (3), and amplifier units (3). Until 1978, according to the Industrial Production Survey, there were more than 1,000 firms, divided into eight ISIC four-digit sectors within the CE industry (including electronic watches and clocks) producing a wide gamut of products. As recent survey statistics show, electronic watches and clocks and transistorized radios are still the two largest sectors in the CE industry in terms of number of firms.

However, firms in these two sectors, just like others, were characterized by their tiny size in terms of workers or output per establishment. This situation has still not changed. In some sectors, such as electronic watches and clocks, the average number of persons engaged per establishment even decreased annually. The rapid growth of small entrepreneurs jumping onto the bandwagon of hot products may be one of the basic reasons. The fluctuation in the number of establishments might also reflect the possible shifting between production lines. The persistently declining size of firms in electronic toys, radios, sound reproducing, and recording equipments should partly explain why the number of electronic watches/clocks firms could inccrease dramatically during 1980–1983.

As for the T/G industry, early development contributes to its integration of the downstream and upstream segments. According to the 1971 census of manufacturing establishments, the first comprehensive industrial survey, there were more than 9,700 firms (1,769 for textiles and 7,937 for garments) and 303,746 employees (85,575 for textiles, 218,171 for garments) in that year producing 28 ISIC four-digit product groups. The 21 product groups in the textile segment included spinning, weaving, knitting of all materials, bleaching, dyeing, and finishing. The quantity and quality were suitable for both export and use by local downstream clothing firms. The remaining seven product groups manufacturing all kinds of wearing apparel covered the widest range of production that can possibly be found in the garment industry of any developing countries.

The firms in the T/G industry were found to be small in size. The average textile firm had 48.4 employees and a garment establishment employed 27.5 persons on average in 1970. The same situation persists in the garment segment, whereas the textile sector has persistently experienced a declining firm size on an average.

B. Degree of Concentration

The CE industry in Hong Kong has been polarized since its early stage of growth. The Industrial Survey (electronics only) of 1970 showed that the two largest firms in the finished products sectors employed 30% of workers within the sector. The smallest 75 firms, which represented 68%, employed only 13% of the employees in the entire sector.

The most recent figure for a specific concentration indicator, furnished in the 1978 Survey of Industrial Production, showed that the largest three firms produced 8.7% of the total output of the CE, and owned 9.6% of the fixed assets of the whole industry. Results from the most recent Industrial Production Survey (1984) also show that the largest 106 firms, which represented less than 10% of the firms in the sector (manufacturing consumer electronic and electronic products), employed more than 60% of the workforce in this sector and produced more than 70% of the total output of CE in that year.

The situation in the T/G industry is similar. The "big three" in the textile segment in 1978 produced 7.6% of the total segment output, and owned 8.7% of the fixed assets of the whole. The big three in the garment sector, on the other hand, contributed 5% output and owned 13.4% of the fixed assets. The findings from the 1984 Industrial Production Survey indicate that the largest 104 firms (of garment manufacture) and 111 establishments (of textile manufacture), which represent 1 and 2.3% of the firms in the respective sectors, employed 18.3 and 29.8% of the workforce in their sectors and contributed 25.6 and 44.9% of the total output for the garment and textile segments, respectively (Table 8).

C. Ownership and Foreign Investment

Hong Kong as a free economy in which only infrastructure is provided as an incentive for overseas investors has attracted a considerable amount of foreign investment since the 1950s. The manufacture of many CE products has depended on transferred technology and has been initiated by subsidiaries of multinational corporations (MNCs). Local textile and garment firms have also been inspired by foreign firms in design, technology, and management. However, local firms have dominated the CE and T/G industries since the very beginning. This is particularly true in terms of number of establishments. There were 27 firms in T/G and 16 firms in electronics (no separate figures for CE) involving foreign capital in 1971. The numbers have increased to 105 and 115, respectively, in 1986, which represent only a minor part of the T/G and electronics industries.

However, foreign investments in the T/G and electronics industries have constituted the major part of the overall overseas investment in the Hong Kong manufacturing sector in terms of number of firms, employment, and investment (Table 9).

A breakdown of investment by source country shows that the United States was the largest investor in 1986 in the electronics industry (having more than 60% of investment), followed by Japan, Netherlands, and China. As to the T/G industry, the United States firmly holds the top position in terms of investment (with a share of 38% of investment), but ranked second in terms of number of

Table 8. Size Distribution of Consumer Electronics and Textile and Garment Industries in Hong Kong, 1984

Size (value of gross output in HK$, Mn.)	*Number of establishments*			*Number of persons employed (1,000 persons)*			*Gross output (HK$,Mn.)*		
	CE	*T*	*G*	*CE*	*T*	*G*	*CE*	*T*	*G*
Less than 1	302 (27.3)	2,992 (61.3)	6,405 (62.1)	2.6 (2.7)	12.2 (10.7)	36.9 (12.4)	120 (0.5)	783 (2.7)	2,200 (5.3)
1–9	464	1,247	2,875	12.5	29.7	99.7	1,751	4,421	10,792
10–19	149	328	606	10.5	17.7	51.2	1,971	4,499	7,642
20–49	85	201	350	12.2	20.5	54.6	2,852	6,325	10,115
50 and over	106 (9.6)	111 (2.3)	104 (1.0)	58.1 (60.6)	33.9 (29.8)	54.2 (18.3)	16,058 (70.5)	13,048 (44.9)	10,559 (25.6)
Total	1,106	4,879	10,323	95.9	114.0	296.5	22,764	29,076	41,308
	(100.0)	(100.0)	(100.0)	(100.0)	(100.0)	(100.0)	(100.0)	(100.0)	(100.0)

Source: Compiled and calculated from *1984 Survey of Industrial Production* (Census and Statistics Department, Hong Kong, 1986).
Figures in parenthesis are percentages.

Table 9. Overseas Investment in Hong Kong Manufacturing Sector, Selected Years

	1971		*1973*		*1984*		*1986*	
		(%)		(%)		(%)		(%)
Establishment of overseas interests	112	(100.0)	210	(100.0)	442	(100.0)	509	(100.0)
Textile/garment	27	(24.1)	56	(26.7)	89	(20.1)	105	(20.6)
Electronics	16	(14.3)	48	(22.9)	82	(18.6)	115	(22.6)
Employment (1,000 workers)	—		63.0	(100.0)	89.0	(100.0)	86.4	(100.0)
Textile/garment	—		9.7	(15.4)	17.2	(19.3)	16.6	(19.2)
Electronics	—		30.2	(48.0)	34.8	(39.1)	32.3	(37.4)
Investment HK$, mn.	759.9	(100.0)	1,392.1	(100.0)	11,448.3	(100.0)	15,527	(100.0)
Textiles/garment	160.9	(21.2)	306.5	(22.0)	1,115.0	(9.8)	1,322	(8.5)
Electronics	264.7	(34.9)	304.0	(21.8)	4,062.0	(35.5)	5,021	(32.3)

Source: The Survey of Overseas Investment in Hong Kong's Manufacturing Industry, 1984, 1986 and data released by Industry Department, Hong Kong.

establishments in the same year. The major investors in this industry were the United States, U.K., and Japan. It is worth noting that the average scale of firms with foreign investment is significantly larger than that of the local ones.[3]

D. Value Added and Labor Share

Among the major manufacturing industries in Hong Kong, the electronics industry has been the one that depends relatively heavily on raw materials as inputs, and its value added was below one-third of its output. But the consumer electronics industry relied even more on material inputs. From Table 10, it is observed that the value added of CE has ranged from 21 to 23% of gross output during 1979–1984, which is the lowest among the three. The garment segment firmly takes its top position during the same period and the figures of the value added as the percentage of output has steadily increased from 29% in 1979 to 32% in 1984.

The labor share, on the other side, has shown signs of a stable decline for the textile and garment industry since 1979, but it fluctuated for CE during 1979–1984. These facts may indicate a few improvements in capital investment in the T/G industry, and the rapidly changing composition of CE production, and also reflect a stagnant wage rate during the same period. However, the significant labor-intensive nature of the local T/G and CE industries still remains.

The skill level of manpower in the T/G and electronics industries, on the other hand, had shown signs of improvement. The growing share of the high skilled labor in the electronic (no disaggregated figures for CE) industry has been observed since the early 1970s. From Table 11 it is clear that the proportion of

Table 10. Value added and Labor Share of CE and T/G Industries in Hong Kong, Selected Years

	National accounts value added as a percentage of gross output			*Total labor cost as a percentage of value added*		
Year	*CE*	*T*	*G*	*CE*	*T*	*G*
1973	—	32	30	—	49	69
1979	21	23	29	61	68	79
1980	20	23	29	72	70	79
1981	22	22	30	55	68	73
1982	23	23	33	52	65	76
1983	23	24	33	57	58	73
1984	22	25	32	59	60	75

Source: Compiled from *Survey of Industrial Productions*, various years, (Census and Statistics Department, Hong Kong).

Table 11. Skill Level of Electronics, Textile, and Garment Employees, Selected Years

Year	*Industry*	*Industry total*	*Technologist*[a] (%)	*Technician*[b] (%)	*Craftsman*[c] (%)	*Operative and unskilled*[d] (%)
1966	E	20,322	—	4.5	7.3	88.2
1967	T	85,045	—	5.3	10.8	83.9
1969	G	114,189	—	4.0	3.0	93.0
1974	E	48,960	1.5	6.3	16.7	75.5
1975	T	68,040	1.1	4.9	13.3	80.7
1975	G	184,128	0.7	4.4	1.2	93.7
1979	T	70,341	2.1	7.0	15.4	75.5
1980	E	92,968	2.4	10.7	10.0	76.8
1981	G	239,558	1.4	5.4	3.7	89.5
1984	E	107,375	3.9	11.7	9.3	72.9
1985	T	49,927	1.6	7.7	16.9	73.8
1985	G	262,904	1.4	6.5	4.6	87.5

Source: Manpower Survey Reports on Textile Industry, Clothing Industry, and Electronic Industry, various issues (Hong Kong Training Council, various years).

[a] A technologist is a person who applies his professional skills to a wide range of engineering activities.

[b] A technician is a person who performs technical duty normally under the supervision of a technologist.

[c] A craftsman is a worker who can apply his skills to a wide range of jobs within his crafts.

[d] An operative is a semiskilled worker who engages in repetitive production work that requires a restricted range of skills.

the employed technologists among the total number of workers increased from 1.5 to 3.9% between 1974 and 1984. The share of technicians also increased from 4.5% in 1966 to 11.7% in 1984.

In relative terms, the proposition of skilled personnel (including technologist and technician) is lower for the T/G than for the electronics industry. Only 1.1 and 0.7% of employees were technologist for the textile segment and garment segment, respectively, in 1975. The share has increased to 1.6 and 1.4%, respectively, in 10 years of time, but is still significantly lower than that of electronics. The share of technicians for the T/G industry is similar. There was improvement in the last decades, when the proportion increased from 5.3% in 1967 to 7.7% in 1985 for the textile segment, and from 4% in 1969 to 6.5% in 1985 for the garment sector. However, the achievement is not so impressive if compared to that of electronics.

The significant manpower up-grading in electronics may be necessary to increase the production flexibility needed for its survival, but it is not enough. As compared to Taiwan, which started her electronics industry about the same time as Hong Kong, the proportion of technologists in Hong Kong seems to be far behind the level needed for developing local R&D and product engineering.[4]

IV. CHANGING ENVIRONMENT AND ADJUSTMENT

A. Changes in the External and Internal Environments

The Long-Term Arrangement (LTA) regarding international trade in cotton textiles that came into force in October 1962 may be the first significant event signaling the change of free trade. The LTA was negotiated to protect the textiles industry in the developed countries from market disruption by cotton textiles imported from developing countries. The development of the man-made fibers sector and overseas investment from Taiwan and Hong Kong to ASEAN resulted partly from this agreement.

In 1973, the first Multi-Fiber Agreement (MFA1) was formulated covering the period 1974–1977. Under the MFA1, synthetic fibers and yarns that were not covered in the LTA became subject to quotas. The Agreement also set minimum growth rates for quotas and created an independent Textile Surveillance Body to supervise the implementation.

In 1978, the MFA2 covering 1978–1981 was launched. It was more restrictive than MFA1 because it removed the minimum annual growth rate of 6% for quotas. From 1982 to 1986, there was MFA3. Under this improved agreement, fairly detailed net restrictions by means of bilateral quota were developed. From Table 12, it is noted that around 90% of the Hong Kong textile and garment

Table 12. Exports of the T/G Products under Restrictions
HK$ in millions: (Percentage)

Market	*1980*	*1981*	*1982*	*1983*
E.C.C.	8,736	9,306	9,005	9,543
	(91.9)[a]	(94.0)	(91.8)	(93.7)
United States	7,706	10,187	10,687	14,146
	(90.2)	(87.9)	(88.6)	(84.0)
Canada	602	737	828	1,193
	(83.3)	(80.4)	(83.6)	(85.0)
Sewden	504	583	718	621
	(86.5)	(88.1)	(89.9)	(89.0)
Austria	63	67	74	99
	(23.2)	(24.9)	(30.7)	(34.7)
Finland	16	31	27	24
	(14.7)	(27.1)	(18.4)	(21.2)
Total	17,663	20,911	21,339	25,626
	(65.4)	(64.4)	(65.7)	(65.3)

Source: Calculated from the statistics furnished by the Trade Department.

[a] The ratio of (export value of T/G products under restrictions)/(domestic exports of T/G products).

exports were restricted in various forms by E.E.C. and the United States in the period 1980–1983.

In addition, since the United States is the major market for most exporters in the region, it was not long before the textile industry had to face another round of protectionism. This time it appears in HR 1562 (the so-called Jenkins Bill). The bill was the first of some 300 bills to be read in both Houses of the U.S. Congress. It was well supported in the Congress as the U.S. trade deficit mounted and it also appeared that the U.S. administration could not respond to the protectionist mood with alternative measures in the following year. By December 3, 1985, the final version was approved by the U.S. Congress and subsequently vetoed by the President.

Although the bill was not signed by the President, its death does not mean that the protectionist sentiment has subsided in the United States. Democratic Representative Ed Jenkins said, "If no positive action is taken by the administration, this will not be the last textile bill you will see."[5] It can be expected tht the United States may eventually take unilateral actions to limit imports. Canada is also likely to further curb import of textile and apparels, whereas E.E.C., Japan, Austria, Switzerland, and the Nordic countries favor the extension of MFA in its present form. In any event, the T/G industry in Hong Kong is facing the most vulnerable period of its history.

The protectionism faced by the CE industry in Hong Kong is milder, since the local CE exports occupy an insignificant share in the world market at present. This industry is also characterized by relatively unlimited chances of product variation or combination made possible by the development of microelectronics. The current effort of local firms to widen their range of products seems an effective means to escape from the NTBs or graduation from GSP in the major overseas markets.

Furthermore, there are domestic challenges, chiefly the continuous increase of labor cost since the 1960s. It has lead to a deterioration in Hong Kong's advantage in labor-intensive productions (Table 13). In addition to protective measures

Table 13. Comparison of Wage Cost, 1984, Selected Asian Countries

	Taiwan	*Hong Kong*	*Korea*	*Thailand*	*Indonesia*	*P.R.C.*
Total cost per working hour (US$)	1.64	1.65	1.89	0.56	0.22	0.26
Working days per year	356	354	353	353	353	—
Working hours per year	8,544	8,496	8,472	8,472	7,413	—

Source: Werner International, Brussels, 1985; adopted from Taiwan Research Institute of Economics, *Annual Report on Textile Industry, 1985.*

adopted by the developed countries, the rising wage rates have made Hong Kong a less attractive place for MNCs to set up their T/G or CE establishments. Without physical capital investment, technology transfer (R&D, production process in particular) is very much limited. The domestic manufacturers have to invest more resources in searching for and locating optimum technologies in order to upgrade their products and meet the external competition.

However, as far as the T/G and CE industries are concerned, small firms (with 99 or less persons engaged) constitute the majority. More than 90% of the CE or T/G firms are of small scale in Hong Kong and it is difficult for the industry itself to be engaged in any comprehensive industrial upgrading project aiming at tomorrow's technology.

B. Responses

The constraints just mentioned may well indicate that the industrial adjustment in Hong Kong will be undertaken along the following ways:

1. To invest in an area with plenty of unused quota, lower labor cost, and fiscal incentives provided;
2. To move part of the operations to neighboring countries to produce low value added but highly labor intensive operations; and
3. To produce relatively high value added products aiming at a high end market segment through improvement in production technology or technology joint venture.

These measures will enable the small-firms-dominated industries to flourish in a laissez-faire setting.

In order to circumvent quota restrictions that developed countries had imposed on Hong Kong's T/G products, a few firms have set up their establishments in the forms of wholly owned or joint ventures in Singapore, Thailand, and the Philippines since the 1960s.

Because there is no official statistics on Hong Kong's overseas investment, we have resorted to secondary sources.[6] Hong Kong's investment in T/G industries in Singapore has been quite significant since the mid-1960s. Among the 25 textile firms involving 50% or more foreign interests in 1984, five came from Hong Kong. And of the 21 garment manufacturers with major overseas interests in the same year, 9 came from Hong Kong.

Hong Kong investment in the Philippines and Thailand's garment segment is also substantial. The segment's exports after 1970 have been said to be mostly the effort of their foreign (Taiwan and Hong Kong in particular) firms.

Labor costs and foreign government's fiscal incentives, such as tax holidays might be secondary incentives in this regard, as very few CE firms established their subsidiaries overseas before the 1980s.

For those firms engaged in producing low value added items aiming at the low end market, relocating part of their operations in neighboring countries to manufacture low VA but highly labor-intensive parts is an optimum option for the T/G or CE firms in Hong Kong. Because of geographical convenience, some local firms have subcontracted part of these operations to Chinese firms in the Special Economic Zones since early 1980. However, this strategy has its limits even in the short run. For example, problems with the certificate of origin regulations may arise, China may not have sufficient quotas for the T/G products, and also labor costs have increased. To solve these problems, a few local CE firms have established their joint venture settings in the nearby Special Economic Zone in China. But the long-term effect is undetermined.

Producing high value added products aiming at a high end market segment through improvement of production technology may be a practical solution for both T/G and CE firms. However, lack of investment in R&D and low economies of scale are troubling the CE firms that have been experiencing a rapid and unsteady technology development. As a result, the adjustment of the CE industry has basically followed the past trend. Even consumer electronics has progressed from mainly assembling simple transistor radios in the 1960s to the manufacturing of a wide range of commodities in response to changes in fashion, market, and technology. Its basic development strategy is to turn out the matured, standardized or fad, easy-to-copy products.[7] However, this path of evolution may be vulnerable. For example, after 20 years of development and diversification within the radio production line, it showed no significant increase in the unit price received. The Hong Kong product can accept only the lowest price for its radio sets as compared with other leading exporters, chiefly Japanese, during 1979–1981 (Table 14).

By examining the Unit Value Index (UVI) for radios, watches and clocks, and domestic electric appliances during 1978–1985, one can also note that the increase (if any) was insignificant and below average. For watches and clocks it was even worse: it has declined since 1979 (Table 15).

By way of contrast, the T/G industry has worked well to follow this approach. From the same table, it is noted that the textile and garment products have both lifted their UVI by 27 and 48%, respectively, within 5 years. The reasons for the success of the T/G industry may include (1) a longer history than other Asian competitors, (2) the matured nature of basic technology, and (3) its successful shift from subcontracting to partnership with foreign buyers including leading Western department stores or fashion designers. However, the widely applied quantity restraints in the form of export quota may be another major force, or incentive, to force the clothing firms to upgrade their products and aim at the upper end of the market. Absence of this factor has led CE firms to pursue horizontal diversification and stay in the low-end of the market segment as before. Under such circumstances, to maintain its market share, the CE industry

Table 14. Hong Kong's Radio Export Position, 1979–1981

	Hong Kong	*Japan*	*Taiwan*	*Singapore*
Quantity in 1,000 units				
1979	54,011	36,888	16,873	17,764
1980	61,742	42,159	18,208	21,749
1981	57,076	41,800	19,759	18,007
Value in HK$Mn.				
1979	3,240	12,468	2,264	1,596
1980	3,957	14,972	2,618	2,281
1981	3,921	17,783	3,380	2,727
Unit price in HK$ (1979 = 100)				
1979	60.0	338.4	134.2	89.8
(%)	(100.0)	(100.0)	(100.0)	(100.0)
1980	64.1	355.1	143.8	104.9
(%)	(106.8)	(104.9)	(107.2)	(116.8)
1981	68.7	425.4	171.1	151.3
(%)	(114.5)	(125.7)	(127.5)	(168.6)

Source: Compiled from "Hong Kong's Export Position of Radios Compared with Other Countries as an Exporter of Selected Products" (Hong Kong Trade Development Council) and *Study on the Hong Kong Electronics Industry*, p. 25 (Hong Kong Productivity Centre, 1985).

has been facing increasing competition from both the other NICs and developing countries, including China.

C. Actions Taken at the Firm Level: Survey Findings

Although the sample firms in the T/G businesses have expressed concern over rising protectionism, no CE manufacturers in the sample regarded protectionism as a serious threat in the short run. They usually turned out products according to overseas market standard or even specifications, and nontariff barriers (NTBs) such as quota or import testing seem to be of no great concern to them. The customs procedures or tariffs levied have had no major impact on them so far.

Consequently, the T/G firms in the sample are found to be worried about NTBs and market competition and respond accordingly, whereas the CE firms are most concerned about changes in market conditions such as keen competition and shifts in consumer taste.

To cope with and adjust to these changes, the sample firms have taken or will take a series of actions (Table 16). Among them, diversification of production

Table 15. Unit Value Index of Domestic Exports, Selected Commodities (Base Year 1981 = 100)

Commodity	*1969*	*1978*	*1979*	*1980*	*1981*	*1982*	*1983*	*1984*	*1985*
All domestic merchandise exports	33	72	84	92	100	106	117	131	131
Radios of all kinds	52	77	85	89	100	99	101	111	106
Watches and clocks	55	116	120	111	100	92	95	94	86
Domestic electrical appliances	—	—	—	—	100	101	107	116	107
Clothing	31	67	81	91	100	110	121	146	148
Textile fabrics	39	72	88	93	100	105	114	133	127

Source: Compiled from *Hong Kong Review of Overseas Trade, 1978–1984* (Census and Statistics Department, various years.)

Table 16. Actions Taken in Response to Market Changes

Actions	Number of firms: Has been taken T/G	Has been taken CE	Will be taken T/G	Will be taken CE	Total T/G	Total CE
1. Diversity of production lines	14	12	1	5	15	17
2. Product differentiation	16	12	1	2	17	14
3. Vertical integration (R&D, design, marketing, etc.)	11	4	1	1	12	5
4. Investments in automation to decrease production cost	15	11	3	1	18	12
5. To increase R&D investments	7	7	8	5	15	12
6. To develop the high-quality–high-price products.	15	8	3	3	18	11
7. Lowering price[a]	18	8	3	2	21	10
8. Diversification of overseas markets	15	7	3	6	18	13
9. To turn to local markets	6	6	2	2	8	8
10. To develop "own brand"	6	5	2	4	8	9
11. To develop new marketing channels	8	6	7	6	15	12
12. To incorporate more foreign capitals or cooperation in various forms	1	0	5	3	6	3
13. More subcontracts to local firms	8	3	1	4	9	7
14. More subcontracts to P.R.C. firms	6	6	3	5	9	11
15. To set up a subsidiary in P.R.C.	5	5	4	6	9	11
16. To set up a subsidiary in other areas	6	0	7	0	13	0

[a] Lowering price is considered a very short run action to cope with market competition rather than a strategy.

lines and product differentiation are the most popular strategies adopted so far for both textile/garment and consumer electronics industries. It may be worth noting that the textile and garment industry may have their production line (product category) more narrowly defined vis-à-vis the CE industry. Occasionally a diversity of T/G production lines may be just a product differentiation in the view of CE firms since only a few changes in process, capital, and other considerations such as layout are involved. Another similar strategy that is popular in the two industries is investment in automation to decrease production cost.

As for significant differences between the two industries (in terms of popular strategies adopted), it is found that many more T/G firms have taken or will take the following strategies (in order of frequency):

1. To set up a subsidiary overseas.
2. To develop high-quality–high-price products.
3. To pursue vertical integration (R&D, design, marketing, etc.).
4. To carry out diversification of overseas markets.

The six firms in the T/G industry that have overseas subsidiaries and seven others considering such subsidiaries have indicated that their major motives are as follows: (1) to escape from quota restrictions, (2) to decrease labor cost, and (3) to penetrate the new target market(s).

These findings have generally been consistent with the previous observations of the secondary sources at the more aggregated level. However, because the size of the surveyed sample was very small, care should be taken in interpreting the findings.

V. CONCLUSION

Hong Kong has experienced a rapid economic growth since the 1960s as a result of its successful industrialization and export promotion strategy. The textiles/garments and electronics products, among others, have played a major role during this period. Today, they have become the two largest industries in terms of exports and employment. They are also among the most export-oriented industries with more than half of their output sold to overseas markets.

As Hong Kong is an open economy with free trade, the industries must compete with imported products in the domestic market on the one hand and with other competitors in the overseas markets on the other. However, according to our longitudinal observation, the development and evolution of the industries in Hong Kong have been essentially led by export growth. The major concern of the CE industry is how to respond and adjust to the changing world market conditions, whereas the T/G industry has to struggle to cope with various NTBs.

In the domestic markets, local firms have their market share in the segment of middle and lower end products. No firm has ever seriously expected protection or assistance from government under the laissez-faire economic system. As far as foreign markets are concerned, no serious complaints about protectionism were made. Although a few Hong Kong CE products did enjoy conventional tariffs and duty-free entry status and benefitted from GSP schemes during the past decade, the possible "graduation" from the scheme in the future has ironically not drawn much attention from the business community. Market mechanism and consumers' demand are and will be the two vital factors to influence the operations and policy making of the firms.

For the textile and garment industry, it is different. Quota constraints and other NTBs have applied to most of Hong Kong's T/G exports in her major markets, E.E.C. and the United States. The prospect is not optimistic.

The philosophy of positive noninterventionism pursued by the Government precludes industrial policy on subsidy of any forms for industrial firms. As a manifestation of the entrepreneurship of the small manufacturers, the CE firms in Hong Kong, with some exceptions, have flourished in producing matured or fad products by using standardized labor-intensive technologies and imported materials as well as intermediate inputs. With respect to the T/G firms, they have to pursue high end market, product upgrading under the quota restrictions and at the same time to diversify the overseas markets as well as investment.

More specifically, under these circumstances, the industries developed their own patterns of production and growth path. The high productivity and industry of the labor force, the excellent infrastructure and communication facilities, and the innovation of the enterprising manufacturers have made the industries in Hong Kong well known for their great flexibility in meeting market changes and their ability to satisfy overseas buyers' requirements with respect to price, quality, design, and delivery time.

In the CE industry, the keen competition among the large number of small firms and the cut-throat pricing practices have been regarded as one of the comparative advantages of the industry in Hong Kong. Subcontracting, on the other hand, is also an effective tool to enable firms to cope with demand fluctuations and at the same time to avoid risky expansion of their production capacity. This policy is widely recognized as one of the major sources of flexibility of the CE industry in Hong Kong. In addition, the local firms are also acclaimed for their ability to accommodate small size orders with large varieties by modifying standardized production processes or utilizing "open stock" parts and components. This is true not only with marketing, but also with production.

To the textile and garment firms, market competition has been reinforced by neoprotectionism. In order to circumvent quota restrictions, some firms have established overseas joint ventures or wholly owned subsidiaries. To cope with quantity limits, the T/G firms have also upgraded their products to maximize the value per unit. Because of her longer history in T/G exports, Hong Kong has earned a relatively larger lease for growth under the MFAs. In this sense, the quota system itself has turned out to be a protective umbrella to ensure the market share for Hong Kong's T/G industries in the developed countries and enhance the success of its industrial upgrading.

The textile/garment industry and consumer electronics have successfully adjusted in various ways to internal and external environmental changes. However, there is one question that every researcher has to address: Can the industries, consumer electronics in particular, continue their growth along these lines, over the long run? As more and more developing economies develop their own T/G and CE industries and enjoy comparative advantages in production due to cheaper labor, the industries in Hong Kong will increasingly find it harder to hold their market shares. Even under the quota system, the T/G firms may lose ground due to rising costs. Two conflicting arguments can be advanced. The first one advocates that the Hong Kong Government must take an active role in improving the industry's technological capacity by creating an environment conducive to the formation of a more technology-intense industry. This view was clearly expressed in the conclusion of the HKPC Report of Study on the Hong Kong Electronics Industry. The other strongly supports the Government's policy of positive noninterventionism and maintains that market mechanism and entrepreneurs can solve the problems because they know them best.

Nonetheless, there is a common ground between the two views. Both of them emphasize the importance of the industry moving up the market along the line of the comparative advantages that have been mentioned before. In other words, the upgraded industry will not be producing high-technology products involving substantial investment in R&D, or manufacturing those capital- and skill-intensive parts and components such as digital, very large scale IC, fibers for special purpose, or fashions by designer. Hong Kong does not possess comparative advantages yet in producing these types of goods for export. Instead, many industrialists and researchers agreed that Hong Kong should steadily improve value added performance by designing new products, product differentiation, competitive pricing, and enhancing flexibility in both production and marketing as they have done so well in the past. The ways to increase value added performance include, inter alia, nonmanufacturing efforts such as technical upgrading, market research, developing own brands, and after-sales services. Taking the trend of technological progress into consideration, technology-intensive electronics production is an opportunity for Hong Kong tomorrow. As far as the small size of the firms is concerned, forming some sort of an "operation group" consisting of one or two core firms that are larger in size and many satellite firms that are closely related to each other may be a feasible way to achieve large-scale economies in production and marketing. The group can perform not only the tasks of product design, quality control, and testing, but also market research and promotion of its own brand-name products.

NOTES

1. For details, reader can refer to *Study on the Hong Kong Electronics Industry* (1984), Fang and Chee (1983), Yu (1982), and Chen (1971).

2. Relative Export Performance represents the ratio between "world market share for a particular commodity of a given country" and "world market share for all exports from the same country," e.g., the indicator

$$R_{ij} = \frac{x_{ij}}{\sum_{i=1}^{m} x_{ij}} \Bigg/ \frac{\sum_{j=1}^{n} x_{ij}}{\sum_{i=1}^{m}\sum_{j=1}^{n} x_{ij}}$$

where i stands for the ith country, i = 1, 2, . . ., m, and j represents the jth commodity (commodity group), j = 1, 2, . . ., n.

See Balassa (1965) and JETRO (Japan External Trade Organization): White Paper on International Trade (1977). Four classes have been defined according to value of the commodity's R.

A ($R>2.5$):	Goods with strong comparative advantage
B ($1.25<R<2.5$):	Goods with rather strong comparative advantage
C ($0.8<R<1.25$):	Goods with average comparative advantage
D ($R<0.8$):	Goods with weak comparative advantage.

For further details, reference may be made to Aquino (1981) and Balassa (1981).

3. The direct and indirect contributions of foreign manufacturing firms to developing countries have been extensively discussed in Cohen (1975), Kojima (1977), Lall and Streeten (1977), Nabseth and Ray (1974), and Sciberras (1977).

4. According to the figures provided by Research Department, Bank of America, it is shown that Hong Kong had the least number of postsecondary graduates majoring in electronics or electrical engineering (EE) in 1980 (Source: *Commonwealth 16*, October 1982):

	Hong Kong	*Singapore*	*Korea*	*Taiwan*
Electronics graduates	187	—	1,339	4,230
EE graduates	243	—	1,007	3,715
Total	430	83	2,346	7,945

Also see Tuan (1987).

5. *Congressional Quarterly*, the United States Congress, December 7, 1985, Washington, D.C., p. 2557.

6. See Chia (1987), with special reference to Pan Eng Fong for Singapore, Tuanjai Ajanant for Thailand, and Bienvenido P. Alano for the Philippines.

7. Up to a certain degree, such behavior, or strategy can be well interpreted by the Product Cycle Theory. For empirical studies, see Lu (1984), Vernon (1966, 1979), and Wells (1969). However, for the Hong Kong CE case, further in-depth exploration is needed.

REFERENCES

Aquino, A. ''Changes over Time in the Pattern of Comparative Advantage in Manufactured Goods: An Empirical Analysis for the Period 1962–1974.'' *European Economic Review 15* (1), 1981, 41–62.

Balassa, B. ''Trade Liberalization and Revealed Comparative Advantage.'' *Manchester School of Economics and Social Studies* May 1965, 99–123.

———''A 'Stages' Advantage to Comparative Advantage. *The Newly Industrializing Countries in the World Economy*. New York: Pergamon Press, 1981.

Chen, Edward K. Y. *The Electronics Industry of Hong Kong: An Analysis of Its Growth*. Unpublished M. Phil. thesis, Hong Kong, Hong Kong University, 1971.

Chia, S. Y. (ed.) *Trade, Protectionism and Industrial Adjustment* Vol. 1 (The Textile and Garment Industry). Singapore: ISEAS-NSI, Singapore: 1987.

Cohen, B. I. *Multinational Firms and Asian Exports*. New Haven, Yale University Press, 1975.

Fang, Chan-Hsiung and Chee Ming-Choo. *A Comparison of Foreign Firms in the Electronic Industry of Hong Kong*. KCIE Monograph No. 13, Kagoshima Center of International Economy, Japan, December 1983.

Kojima, K. *Japan and a New World Economic World*. Croom Helm, 1977.

Lall, S. and Paul Streeten. *Foreign Investment, Transnationals and Developing Countries*. London: Macmillan Press, 1977.

Lin, T. B., V. Mok, and Y. P. Ho. *Manufactured Exports and Employment in Hong Kong*. Hong Kong: The Chinese University of Hong Kong Press, 1980.

Lin, T. B. and Chyau Tuan. *Hong Kong's Exports and Economic Structure—Analysis and Forecasts*. Taiwan: The Chung-Hua Institution for Economic Research, 1985.

——— *Economic Cooperation through Foreign Investment—with Special Reference to the Textile Industry in the Asia–Pacific region*. Occasional paper, Economic and Social Committee of Asia Pacific, United Nations, 1987.

Lu, Linyu, *A Case Study of the Product Cycle Theory–Nine Products in Taiwan*. Taiwan, The Chung-Hua Institution for Economic Research, 1984.

Nabseth, L. and G. F. Ray. *The Diffusion of New Industrial Processes: An International Study*. London: Cambridge University Press, 1974.

Sciberras, E. *Multinational Electronics Companies and National Economic Policies*. Greenwich, CT: JAI Press, 1977.

Study on the Hong Kong Electronics Industry. Hong Kong Productivity Centre, April 1984.

Tuan, Chyau. ''Industrial Evolution and Technological Human Resource Development: With special Reference to the Consumer Electronics in Taiwan and Hong Kong.'' *Taiwan Economic Research Monthly 10*(4), April 1987.

Vernon, W. Ruttan. ''International Investment and International Trade in the Product Cycle.'' *Quarterly Journal of Economics 80*, 1966, 190–207.

——— ''The Product Cycle Hypothesis in a New International Environment.'' *Oxford Bulletin of Economics and Statistics 41*(4), 1979, 255-267.

Wells, Louis T., Jr. ''Test of a Product Cycle Model of International Trade: U.S. Exports of Consumer Durables.'' *Quarterly Journal of Economics 83*(1), 1969, 152–162.

Yu, I. K. *Multinational Firms and Economic Development: A Case Study of Electronics Industry in Hong Kong*. Unpublished M. Phil, thesis, Hong Kong, The Chinese University of Hong Kong, 1982.

AMERICAN EXECUTIVES' ATTITUDES TOWARD THE INVESTMENT CLIMATE IN HONG KONG

Kin-chok Mun

I. INTRODUCTION

This study investigates the attitudes of American executives in Hong Kong toward the local investment climate and toward the role of Hong Kong in trade with China. The survey data presented examine whether the change in the future political status of Hong kong is viewed as constraining or enhancing American direct investment. American firms have been the major foreign investor in Hong Kong over the past 30 years. The rise in the number of American residents in Hong Kong relative to the British and America's desire to address its trade

Research in Asian Economic Studies.
Asian Industrialization: Changing Economic Structures,
Volume 1, Part A, pages 187–202.
Copyright © 1988 by JAI Press Inc.
All rights of reproduction in any form reserved.
ISBN: 0-89232-987-4

imbalance by increasing its presence in Asia are potentially positive forces, whereas protectionism looms as a negative countervailing force.

Hong Kong will become a Special Political Area of China in 1997 in accordance with the Sino-British Joint Declaration of 1984. During the transitional period, perceptions conveyed by American executives to their parent companies become the critical vehicle for heightening or lowering expectations concerning the political and economic viability of Hong Kong.

The objectives of the present study are as follows:

1. To investigate the attitudes of American executives in Hong Kong toward the investment climate here in three future periods: 1987–1990, 1990–1997, and after 1997.
2. To identify the factors which are of the greatest concern to American executives in Hong Kong during these three periods.
3. To identify similarities and differences between attitude patterns of American executives in the three periods investigated.
4. To compare attitudes of American executives with those of Hong Kong executives.
5. To compare the investment climate in Hong Kong with that in the other three small dragons in Asia (South Korea, Taiwan, and Singapore) as viewed by the American executives in Hong Kong.

II. SELECTING THE FACTORS FOR ASSESSMENT

In analyzing the business environment in any country or locale, the first step is to select relevant factors as the basis for assessment. These screening factors can be classified into two major categories: "hard" and "soft" factors.

"Hard" factors refer generally to the physical infrastructure, such as transportation, communications, and energy, whereas "soft" factors are basically structural ones that reflect the political, economic, financial, and market environment of a country. "Hard" factors are strongly correlated with the level of economic development of a country. Generally, the better the "hard" factors, the higher the level of economic development. Similarly, a positive relationship exists between "soft" factors and level of economic development. In past years, scholars and research firms have proposed different methods for assessing investment climate, emphasizing environmental factors, most of which were obviously "soft" in nature (Stobaugh, 1969; Business International Corporation, 1981; Ingo, 1982).

In 1979, Mun and Ho conducted a survey on investment climate in Hong Kong by using 20 "soft" factors. In 1984 and in 1986 the Industrial Department of the Hong Kong Government conducted two surveys on "Overseas Investment in Hong Kong's Manufacturing Industries." Of the 10 most favorable factors chosen by the foreign investors, only 2 were considered "hard" factors (Mun and Ho, 1979: 18, 45).

Following the methods previously used, 15 environmental factors were selected as the bases for assessment in this survey, Fourteen are defined as "soft" whereas only one (infrastructure) is a "hard" factor. Factors selected in this survey are as follows:

I. Political Environment
   1. Political stability
   2. Government's liberal economic policy
   3. Private enterprise system
   4. Government administration

II. Economic Environment
   1. Economic growth
   2. Export growth
   3. Free port

III. Financial environment
   1. A free money market
   2. Tax rates
   3. Banking system

IV. Marketing environment
   1. Marketing opportunities in Hong Kong
   2. Marketing opportunities in China

V. Labor conditions
   1. Labor productivity
   2. Industrial relations

VI. Infrastructure

The 15 factors selected are classified into 6 "aggregate" groups. The infrastructure in Hong Kong, such as international communication and transportation facilities, has long been well-developed in comparison with those of neighboring countries. For this reason, one single factor is adequate for representing infrastructure in Hong Kong. As the remaining 14 factors are "soft" in nature, the method used for assessing investment climate in this study is a soft factor approach. Thus, political, economic, and financial factors have major weights in the present assessment.

Five-point scales were used for investigating attitudes of the respondents: very good, good, fair, poor, and very poor. Respondents were asked to rate each factor for three different time periods: 1987–1990, 1990–1997, and after 1997. The 15 factors were unweighted because the main objective of this study, as stated above, was to identify changes in the patterns of attitudes of American executives for three time periods. A profile analysis was considered most appropriate for this purpose.

The mail survey method was decided upon for investigating American executives' attitudes toward the investment climate in Hong Kong. Repondents were randomly selected from the Membership Directory of the American Chamber of Commerce in Hong Kong (1986). Three hundred questionnaires were sent to the selected American firms, of which 86 were returned; the response rate was 28.6% as shown in Table 1. For purposes of comparison, another 290 questionnaires were sent to local or Hong Kong firms selected from companies listed in the Hong Kong External Trade Yearbook (1986). By comparing the attitudes of American executives with those of Hong Kong executives, similarities and differences in emphasis of assessment factors were identified. The response rate of the Hong Kong sample was 15.8%, lower than that of the American sample.

The reason for choosing exporters as the surveyed repondents was based on the fact that most foreign manufacturing firms are export oriented. Their attitudes were considered very relevant to the assessment of investment climate in Hong Kong. The survey was conducted in August 1986.

Table 1. Response Rates of the Samples

Respondent	*Number of questionnaires sent out*	*Number of questionnaires returned*	*Response rate (%)*
American firms	300	86	28.6
Hong Kong firms	290	46	15.8
Total	590	132	22.4

III. SURVEY FINDINGS

The findings in this survey can be summarized as follows:

A. From an Excellent to a Moderate Climate

The general investment climate in Hong Kong would change from an excellent situation to a moderate one during the three time period for comparison. Table 2 shows the overall means of American and Hong Kong executives' views on the 15 environmental factors.

In the American executive sample, the overall mean of the 15 factors declined from 4.246 in the first period (1987–1990) to 3.799 and 3.184 in the second (1990–1997) and third periods (after 1997), respectively. The Hong Kong executives had views similar to the American executives. Comparing changes in attitudes of American executives with those of Hong Kong executives, the former should be considered somewhat more optimistic than the latter.

Profile analysis or disaggregate analysis of the 15 factors is presented in Table 3. For purposes of comparisons the mean values of these factors in the American and Hong Kong samples are shown in Figure 1. During the first period, American executives considered the private enterprise system (mean = 4.65), a free money market (4.64), free port (4.59), infrastructure (4.44), and banking system (4.42) as the five most favorable factors for Hong Kong. In the second period, mean ratings of these five factors declined. However, they remain favorable relative to other factors.

All factors received lower ratings during the third period than during the second period, reflecting worries of American executives. Relatively, free port, marketing opportunities to China, infrastructure, banking system, and labor productivity are most favorable during the third period. The two most troublesome factors for American executives in the third period, as judged by their relatively low mean values, are government administration (2.6) and government's liberal economic policy (2.87). This shows that political factors are exceptionally important to American executives during the third period. The significant change

Table 2. Overall Means of Fifteen Environmental Factors

Time period	*American executives*	*Hong Kong executives*	*Total sample*
1987–1990	4.246	4.033	4.139
1990–1997	3.799	3.335	3.676
After 1997	3.184	2.880	3.032

Table 3. Summary of U.S. Executive Views on Hong Kong's Investment Climate

Factors	*Percentage distribution*						*Mean*	*Standard Deviation*
	Very good	*Good*	*Fair*	*Poor*	*Very poor*	*Total*		
1. Political stability								
(a) Present to 1990	35	57	7	1	—	100	4.26	0.639
(b) 1990–1997	2	42	42	12	2	100	3.33	0.762
(c) After 1997	2	27	46	20	5	100	3.01	0.876
2. Export growth								
(a) Present to 1990	24	60	16	—	—	100	4.07	0.632
(b) 1990–1997	10	49	32	8	1	100	3.57	0.826
(c) After 1997	5	31	44	16	4	100	3.17	0.891
3. Industrial relations								
(a) Present to 1990	22	66	12	—	—	100	4.11	0.575
(b) 1990–1997	4	48	39	7	2	100	3.43	0.775
(c) After 1997	1	26	60	13	—	100	3.16	0.649
4. Economic growth								
(a) Present to 1990	27	57	16	—	—	100	4.11	0.651
(b) 1990–1997	6	41	39	13	1	100	3.37	0.827
(c) After 1997	1	26	51	15	7	100	3.00	0.864
5. Marketing opportunities in China								
(a) Present to 1990	8	31	46	14	1	100	3.32	0.858
(b) 1990–1997	4	55	34	7	—	100	3.55	0.681
(c) After 1997	10	45	37	7	1	100	3.70	0.813

6. Marketing opportunities in H.K.								
(a) Present to 1990	21	69	10	—	—	100	4.11	0.554
(b) 1990–1997	5	58	30	6	1	100	3.59	0.726
(c) After 1997	3	38	46	11	2	100	3.28	0.782
7. Labour productivity								
(a) Present to 1990	41	56	3	—	—	100	4.37	0.554
(b) 1990–1997	16	66	15	3	—	100	3.97	0.641
(c) After 1997	4	47	38	10	1	100	3.41	0.773
8. Private enterprise system								
(a) Present to 1990	66	33	1	—	—	100	4.65	0.505
(b) 1990–1997	22	66	12	—	—	100	4.11	0.575
(c) After 1997	5	22	49	18	6	100	3.02	0.913
9. Government's liberal economic policy								
(a) Present to 1990	42	45	13	—	—	100	4.29	0.684
(b) 1990–1997	16	55	24	5	—	100	3.83	0.754
(c) After 1997	2	19	51	20	8	100	2.87	0.892
10. Free port								
(a) Present to 1990	62	36	2	—	—	100	4.59	0.540
(b) 1990–1997	45	45	8	2	—	100	4.35	0.682
(c) After 1997	15	41	34	9	1	100	3.59	0.899
11. Infrastructure								
(a) Present to 1990	51	43	5	1	—	100	4.44	0.645
(b) 1990–1997	29	57	9	4	1	100	4.09	0.796
(c) After 1997	7	42	33	15	3	100	3.37	0.911

cont.

Factors	Percentage distribution						Mean	Standard Deviation
	Very good	*Good*	*Fair*	*Poor*	*Very poor*	*Total*		
12. Tax rates								
(a) Present to 1990	41	52	6	—	1	100	4.10	0.650
(b) 1990–1997	19	64	15	2	—	100	3.99	0.664
(c) After 1997	4	37	33	24	2	100	3.16	0.912
13. Government administration								
(a) Present to 1990	28	52	15	4	1	100	4.02	0.826
(b) 1990–1997	9	42	36	9	4	100	3.44	0.915
(c) After 1997	1	8	49	32	10	100	2.60	0.829
14. Banking system								
(a) Present to 1990	46	49	5	—	—	100	4.42	0.583
(b) 1990–1997	30	57	12	1	—	100	4.16	0.666
(c) After 1997	4	50	42	3	1	100	3.51	0.684
15. A free money market								
(a) Present to 1990	65	34	1	—	—	100	4.64	0.507
(b) 1990–1997	36	50	14	—	—	100	4.22	0.676
(c) After 1997	1	30	52	10	7	100	3.08	0.853

Figure 1. Attitudes of American and Hong Kong executives toward investment climate in Hong Kong: mean values (five-point scale). Mean values of American and Hong Kong executives' views on 15 environmental factors in three periods are represented by 1, 2, 3 and a, b, c, respectively.

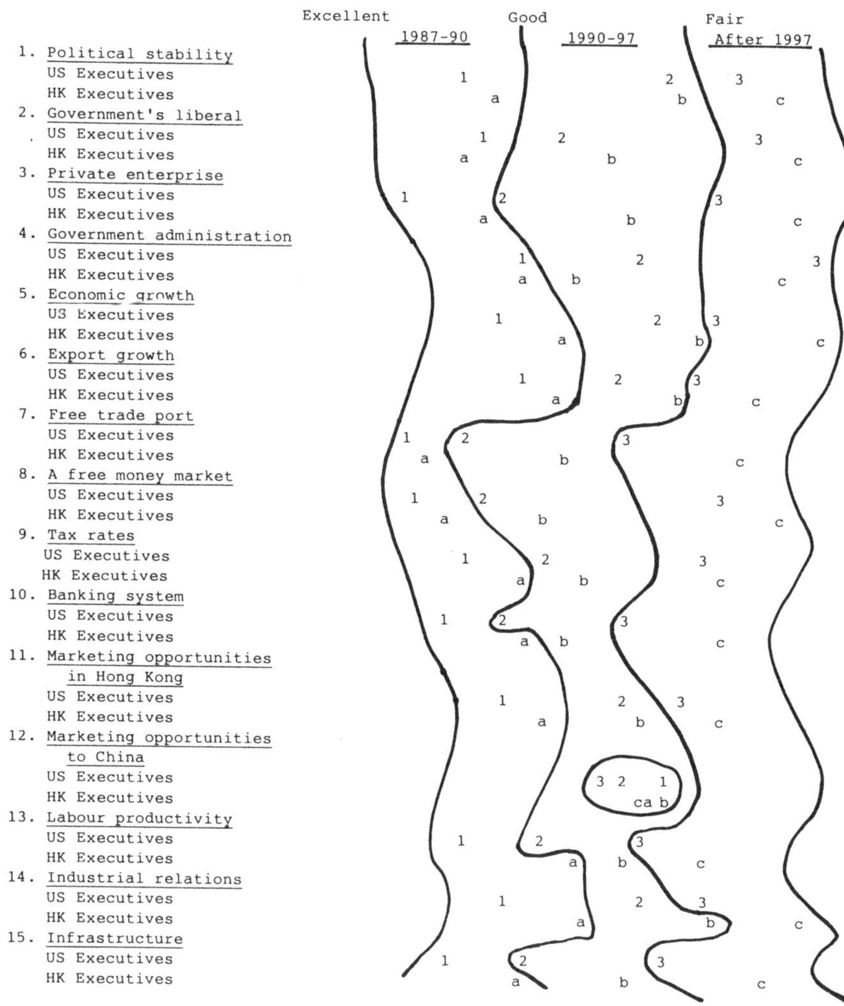

between the first and third periods lies in the factor "a free money market" as judged from the difference of its two mean values. This, again, indicates the concern of American executives about the free movement of capital and convertibility of currency.

B. Similar Attitude Patterns of American and Hong Kong Executives

Comparing changes in attitude patterns between American and Hong Kong executives, similarities exist between the two groups, as indicated by the estimates of Pearson coefficients shown in Table 4. The Pearson coefficients of the attitude patterns of American and Hong Kong executives in the three periods are 0.8508, 0.8204, and 0.7361, respectively. This reflects a strong similarity in attitude change between the two executive groups, suggesting a "Hong Kong residency" perspective that is congruent with regard to assessment of later business conditions.

Table 4. Pearson Coefficients of Attitude Patterns of the American and Hong Kong Executives[a]

	A1	*A2*	*A3*	*H1*	*H2*	*H3*
A1	—	0.6963	-0.0409	0.8508	—	—
A2		—	0.4555	—	0.8204	
A3			—	—	—	0.7361
H1				—	0.7039	-0.4062
H2					—	0.3592
H3						—

[a] A1, A2, A3, attitude patterns of the American executives in three periods. H1, H2, H3, attitude patterns of the Hong Kong executives in three periods.

C. A Significant Change in Attitude Patterns between First and Third Periods

By comparing changes in attitude patterns of American executives in three periods, a relatively strong correlation coefficient of 0.6963 separated the first and second periods, whereas a moderate correlation coefficent of 0.4555 differentiates between the second and third periods. An almost negligible coefficient separates the first and third periods. There is already a significant shift in mean ratings of the 15 factors in the three periods. Based on these correlation coefficients, it can be stated that the American executives surveyed expect a significant change in the relative position of the 15 environmental factors between the first and the third period.

D. Growing Marketing Opportunities to China

In comparison with other factors, the factor "marketing opportunities to China" is slightly improved in the second and third periods over the first period. The main reason for this difference is probably future expectations of the growing role of Hong Kong in The United States–China trade. A survey conducted in 1985 (Mun and Chan, 1986) also supports this view, as shown in Table 5.

Seven factors emerge as most favorable for Hong Kong in its interface with United States–China trade, according to American executives in Hong Kong. They are the excellent geographic location, international communication facilities, housing (compared with China), recreation facilities (compared with China), available China experts, banking service support, and information collection about China's development. Each of these seven factors has a mean value of 4 or greater. Warehousing, with a mean value of 3.96, is close to this group of most favorable factors. The results of the first survey supporting the favorable attitudes of American executives toward marketing opportunities to China is validated by the second survey.

E. Declining Favorable Position among Four Asian Small Dragons

Respondents were also asked to compare the general investment climate of Hong Kong with that of other small dragons in Asia (South Korea, Taiwan, and Singapore) during the three periods. The results are described in Figure 2. In the first period, Hong Kong is considered as the most favorable place for direct investment among Asia's four small dragons (61%), but its favorable position declines in the second (25%) and third periods (24%). In addition to competition with other Asian small dragons in the export of light industrial products, Hong Kong also faces future competition for international investment.

Table 5. Attitudes of U.S. Executives toward the Role of Hong Kong in U.S.–China Trade

	Percenage distribution							
	Most important	*Important*	*Medium*	*Less important*	*Unimportant*	*Total*	*Mean*	*Standard Deviation*
1. Geographic location	54	42	2	2	—	100	4.48	0.641
2. International communication facilities	63	33	4	—	—	100	4.58	0.572
3. Housing an housing facilities	50	35	15	—	—	100	4.34	0.738
4. Recreation facilities	43	39	16	2	—	100	4.23	0.790
5. Available China experts	45	35	16	4	—	100	4.21	0.856
6. Warehousing and transportation facilities	27	52	12	9	—	100	3.96	0.885
7. Banking service facilities	47	31	14	6	2	100	4.15	1.007
8. A strategic location for analyzing policy change in China	23	54	15	8	—	100	3.92	0.837
9. Information collection about China's development	31	43	20	6	—	100	4.00	0.872

10. The third leading financial center in the world	33	37	20	8	2	100	3.92	1.017
11. A place for training Chinese managers	26	35	24	12	3	100	3.66	1.108
12. Connections to Chinese trading companies in Hong Kong	24	32	22	16	6	100	3.52	1.199
13. An agent for transferring technology to China	18	28	28	20	6	100	3.27	1.201

Figure 2. Company executive's attitudes toward the most flavorable place for direct investment among Asia's four small dragons. H, Hong Kong; K, South Korea; S, Singapore; T, Taiwan.

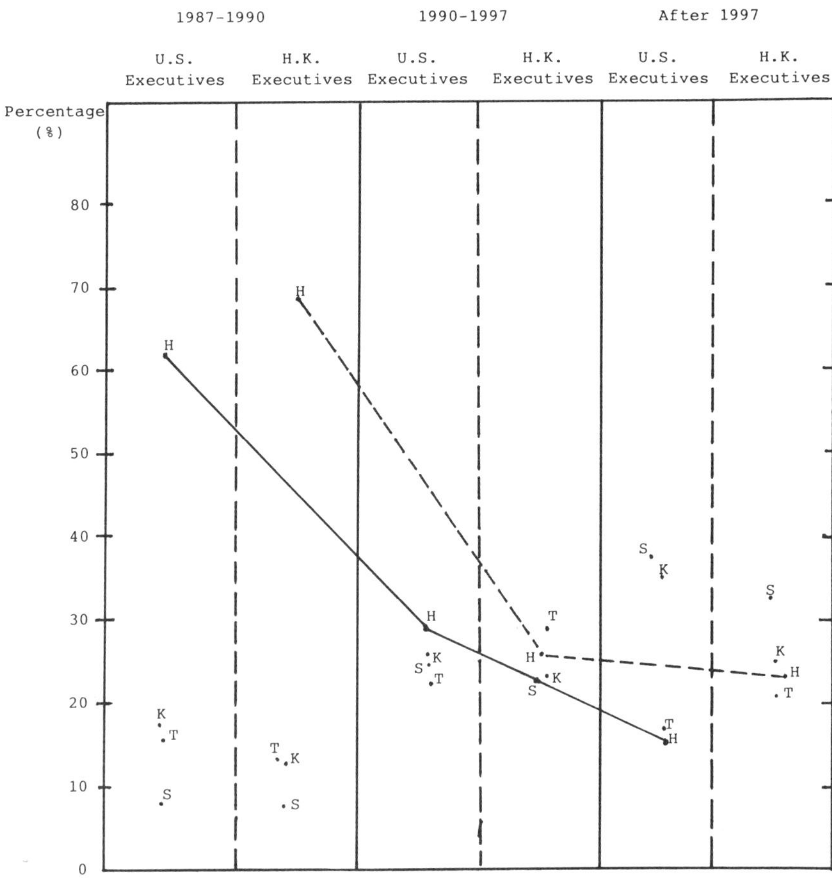

IV. LIMITATIONS OF THE SURVEY

The primary limitations of this survey are as follows: First, the attitudes of American executives represent general views of exporters, not those of executives in specific sectors. Second, attitudes of respondents many be influenced by a general "prediction," popularized by the prevalent public opinion that Hong Kong faces an unstable situation by 1990. Third, American executives living in Hong Kong are likely to have particularly favorable attitudes toward Hong Kong in comparison to Asia's other small dragons (during the first period). Fourth, it is possible that American executives will change their ratings (positively or negatively) on these 15 factors when the Basic Law is promulgated and some uncertainties about the Sino-British declaration are reduced.

V. CONCLUSION

The findings of this survey indicate that American executives in Hong Kong still worry about the future investment climate in Hong Kong. Before promulgation of the Basic Law, foreign firms are uncertain about whether policies will be favorable to investors. Furthermore, there may be concerns about whether the Basic law will truly prevail over political factors in the future.

Second, the future of Hong Kong will be substantially affected by the political–economic development in China. If China can demonstrate continuity in her economic development and maintain her political stability, American investors will probably have more favorable attitudes toward the investment climate in Hong Kong.

Third, growing protectionism in the United States will influence American investors' attitudes. Since the United States is the most important export market for Hong Kong, with 45% of total exports, any restrictions on exports from Hong Kong would be unfavorable to American investments in Hong Kong.

Fourth, the technological environment of Hong Kong is becoming increasingly unfavorable in comparison with that in South Korea and Taiwan. In comparison to other dragons, Hong Kong lacks basic research and governmental support for technology transfer. High technology provides a climate conducive to foreign investments. Low technology levels and higher fuel costs bring about competitive disadvantages for foreign manufacturers in the world market. Although the first three uncertainties are beyond the control of Hong Kong, the fourth one can be reduced by introducing various incentives for improving technology and by increased government funding for research and development.

Hong Kong desperately needs policies which encourage technology transfer at the grass roots level. Funding of a strategy for technology enhancement would increase Hong Kong's value to China and Hong Kong's credibility vis-à-vis competitive countries. If investment climate is to be improved, technology must be viewed as a route to enhanced creativity within the business community. Along with technology transfer should come incentive mechanisms for obtaining and channeling venture capital into Hong Kong.

REFERENCES

Hong Kong Government Industry Department. *Report on the Survey of Overseas Investment in Hong Kong's Manufacturing Industry*, 1984 and 1986.

Ingo, Walter. "Country Risk Assessment." In Walter and Murray (eds.) *Handbook of International Business*, New York: John Wiley, 1982, 10–16 and 21.

Mun, Kin-chok and Tsang-sing Chan. "The Role of Hong Kong in United States–China Trade." *Columbia Journal of World Business* Spring 1986.

Mun, Kin-chok and Suk-ching Ho. "Foreign Investment in Hong Kong." In Lin-Lee-Simonis (ed.) *Hong Kong: Economic, Social and Political Studies in Development*, N. E. Sharpe Inc. and Dawson, 1979, 279–285.

Managing and Evaluating Country Risk. Business International Corporation, New York, 1981, 31–35.

Stobaugh, Robert B. "How to Analyze Foreign Investment Climates." *Harvard Business Review* September–October 1969, 100–108.

HONG KONG–UNITED STATES TRADE: ITS DETERMINANTS

W. L. Chou and Y. C. Shih

I. INTRODUCTION

Hong Kong, with scarce endowments in natural resources and food production, relies almost entirely on trade with the rest of the world. Hong Kong's imports cover a wide range of tradable goods. To pay for imports, Hong Kong has made great efforts to earn foreign exchange through exports. Hence, the industries of Hong Kong are primarily export oriented.

The importance of foreign trade to the Hong Kong economy can be seen from the ratio of trade to gross domestic product (GDP). During the past decade, for instance, merchandise trade including domestic exports, reexports, and imports, averaged more than 150% of Hong Kong's GDP. In view of the openness of the

Research in Asian Economic Studies.
Asian Industrialization: Changing Economic Structures,
Volume 1, Part A, pages 203–230.
Copyright © 1988 by JAI Press Inc.
All rights of reproduction in any form reserved.
ISBN: 0-89232-987-4

Hong Kong economy and the fact that the United States has been the most important trading partner of Hong Kong and provides the largest market for Hong Kong's exports, a study of the bilateral trade between Hong Kong and the United States would help to understand the shaping of Hong Kong's trade flows and economic performance. Furthermore, Hong Kong has had a long-time trade surplus with the United States, and the U.S. trade deficit has grown substantially every year since 1980. An analysis of the bilateral trade flows would reveal more clearly the factors contributing to the Hong Kong–U.S. trade imbalance.

This study first analyzes the aggregate trade flows between Hong Kong and the United States. After reviewing developments in the bilateral trade, we examine the behavior of Hong Kong's major merchandise imports and exports with the United States. For many years Hong Kong has found its largest market in the United States for almost all its principal commodity exports, ranging from garments to jewelry. At the same time, the United States is also one of the main suppliers of Hong Kong's imports, particularly of capital goods. An overview of Hong Kong's trade flows with the United States and the major U.S. barriers to Hong Kong's exports are presented in Section II. Section III discusses briefly the Hong Kong trade balance with the United States. Although Hong Kong has had a chronic trade deficit with the rest of the world as a whole (except 1985 and 1986) since 1947, it has run a surplus with the United States for many years, primarily due to the sluggish growth of imports from the United States. Section IV gives a statistical analysis of the pattern of Hong Kong trade flows with the United States, and explains the bilateral trade in terms of incomes, prices, and exchange rates. Trade flows are examined at aggregate and disaggregated levels. The equations for imports and exports in real terms are estimated by using both the ordinary least squares (OLS) and the seemingly unrelated regressions (SUR) techniques. Summary and conclusions are presented in Section V.

II. HONG KONG–U.S. TRADE: AN OVERVIEW

Before 1950, Hong Kong was mainly a small entrepot base dealing in the distribution and repackaging of commodities to and from China. The situation was drastically changed since the Korean War, and Hong Kong has grown rapidly, becoming a trading center and the thirteenth largest trading entity in the world.[1]

A. Exports

Hong Kong is the largest exporter in the world by value of clothing and toys and the biggest by volume of watches and clocks.[2] Its domestic exports (different from reexports) have found their major consumer markets in North America and Western Europe, and the largest importer of Hong Kong's merchandise is the United States. Over the period from 1976 to 1986 the growth rate averaged

22.9% per year, and the value of exports to the United States has increased by 471%. Only in one year in this period, 1985, did the value fall below the level in the preceding year. However, as shown in Table 1, exports in real terms dipped in 1982 as well as in 1985.

The importance of the U.S. market for Hong Kong domestic exports is further evidenced in the percentage share of total domestic exports. An average of 41% of Hong Kong's products has been exported to the United States after 1980, compared to an average of 36% for the period from 1976 to 1980. The higher U.S. market share ratio after 1980 suggests an increasing reliance on the U.S. market for Hong Kong's domestic exports.

The top four categories of commodities that account for more than half of Hong Kong's domestic exports in 1985 are, in order of their export value, clothing, watches and clocks, textiles, and plastic toys, and the United States has been by far the largest market for all but textiles. Even in textiles the United States used to lead other countries in importing from Hong Kong until 1982 when China began to emerge as the largest buyer. In addition, the United States is also the main outlet for a number of other products exported by Hong Kong, including electrical and nonelectrical household equipment, electronic components for computers, and jewelry.

As previously mentioned, Hong Kong is the biggest exporter of garments in the world: approximately one-third of its domestic exports fall in this category. It can be seen from Table 2 that the amount of clothing exported to the United States as a percentage of Hong Kong's total exports of clothing increased steadily from 34.7% in 1980 to 55.2% in 1985. Table 2 also indicates the growing importance of the U.S. market for Hong Kong's exports of watches and toys. For commodities of smaller export value the reliance of Hong Kong on the U.S. market becomes even greater. The United States imported, for example, an average of 81.6% of Hong Kong's electronic parts for computers, and 61.2% of electrical and nonelectrical household equipment for export, over the 10-year period from 1976 to 1985. Besides, the U.S. market share in jewelry and broadcast receivers has also grown significantly in recent years, strengthening its leading position in Hong Kong's export market.

B. Protection and Exports

With virtually all of its imports subject to no or low trade barriers, Hong Kong has little room for tariff concessions and retaliation against trade protection, but it has to face a wide range of trade restraints imposed by countries intending to protect their domestic industries and markets.

In recent years there have been increasing pressures in the United States for dealing with its trade deficit through a more general restriction on imports. Since the United States has long been Hong Kong's largest trading partner and the major impact of protection on Hong Kong's exports is in textiles and clothing, it

Table 1. Hong Kong's Domestic Exports to the United States, 1976–1986

	1976	*1977*	*1978*	*1979*	*1980*	*1981*	*1982*	*1983*	*1984*	*1985*	*1986*
Value (in billions of current H.K. dollars)	11.2	13.6	15.1	18.8	22.6	29.2	31.2	43.8	61.4	57.7	64.2
Annual growth rate (percentage change on previous year)	53.2	20.6	11.6	24.3	20.2	29.3	6.9	40.3	40.1	-6.0	11.3
Percentage share of H.K. total domestic exports	34.4	39.7	37.2	33.6	33.1	36.3	37.6	42.0	44.5	44.4	41.7
Value (in billions of H.K. dollars, deflated by export unit value index, 1981 = 100)	17.0	19.6	21.0	22.9	25.4	29.2	28.9	36.2	43.8	40.9	44.6

Source: Compiled and calculated from *Hong Kong Annual Digest of Statistics* and *Hong Kong Monthly Digest of Statistics*, Hong Kong, Census and Statistics Department, various issues.

Table 2. Domestic Exports to the United States as a Percentage of Total Domestic Exports, by Commodities, 1976–1985

	1976	*1977*	*1978*	*1979*	*1980*	*1981*	*1982*	*1983*	*1984*	*1985*
Clothing	32.0	39.0	39.9	35.8	34.7	38.7	40.2	47.0	50.6	55.2
Watches and clocks	29.7	31.8	29.1	24.7	25.8	27.4	35.0	37.3	39.1	40.4
Textiles	19.0	19.1	16.6	12.8	13.3	14.0	11.7	14.8	14.7	14.2
Toys	51.1	50.0	45.9	44.2	40.5	45.1	49.9	48.9	60.7	59.2
Household equipment	59.0	57.9	52.3	59.3	61.8	62.6	61.9	66.9	67.9	62.7
Electronic parts for computers	79.9	80.9	83.2	86.9	88.3	93.1	89.5	81.3	66.1	66.7
Jewelry	47.6	46.8	45.9	41.8	34.4	38.4	36.4	43.9	50.3	51.5
Broadcast receivers	44.2	44.8	37.9	26.8	29.7	33.7	40.8	44.5	53.3	49.2

Source: Calculated from *Hong Kong Annual Digest of Statistics*, various issues.

is natural that Hong Kong feels threatened by a resurgence of protectionism in the United States.

U.S. trade protections against Hong Kong have existed for more than 20 years since the United States and Hong Kong entered into textile trade in the late 1950s. In 1974, the Arrangement Regarding Trade in Textiles, commonly known as the Multi-Fiber Agreement (MFA), was created to avoid market disruptions on trade in textile products made from cotton, wool, and man-made fibers. The Arrangement provides a general framework within which Hong Kong enters bilateral agreements with various developed countries. Under the Hong Kong–U.S. Textile Agreement, 1982–1987, for instance, a growth rate of about 6% a year was allowed for Hong Kong's garment and textile exports to the United States. Specific quantitative limits have been imposed on various categories of sensitive textile products, and the nonrestricted categories are subject to the threat of "call-halt," a system under which the United States can stop the import of a particular category of product at any time it deems necessary. Such trade restraints would inevitably restrict Hong Kong's trade growth. Furthermore, the rules of origin unilaterally imposed by the United States would affect significantly the knitting industry subcontracting in China and tend to disrupt Hong Kong's normal trade practices.

Trade flows between Hong Kong and the United States would be further distorted should the Textile and Apparel Trade Enforcement Bill, also known as the Jenkins Bill, be brought into effect. It is estimated that the Bill, if enacted, could substantially reduce both Hong Kong's MFA and non-MFA textile and apparel exports.[3]

To keep its export-oriented economy rolling, Hong Kong needs to continue its long-term trade growth in spite of the threat of increasing trade restraints. In the case of facing higher import tariffs Hong Kong may preserve its export market by reducing its export prices. Large price changes require significant cost and resource adjustments that may take a long period of time. The economy in Hong Kong has been known for its market efficiency and resilience in adapting itself to external shocks, and it seems that Hong Kong is prepared to meet with the challenge of mounting protectionist sentiment.

However, price and cost adjustments may not be effective in dealing with nontariff barriers such as quotas. Unlike tariffs they impose absolute limits on trade and inhibit market responses. Thus, they are direct and inflexible, irrespective of market adjustments. To cope with quantitative trade restrictions Hong Kong has managed to obtain big quota entitlement through negotiations. But more importantly, manufacturers make efforts to move into higher priced sectors by improving the quality of exports on the one hand and switch gradually to the products that are not, or less subject to trade restraints on the other. Consequently, although hampered by trade protections, apparel exports to the United States may not be necessarily impeded by tightened controls on trade flows.

Table 3 presents some figures on Hong Kong's exports of clothing articles from 1976 to 1985. In spite of progressively harsh protection measures imposed

Table 3. Hong Kong's Domestic Exports of Clothing, 1976-1986

	1976	*1977*	*1978*	*1979*	*1980*	*1981*	*1982*	*1983*	*1984*	*1985*	*1986*
Clothing exports (in billions of current H.K. dollars)	14.3	13.9	15.7	20.1	23.3	28.3	28.8	34.4	46.7	44.9	52.2
Percentage of H.K. total merchandise exports	43.8	39.7	38.6	36.0	34.1	35.2	34.7	32.9	33.9	34.6	33.9
Exports of apparel to the U.S. (in billions of current H.K. dollars)	4.6	5.4	6.3	7.2	8.1	10.9	11.6	16.2	23.6	24.8	N.A.
Percentage of H.K. total clothing exports	32.0	39.0	39.9	35.8	34.7	38.7	40.2	47.0	50.6	55.2	N.A.
Annual growth rate (%)	48.4	17.4	16.7	14.3	12.5	34.6	6.4	39.7	45.7	5.1	N.A.

Sources: Calculated from *Hong Kong Annual Digest of Statistics* and *Hong Kong Monthly Digest of Statistics*, various issues.

in recent years, Hong Kong's total clothing exports managed to grow steadily in most of the years under observation. Even in 1985 when Hong Kong's exports of all merchandise and clothing articles both decreased, the values of clothing exports to the United States still continued to climb, thus increasing the U.S. share in Hong Kong's total exports of clothing from 34.7% in 1980 to 55.2% in 1985. Actually the average annual growth rate of clothing exports to the United States for the period after 1980 (26.3%) is higher than that before 1980. However, as a percentage share of Hong Kong's exports of all merchandise, clothing articles declined noticeably after 1976, although the percentage share was fairly stable for the period from 1980 to 1986. The decrease in clothing's share of total exports reflects to a certain extent Hong Kong's progress in product diversification for export, lessening Hong Kong's dependence on apparel exports.

C. Imports

Since Hong Kong lacks natural resources and agricultural products, imports are as important as exports, if not more so. The value of total merchandise imports usually exceeds that of exports. Being a major entrepot base Hong Kong imports not only for domestic use but also for reexports. In our analysis only retained imports, total imports net of reexports, from the United States are considered.

The larger part of Hong Kong's imports have come from neighboring countries in Asia, but the United states, ranked third after China and Japan, is among the main suppliers in the Hong Kong's import market. In terms of trade value, however, the importance of the United States in Hong Kong's imports is far less than in exports. As it is shown in Table 4, retained imports from the United States account for an average of 11.1% of Hong Kong's total retained imports over the period from 1976 to 1986. In comparison 38.6% of Hong Kong's domestic export sales have been made to the United States for the same period. Table 4 also indicates that the growth rate of imports from the United States decreased on average from 14.4% before 1980 to 5.2% after 1980, and imports valued at constant prices dipped in 3 successive years after 1980 and again in 1985 and 1986, all contributing to the shrinkage of the U.S. share in the Hong Kong market.

For commodities classified by end-use, the United States has been one of the major suppliers of raw materials and semimanufactures, capital goods, consumer goods, and foodstuffs, and it was Hong Kong's largest supplier of capital goods until 1976. The percentage share of Hong Kong's imports by the United States in each category is given in Table 5. It can be seen that, in terms of market share, imports of raw materials and foodstuffs from the United States remained stable over the period under observation. However, in recent years, China and Taiwan have increased their sales in consumer goods in Hong Kong,

Table 4. Hong Kong's Retained Imports from the United States, 1976–1986

	1976	*1977*	*1978*	*1979*	*1980*	*1981*	*1982*	*1983*	*1984*	*1985*	*1986*
Value (in billions of current H.K. dollars)	4.1	4.8	5.9	8.8	10.1	10.4	10.5	13.1	15.9	12.4	12.8
Annual growth rate (%)	19.5	19.0	22.3	36.6	24.4	3.5	1.1	24.9	20.7	-21.7	2.9
Percentage share of total retained imports	11.8	12.5	11.9	12.3	12.3	10.8	10.7	11.0	10.6	9.8	8.3
Value (in billions of H.K. dollars deflated by import unit value index, 1981 = 100)	6.7	7.7	9.0	10.3	11.7	10.4	8.9	9.3	10.2	8.0	8.1

Sources: Calculated from *Hong Kong Annual Digest of Statistics* and *Hong Kong Monthly Digest of Statistics*, various issues.

Table 5. Growth Rate of U.S. Imports from Hong Kong and Their Percentage Share of Hong Kong's Total Imports, by End-use, 1976–1985 (Percent)

	1976	*1977*	*1978*	*1979*	*1980*	*1981*	*1982*	*1983*	*1984*	*1985*
Raw materials and semi-manufactures										
Growth rate	73.5	15.7	25.7	45.9	17.2	2.9	0.5	35.4	44.0	–25.2
Percentage share	8.8	9.6	9.2	9.5	9.0	8.5	8.7	8.8	9.6	7.4
Consumer goods										
Growth rate	30.4	–0.2	48.7	26.1	22.6	9.8	12.0	8.3	7.5	9.9
Percentage share	14.6	11.8	12.0	11.8	10.6	9.2	9.9	8.9	7.6	7.3
Capital goods										
Growth rate	14.6	24.1	7.8	52.3	46.3	9.7	5.2	16.1	39.7	–8.0
Percentage share	26.9	28.0	24.0	24.6	27.2	22.5	22.3	22.9	22.0	18.3
Foodstuffs										
Growth rate	19.8	20.9	13.0	15.5	21.5	24.8	12.7	15.9	6.9	10.4
Percentage share	11.5	12.8	12.8	12.6	12.7	13.0	12.8	12.6	12.9	14.2

Source: Calculated from *Hong Kong Annual Report Digest of Statistics*, various issies.

whereas Japan and Taiwan take an increasingly larger share in the market for capital goods, causing the United States to lose ground in the Hong Kong's import market since 1980.

III. HONG KONG TRADE BALANCE WITH THE UNITED STATES

As pointed out, the value of Hong Kong's total imports usually exceeds that of exports. Therefore, throughout the period of analysis, Hong Kong had a deficit on visible trade up to 1985, which was met by a surplus in services and capital movement.[4] Notwithstanding the multilateral trade deficit, Hong Kong has run a persistent trade surplus with the United States and as seen in Table 6, the amount of bilateral surplus has actually grown every year since 1976.

An alternative and probably more rational yardstick of trade surplus is the surplus gap that measures the extent of surplus relative to exports. As Table 6 indicates, the surplus gap decreased in the late 1970s, but increased steadily in the 1980s, rising from 55.5% in 1980 to 80.1% in 1986.

The reason for the widening of the surplus margin is that the growth rate of Hong Kong's exports to the United States exceeds that of imports from the United States every year during the 1980s (See Tables 1 and 4). Even in 1985 when Hong Kong's exports to the United States actually decreased and had a negative growth rate, imports fell even more, thus enlarging the surplus gap.

A closer examination of Table 5 reveals that it is the erratic variations in imports of raw materials and capital goods and sluggish growth in foodstuffs and consumer goods that account for relatively lower growth rates of total imports when compared with that of Hong Kong's exports to the United States. The value of retained imports from the United States shows only a 27% growth between 1980 and 1986 whereas the value of domestic exports increased by 184% over the same period. If reexports are added to retained imports, the growth rate shoots up to 76%, but is still much less than that of Hong Kong's exports to the United States.

One thing that should be pointed out in analyzing the bilateral trade balance with the United States is that the value of retained imports at constant dollars actually declined by 30% from 1980 to 1986 whereas that of domestic exports to the United States increased by 71%. Therefore, the growth of the nominal value of retained imports was caused only by the increase in prices of U.S. products. As a matter of fact, the price of U.S. exports to Hong Kong has increased much more rapidly than that of the U.S. major competitors in Asia, namely China, Japan, and Taiwan.[5]

Table 6. Hong Kong Trade Balance (in Billions of Current H.K. Dollars)

	1976	*1977*	*1978*	*1979*	*1980*	*1981*	*1982*	*1983*	*1984*	*1985*	*1986*
Hong Kong multilateral trade balance	–1.7	–3.9	–9.1	–9.9	–13.4	–16.2	–15.5	–14.7	–1.9	3.7	0.6
Hong Kong–U.S. bilateral trade balance	7.1	8.7	9.2	10.7	12.5	18.8	20.7	30.7	45.5	45.3	51.4
Surplus gap with the U.S. (%)	63.8	64.3	60.8	57.0	55.5	64.4	66.3	70.0	74.2	78.5	80.1

Sources: Calculated from *Hong Kong Annual Digest of Statistics* and *Hong Kong Monthly Digest of Statistics*, various issues.

IV. AN ECONOMETRIC ANALYSIS OF BILATERAL TRADE FLOWS[6]

We now move on to the specification and estimation of an econometric model that will guide our empirical analysis of bilateral trade flows between Hong Kong and the United States. The model attempts to explain demand behavior of Hong Kong's exports to, and imports from, the United States. There are two sets of demand equations in the model. The first set of equations describes export relations and is specified in simple linear form as follows:

$$X_i = a_i + b_i YUS + c_i E + d_i PX + e_i D_i + u_i, \; i = 1, 2, \ldots 5 \qquad (1)$$

where X_1 to X_4 represent four major commodity groups exported to the United States and X_5 denotes the aggregate domestic exports to the United States, *YUS* is the national income of the United States, *E* is the exchange value of the Hong Kong dollar, *PX* is prices of Hong Kong exports relative to prices of the U.S. domestically produced goods, and D_i's are dummy variables used for periods in which there are recessions in the whole economy or in particular industries and u_i is the stochastic error term. The dependent variables (X_i) are expected to be positively related to the income variable *YUS*, but inversely related to the exchange rate variable *E* and the price variable *PX*. The coefficients *a*, *b*, *c*, *d*, and *e* are to be estimated.

Similarly, the import equations are specified as follows:

$$M_j = k_j + l_j YHK + n_j PM + v_j, \; j = 1, 2, \ldots, 5 \qquad (2)$$

where M_1 to M_4 represent four major commodity groups imported from the United States and M_5 denotes the total retained imports from the United States, *YHK* is the income of Hong Kong, *PM* is prices of imports from the United States relative to prices of alternative import suppliers, and v_j is the stochastic error term. The dependent variables (M_j) should vary positively with the income variable *YHK* but negatively with the price variable *PM*. The coefficients *k*, *l*, and *n* are to be estimated.

The commodities chosen for export analysis include clothing and clothing accessories (X_1), plastic toys and dolls (X_2), watches and clocks (X_3), and electronic components and parts for computers (X_4). Meanwhile, the major categories of merchandise imports from the United States are foodstuffs (M_1), raw materials and semimanufactures (M_2), consumer goods (M_3), and capital goods (M_4). Since the demand for traded merchandise by commodity type is potentially related to one another, though not strictly simultaneously, the off-diagonal elements of the residual covariance matrix are expected to be nonzero. Zellner's seemingly unrelated regression (SUR) approach can be used and efficient estimates can be obtained. According to Zellner (1962), efficiency in estimation can be gained if the system of seemingly unrelated regression (SUR) equations is viewed as a single large equation to be estimated. This single system equation is estimated through the use of generalized least-squares method.

Table 7. Estimated Correlations across Four Export Equations[a]

	X_1	X_2	X_3	X_4
X_1	1.0000	0.6038	0.1250	0.6213
X_2	0.6038	1.0000	−0.1457	0.0867
X_3	0.1250	−0.1457	1.0000	0.2715
X_4	0.6213	0.0867	0.2715	1.0000

[a] Variables are in per capita terms.

Table 8. Estimated Correlations across Four Import Equations[a]

	$log(M_1)$	$log(M_2)$	$log(M_3)$	$log(M_4)$
$\log(M_1)$	1.0000	0.0392	−0.1007	−0.4395
$\log(M_2)$	0.0392	1.0000	−0.0435	−0.0188
$\log(M_3)$	−0.1007	−0.0435	1.0000	0.0722
$\log(M_4)$	−0.4395	−0.0188	0.0722	1.0000

[a] Variables are in per capita terms.

The estimated cross-model correlation coefficients for export and import equations are presented separately in Table 7 and Table 8, and some of them are fairly high. The equations for X_1, X_2, X_3, and X_4 were thus estimated individually using ordinary least-squares (OLS) method, and jointly using SUR. The equation for total Hong Kong's domestic exports to the United States (X_5) was estimated by OLS. Analogously, the same estimation procedure was adopted for M_1, M_2, M_3, and M_4, and for Hong Kong's total retained imports from the United States (M_5).

The data used for the model estimation, annual observations for the 1968–1985 time period, were derived from several sources. Data on Hong Kong's exports, imports, population, the price deflator of domestic exports, and unit value indexes of imports from the United States, China, and Japan were taken from *Hong Kong's Annual Digest of Statistics*, various issues. Data on Hong Kong's domestic demand and the effective exchange rate index were taken from *Hong Kong Monthly Digest of Statistics*, various issues. Data on value added in Hong Kong's manufacturing sector were taken from *Estimates of Gross Domestic Products*, various issues. Data on U.S. GNP, population, and the wholesale price index were collected from IMF's *International Financial Statistics* (Washington, D.C.), whereas U.S. personal consumption expenditures were taken from *Survey of Current Business*, various issues. All variables were measured in constant (1980) dollars and in per capita terms.

A. Estimation Results

The estimated equations for total and disaggregated exports and imports between Hong Kong and the United States are presented in Table 9 through Table 12. In each of the tables we report the values of the estimated coefficients along with their respective *t*-statistics. The coefficient of determination, R^2, the Durbin–Watson statistic (DW), and the standard error of the estimate, SE, are also presented. Variables used in the estimated export and import equations are listed in Tables A1 and A2 of the Appendix. As can be seen in Table 9, the seemingly unrelated regression estimation reduces the standard errors of the estimates and changes the magnitude of the coefficients as well. Estimation using OLS yields results with higher standard errors.

For the export equations the following are worth noting: (1) The results for the U.S. personal consumption expenditures variable (CPUS), which appears as an income variable in equations X_1, X_2, and X_4, are significant and of the expected positive sign when estimated by SUR. The lagged income variable, (*CPUS-1*), in equation X_3 is equally significant by SUR. (2) With respect to the relative price variable (*PX5/PUSW*), the coefficient estimates show the expected negative sign only in the equation for X_3 with a significant *t*-statistic. Therefore, the equations for X_1, X_2, X_4, and X_5 were reestimated with the relative prices omitted and the exchange rate variable (*EX*) added. The coefficient estimates of the *EX* variable are of the expected negative sign in the equations for X_1, X_2, and X_5, where the

Table 9. Estimated Equations for Domestic Exports

LHS variable	Estimation technique	Explanatory variables (CPUS)	(EX)	(CPUS–1)	(PDEC/PUSW)	(D)	(LHS–1)	CNST	Adjusted R^2	SE	DW
	OLS	0.0044	–16.5552			–5.1911	0.7114	–3.2965	0.9614	3.0216	1.879
		(1.691)	(1.326)			(3.188)	(3.534)	(.180)			
X_1											
	SUR	0.0056	–9.9278			–4.9806	0.6956	–17.4355			1.643
		(2.815)	(1.132)			(5.403)	(5.591)	(1.097)			
	OLS	0.0013	–11.1704			–1.2923		8.5743	0.7910	1.1771	2.011
		(2.216)	(3.267)			(2.046)		(1.211)			
X_2											
	SUR	0.0014	–10.6860			–1.0947		7.6738			2.146
		(2.317)	(3.148)			(2.441)		(1.090)			
	OLS			0.0014	–5.1329		0.8521	–3.4004	0.9895	0.3884	2.993
				(4.404)	(3.249)		(13.373)	(1.551)			
X_3											
	SUR			0.0015	–4.8406		0.8286	–4.1895			2.915
				(4.805)	(3.216)		(13.462)	(1.974)			

	OLS	0.0016	−2.1085	0.6285	−9.2947	0.8184	1.3674	1.716
		(1.741)	(2.468)	(2.772)	(1.546)			
X_4								
	SUR	0.0019	−1.6956	0.5342	−11.1214			1.647
		(2.346)	(2.709)	(2.831)	(2.090)			

Notes: LHS variable stands for the left-hand-side variable i.e., the dependent variable.

CPUS, CPUS-1, and the four LHS variables are in per capita terms. They were divided by the U.S. population (USN).

D ($i = 1,2,4$) are dummy variables. CNST is the constant term.

t-statistics in absolute value are in parentheses.

System weighted R^2 for the combined model = 0.9763; system weighted mean squared error (MSE) = 0.9611 with 51 degrees of freedom.

Table 10. Estimated Equation for Total Domestic Exports

		Explanatory variables							
LHS variable	*Estimation technique*	*log(EX)*	*log(CPUS)*	*log(LHS-1)*	D_5	*CNST*	*Adjusted* R^2	*SE*	*DW*
$\log(X_5)$	OLS	–0.4596	1.1190	0.5685	–0.1557	–7.9850	0.9771	0.0696	1.595
		(1.314)	(2.459)	(2.653)	(4.045)	(2.411)			

See notes on Table 9.

Table 11. Estimated Equations for Imports by Commodity

LHS variable	Estimation technique	Explanatory variables: log (PMUS/PMC)	log (PMUS/PMJ)	log (PDD)	log(XM)	CNST	Adjusted R^2	SE	DW
log(M_1)	OLS	−0.9392 (5.949)[d]		0.8106 (13.588)		−3.7295 (18.950)	0.9249	0.0793	2.203
	SUR	−0.9905 (6.365)		0.8216 (13.907)		−3.7586 (22.269)			2.196
log(M_2)	OLS		−1.1159 (2.753)		1.1450 (8.105)	−2.2354 (10.624)	0.8107	0.1756	2.287
	SUR		−1.1233 (2.771)		1.1467 (8.027)	−2.2374 (10.635)			2.286
log(M_3)	OLS		−0.6535 (3.695)	0.5902 (10.641)		−2.5081 (15.716)	0.8853	0.0799	1.454
	SUR		−0.6467 (3.659)	0.5900 (10.638)		−2.5078 (15.717)			1.462

cont

LHS variable	Estimation technique	Explanatory variables: log (PMUS/PMC)	log (PMUS/PMJ)	log (PDD)	log(XM)	CNST	Adjusted R^2	SE	DW
	OLS		−0.8977		1.0533	−2.2156	0.9338	0.0891	2.243
			(4.365)		(14.534)	(20.758)			
$\log(M_4)$									
	SUR		−0.8605		1.0482	−2.2107			2.206
			(4.250)		(14.549)	(20.796)			

Notes: LHS variable stands for the left-hand-side variable, i.e. the dependent variable all divided by Hong Kong's population.
PDD and XM are measured in per capita terms.
System weighted R^2 for the combined model = 0.9369; system weighted MSE = 0.9981 with 60 degrees of freedom.
See also Notes Table 9.

Table 12. Estimated Equation for Total Imports from the United States

LHS variable	*Estimation technique*	*Explanatory variables*			*Adjusted R^2*	*SE*	*DW*
		log(PMUS/PMJ)	*log(TDD)*	*CNST*			
log(M_5)	OLS	−0.5666 (4.220)	0.8259 (19.837)	−1.9023 (15.228)	0.9633	0.0607	1.990

Notes: M_5 and TDD are measured in per capita basis.
See Notes: Table 9, and 11.

t-statistics in absolute values are greater than one. (3) The dummy variables, designed for periods in which there were economic recession or slack in business in particular industries and used in the equations for X_1, X_2, X_4, and X_5 have significant coefficient estimates. (4) The lagged dependent variable (*LHS-1*) appears in all but the equation for X_2, and their coefficient estimates are significant.

In the import equations the relative price variable, either (*PMUS/PMC*) or (*PMUS/PMJ*), was used to account for the substitution effect of Hong Kong's imports from different sources. As seen in Tables 11 and 12, the two relative price variables are significant, and of the expected negative sign in all five import equations, reflecting the important role of relative prices in determining Hong Kong's demand for the U.S. exports. The results are consistent with the practice followed by Hong Hong's attempts to import as competitively as it can in order to enhance its competitiveness for its exports to the world markets.

The income variable assumes several forms in the import equations. Private domestic demand (*PDD*) was chosen in the equations for M_1 and M_3, output the value added of Hong Kong's manufacturing industries (*XM*) in the equations for M_2 and M_4, and the aggregate domestic demand (*TDD*) in the equation for M_5. All coefficient estimates are statistically significant. Thus, the results tend to support the a priori hypothesis.

Since there are no lags in the estimated import equations, adjustment of actual import quantities to their equilibrium levels is hence expected to complete within 1 year. On the other hand, the estimated coefficient of lagged domestic exports is significantly different from zero in all domestic export equations but X_2, implying there is some degree of dynamic adjustment in these equations.

The estimated income and price elasticities for Hong Kong's domestic exports and imports are presented in Table 13. As expected, the short-run income elasticities of domestic exports are smaller than the equilibrium income elasticities. Table 13 indicates that the price elasticities for M_2 and M_4 are greater than one, suggesting that there exist good substitutes for American raw materials and semimanufactures and U.S.-produced capital goods in the Hong Kong market (mainly from Japan, China, and Taiwan). When all goods are counted, the price elasticity is –0.5666, implying that a 1% increase in import prices of U.S. products relative to import prices of Japanese products will lower the volume of imports from the United States by about 0.6%. Not much can be said about the role of the prices in Hong Kong's domestic exports to the United States, with the exception of the exports of watches and clocks (X_3). The price elasticity of Hong Kong's exports of watches and clocks to the United States presented in Table 13 is –1.2089, suggesting that Hong Kong-produced watches and clocks have good substitutes in the U.S. market.

In Tables 9 and 10 the exchange rate variable is shown to have a significant effect on Hong Kong's domestic exports of clothing and clothing accessories (X_1) and of plastic toys and dolls (X_2), which account for more than 50% of Hong Kong's total domestic exports to the United States. The elasticity of X_1 with

Table 13. Estimated Mean Elasticities of Export and Import Demands

Demand		Elasticity with respect to: Income	Relative prices	Exchange rate
Domestic exports				
X_1	SR	1.2135		−0.2784
	LR	3.3168		−0.7609
X_2	SR	1.3498		−1.3397
X_3	SR	2.4942	−1.2089	
	LR	8.7911	−4.2609	
X_4	SR	3.2951		
	LR	6.2806		
X_5	SR	1.1190		−0.4596
	LR	2.5993		−1.0651
Imports				
M_1		0.8216	−0.9905	
M_2		1.1467	−1.1233	
M_3		0.5900	−0.6467	
M_4		0.8605	−1.0482	
M_5		0.8259	−0.5666	

SR, short run; LR, long run.

respect to *EX* is smaller than one, whereas that of X_2 is greater than one. The exchange rate variable also has a significant effect on the aggregate domestic exports to the United States (X_5). The exchange-rate elasticity of X_5 presented in Table 13 implies a 1% increase in Hong Kong's effective exchange rate index would lower the volume of domestic exports to the United States by about 0.46%.

As regards income elasticities, Hong Kong's aggregate domestic exports are much more sensitive to income than are Kong Kong's imports. Equal increases in income of one percentage point in Hong Kong and the United States would raise the volume of Hong Kong's domestic exports to the United States by about 2.6% but would raise the volume of Hong Kong's imports from the United States by only 0.83% in the long run. Thus, balanced income growth in Hong Kong and the United States would result in unbalanced bilateral trade. This differential sensitivity to income implies that Hong Kong's real income must grow much faster than the United States to maintain balanced increases in imports and exports provided that there is no change in relative prices.

V. CONCLUSION

The main points of empirical results can be summarized as follows:

1. Hong Kong's aggregate domestic exports to the United States respond to the following variables: the U.S. gross national products (+), the exchange rate (–), and the dummy variable, D_5 (–). Domestic exports to the United States by commodity respond to different variables. Domestic exports of clothing and clothing accessories respond to personal consumption expenditures in the United States (+), the exchange rate (–), and the dummy variable D_1 (–). Domestic exports of plastic toys and dolls respond to the U.S. personal consumption expenditures (+), the exchange rate (–), and the dummy variable D_2 (–). An increase in the prices of Hong Kong's domestic exports relative to the U.S. wholesale prices has a negative effect on domestic exports of watches and clocks, which, other things being equal, respond positively to an increase in the lagged values of expenditures of the private sector in the United States. Domestic exports of electronic components and parts for computers respond to two variables: the U.S. personal consumption expenditures (+), and the dummy variable D_4 (–).

2. Since the United States has been the largest market of Hong Kong's domestic exports for many years, changes in U.S. trade policies could affect Hong Kong's domestic exports to this market significantly. Restrictions on imports are growing as the United States struggles with its trade deficit problem. We have made no attempt to analyze in our estimation the impact of changes in U.S. tariff and nontariff barriers on Hong Kong's domestic exports. The export models, particularly the one for exports of clothing and clothing accessories, are likely to be misspecified when variables representing U.S. trade policies are omitted.

3. On the import side, Hong Kong's aggregate demand for U.S. merchandise imports responds to the relative price (*PMUS*/*PMJ*) variable (–), and the variable representing aggregate domestic demand (+). At the disaggregated level, imports of foodstuffs respond to the relative price (*PMUS*/*PMC*) variable (–), and expenditures of the private sector in Hong Kong (+). An increase in the prices of imports from the United States relative to the prices of imports from Japan has a negative effect on imports of U.S.-produced raw materials and semimanufactures, consumer goods, and capital goods, whereas an increase in the value added of the manufacturing sector (*XM*) in Hong Kong has a positive effect on imports of American raw materials and semimanufactures, and capital goods, and an increase in the private sector expenditures has a positive effect on imports of consumer goods from the United States.

4. Our empirical results indicate Hong Kong's imports of U.S.-produced raw materials and semimanufactures, and capital goods are much more price elastic than other types of commodities imported from the United States, implying good substitutes for these imports exist. In fact, a large part of Hong Kong's

imports of raw materials and semimanufactures increasingly come from its neighboring countries such as China, Japan, and Taiwan, and capital goods are mainly imported from Japan.

5. U.S. imports from Hong Kong are more income elastic than U.S. exports to Hong Kong, suggesting an increasing Hong Kong trade surplus with the United States is expected during U.S. economic recovery periods. This can be confirmed by the statistics on Hong Kong's visible trade balances with the United States presented in Section III. It can also be seen in Table 6 that Hong Kong's trade surplus increased more rapidly during 1976–1978, 1980–1981, and 1983–1984, in which the U.S. GNP grew at higher rates. To prevent further deterioration of trade deficit with Hong Kong, U.S. exports to Hong Kong must grow at a proportionately higher rate than imports.

APPENDIX: VARIABLE DEFINITIONS

Table A1. The Variables in the Export Equations

Variable	*Description*
CPUS	Personal consumption expenditures in the United States, in constant (1980) dollars, US$ billion
X_1	Hong Kong's domestic exports of clothing and clothing accessories to the United States, in constant (1980) dollars, HK$ billion
X_2	Hong Kong's domestic exports of plastic toys and dolls to the United States, in constant (1980) dollars, HK$ bn
X_3	Hong Kong's domestic exports of watches and clocks to the United States, in constant (1980) dollars, HK$ bn
X_4	Hong Kong's domestic exports of electronic components and parts for computers to the United States, in constant (1980) dollars, HK$ bn
X_5	Hong Kong's aggregate domestic exports of goods to the United States, in constant (1980) dollars, HK$ bn
D_1	Dummy variable, 1 in 1972–1974, 1980, and 1982; 0 otherwise
D_2	Dummy variable, 1 in 1973–1975, 1983, 0 otherwise
D_4	Dummy variable, 1 in 1975–1976, 1982, and 1985; 0 otherwise
D_5	Dummy variable, 1 in 1973–1975, 1982, and 1985; 0 otherwise
EX	Hong Kong's trade-weighted effective exchange rate index, December 18, 1971 = 100
PUSW	U.S. wholesale price index, 1980 = 100
USGNP	Gross national products of the United States, in constant (1980) dollars, US$ bn
USN	Population in the United States, 100 million persons

Table A2. The Variables in the Import Equations

Variable	*Description*
M_1	Hong Kong's imports of foodstuffs from the United States, in constant (1980) dollars, HK$ billion
M_2	Hong Kong's imports of raw materials and semimanufactures from the United States, in constant (1980) dollars, HK$ bn
M_3	Hong Kong's imports of consumer goods from the United States in constant (1980) dollars, HK$ bn
M_4	Hong Kong's imports of capital goods from the United States, in constant (1980) dollars, HK$ bn
M_5	Hong Kong's aggregate imports of goods from the United States, in constant (1980) dollars, HK$ bn
PDD	Hong Kong's domestic demand in the private sector, in constant (1980) dollars, HK$ bn
PMC	Unit value index of Hong Kong's imports from China, 1980 = 100
PMJ	Unit value index of Hong Kong's imports from Japan. 1980 = 100
PMUS	Unit value index of Hong Kong's imports from the United States, 1980 = 100
TDD	Hong Kong's aggregate domestic demand, in constant (1980) dollars, HK$ bn
XM	Value added in Hong Kong's manufacturing sector, in constant (1980) dollars, HK$ bn

NOTES

1. Hong Kong Government, *Hong Kong, 1987*, Government Printer, 1987, 5.
2. Ibid.
3. The estimated cutback in Hong Kong's exports is approximately 13% for MFA products and 70% for non-MFA products. See Sung (1985).
4. See Shih (1986).
5. With unit value index of imports in 1981 equal to 100, the indices in 1985 for the United States, China, Japan, and Taiwan are 156, 125, 120, and 126, respectively.
6. For general references for this study, see (Haynes, et al. (1986); (Petri, 1984); and (Reinhart, 1986).

REFERENCES

Census and Statistics Department. *Hong Kong Annual Digest of Statistics*, Hong Kong, Government Printer, various issues.

——— *Hong Kong Monthly Digest of Statistics*. Hong Kong Government Printer, various issues.

Haynes, Stephen E., Michael M. Hutchison, and Raymond F. Mikesell. *Japanese Financial Policies and the United States Trade Deficit*. Essays in International Finance No. 162. Princeton, NJ: Princeton University International Finance Section, April 1986.

Hong Kong Government, *Hong Kong, 1987*. Hong Kong, Government Printer, 1987.

International Monetary Fund, *International Financial Statistics, 1986* Washington, D.C., IMF, 1986.

Petri, Peter A. *Modeling Japanese–American Trade: A Study of Asymmetric Interdependence*. Cambridge, MA: Harvard University Press, 1984.

Reinhart, Vincent. "Macroeconomic Influences on the U.S.–Japan Trade Imbalance." *Quarterly Review*, New York: Federal Reserve Bank of New York, Spring 1986, 6–11.

Shih, Elbert Y.C. "International Financial Relations." In R. H. Scott, K. A. Wong, and Y. K. Ho (eds.) *Hong Kong's Financial Institutions and Markets*, Hong Kong: Oxford University Press, 1986, 132–152.

Sung, Kayser. "What Protection Against Protectionism?" *Textile Asia* Hong Kong, *16* (12), December 1985, 18–19 and 161.

Zellner, Arnold. "An Efficient Method of Estimating Seemingly Unrelated Regressions and Tests for Aggregation Bias." *Journal of the American Statistical Association 57*, June 1962, 348–368.

SECTION III

ASEAN:
THE PHILIPPINES / INDONESIA

THE CHARACTERISTICS AND ROLE OF SMALL AND MEDIUM INDUSTRIES IN THE PHILIPPPINES

Jean-Pierre Dumas

I. INTRODUCTION

The case for promoting small and medium industries (SMIs) in developing countries is well known. SMIs are usually considered to have the following desirable features: they are labor intensive, and they have a tendency to absorb unskilled or semiskilled labor; they use relatively less capital per job than larger enterprises; they help to mobilize domestic savings that may have otherwise not been used productively; wages and salaries paid are generally closer to the

Research in Asian Economic Studies.
Asian Industrialization: Changing Economic Structures,
Volume 1, Part A, pages 233–257.
Copyright © 1988 by JAI Press Inc.
All rights of reproduction in any form reserved.
ISBN: 0-89232-987-4

opportunity cost of labor than those paid by large firms; they have a tendency to be located in rural areas, promoting regional industrial employment; they cater to a wide variety of markets ranging from the low-income consumer goods market to the export market; and they play a useful role in the industrial process as subcontractors for larger enterprises.

However, SMIs have often faced a hostile environment. They rarely have competitive access to credit from institutional financing agencies because of the intrinsic risk and the transaction costs attached to loans to small units. Generally, the industrial policy of governments has been biased against SMIs. Traditionally, industrial policies have consisted of (1) protecting existing industries through quota and tariffs, (2) legislating investment incentives generally in favor of large firms, and (3) directly undertaking public sector investments, often with foreign aid or commercial loans. All these policies have discriminated against SMIs. Larger firms are better equipped to obtain import permits and scarce foreign exchange for capital equipment and inputs. Investment incentives are in general directed toward large enterprises, and public investments have been made in favor of large, capital-intensive projects. The conditions and requirements of the bureaucratic system demand much time and effort (and sometimes money), making it difficult for small firms to overcome hurdles.

In addition to this nonconducive environment, SMIs are not always as efficient as suggested. Their traditional limitations are also well known: management capability is often weak, accounting procedure is sometimes limited or nonexistent, and the quality of their output is uneven. All these factors explain a relatively high mortality rate for SMIs, which makes them risky ventures for bankers.

This research will be limited to the analysis of the role of SMIs in the industrial development of the Philippines, utilizing information that comes mainly from the 1972 and 1983 industrial censuses.

II. THE ROLE OF THE MANUFACTURING SECTOR IN THE ECONOMY

Before examining the role of SMIs in the Philippines, it might be useful to look at the manufacturing sector as a whole. Although the value added of the manufacturing sector increased from an estimated 9% of the GNP for the period 1946–1950 to a quarter of the GNP after 1971, the share of manufacturing employment stayed constant and even declined during the same period (Table 1). The manufacturing sector as a whole, therefore, has made little contribution to the absorption of the increasing labor force in the Philippines.[1]

It is generally accepted that the share of the manufacturing sector increases with the level of development (as measured by GNP per capita). The weight of Philippine manufacturing value added (VA) is relatively high when compared to that of the other developing countries with higher GNP per capita (Table 2).

Table 1. Weight of the Manufacturing Sector in the Philippines

	1946–1950	*1956–1960*	*1966–1971*	*1972*	*1975*	*1978*	*1980*	*1983*	*1984*	*1986*
VA of the mfg. sector as a % of the GNP at constant prices	9.4	15.4	14.7	24.1	24.1	25.4	25.0	25.5	25.4	24.4
Share of employment in the mfg. sector as a % of total employment	—	12.5	—	10.5	11.4	9.4	10.6	9.8	9.5	9.2

Sources: Baldwin (1975: 3). National Economic and Development Authority (NEDA), Philippine Statistical Yearbook, 1987. National Census and Statistics Office (NCSO).

Table 2. Structure of the Manufacturing Sector in some Developing Countries

	Manufacturing VA / GDP (1985) (%)	*GNP per capit (dollar 1985)*
Bangladesh	8	150
Burma	10	190
Niger	4	250
India	17	270
Sudan	9	300
Pakistan	20	380
Indonesia	14	530
Philippines	25	580
Ivory Coast	17	660
Thailand	20	800
Peru	20	1010
Ecuador	19	1160
Colombia	18	1320
Korea, Republic of	28	2150
Hong Kong	24	6230

Source: The World Bank, *World Development Report 1987*.

The increase of the manufacturing sector share in the GNP of the Philippines may be explained, inter alia, by the build-up of the manufacturing sector through an import-substitution policy that protected the manufacturing sector relatively more than other sectors of the economy (Baldwin, 1975). This resulted in a transfer of resources from the primary sector to the manufacturing sector. This import-substitution policy and other ''industrial policies,'' such as subsidies and creeping government control through its ownership of industrial assets, created an environment that favored capital-intensive manufacturing projects with some dubious economic returns. This policy was made possible due to an intensive external borrowing policy during the 1970s. The total outstanding debt (disbursed) increased by 29% p.a. (per annum) (in U.S. dollar terms) for the 1975–1980 period.

Given the weight of the manufacturing sector in the economy, the growth of this sector has followed quite closely the GNP rate of growth. The manufacturing sector grew in real terms by 6.7% p.a. from 1975 to 1981, slowed down in 1982–1983, and tumbled by –7% in 1984–1985, which corresponded to a political, financial, and economic crisis in the Philippines. In 1987, the manufacturing sector VA rebounded by 7% in real terms (Table 3).

Hooley (1985) has made a detailed study on the source of the manufacturing sector growth during the 1960s and the 1970s. The total factor productivity growth (TFPG) of the manufacturing sector, i.e., the economic growth not accounted for by capital, labor, and intermediate inputs, was 0.6% p.a. for the period 1956–1970 and –1.2% p.a. for the period 1971–1980. The factor that had the highest weight in the Philippine manufacturing growth was intermediate inputs. The relatively high growth of the manufacturing sector in the Philippines can be explained by a higher growth of factor inputs (intermediate inputs, capital, and labor). For other Asian countries studied, TFPG was always positive (Table 4).

The decline in total factor productivity growth and the low employment in the manufacturing sector seem to be the consequence of increasing capital labor ratio in the manufacturing sector (Table 5). This capital deepening, on the other hand, was the result of the high level of debt financing during the 1970s with subsidized interest rates.

In the 1970s efforts were made to push nontraditional exports through the establishment of export-processing zones allowing exporters to bring in duty-free inputs, and the devaluation of the Peso in 1970. The results were spectacular. Until 1970, about 80% of Philippine exports were accounted for by 10 unprocessed primary products: copra, sugar, banana, logs, lumber, desiccated coconut, coconut oil, abaca, copper concentrates, and gold; their total export share dropped

Table 3. Philippines: Growth of the GNP and the Manufacturing Value Added at 1972 Prices

	1972–1981	*1982*	*1983*	*1984*	*1985*	*1986*	*1987*
Manufacturing sector (%)	6.7	2.4	2.3	–7.1	–7.6	0.8	7.4
GNP (%)	6.3	1.6	1.1	–7.1	–4.2	1.5	5.1

Source: NEDA, *Philippines Statistical Yearbook*, 1987.

Table 4. TFPG in Some Asian Countries

	Philippines		*Indonesia*	*Japan*	*Korea*	*Thailand*
	1956–1970	*1971–1980*	*1975–1982*	*1953–1973*	*1960–1977*	*1963–1976*
TFPG	0.6	–1.2	1.7	2.1	3.8	0.7

Table 5. Philippines: Capital[a]–Labor Ratios for the Manufacturing Sector

1972	*1983*
20,440	25,268

[a] Capital was estimated at 1972 prices.

to 24% in 1985. Nontraditional exports that constitute the bulk of total exports are mainly concentrated in three products: semiconductors, garments, and handicrafts. Most of these outputs come mainly from small establishments with low capital–labor ratios and a high propensity to export. Unfortunately, exportation is not captured at all by statistical surveys.

In terms of value added (VA), the dominant industry in the Philippine manufacturing sector is the food processing section that accounted for 40% of the manufacturing VA in 1985. In this sector, there is a reasonable proportion covered by SMIs. The other sectors in order of magnitude are chemicals[2] and chemical products[3] (8% of the manufacturing VA) with some SMIs producing chemical products. Electrical machinery[4] accounted for 7% of the manufacturing VA. On the other hand, furniture and fixtures accounted for only 0.5% of the manufacturing VA, and leather and wood products 2.5%. Typically, the importance of labor-intensive sectors such as clothing and footwear, furniture and leather products, wood products, and printing is not as great as might have been expected in a labor abundant economy as is the Philippines (Table 6).

Given the collapse of many capital-intensive sectors during the crisis (1983–1984), the manufacturing VA by subsectors has reverted to a structure more akin to the early 1950s, with food, beverage, and tobacco accounting for about half of the manufacturing VA. Paper and paper products, chemical products, and transport equipment (automotive industry) have seen their shares declining considerably with the economic crisis.

In the conclusion, the apparent high manufacturing growth in the Philippines during the 1960s and the 1970s was mainly achieved by an expansion in domestic demand and import substitution[5] fueled by large external borrowing, an inefficient use of intermediate goods and capital within industries as can be seen through the analysis of the TFPG, and a misallocation of resources away from the more efficient industries toward less efficient (see Hooley, 1985).

The increasing role of the State in manufacturing in the 1970s explains these negative results. The import-substitution policy along with an overvalued exchange rate, the cascading tariff structure, and low interest rate resulted in the overuse of capital and intermediate goods. The binge in external borrowing during the 1970s also explains the abuse in capital imports that were not fully utilized.

Table 6. Gross Value Added in Manufacturing by Industry Group (%) Calculated at 1972 Prices

Industry group	*1960*	*1970*	*1975*	*1980*	*1985*
Food manufactures	27.63	24.04	36.01	36.33	39.98
Beverage industries	7.66	8.02	2.89	3.16	3.68
Tobacco manufactures	4.82	6.87	5.46	4.48	4.49
Textile manufactures	5.78	6.51	5.10	4.53	3.39
Footwear, wearing apparel	3.75	1.69	4.17	4.40	6.00
Wood and cork products	4.24	4.06	2.51	2.87	2.48
Furniture and fixtures	0.91	0.43	0.58	0.57	0.50
Paper and paper products	2.60	2.97	0.90	0.82	0.73
Publishing and printing	3.46	2.56	1.55	1.40	1.80
Leather and leather products	0.44	0.17	0.30	0.29	0.32
Rubber products	3.18	3.10	1.74	1.30	1.30
Chemical and chemical products	9.77	12.77	8.58	10.20	7.88
Products of petroleum and coal	0.00	7.13	7.71	5.92	5.33
Nonmetallic mineral products	3.62	3.84	2.73	2.48	1.73
Basic metal industries	1.54	4.00	3.34	3.68	4.95
Metal products	5.49	2.56	4.20	4.49	3.45
Machinery except electrical	1.88	0.95	2.97	3.13	1.89
Electrical machinery	3.13	3.61	3.88	4.98	7.40
Transport equipment	2.94	3.45	4.19	3.82	0.63
Miscellaneous manufactures	7.16	1.27	1.18	1.14	2.07
Total manufacturing	100.0	100.0	100.0	100.0	100.0

Source: NEDA and NCSO.

III. DEFINITION OF SMIs

Any definition of the universe of SMI is deemed to include some degree of arbitrariness. The definition selected is based on the number of employees, not on the value of fixed assets or sales. This had the advantage of escaping the reevaluation problem caused by inflation.

Generally, a distinction is drawn between household manufacturing and establishments[6] employing (1) less than 10 workers, (2) from 10 to 100 workers (segment considered as SMI), and (3) more than 100 workers (large firms).

Employment in household manufacturing is estimated as the difference between the estimates of manufacturing employment provided in the population census and those provided by the census of establishments.

The household sector is quite small in terms of its share in total VA, yet it is still the largest source of employment in the Philippine manufacturing sector; it was estimated as more than half of the total manufacturing in 1975 and 1983. This may be explained as "a solution" to the high unemployment rate in the country, households being characterized by easy entry and low productivity. In addition, high interisland transportation costs provide natural protection to producers in rural areas and outlying islands. The size of the household sector declined from about 75% of the manufacturing employment in 1956 to 63% in the mid-1960s, and to 53% in 1975–1983 (Table 7).

The definition of the SMI sector, somewhat arbitrary, may change dramatically the conclusion of any study on SMIs. If, for example, the cottage industry is included in the SMI sector, then this sector accounted for 70% of total manufacturing employment in 1983. If the SMI sector includes establishments from 1 to 99 employees, it accounted for 17% of total manufacturing employment and if the SMI sector only includes establishments from 10 to 99 employees it accounted for 7% of total manufacturing employment. This is why international comparison of firm size is so difficult in the absence of a standard definition of the SMI universe.[7] In this study, the SMI sector covers manufacturing establishments that employ between 10 and 99 workers.

Table 7. Philippines: Employment[a] in the Manufacturing Sector According to Size of Activity (in Thousands) (Including the Household Sector)

	1975		*1983*	
Firm's size	*Number*	*%*	*Number*	*%*
Household	882	53	998	53
Establishments				
less than 10 employees	207	13	187	10
10 to 99 employees	132	8	127	7
100 to 199 employees	56	3	71	4
200 and over	374	23	504	27
Total	1,651	100	1,887	100

Source: Anderson and Khambata (1981: p. 80). NEDA, *Philippine Statistical Yearbook*, 1987.

[a] Total employees inclusive of those who work for noncash wage payment.

IV. THE RELATIVE WEIGHT OF THE SMI SECTOR IN THE ECONOMY

The results of the 1972 and 1983 censuses that give statistics by size and by industry for the manufacturing sector have been provided by the NCSO for this study. The summary of the 1983 census is given in Table 8.

The universe of small and medium establishments[8] (establishments with 10 to 99 employees) accounted for 8% of total manufacturing establishments, 15% of total paid employees, 10% of fixed assets, and 13% of total sales. Their role at the macroeconomic level was rather limited. In 1983, they contributed to about 2% of the GNP and 6% of the manufacturing VA (Table 9).

Large manufacturing firms[9] in the Philippines have for the last two decades dominated the manufacturing sector. With only 1% of total manufacturing establishments they accounted for 64% of paid employees,[10] 79% of the manufacturing VA, and 77% of the fixed assets of the sector in 1983 (Table 8).

Table 8. Philippines: Selected Statistics for Manufacturing Establishments 1983 by Size (in percent)

Size	*Number of establish-ment*	*Number of paid employees*	*VA*	*FA*	*Total compen-sation*	*Total sales*
Total mfg. sector	100.0	100.0	100.0	100.0	100.0	100.0
Less than 10 employees	89.8	11.8	2.4	3.2	3.8	1.1
10–99 employees	8.1	15.4	10.4	10.2	11.3	12.5
100–199 employees	0.9	9.0	8.3	9.8	9.8	8.4
200 and above	1.3	63.8	78.9	76.8	75.1	78.0

Source: NCSO, *Manufacturing Census* 1983.

Table 9. Contribution of SMI's to GNP in the Philippines (at Current Prices)[a]

SMIs VA	*1972*	*1975*	*1983*
Percentage of total manufacturing VA	9.4	7.7	6.2
Percentage of total GNP	2.2	1.9	1.6

[a] The discrepency from these data and the data in Table 8 regarding the VA share is due to the fact that the manufacturing VA and other statistics in Table 9 come from a sample whereas in Table 8 manufacturing VA is calculated from the national *Manufacturing Census*, 1983.

A. Composition of the SMI Sector

SMIs tend to be traditionally concentrated in the production of "light" consumer goods. In the Philippines, SMIs are mainly concentrated within the food manufacturing subsector (32% of the VA of the SMI sector in 1983), in chemicals (15%), and fabricated metal products[11] (7%). The other light consumer goods such as beverages, tobacco, textile, wearing apparel,[12] and pottery[13] are mainly produced by large firms (Table 10).

Table 10. Composition of VA in SMIs: Percentage of Industries to Total Manufacturing

Code	*Sector*	*1972*	*1983*	*1986*
311/12	Food manufacturing	21.0	32.3	30.2
313	Beverage	2.3	2.4	0.9
314	Tobacco	0.7	0.1	0.1
321	Manufacture of textiles	5.0	3.3	3.9
322	Wearing apparels	3.1	2.3	2.2
323	Leather and leather products	0.5	0.3	0.4
324	Footwear	0.5	0.7	0.5
331	Wood (except furniture)	8.2	4.1	3.8
332	Furnitures	2.3	2.1	1.5
341	Paper and paper products	2.8	2.1	3.5
342	Printing, publishing	5.6	4.4	4.7
351	Industrial chemicals	4.8	8.2	6.5
352	Other chemical products	9.7	7.1	10.9
353	Petroleum refineries	—	—	—
354	Miscellaneous products of petroleum and coals	0.2	0.2	0.7
355	Rubber products	2.8	1.9	4.3
356	Plastic products	4.1	3.0	3.1
361	Pottery	0.05	—	0.3
362	Glass and glass products	0.5	0.5	—
369	Other nonmetallic mineral products	1.8	2.2	2.1
371	Iron and steel basic industries	2.8	3.0	4.6
372	Nonferrous metals	0.5	0.6	0.5
381	Fabricated metal products	7.5	7.4	3.6
382	Non-electrical machinery	3.4	4.1	3.4
383	Electrical machinery	2.4	2.4	3.6
384	Transport equipment	6.0	3.0	2.4
385	Professional and scientific goods	0.1	0.3	0.8
386	Repair of furniture	—	0.4	0.3
390	Other manufacturing industries	1.1	1.2	1.9
	Total VA in the SMI sector	100	100	100

Source: Manufacturing Census, NCSO, Philippines.

V. GROWTH OF OUTPUT BY SIZE OF ESTABLISHMENT

The rate of growth of the output (in real terms) for the period 1972–1983 was higher for large firms[14] (+6.4% p.a.) than for SMIs (5% p.a.). This confirms our intuition that the environment was more favorable to the development of large firms than of SMIs for this period. Nevertheless the range is too small to draw definitive conclusions (Table 11).

The most dynamic sector in terms of creation of new establishments is the sector of large firms. For the period 1972–1983, the number of large firms (more than 100 workers) increased by 4.6% p.a. against 1.8% only for the number of SMIs (Table 12).

Table 11. Philippines: Rates of Growth of the Output in the Manufacturing Sector by Size of Establishment (at 1972 Prices) (in Thousand Pesos)

Establishment size	*1972*	*1983*	*Annual rate of growth (%)*
10–99 employees	3,602,434	6,186,340	5.0
100–199 employees	2,710,022	4,087,600	3.8
200 and above employees	16,046,842	31,749,200	6.4
Total manufacturing sector	22,359,298	42,023,140	5.9

Source: Manufacturing Censuses, NSCO, Philippines.

Table 12. Philippines: Rates of Growth of Establishment

	Number of firms		
Establishment size	*1972*	*1983*	*Annual rate of growth (%)*
10–99 employees	3,583	4,369	1.8
100–199 employees	307	505	4.6
200 and above employees	437	716	4.6
Total manufacturing sector	4,327	5,590	2.4

Source: Manufacturing Censuses, NSCO, Philippines.

VI. RATE OF GROWTH OF EMPLOYMENT

The rate of growth of employment in the manufacturing sector (formal sector only) is the lowest for SMIs for the period 1972–1983. Therefore, it is difficult to draw the conclusion that the SMI sector is the most dynamic sector in terms of job creation at least during the period 1972–1983.[15]

The rate of growth of employment in the 1970s, and the rate of formation of manufacturing establishments are apparently relatively high in the manufacturing sector (Table 13). Nevertheless, these statistics should be used cautiously, as the increase may be partly due to an increase in statistical coverage of the population from 1972 to 1983.

SMIs are important in terms of employment in the following subsectors: food manufacturing, wood and cork products, printing and publishing, textiles, and wearing apparel. This is shown in Table 14.

The highest increase in employment was in the wearing apparel subsector at 14% p.a. Even if there was better coverage in 1983 than in 1972, the increase in employment in this subsector was real and reflected the boom in wearing apparel exports. However, this increase did not occur in the SMI tranche (3% p.a.) but in large firms (17% p.a.).

Table 13. Philippines: Rates of Growth of Paid Employees in the Manufacturing Sector by Size of Establishment (1972–1983)

Establishment size	*Rate of growth of paid employees (%)*	*Rate of growth of establishments (%)*
10–99 employees	2.7	1.8
100–199 employees	4.7	4.6
More than 200 employees	5.1	4.6
Total manufacturing	4.6	2.4

Source: Philippine National Census of Establishments, 1972 and 1983.

Table 14. Number of Paid Employees in Selected Industries by Firm's Size (1972, 1983)

Code	*Sector*	*1972*	*1983*	*Annul growth rate (%)*
(311/12)	Food			
	10–99 employees	15,850	26,120	4.6
	100–199 employees	4,872	9,371	6.1
	More than 200 employees	64,910	92,713	3.3
	Total	85,632	128,204	3.7
(331)	Wood & wood products			
	10–99 employees	10,480	8,157	−2.3
	100–199 employees	4,339	6,895	4.3
	More than 200 employees	40,320	44,288	0.9
	Total	55,139	59,340	0.7
(342)	Printing & publishing			
	10–99 employees	6,067	8,074	2.6
	100–199 employees	2,293	2,826	1.9
	More than 200 employees	3,834	3,862	0.07
	Total	12,194	14,762	1.8
(321)	Textiles			
	10–99 employees	5,561	7,676	3.0
	100–199 employees	2,961	6,620	7.6
	More than 200 employees	49,273	71,349	3.4
	Total	57,795	85,645	3.6
(322)	Wearing apparels			
	10–99 employees	5,223	7,257	3.0
	100–199 employees	818	4,477	16.7
	More than 200 employees	11,658	63,079	16.6
	Total	17,699	74,813	14.0

Source: Philippine National Census of Manufacturing Establishments, 1972 and 1983.

VII. CAPITAL

The SMI sector accounted for 10% of total fixed assets (FA) of the manufacturing sector in 1983, against 80% for large firms.[16]

Fixed assets in the manufacturing sector increased by 6.6% during the 1972–1983 period (Table 15).

The capital–labor ratio at the manufacturing level increases with size (Table 16), as SMIs expectedly are more labor intensive than the larger size industries.

There was an increase (in constant prices) in the capital–labor ratio in the 1970s, which was more important in the SMI range. Curiously enough, the increase was relatively lower for large firms.

The most capital-intensive sectors are petroleum refineries, cement, chemicals, iron and steel basic industry, paper and paper products, nonferrous metal basic industry, glass and glass product, beverage, transport equipment, and food manufacturing (Table 17). It is interesting to note that the capital–labor ratios increased dramatically during the 1970s for the chemical industry, iron and steel basic industry, paper and paper products, nonferrous metal basic industry, glass and glass product, beverage, and transport equipment. The capital deepening in these sectors may explain the difficulty for the manufacturing sector to be labor intensive. Capital was invested in heavy industry with low employment creation and low propensity to export. On the other hand, traditional labor-intensive sectors did not experience capital deepening during this period: wearing apparel, leather products, footwear, furniture, and electrical machinery (including electronics). In other words, the incentives seem to have worked against the sectors in which the country has the most comparative advantages. This is another illustration of the import-substitution policy consequence that has the effect of promoting sectors in which the country has a "comparative disadvantage."

Table 15. Fixed Assets in Philippine Manufacturing by Size (Million ₱) (at 1972 Prices)

Size by number of employees	*1972*	*1983*	*Annual rate of growth (%)*
10–99	856.064	1,843.730	7.2
100–199	699.152	1,771.040	8.8
200 and above	7,112.020	13,955.900	6.3
Total	8,667.236	17,570.670	6.6

Source: Philippines, National Census of Establishments, 1972 and 1983.

Table 16. Capital[a]–Labor Ratio in the Philippine Manufacturing Sector by Size of Firm

Size by number of employees	*1972*	*1983*
	At current prices	
10–99	9.5	42.8
100–199	16.4	70.0
200 and above	24.4	77.8
Total manufacturing sector	20.4	70.8
	At constant 1972 prices	
10–99	9.5	15.3
100–199	16.4	25.0
200 and above	24.4	27.8
Total manufacturing sector	20.4	25.3

[a] Capital is measured by fixed assets.

Table 17. Philippines: Capital Intensive Industries (in Constant Prices)

		Ratios					
		1972			*1983*		
Code	*Sector*	*FA/L*	*Q/FA*	*Q/L*	*FA/L*	*Q/FA*	*Q/L*
(353)	Petroleum refineries	475	3.6	1,708	167	9.9	1658
(363)	Cement	—	—	—	103	0.9	92
(351)	Chemicals	47	1.8	86	84	2.1	173
(371)	Iron and steel basic industry	75	1.0	74	77	2.2	166
(341)	Paper and paper products	19	2.5	48	73	0.7	53
(372)	Nonferrous metal basic industry	4	10.0	40	72	1.1	81
(362)	Glass and glass products	19	1.9	37	45	0.8	37
(313)	Beverage	10	6.3	63	43	1.4	59
(384)	Transport equipment	10	6.3	63	42	2.9	123
(311)	Food manufacturing	36	2.2	79	31	2.7	83
(369)	Other nonmetallic mineral product	96	0.5	51	25	0.9	23

Source: National Census of Establishments, 1982 and 1983.

Note: FA, fixed assets; L, number of paid employees; Q, output.

VIII. FACTOR PRODUCTIVITY OF SMIs AND THE LARGE-SCALE FIRMS

The case for policy intervention in favor of SMIs rests on evidence that small units on average are more labor-intensive and use factor inputs more productively than their larger counterparts, so that a shift of resources in favor of smaller units would yield a net increase in output as well as increase in the demand for unskilled labor.

As SMIs employ proportionally more unskilled labor than large firms, they tend to have lower labor productivity. Generally, net productivity per employee in the manufacturing sector rises with the size of the firm.

Although SMIs tend to have lower productivity of labor, their capital productivity is generally higher than that of medium and large-scale industry.

To summarize: generally, labor productivity increases with size of the firms, capital productivity declines with size, but follows a more erratic pattern, and capital intensity (FA/L) rises with size.

To obtain the relative efficiency of SMIs versus large firms, the global factor productivity (GFP) is estimated.

The GFP is estimated for the manufacturing sector as a whole and by size. Cobb–Douglas production functions have been estimated based on a cross-section of different Philippine manufacturing industries at three-digit level for the years 1972 and 1983 (Table 18). These years were chosen because the National Census and Statistics Office provided the manufacturing data by size for this period. Sicat (1963), Williamson and Sicat (1968), and Sicat (1967) studied GFP for the manufacturing sector as a whole. Since data breakdown by size was not available before, it is the first time that this computation is made possible.

Table 18. Results of the Cobb–Douglas Production Function for the Philippines Manufacturing Sector (1972–84) (Using VA Only)

Year	*A*	α_e	β_e	$\alpha_e + \beta_e$	R^2
1972	0.077	0.663 (0.232)	0.506 (0.102)	1.17	0.86
1975	0.007	1.138 (0.221)	0.457 (0.113)	1.60	0.85
1983	0.026	0.672 (0.264)	0.595 (0.133)	1.27	0.81
1984	0.056	0.468 (0.155)	0.667 (0.08)	1.14	0.90

Notes: 1. All statistics are based on establishments with 10 or more workers.
2. Standard errors are in parentheses.
3. Subscript refers to estimated values of parameters.

The production function specified is the standard Cobb-Douglas function.

$$Q = AL^{\alpha} K^{\beta} \Pi^{\gamma} \quad (1)$$

where Q = Output at 1972 prices
A = GFP
L = Total paid employees
K = Book value of fixed assets (value net of depreciation) at 1972 prices
Π = Intermediate inputs at 1972 prices
α = Parameter of share of labor income to output
β = Parameter of share of capital income to output
γ = Parameter of share of intermediate inputs to output

The estimated production function incorporated intermediate inputs, since this is the most important factor in the manufacturing process.

To estimate A, α, β, and γ, cross-sectional data of the *i*th industry at the three-digit level for a specific year have been used. Let us rewrite Eq (1) for the ith industry.

$$Q_i = AL_i^{\alpha} K_i^{\beta} \Pi_i^{\gamma} e^{ui} \quad (2)$$

The variables have been weighted by the number of establishments within each industry.

VA by industry is calculated at 1972 prices using the deflators calculated by NEDA for each industry. These deflators are quite different from those used by Hooley (1985). They are regularly published by NEDA, whereas Hooley's producer price index series was discontinued in 1980.

Fixed-asset variables are at net book value and are generally given at historical cost. The value of fixed assets (the weakest data) seems to be rather underestimated in the Philippines. Nevertheless, a deflator for the fixed assets has been calculated for this study.

The equation is estimated using a linear regression model in logarithmic form:

$$\ln Q_i = \ln A + \alpha \ln L_i + \beta \ln K_i + \gamma \ln \Pi_i + u_i \quad (3)$$

A is a scale constant, which represents TFP, α, β and γ are parameters to be estimated, and u is a residual with stochastic properties. The subscript i refers to the *i*th industry. Thus, in this regression no attempt is made to restrict the sum of the regression coefficients α, β, and γ to unity, since the objectives are to estimate A (total factor productivity) and the nature of returns to scale.

A. Analysis of the Results at the Manufacturing Sector Level

Total factor productivity (TFP) in the manufacturing sector is estimated at 1.26 in 1972 and 2.7 in 1983 (Table 19).

Table 19. Reults of the Cobb–Douglas Production Function for the Philippines Manufacturing Sector (1972–1983) (Using Output and Intermediate Inputs)

Year	*A*	α_e	β_e	γ_e	$(\alpha_e+\beta_e+\gamma_e)$	R^2	*Remarks*
1972	1.26	0.11 (0.06)	0.12 (0.03)	0.79 (0.04)	1.02	0.99	Value Mn ₱
1981	0.82	0.16 (0.05)	–0.04 (0.04)	0.91 (0.04)	1.03	0.99	Value Mn ₱
1983	2.70	0.17 (0.15)	0.14 (0.10)	0.81 (0.09)	1.12	0.96	Value Mn ₱

Note: Standard errors are in parentheses.

This corresponds to a relatively high growth of GFP from 1972 to 1983. The results, however, should be considered with extreme caution since they are based on data which are not always very reliable and give different results if one uses VA only[17] (Table 18).

Using Denison methodology[18] to calculate total factor productivity growth (TFPG), a decline of –0.6% p.a. for the 1972–1983 period is shown for the manufacturing sector.

$$\text{TFPG} = \frac{\Delta Q}{Q} - \alpha 72 \frac{\Delta L}{L} - \beta 72 \frac{\Delta K}{K} - \gamma 72 \frac{\Delta \Pi}{\Pi}$$

$$-0.6\% = 5.9 - (0.09 \times 4.6) - (0.3 \times 6.6) - (0.61 \times 6.8)$$

Manufacturing growth is found to be more intermediate input intensive rather than capital intensive in the Philippine manufacturing sector.

Another important finding is that the sum of the elasticities of output respective to inputs, i.e., the sum of estimated α, β, and γ, was slightly higher than one. Therefore, the Philippine manufacturing sector is showing increasing returns to scale.

For the 1972–1983 period, one can observe that the estimated α_e (elasticities of output with respect to labor) were much higher than the actual α_a. The distribution of income in the Philippines is largely against labor, as the present analysis indicates, and the finding is in conformity with that of Sicat (1963). (Table 20).

Table 20. Comparison between Estimated and Actual α, β, and γ

Year	*Estimated* α_e	*Actual* α_a	*Estimated* β_e	*Actual* β_a	*Estimated* γ_e	*Actual* γ_a
1972	0.11	0.09	0.12	0.30	0.79	0.61
1983	0.17	0.06	0.14	0.28	0.81	0.65

Notes:

$$\alpha_e = \frac{\partial Q(L)}{\partial L(Q)}, \beta_e = \frac{\partial Q(K)}{\partial K(Q)}, \gamma_e = \frac{\partial Q(\pi)}{\partial \pi(Q)}.$$

$$\alpha_a = \frac{\text{Salaries for the mfg. sector}}{Q}, \beta_a = \frac{\text{Profit Share}}{Q}, \gamma_a = \frac{\text{Payments for intermediate inputs}}{Q}.$$

The elasticity of output with respect to labor is $\alpha_e = \frac{\partial Q(L)}{\partial L(Q)}$ or the marginal productivity of labor multiplied by the ratio labor to output. Given α_e and the ratio L/Q, one can estimate the marginal productivity of labor $\frac{\partial Q}{\partial L}$ (Table 21).

The next step is to compare the estimated marginal productivity of labor with the average salaries and compensation (at 1972 prices) distributed in the manufacturing sector. One can notice that the factor labor has received a lower income than its marginal productivity. The marginal product of labor was about three times higher than the unit wage (Table 22). This is contrary to the traditional opinion that considers that a priori in a developing country, the price of labor is above its marginal value product, since at least in the manufacturing sector of the Philippines the average salary was much lower than the marginal value product of labor. Care should be exercised when shadow prices are estimated for the factor labor in the manufacturing sector of the Philippines. In economic analysis of projects, not only should average salary not be lowered further, but it may also be revalued to consider the marginal value product of the factor labor. Even if these estimates are crude, they give an order of magnitude of the gap between the price of labor and its marginal productivity. Unit salary (S/L) was declining in real terms in our sample for the 1972–1983 period (–1.4% p.a.).

Real wagers were in 1970 already equal to their level a decade before, partly because of a large pool of workers in the informal sector. In addition, decline in real wage growth is also closely associated with low productivity growth.

Therefore, low overall employment in the manufacturing sector was not due to high labor cost (only 19% of the VA for the 1972–1984 period) but to a capital-intensive industrialization.

We now estimate the marginal productivity of capital $\frac{(\partial Q)}{(\partial K)}$ in the Philippine manufacturing sector (Table 23).

Table 21. Estimate of the Marginal Productivity of Labor in Philippine Manufacturing

	$\frac{\partial Q}{\partial L}$	=	[$\frac{Q}{L}$	x	α_e]
1972	5,082	=	52,747	x	0.11
1983	10,282	=	60,481	x	0.17

Table 22. Comparison of the Marginal Productivity of Labor with Average Salary in the Manufacturing Sector

	$\frac{\partial Q}{\partial L}$	$s = \frac{S}{L}$	$\frac{\partial Q}{\partial L} / s$
1972	5,082	4,497	1.3
1983	10,282	3,863	2.7

Table 23. Estimate of the Marginal Productivity of the Capital in Philippine Manufacturing

	$\frac{\partial Q}{\partial K}$	=	[$\frac{Q}{K}$	x	β_e]
1972	0.31	=	2.58	x	0.12
1983	0.34	=	2.39	x	0.14

The marginal productivity of capital was about 31% (at 1972 prices). The weighted real lending rates of commercial banks were estimated at 6% p.a. Therefore it can be concluded that the marginal productivity of capital was higher than the cost of capital. This result is more consonant with the traditional cost--benefit analysis theory.

The rates of profit (Π/*FA*) of the manufacturing sector were 78% in 1972 and 68% in 1983. These rates of profit are likely to be overestimated, given the strong presumption that *FA* are undervalued. In addition, the profit (Π) is a residual; it is the nonwage component of the VA. It includes tax, depreciation, and interest payments, and therefore it is a very crude measure of profit.

B. Productivity by Size

Productivity by size of firms has also been calculated using the same methodology: cross-section by size. The results are reported in Table 24.

Table 24. Regression Results by Employment Size

	A	α	β	γ	R^2	*Remarks*
1972						
10–99	1.25	0.07 (0.08)	0.02 (0.02)	0.90 (0.03)	0.99	Mn ₱
100–199	4.95	−0.16 (0.56)	0.36) (0.07)	0.66 (0.07)	0.97	Mn ₱
200 and above	2.08	0.05 (0.05)	0.004 (0.03)	0.83 (0.03)	0.99	Mn ₱
Total mfg. sector	1.26	0.11 (0.06)	0.12 (0.03)	0.79 (0.04)	0.99	Mn ₱
1983						
10–99	1.56	0.01 (0.15)	0.08 (0.04)	0.85 (0.03)	0.99	Mn ₱
100–199	3.42	−0.12 (0.45)	0.07 (0.04)	0.78 (0.05)	0.94	Mn ₱
200 and above	1.04	0.11 (0.09)	0.02 (0.04)	0.90 (0.04)	0.98	Mn ₱
Total mfg. sector	2.7	0.17 (0.15)	0.14 (0.10)	0.81 (0.09)	0.96	Mn ₱

The range with the highest GFP was between 100 to 199 paid employees for 1972 and 1983. SMIs (10 to 99 paid employees) had the lowest GFP in 1972 and a low level in 1983. Therefore, inspite of the fact that the data are rather imperfect, it seems that SMIs, at least in the Philippines, do not show a higher GFP than larger firms.

IX. SMIs AND EXPORTS

One traditional issue regarding SMIs is whether they are significantly involved in exportation. According to Little (1987: 230), "big firms have economies of scale in export marketing, and it is generally true that most small units export little or nothing." This is not always true. In the Philippines, for example, SMI exports (mainly embroidery, garments, bamboo and rattan, crafts and needle crafts) were estimated at US$556 million in 1980 or about 10% of total exports of the year. They were ranked as the second most important export item in 1980 after sugar (US$590m.). The exportation of handicraft products, mainly produced by SMIs, fetched US$138m. in 1985 or 3% of total exports.

The rattan furniture industry in the Philippines is a good example of SMIs largely involved in the export business. There is almost no domestic market. To export, the industry does not hesitate to import cheaper inputs or to substitute cheaper local variety. Some enterprises export only semifinished products as sanded items, the finishing and upholstery being carried out abroad. To compete with mass-produced Taiwanese and Indonesian products, Philippine firms have chosen to emphasize design and quality to gain their share of the world market. Philippine producers have a significant comparative advantage in the quality product that enables some firms to export to the European and Japanese markets. Exposure to international markets has resulted in cost-minimizing behavior and a high return to innovation.

Conversely, the wood-furniture industry has not been able to penetrate the world market as has the rattan industry in spite of the Bureau of Investment incentives for furniture exporters. This may be due to relatively high ERP in the industry as compared to the rattan industry which does not provide any incentive for exporting.

The ERP is high in the furniture industry which pays a lower price than the world price for lumber and enjoys high nominal protection for the end product. The protection given to the furniture industry has encouraged inefficient techniques of production and little functional specialization.

X. CONCLUSION

When considered in terms of their contribution to employment and VA, the role of Philippine SMIs is still limited. If the household sector is included, employment in this sector and in small and medium-size industries far outweighs employment provided by large firms. Household manufacturing still remains the major source of employment but its share is on the decline. But, when only manufacturing establishments are considered, employment generated by small- and medium-size establishments is particularly low in the Philippines as compared to other Asian and industrialized countries. The Philippines is still largely characterized by a dualistic manufacturing structure in which employment is concentrated in cottage and large capital-intensive industries. After 40 years of industrialization, low productivity cottage industries have not been incorporated into the modern manufacturing sector. The SMI sector contribution to employment could be substantially increased with a more neutral policy vis-à-vis small-scale enterprises that operate in sector with a low or even negative effective rate of protection.

The global efficiency of Philippine SMIs does not seem to be higher than their larger counterparts.

Therefore, programs in favor or SMIs should primarily consider increasing the level of productivity of these firms.

Relations between medium-scale and large firms are still limited in the Philippines. The subsectors open to international competition (rattan, garment industries) are more involved in subcontracting arrangements, whereas the linkages between assemblers and subcontractors are weak in protected industries (automobile and electronics). There is certainly room to improve the relationships between medium-size and large firms through subcontracting arrangements.

It has been found that in the Philippines, a large part of SMIs are export oriented, contributing decisively to the exports of the country. These firms have generally weathered the 1983 crisis better than import-substitution firms.

The main justification for a program in favor of SMIs does not rest on the second best argument, but on market imperfections specific to this sector.[19] In other words, the role of an SMI program is not to be an alternative to more desirable policies toward agriculture and trade policy. These should be tackled specifically at the right level. It is unlikely that an SMI program, financed by a multilateral bank, can address in depth these questions because the amount of the loan involved is too small for the multilateral institution to have the necessary leverage to change the economic framework. In addition, the counterparts in charge of dealing with the SMI sector are not the same as those in charge of the trade policy of the country; therefore, there is little hope that an SMI program might alter this trade issue.

In the Philippines, macropolicies (trade policy, tax and credit policies) have had the effect of working systematically against SMIs. To palliate this bias, the Government has instructed some programs in favor of SMIs. Policies and programs are often in contradiction with each other.

As expected, the role of institutional credit in financing SMIs is almost nonexistent except for that provided through the Government's programs or for borrowers of good standing.

The risk of financing SMIs and a fortiori microenterprises is compounded by the risk of financing "lemons" that would oblige lenders to charge a rate of interest that would sufficiently cover good and bad projects. The difference between the institutional rate charged and this risk-relating rate is so huge that it is not politically feasible to charge it to SMIs. Therefore, commercial banks generally abstain from granting finance to this sector. However, this source of risk should decline with the accumulation of information and experience within the institutions, and with the development of appraisal, supervision, and internal control procedures. This is the main justification for installing at the start of a lending program a strong extension component that will involve commercial banks progressively in this sector. The program will certainly take a long time. So far, there is little evidence that any of the beneficiary institutions are making substantial progress toward the stage of reducing dependence on external sources to finance SMIs. Most financial institution beneficiaries of multilateral or bilateral loans in favor of SMIs are far from being able to sustain an acceptable level of lending, with small incomes received from repayments.

SMI programs have a tendency to overemphasize fixed-capital equipment, whereas SMIs financial requirements rely more on working-capital finance. Development banks are not always well equipped to play this role.

As usual, the study will conclude that the less regulated the environment is, the better it will be for SMIs. Broad programs designed to provide equal incentives and access to scarce resources for all firms, irrespective of size, are likely to be more beneficial in the long run than special programs tailored exclusively for SMIs. Mardsen (1981: 35) has rightly observed "the best overall tonic for small business is likely to be an economic climate combining minimum regulation with maximum openness."

ACKNOWLEDGMENTS

The views expressed in this chapter are personal, and do not in any way represent the views and policies of the Asian Development Bank. The author wishes to express his thanks to Emma Banaria and Celia Garcia for providing able research assistance, and to Helen M. Kidchulan for proficiently typing the manuscript. Special thanks are due to M. G. Quibria for his invaluable comments.

NOTES

1. Labor force increased by about 4.2% p.a. (per annum) for the 1970–1985 period, whereas employment in the manufacturing sector increased by 2.5% p.a. during the same period.
2. Chemicals: fabrication of acids, gases, fertilizers, pesticides, etc.
3. Other chemicals (code 352) include paints, drugs and medicines, soap, perfume, cosmetics, etc.
4. Electrical machinery: electrical motors, transformers, radio, TV, housewares, etc.

5. See Estanislao et al. (1981).

6. An establishment is a manufacturing activity at a fixed location and having performance of assets in its premises.

7. It is not rare to find studies that consider SMI employing less than 50 workers, for example, without explicitly saying whether the cottage industry is included. Official statistics generally do not provide data on the output of cottage industry.

8. Do not include by definition the household sector.

9. More than 200 employees.

10. Against 15% for SMIs.

11. Cutlery, hardware, welding, coating, shops, etc.

12. Wearing apparels arc produced either by large firms or establishments with less than 10 workers.

13. The VA of the pottery industry (361) accounts for only 0.3% of the total manufacturing VA in 1983.

14. Above 200 employees.

15. Same conclusion for 1967–1972, see Anderson and Khambata (1981).

16. Establishments with more than 200 workers.

17. The result (A) is also quite sensitive to the unit chosen: thousand or million Pesos.

18. In this case, α, β, and γ are actual data, and not estimated. TFPG is equal to the increase in output in real terms minus the weighted increase (in real terms) of the factors of production, as specified in the function.

19. The same reason may be invoked in favor of agricultural credit.

REFERENCES

Anderson, D. and F. Khambata. *Small Enterprises and Development Policy in the Philippines: A Case Study*. The World Bank Staff Working Paper No. 468, The World Bank, Washington, D.C., 1981.

Baldwin, Richard E. *Foreign Trade Regimes and Economic Development: The Philippines*. New York: Columbia University Press for the National Bureau of Economic Research, 1975.

Estanislao, J. P., S. E. Agdamag, and M. T. Lim. *Source of Philippine Industrial Growth, 1966–1978*. Philippine Institute for Development Studies, Manila, 1981.

Hooley, Richard. *Productivity Growth in Philippine Manufacturing: Retrospect and Future Prospects*. Monograph Series No. 9, Philippine Institute for Development Studies, Manila, 1985.

Little, I. M. D. "Small Manufacturing Enterprises in Developing Countries." *The World Bank Economic Review 1*(2), 1987, 203–235.

Mardsen, K. "Creating the Right Environment for Small Firms." *Finance and Development 18* (4), December 1981, 33–36.

Sicat, G. "Production Functions in Philippine Manufacturing." Institute of Economic Development and Research, University of the Philippines, Manila, 1963.

———"Denison's Method of Separating the Sources of Economic Growth and Aggregate Production Function." Institute of Economic Development and Research, University of the Philippines, Discussion Paper No. 67-3, 1967.

Williamson, J. and G. Sicat. "Technical Change and Resource Allocation in Philippine Manufacturing, 1957–1965." Institute of Economic Development and Research, University of the Philippines, Discussion Paper No. 68-21, 1968.

INDUSTRIALIZATION OF INDONESIA: A SURVEY

Sukanto Reksohadiprodjo

I. INTRODUCTION

Industrial development in Indonesia is a part of a long-term effort to restructure the nation's unbalanced economy hitherto dominated by only one activity, i.e., agriculture. Data presented in Table 1 indicate the unbalanced state of the Indonesian economy.

The economic goals of the industrialization plan are (1) to have a strong and balanced economic structure between agriculture and industry, (2) to create more employment opportunities, (3) to ensure equity in economic and business opportunities, (4) to enhance exports, (5) to earn and save foreign exchange, (6)

Research in Asian Economic Studies.
Asian Industrialization: Changing Economic Structures,
Volume 1, Part A, pages 259–286.
Copyright © 1988 by JAI Press Inc.
All rights of reproduction in any form reserved.
ISBN: 0-89232-987-4

Table 1. Contribution of Sectors to Gross Domestic Products (GDP) of Indonesia, 1960–1985

Sectors	*1960*	*1970*	*1980*	*1985*
Agriculture (%)	54	45	30	24
Mining (%)	4	10	10	10
Manufacturing (%)	8	8	15	26
Service (%)	34	37	45	40
Total	100	100	100	100

Source: Republik Indonesia, *Nota Keuangan dan Rancangan Anggaran Pendapatan dan Belanja* Negara, 1987–88, Jakarta.

to support regional economic development, and (7) to utilize available natural energy and human resources.

II. INDUSTRIES IN INDONESIA

In Indonesia, industries are classified into four different groups: (1) basic metal and machineries, (2) basic chemicals, (3) miscellaneous, and (4) small-scale industries.

The purpose of the basic industries (1) and (2) is to provide support for sustained economic growth and progressive strengthening of the economic structure of the country. The technologies used are advanced, and relatively more capital intensive. The miscellaneous industries will target for both economic growth and equity; they will use advanced or intermediate technologies, and they may be either labor intensive or capital intensive. Finally, the small-scale industries will focus exclusively on the goal of economic equity. The technologies used in these industries may be intermediate or simple, and they are relatively more labor intensive.

The basic metal and machineries industries are further classified into (1) machineries, (2) basic metal, (3) electrical machineries and electronics, (4) land and air transport equipment, and (4) ship-building. The basic chemical industries consist of (1) cellulose and rubber, (2) agrochemical, (3) organic chemical, and (4) inorganic chemical. The miscellaneous industries include (1) food processing, (2) textiles, (3) chemicals, (4) electrical and metal appliances, and (5) building materials and other general items. Small-scale industries also have five subgroups: (1) food processing, (2) clothing and leather goods, (3) chemical and building materials, (4) handicrafts and general goods, and (5) metal products.

In 1969 the gross domestic product (GDP) of Indonesia was Rp. 4,820.5 billion, and the contribution of the manufacturing sector was Rp. 399.0 billion, or 8.3%. In 1983, the GDP of the country rose to Rp. 12,482.2 billion, and the manufacturing sector contributed Rp. 1,942.5 billion or 15.1%. The annual percentage increase of the GDP over the 13-year period was 7.2%, whereas the annual percentage increase of the manufacturing sector was higher at 11.9% (both at 1973 constant prices).[1] Over the same time period, the output in the machineries and basic metal industries increased by 17% per annum; that of the basic chemical industries also increased by 17% per annum. Both the miscellaneous industries and the small-scale industries recorded a rate of annual increase of 6% over the same time period.

Of the total value added of the industries. miscellaneous industries contributed approximately 46%, machineries and basic metals 30.8%, chemicals 12.5%, and small-scale industries 10.7%. The value added of the industries is estimated to be Rp. 2,777 billion at the end of the Fourth Five Year Plan (1989). The value added of the industries by the end of the Third Five Year Plan in 1984 was Rp. 1,723.4 billion. The sectoral breakdown is as follows: miscellaneous industries 55.3%, machineries and basic metals 22.6%, small-scale industries 12.9%, and chemicals 9.2%. The growth rate of the industries during the period was 8.9% per annum.

In what follows several summary statistics indicating the state of the economy is presented. Table 2 presents estimates of incremental capital output ratios, and shows the incremental added value investment needs and the investment–labor ratio calculations in terms of a four-fold classifications of Indonesian industries. Table 3 indicates the employment profile as industrialization progresses, and shows percentage of labor absorbed and total labor employment in each of the four industry segments. Tables 4 and 5 describe Indonesia's trade relations with the rest of the world. Table 4 gives a breakdown of the country's exports/imports with a regional disaggregation of the world market, and Table 5 is an index of Indonesia's dependence on imports. Table 6 is an account of U.S.–Indonesia trade.

It is realized that the industrial development in Indonesia has also determined the pattern of its exports and imports (see Table 4). In 1969, Indonesia's total imports consisted of raw materials and supplies (48.8%), capital goods (29.1%), and consumption goods (22.1%). In 1985/86, the shares were 54, 39.8, and 6.2%, respectively (see Table 5). In 1986, raw materials and supplies imported consisted of chemicals, iron and metals, rubber and plastic, yarn, building materials, pulp, materials for pharmaceutical products, electrical equipment, fertilizer, and cement. Capital goods imported included machineries, transport equipment, electrical equipment, electrical generators, and telecommunication equipment. Consumption goods imported are milk, food, beverages, fruits, household wares, textiles, soap and cosmetics, tobacco, rice, and other related products.

Regional disaggregation of the world market for Indonesia's imports is presented in Table 4. Further disaggregation countrywide of Indonesia's imports is as follows in 1985/86: Japan (27.3%), European Countries (20.1%), United States (15.8%), Singapore (6.7%), Australia and Oceania (5.4%), Canada and Latin American (3.9%), China (2.7%), ASEAN countries (1.0%), and other Asian Countries (2.9%).

Table 2. ICOR, Incremental Added Values, Investment, and IL Ratio

Class of industries	*ICOR*	*Incremental added value (billion Rupiahs)*	*Investments*		*IL (US$/L)*
			Billions Rupiahs	*Million US$*	
Machineries and basic metals	3.4	464.5	1,576	3.805	108,714
Chemicals	3.5	192.4	673	1.622	46,342
Miscellaneous industries	2.8	322.0	902	2.173	5,432
Small-scale industries	1.9	74.7	142	0.342	368
Total	3.08	1,053.6	3,296	7.942	

Source: Department Perindustrian (Ministry of Industry), *Rencana Pembangunan Lima Tahun Keempat Sektor Industri* (Tahun 1984/1985–1988/1989), 21.

Table 3. Labor Absorbed by the Industrial Sector

Class of industries	*Percentage of labor absorbed*	*Total labor (people)*
Machineries and basic metals	2.5	35,000
Chemicals	2.5	35,000
Miscellaneous	28.5	400,000
Small-scale	66.5	930,000
Total	100.0	1,400,000

Source: Same as for Table 2, p. 22.

Table 4. Indonesia's Exports and Imports, 1981/1982 and 1985/1986, in Percentages

	1981/1982	*1985/1986*
Indonesia's exports to		
Asia	64.7	65.4
America	25.9	24.5
Europe	5.6	7.9
Australia	3.5	1.2
Africa	0.2	1.0
Total	99.9	100.0
Indonesia's imports from		
Asia	58.7	53.1
Europe	20.3	20.1
America	16.0	19.7
Australia	3.3	5.4
Africa	1.7	1.7
Total	100.0	100.0

Source: Biro Pusat Statistik, *Indikator Ekonomi*, several issues.

Table 5. Indonesia's Imports by Types of Goods, 1981/1982 and 1985/1986, in Percentages

Imports of	*1981/1982*	*1985/1986*
Raw materials	48.8	54.0
Capital goods	29.1	39.8
Consumption goods	22.1	6.2
Total	100.0	100.0

Source: Same as for Table 4.

Table 6. Commodities Exported to, and Imported from the United States by Indonesia, 1985/1986, in Percentages

Export		*Import*	
Oil	73.6	Machineries	24.6
Rubber	9.3	Chemicals	16.6
Coffee, cocoa	4.6	Cereals	14.4
Wood manufactured	3.0	Aircrafts	7.9
Tin	1.2	Oil	1.4
Tobacco manufactured, Wood unmanufactured, Vegetable oil	8.3	Road, Textiles, Iron steel, Metal manufactured, Ships	36.5
Total	100.0	Total	100.0 (adjusted for rounding error)

Source: Same as for Table 4.

III. PROBLEMS ENCOUNTERED

Although production of the industrial sector increased over time, there are still problems to be resolved.

1. The role of the industrial sector in the national economy is still small and the linkages between the industrial sector and the other sectors in the economy continues to be suboptimal. Indeed, the linkages within various segments of the industrial sector itself, as it grows, warrants further attention.
2. Second, the interregional distribution of the development activities in the industrial sector in Indonesia continues to be uneven. Most of them are located in Java whereas other regions continue to lag behind.
3. Third, capital is in short supply. Knowledge of technoloy, design, and engineering is inadequate and managerial skill is in need.
4. Fourth, domestic and export markets should be further explored to enable further increases in capacity utilization. Underutilization of existing industrial capacity is certainly a discouragement to new investment and therefore acts as a hindrance to progressive growth of the economy.
5. Fifth, the Indonesian society may not be fully prepared to face the challenges of the fast changing situation following industrialization.
6. Finally, the business climate in an economic regime as it progresses through stages of accelerated industrialization must be able to create a higher order of certainty.

It is argued that the contribution of the industrial sector should be about 30% of the GDP of the country. Programs of industry links have been constructed. The government based its progrems on *industry trends* that covered economic activities of sugarcane, wood, oil and gas, palm oil, forest products, miscellaneous products, basic chemicals, machineries and basic metals, and small-scale industries.

Industrial development should be dispersed between regions. There are *five growth regions*: North Sumatra, South Sumatra, Java and Bali, South Sulawesi, and East Kalimatan. In each region, the government plan calls for establishment of several industrial zones for machineries and basic metal industries, chemicals, etc. (upstream, basic and large industries, state enterprises, private enterprises, and joint enterprises between state and private investors).

Within each industrial zone, the government plan then calls for establishment of industrial estates for upstream, intermediate, and medium-size industries (joint and private enterprises). These industries would then become the support base for the small-scale industries (private firms).

Shortages of capital and entrepreneurial skill are to be eliminated through programs involving direct foreign investment inflows and domestic capital investment. Since 1967, direct foreign investments in the manufacturing sector have been approximately US$ 11,918.9 million in 592 projects, or about 75.7% of total direct foreign investment. Since 1968, domestic capital investments in the manufacturing sector have been Rp. 20,643,702 million in 2,619 projects, or 68.2% of total domestic capital investment.

Of the total US$ 15,741.2 million direct foreign investment (since 1967), Japan is first with a total investment of $US 5,269.5 million or 33.5%, followed by other countries with a total investment of US$ 2,520.6 million or 16.0%. Hong Kong with its investment of US$ 1,883.8 million accounts for 12%, and the share of the United States with its total investment of US$ 1,168.5 million is 7.4%

Non-oil and gas exports of Indonesia in 1983 were directed primarily to eight countries: Singapore (US$ 1,094.8 million or 23,315.2 million kgs), Japan (US$ 1,038.5 million or 4,507.3 million kgs), the United States (US$ 871.9 million or 934.9 million kgs), West Germany ($US 262.8 million or 667.1 million kgs), the United Kingdom (US$ 154.6 million or 250.8 million kgs), South Korea (US$ 56.8 million or 415.8 million kgs), Australia (US$ 42 million or 23.1 million kgs), and the Philippines (US$ 31.6 milion or 213.4 million kgs). Commodities exported in 1984 included crumb rubbers, plywood, sawed woods, finished clothing, aluminum, othjer products, crepe (RSS) textiles, transitors, pellets, chemicals, fertilizer, vegetable oil, leather and leather goods, finished woods, other textiles, strearin, electric appliances, and miscellaneous products.

IV. CENSUS OF INDUSTRIES

Indonesia recently conducted two censuses of industries, one in 1974/1975 and another in 1986 (part of economic census).

In the 1974/1975 census of industries there were about 1,288,615 units of establishments in Indonesia. In the 1986 census, the number of units increased to 1,534,000. In the 1974/1975 census the number of workers employed were reported to be 4,900,000. In the 1986 census, the number rose to 5,287,000. Table 7 shows the number of workers in the large- and medium-scale subgroups of industries in both the censuses. Evidently, both the number of establishments and number of workers employed increased over time for each of the subgroups of industries. On an average, for the whole range of large- and medium-scale industries, the annual rates of increase for the number of establishments and the number of workers employed over the time periods are 5.60 and 8.86%, respectively.

Table 8 indicates the numbers of establishments and of workers employed in the large and medium manufacturing industries in the provinces (except East Timor) in Indonesia. Table 9 presents the same two sets of data for the small-scale industries and its subsectors. The numbers of units of establishment and of workers employed increased, on an average, by an annual rate of 7.37 and 8.13%, respectively. Table 10 presents the related sets of data on small-scale industries and its growth in all provinces in Indonesia.

Tables 11 and 12 relate to household industry. Table 11 presents the numbers of establishments and of workers employed in various subsectors of the house-

Table 7. Number of Establishments and Workers in the Large- and Medium-Scale Industries in Indonesia and Their Growth According to Subindustries, 1974/1975 and 1986 (Excluding East Timor)

	Number of establishments			*Number of workers*		
Subindustries	*1974/1975 industry census*	*1986 economic census*	*Percentage increase*	*1974/1975 industry census*	*1986 economic census*	*Percentage increase*
Food and beverages	2,367	3,880	4.60	268,388	519,449	6.19
Textile, finished clothing and leather	2,066	2,869	3.03	174,246	381,360	7.38
Wood and wood products	407	1,204	10.36	22,368	181,883	20.99
Paper and paper products	289	604	6.93	21,982	56,680	8.99
Chemical and chemical products	899	1,626	5.53	83,802	248,631	10.39
Nonmetal extractives	480	1,249	9.08	24,579	88,995	12.40
Basic metals	18	30	4.75	2,060	15,647	20.24
Metal products, machineries, and equipment	500	1,283	8.94	55,867	179,375	11.19
Other manufacturing	65	157	8.35	8,394	12,015	3.31
Total	7,091	12,902	5.60	661,704	1,684,035	8.86

Sources: Biro Pusat Statistik, *Sensus Industri* 1974/1975: *Industrial Besar dan Sedang di Indonesia*, Bagian I (Central Bureau of Statistics, Industry Census 1974: Large and Medium Manufacturing Industries in Indonesia, Vol. I). Biro Pusat Statistik, *Sensus Ekonomi* 1986: *Statistik Industri Besar dan Sedang*, Vols. I and II (Central Bureau of Statistics, 1986 Economic Census: Large and Medium Manufacturing Industries Statistics, Vols. I and II).

Table 8. Number of Establishments and Workers in the Large and Medium Manufacturing Industries in the Provinces in Indonesia, 1974/1975–1986 (Excluding East Timor)

	Number of establishments			*Number of workers*		
Provinces	*1974/1975 industry census*	*1986 economic census*	*Percentage increase*	*1974/1975 industry census*	*1986 economic census*	*Percentage increase*
Aceh	25	45	5.49	2,887	11,110	13.03
North Sumatra	272	687	8.79	25,258	88,965	12.13
West Sumatra	45	110	8.46	4,288	11,428	9.32
Riau	49	135	9.65	3,244	20,356	18.17
Jambi	30	104	11.97	3,701	13,815	12.72
South Sumatra	73	173	8.16	11,111	35,395	11.11
Bengkulu	3	9	10.50	63	673	24.03
Lambung	65	166	8.90	4,319	22,919	16.38
Jakarta	878	1,798	6.73	87,943	231,910	9.22
West Java	1,598	3,134	6.31	116,629	392,535	11.66
Central Java	1,584	2,168	2.89	147,862	270,253	5.64
Yogyakarta	155	205	2.57	13,804	17,452	2.15
East Java	1,819	3,038	4.77	205,970	412,504	6.52
Bali	63	243	13.31	5,811	15,616	9.40
West Nusa Tenggara	67	80	1.63	3,288	3,739	1.18
East Nusa Tenggara	14	24	5.02	785	1,370	1.59
West Kalimantan	58	79	2.85	8,022	20,909	9.10
Central Kalimantan	21	79	12.80	1,224	15,838	26.21
South Kalimantan	60	141	8.08	4,434	23,429	16.34

East Kalimantan	23	104	14.70	958	34,127	38.38
North Sulawesi	18	72	13.43	1,013	4,562	14.66
Central Sulawesi	5	34	19.04	190	4,807	34.14
South Sulawesi	114	158	3.01	6,174	18,026	10.23
Southeast Sulawesi	30	61	6.66	941	2,058	7.37
Moluccas	10	34	11.77	1,023	8,961	21.81
West Irian	12	20	4.75	762	1,259	4.67
Total	7,091	12,902	5.60	661,704	1,684,014	8.86

Source: BPS, *Sensus Industri* 1974/1975: *Industri Besar dan Sedang di Indonesia*, Vol. I. BPS, *Sensus Ekonomi* 1986.

Table 9. The Number of Establishments and Workers of Small-Scale Industries and Their Growth, 1974/1975 and 1986 (Excluding East Timor)

	Number of establishments			Number of workers		
Subindustries	*1974/1975 industry census*	*1986 economic census*	*Percentage increase*	*1974/1975 industry census*	*1986 economic census*	*Percentage increase*
Food and beverages	24,275	36,950	4.29	151,194	281,431	6.41
Textile, finished clothings, leather	5,792	14,862	9.88	55,375	121,993	8.22
Wood and wood products	5,456	15,494	11.00	41,680	111,553	10.35
Paper and paper products	867	2,705	12.05	8,067	23,141	11.11
Chemical and chemical products	1,382	2,551	6.32	12,422	22,517	6.13
Nonmetal extractive materials	6,749	12,148	6.05	46,916	89,326	6.65
Basic metals	—	—	—	—	—	—
Metal products, machines, and equipment	2,957	4,901	5.18	22,113	36,842	5.24
Other manufacturing	708	8,503	28.22	5,473	63,398	27.76
Total	48,186	98,114	7.37	343,240	750,201	8.13

Sources: BPS, *Sensus Industri* 1974/1975: *Industri Kecil di Indonesia*, jilid 1 (Central Bureau of Statistics, 1974/75, Industry Census: Small scale industry of Indonesia, Vol. 1).
BPS, *Sensus Ekonomi* 1986, Vols. 1 and 2 (Central Bureau of Statistics, 1986 Economic Census, Vols. 1 and 2).

Table 10. The Number of Establishments and Workers in Small-Scale Industries and Their Growth in Provinces in Indonesia 1974/1975 and 1986 (Including East Timor)

Provinces	*Number of establishments*			*Number of workers*		
	1974/1975 industry census	*1986 economic census*	*Percentage increase*	*1974/1975 industry census*	*1986 economic census*	*Percentage*
Aceh	741	1,028	3.33	5,016	6,874	3.20
North Sumatra	1,985	3,742	6.55	15,750	29,364	6.53
West Sumatra	1,220	1,326	0.84	7,710	9,291	1.88
Riau	684	992	3.79	4,782	7,628	4.78
Jambi	440	568	2.59	2,608	3,678	3.50
South Sumatra	1,922	1,608	-1.77	12,185	11,778	-0.34
Bengkulu	116	201	5.65	847	1,338	4.68
Lambung	470	1,135	9.22	3,633	8,645	9.06
Jakarta	1,983	8,352	15.46	18,510	71,187	14.47
West Java	10,077	17,624	5.75	71,467	133,163	6.42
Central Java	9,213	27,193	11.43	74,235	211,269	11.03
Yogyakarta	1,160	2,680	8.73	9,291	19,265	7.56
East Java	11,418	20,094	5.82	71,154	155,424	8.13
Bali	710	1,819	9.86	5,630	14,185	9.68
West Nusa Tenggara	555	1,232	3.30	3,348	8,497	9.76
East Nusa Tenggara	264	384	3.82	2,041	2,675	2.74
West Kalimantan	497	592	1.76	3,104	4,308	3.33
Central Kalimantan	191	432	8.50	1,508	3,086	7.42

(cont)

Table 10. cont.

Provinces	*Number of establishments*			*Number of workers*		
	1974/1975 industry census	*1986 economic census*	*Percentage Percentage increase*	*1974/1975 industry census*	*1986 economic census*	*Percentage increase*
South Kalimantan	509	1,020	7.20	3,694	7,190	6.89
East Kalimantan	147	531	13.70	1,267	4,131	12.55
North Sulawesi	452	682	4.20	3,221	4,777	4.02
Central Sulawesi	296	614	7.52	1,839	4,094	8.33
South Sulawesi	2,528	3,371	2.92	15,843	22,057	3.63
Southeast Sulawesi	386	464	1.86	2,678	3,088	1.43
Moluccas	100	256	9.86	855	1,710	7.18
West Irian	122	174	3.61	1,021	1,199	1.62
Total	48,186	98,114	7.37	343,240	750,201	8.13

Source: BPS, *Sensus Industri 1974/1975: (Central Bureau of Statistics, 1974/1975 Industry Census). BPS, Sensus Ekonomi* (1986) (Central Bureau of Statistics, 1986 Economic Census).

Table 11. The Number of Establishments and Workers of Household Industries and Their Growth from 1974/1975 to 1986 According to Subsector of Industries (Excluding Riau, East Nusa Tenggara, Central Kalimantan, East Kalimantan, Central Sulawesi, Southeast Sulawesi, Moluccas, Irian Jaya, and East Timor)

	Number of establishments			*Number of workers*			
Subsectors	*1974/1975 industry census*	*1986 economic census*	*Percentage increase*	*1974/1975 industry census*	*Adjusted industry census*	*1986 economic census*	*Percentage increase*
Food and beverages	431,109	423,886	–0.16	1,395,897	1,079,301	1,044,119	–0.32
Textile, finished clothings, leather	137,527	134,459	–0.22	428,839	326,581	191,072	–5.02
Wood and wood products	530,578	441,177	–1.76	1,630,332	1,204,341	725,525	–4.76
Paper and paper products	2,628	8,881	12.42	9,630,332	7,625	16,635	7.79
Chemical and chemical products	5,317	7,561	3.44	20,946	17,904	13,082	–2.97
Iron-metalic extractive materials	80,435	103,214	2.43	262,711	222,124	260,451	1.54
Basic metals	—	—	—	—	—	—	
Metal products, and equipment	15,432	32,658	7.47	55,773	49,767	84,413	5.21
Other manufacturing	20,125	190,386	24.12	64,545	56,207	390,270	20.49
Total	1,223,151	1,342,222	0.90	3,862,521	2,963,850	2,725,567	–0.80

Sources: BPS, *Sensus Industri* 1974/1975: *Industri Kerajinan Rumahtangga*, jilid I dan II. (Central Bureau of Statistics, 1974/75, Industry Census: Household Manufacturing, Vols. I and II). BPS, *Sensus Ekonomi* 1986 (Central Bureau of Statistics, 1986 Economic Census).

Table 12. The Number of Establishments and Workers in Household Industries and Their Growth from 1974/1975 to 1986 in Provinces in Indonesia

	Number of establishments			*Number of workers*			
Provinces	*1974/1975 industry census*	*1986 economic census*	*Percentage increase*	*1974/1975 industry census*	*Adjusted industry census*	*1986 economic census*	*Percentage increase*
Aceh	24,574	17,661	−3.13	73,562	49,046	27,866	−5.29
North Sumatra	15,560	26,560	5.28	52,407	40,720	46,532	1.29
West Sumatra	22,942	26,152	1.27	65,879	49,185	46,399	−0.56
Jambi	8,207	6,372	−2.45	27,399	22,367	11,469	−6.22
South Sumatra	11,523	22,813	6.52	38,736	29,252	48,953	5.08
Bengkulu	4,850	4,490	−0.74	14,837	10,542	7,385	−3.36
Lambung	8,533	29,098	12.74	28,773	20,997	61,428	10.87
Jakarta	16,345	19,228	1.57	57,949	49,878	39,151	−2.30
West Java	149,500	222,595	3.90	472,399	368,554	520,221	3.37
Central Java	520,892	421,115	−2.02	1,633,451	1,243,797	889,239	−3.18
Yogyakarta	86,310	67,582	−2.32	267,860	183,964	136,292	−2.84
East Java	171,716	261,134	4.11	568,971	457,284	556,862	1.91
Bali	21,613	31,087	3.56	64,442	43,432	54,822	2.26
West Nusa Tenggara	30,050	43,384	3.59	80,292	62,869	61,173	−0.26
West Kalimantan	12,078	12,820	0.57	39,000	28,600	18,998	−3.87
South Kalimantan	22,667	39,947	5.60	73,761	57,996	53,166	−0.83
North Sulawesi	29,138	21,733	−2.78	98,184	80,063	30,791	−8.78
South Sulawesi	66,353	67,881	0.22	204,619	165,274	114,820	−3.44
Total	1,223,151	1,342,222	0.90	3,862,521	2,696,850	2,725,567	−0.80

Sources: BPS, *Sensus Industri* 1974/1975: *Industri Kerajinan Rumah tangga*, jilid I (Central Bureau of Statistics, 1974/1975, Industry Census: Household industry, Vol. I).
BPS, *Sensus Ekonomi*, 1986 (Central Bureau of Statistics, 1986 Economic Census).

hold industry, while Table 12 include the two sets of data in the category in the provinces of Indonesia. It should be noted that in the household industry category, although in 1986 the number of units of establishments increased from 1974/1975 by 0.9%, the number of workers employed over the time period decreased by 0.8%.

V. THE INDUSTRIAL POLICY OF INDONESIA: THE THREE PHASES

The progress of Indonesia's industrialization must be attributed to the industrial policy the country adopted. The goals of this policy are summarized below (Biro Pusik Statistik, 17–18):

1. To create employment opportunities and business opportunities, to increase export, to earn and save foreign exchange, to support regional economic development, and to optimally utilize natural and energy resources and human resources (as stated in the introduction).
2. To produce industrial machineries and develop a capital goods base.
3. To ensure availability of raw materials and intermediate goods as will be necessary for an efficient functioning of the industrialized economy.
4. To support the agricultural sector, and other related sectors that make use of agriculture products.
5. To improve interindustry linkages and also the linkages between the industrial sector and other sectors of the economy.
6. To augment the contribution of the industrial sector to the economy with a view to restructuring the national economy.
7. To improve intersectoral linkages within the industrial sector to achieve higher yields of value added.
8. To provide a support base to the small-scale and handicraft industry sectors for a higher rate of labor absorption.
9. To accelerate the growth of industrial centers in the regions that are endowed with supplies of potential natural resources.
10. To intiate steps toward promoting private businesses by way of establishing adequate facilities and general conditions that support the growth of industries, and also by way of increasing education and training related to technological expertise and skill and management capabilities, particularly for small-scale businessmen and professionals who are ready for independent business.
11. To enhance skill and expertise in technology, techniques, design, and engineering that are essential to a successful industrialization process and that will contribute to the creation of a base for the economic "take off" for Indonesia.

12. To introduce measures to prevent pollution and damage to the environment, to control waste of natural resources, and to contain conspicuous consumption.
13. To encourage optimum use of domestic products in the execution of industrialization policy.
14. To direct the industrial development program with a view to ensuring national stability within the framework of national security.
15. To create a strong base for the subsequent Five Year Development Plans.

The strategies by the Ministry include increases of produciton, increased earnings of foreign exchange, and human resource development. The results of the industrialization program were increased outputs of basic metal, basic chemical, and miscellaneous industries. Some of the industries, however, experienced declines in their outputs since 1982–1983 because of recessions in the international market and also in Indonesia. The increased output in several industrial sectors contributed to the increase of GDP (see Table 13). The proportion of the industrial sector output in the GDP increased over time, even though the rate of growth fluctuated during the 1982–1983 recession. In terms of manufacturing industries, the sectors's contribution to GDP rose from 8.3% in 1969 to 15.1% in 1983, and to a projected rise to 16.3% in 1985 (see, Table 13b). In terms of percentage increase, the manufacturing sector recorded an average growth rate of 11.9% over the 1969–1983 period, and this rate would have been much higher but for the recessions and its serious adverse impacts in 1982 and 1983 (see, Table 13c).

The process of industrialization began in Indonesia in 1967 with the introduction of Law No. 1 of the year concerning foreign investment, followed by Law No. 6 of 1968 that related to domestic investment. The three phases of industrialization in Indonesia may be identified as follows: first, the import substitution phase from 1967 through 1975, second, the phase of the development of upstream industries, 1975–1982, and third, the difficult period from 1982 on.

The import substitution phase was characterized by the following three steps. First, assembly-type industries producing consumption goods, such as cars, motor cycles, television sets, radios, refrigerators, air conditioners, and sewing machines, were established. They were end-process activities with imported completely knocked down kits in which components were purchased from the principal companies. Second, protection of these industries was given by the Government of Indonesia. Import of products produced by these industries was totally prohibited, and these industries were given tax holidays. Third, most of these industries were established by foreign investors whose motivation was to exploit the potential domestic market for their products.

The phase of developing upstream industries was marked by the following four characteristics. First, there was market saturation for final consumer goods produced by import-substitution policy-induced manufacturing industries. Second, the establishment of basic industries, machine industries, spare-parts industries, and high-tech industries was undertaken under public enterprises. These were designated as strategic industries. Third, a deletion program for basic metal industries was initiated. They were supported to undertake in-house manufacture of certain components or to buy some compenents from other firms (unaffiliated ones) that produced these components (out-house manufactures), i.e., small-scale subcontractors, if possible. Fourth, a policy providing expansion of protection of intermediate and capital goods industries was initiated.

Table 14 shows the structural changes in the manufacturing sector in Indonesia. The following points are to be noted:

1. There was a sharp decline of the contribution of consumption goods industries (except the durable consumption goods) to the value added of total industry output. It fell from 80.8% in 1971 to 47.6% in 1980.
2. There was a percipitate increase in the contributions of intermediate goods industries and of capital goods industries to the value of total industry. Over the same time period, the rates of these two industry sectors rose from 13.1 to 35.5% and from 6.1 to 16.9%, respectively.
3. The contribution of food, beverage, and tobacco industries to the added value of the industrial sector declined from 63.8 to 31.7%.
4. The contribution of the wood product industries increased from 1.4 to 7.0%, chemical industries increased from 0.8 to 4.3%, other chemical goods increased from 3.8 to 7.1%, rubber industries rose from 1.3 to 4.8%, and nonmetal mineral goods industries increased from 2.5 to 5.9%
5. The contribution of iron and steel industries sharply increased from zero in 1971 to 3.1% in 1980.
6. The growth of capital goods industries was very fast, averaging 29.2% per annum. The contribution of nonelectrical machinery industries rose from 2.5 to 5.3%, that of transport equipment industry went up from 0.9 to 6.4%, and contributions of metal goods industry rose from 2.3 to 3.5%.
7. The composition of imported goods changes as well. In 1969–1970, the imported consumption goods as a percentage of total import was 22.1%, and in 1984–1985 it declined to only 5.6%. Over the same time period, the percentage of imported intermediate goods increased from 48.8 to 53.1%, and the percentage of capital goods import rose from 29.1 to 41.3%.

The third phase of Indonesia's industrial development has been plagued by problems. These problems can be summed up as follows:

1. The structure of the industry has developed certain difficult characteristics.

Table 13. Gross Domestic Product, 1969–1983

Sectors	1969	1970	1971	1972	1973	1974	1975	1976	1977
a. Billion Rupiah, at 1973 Constant Prices									
1. Agriculture	2,263.0	2,356.0	2,441.0	2,479.0	2,710.0	2,811.0	2,811.2	2,943.7	2,981.3
a. Food	1,373.0	1,402.0	1,436.0	1,415.0	1,573.0	1,681.0	1,696.1	1,755.5	1,734.2
b. Other	890.0	954.0	1,005.0	1,064.0	1,137.0	1,130.0	1,115.1	1,188.2	1,247.1
2. Mining and extractives	452.0	522.0	551.0	674.0	831.0	859.0	828.1	952.3	1,070.0
3. Manufacturing	399.0	435.0	490.0	564.0	650.0	755.0	847.9	930.0	1,057.7
4. Electricity, gas, drinking water	19.6	22.5	24.7	26.2	30.4	37.0	41.2	46.3	49.0
5. Construction	114.0	143.0	171.0	222.0	262.0	320.0	364.8	384.5	463.8
6. Transportation and communication	158.0	165.0	210.0	229.0	257.0	288.0	302.7	342.6	438.7
7. Trade, financial institutions other service sectors	1,414.9	1,538.5	1,657.0	1,873.0	2,013.0	2,199.0	2,434.9	2,556.9	2,821.5
Total	4,820.5	5,182.0	5,544.7	6,067.2	6,753.4	7,269.0	7,630.0	8,156.3	8,882.0

Sectors	1978	1979	1980	1981	1982	1983	1984	1985
a. Billion Rupiah, at 1973 Constant Prices								
1. Agriculture	3,134.8	3,255.6	3,424.9	3,593.5	3,669.8	3,845.6		
a. Food	1,835.8	1,908.8	2,073.4	2,261.2	2,294.4	2,412.3		
b. Other	1,299.0	1,346.8	1,351.5	1,332.3	1,375.4	1,433.3		
2. Mining and extractives	1,048.8	1,046.9	1,034.6	1,069.1	939.8	966.5		
3. Manufacturing	1,235.6	1,395.3	1,704.6	1,877.8	1,900.7	1,942.5		
4. Electricity, gas, drinking water	56.9	68.6	77.9	89.9	105.5	112.8		
5. Construction	528.9	562.8	639.3	720.2	757.8	804.5		
6. Transportation and communication	514.2	559.8	609.4	676.9	716.6	752.5		
7. Trade, financial institutions other service sectors	3,047.3	3,275.9	3,678.5	4,027.2	4,235.2	4,427.8		
Total	9,566.5	10,164.9	11,169.2	12,054.6	12,325.4	12,842.2		

Table 13. cont.

Sectors	1969	1970	1971	1972	1973	1974	1975	1976
			b. Proportion					
1. Agriculture	46.9	45.5	44.0	40.8	40.1	38.7	36.8	36.1
a. Food								
b. Other								
2. Mining and extractives	9.4	10.0	9.9	11.1	12.3	11.8	10.9	11.7
3. Manufacturing	8.3	8.4	8.8	9.3	9.6	10.4	11.1	11.4
4. Electricity, gas, drinking water	0.4	0.4	0.4	0.4	0.5	0.5	0.5	0.6
5. Construction	2.4	2.8	3.2	3.7	3.9	4.4	4.8	4.7
6. Transportation and communication	3.3	3.2	3.8	3.8	3.8	4.0	4.0	4.2
7. Trade, financial institutions other service sectors	29.3	29.7	29.9	30.9	29.8	30.2	31.9	31.3
Total	100.0	100.0	100.0	100.0	100.0	100.0	100.0	100.0

Sectors	*1977*	*1978*	*1979*	*1980*	*1981*	*1982*	*1983*	*1985 estimated*
			b. Proportion					
1. Agriculture	33.6	32.8	32.0	30.7	29.8	29.8	29.9	28.5
a. Food								
b. Other								
2. Mining and extractives	12.0	10.9	10.3	9.3	8.9	7.6	7.4	9.7
3. Manufacturing	11.9	12.9	13.7	15.3	15.6	15.4	15.1	16.3
4. Electricity, gas, drinking water	0.6	0.6	0.7	0.7	0.7	0.9	0.9	1.2
5. Construction	5.2	5.5	5.5	5.7	6.0	6.1	6.3	6.8
6. Transportation and communication	4.9	5.4	5.5	5.4	5.6	5.8	5.9	5.9
7. Trade, financial institutions other service sectors	31.8	31.9	32.3	32.9	33.4	34.4	34.5	31.6
Total	100.0	100.0	100.0	100.0	100.0	100.0	100.0	100.0

Table 13. cont.

Sectors	1969	1970	1971	1972	1973	1974	1975	1976
c. Percentage Increases								
1. Agriculture	4.1	4.1	3.6	1.6	9.3	3.7	0.01	4.7
a. Food								
b. Other								
2. Mining and extractives	15.5	15.5	5.6	22.3	23.3	3.4	–3.6	15.0
3. Manufacturing	9.0	9.0	12.6	15.1	15.2	16.2	12.3	9.7
4. Electricity, gas, drinking water	14.8	14.8	9.8	6.1	16.0	21.7	11.4	12.4
5. Construction	25.4	25.4	19.6	29.8	18.0	22.1	14.0	5.4
6. Transportation and communication	4.4	4.4	27.3	9.0	12.2	12.1	5.1	13.2
7. Trade, financial institutions other service sectors	8.7	8.7	7.7	13.0	7.5	9.2	10.7	5.0
Total	7.5	7.5	7.0	9.4	11.3	7.6	5.0	6.9

Sectors	1977	1978	1979	1980	1981	1982	1983	Average
				c. Percentage Increases				
1. Agriculture	1.3	5.2	3.9	5.2	4.9	2.1	4.8	3.8
a. Food								
b. Other								
2. Mining and extractives	12.4	–2.0	–0.2	–1.2	3.3	–12.1	1.8	5.5
3. Manufacturing	13.7	16.8	12.9	22.2	10.2	1.2	2.2	11.9
4. Electricity, gas, drinking water	5.8	16.1	20.6	13.6	15.4	17.4	6.9	13.3
5. Construction	20.6	14.0	6.4	13.6	12.7	5.2	6.2	14.9
6. Transportation and communication	20.1	17.2	8.9	8.9	11.1	5.9	5.0	11.7
7. Trade, financial institutions other service sectors	10.3	8.0	7.5	12.3	9.5	5.2	4.5	8.4
Total	8.9	7.7	6.3	9.9	7.9	2.2	4.2	7.2

Sources: Republik of Indonesia, *The Fourth Five-Year Development Plan* 1984/85–1988/89, Jakarta, 1984.

Table 14.
The Growth and Structural Change of Added Value of Manufacturing Industries, 1971 and 1980

	ISIC Code	*Subsubsectors of industry*	*Percentage of total 1971*	*1980*	*Rate of growth yearly average 1970–1981*
1.	Consumption goods		80.8	47.6	
	3110	Food products	33.9	11.1	13.61
	3130	Beverages	2.0	1.5	9.26
	3140	Tobacco	27.9	19.1	9.64
	3210	Textile	13.2	12.4	10.83
	3220	Finished clothing	0.1	0.4	12.56
	3240	Shoes	0.6	0.8	9.05
	3320	Furnitures	0.3	0.2	18.72
	3420	Printing and publishing	2.0	1.5	24.32
	3610	Porcelain	0.6	0.2	10.15
	3900	Other	0.3	0.4	12.04
2.	Intermediate goods		13.1	35.5	
	3230	Leather goods	0.3	0.2	31.48
	3310	Wood products	1.4	7.0	19.15
	3410	Paper products	2.0	1.5	14.73
	3510	Chemical	0.8	4.3	19.62
	3520	Other chemicals	3.8	7.1	4.53
	3530	Refineries	n.a.	n.a.	7.73
	3540	Oil products and coal	0	0	n.a.
	3550	Rubber products	1.3	4.8	22.21
	3560	Plastic products	0.5	0.7	33.23
	3620	Glass products	0.5	1.1	17.56
	3690	Nonmetal mineral products	2.5	5.9	27.79
	3710	Iron and steel	—	3.1	51.35
	3720	Noniron metal	—	0	—
3.	Capital goods		6.1	16.9	
	3810	Metal products	2.3	3.5	18.86
	3820	Machine products	0.4	1.6	19.01
	3830	Electrical machines	2.5	5.3	29.20
	3840	Transport equipment	0.9	6.4	7.31
	3850	Professional and scientific	0.0	0.1	12.04
	Total (industrial sector)		100.0	100.0	11.88
	Added value of industrial sector (billion Rp, current prices)		135,900	2,130,000	—

Sources: Roepstorff (1985: Table 5, p. 37).

a. There is a concentration of industries in the production of consumption goods; most companies are of assembly-type and function as import-substitute producers, with much of their raw materials and intermediate goods being imported.

b. Natural resources available in the country are not domestically utilized, but are used mostly for exports.

c. Fast development of downstream industries have taken place when the development of upstream industries faces difficult problems.

d. Import of consumption goods did decline, but imports of intermediate and capital goods have been increasing at a much faster rate.

e. The role of industry in the economy is still ill-defined. Linkages between the industrial sector and other sectors of the economy, and also interindustry linkages continue to be quite inadequate.

2. The proportion of manufactured goods export to the total export is relatively low. Some contributing factors are listed here.

a. The scale of operation for industries is in general relatively small and machineries used are old fashioned; as a result, outputs are of low quality and costs of transport and electricity are relatively high.

b. There is a continued shortage of skilled labor

c. Export trade is limited by its country destinations, and also by the types of products for exports. Concentration of exports to Japan, the United States, and the European Economic Community persists. The types of commodities exported also remain limited. A diversification of the export trade by exploration of new market destinations and also by broadening of the product categories is overdue.

d. Export-trade enterprises are limited in numbers.

e. Protectionist trade policies of the developed industrialized countries limit Indonesian exports.

3. The manufacturing industries have limited competitive strength. Some specific reasons for this development are cited below.

a. Low utilization of capacities, especially in automobile manufacturing, steel industry, electronics, paper, textiles, and petroleum refinery limits competition is pervasive.

b. Protection given by the Government of Indonesia does not provide incentives to competition.

c. The high cost of business limits entry of new firms, and thus inhibits competition.

d. A generally pervasive low level of efficiency is yet another limiting factor.

e. Laxity in the enforcement of Indonesian Industrial Standards acts as a deterrent to competition in terms of quality of products.

4. There is a concentration of industries in one region, namely Java.
5. Indonesia does not have adequate software; basic and applied research is lacking.
6. The role of small-scale industries continues to be at the bottom level, although it is generally recognized that in the subsector business and employment opportunities and export of non-oil products can be increased. The market link between the small- and large/medium-scale industries is nonexistent. The quality of products of the subsector has remained relatively poor, and the subsector does not have access to capital and other related facilities, nor to technology, and entrepreneurial and managerial skill.

VI. CONCLUSION

A set of recommendations is in order. First, the industrial climate and regulations should be reviewed and adjusted further to attract industrial investors. Second, more infrastructure facilities should be developed in outer Java. Third, incentives by way of low tax rate, fast services, low interest rate, and favorable business regulations should be provided to both foreign and indigenous investors. Fourth, marketing strategy, efficiency, and quality of products should always be considered to create new markets. Fifth, industrial development goals, strategies, and policies should be better communicated to the people of Indonesia so that there is a better appreciation of the policy actions that may follow. Sixth, export diversification both in terms of types of commodities and market destinations should receive high priority.

NOTE

1. Excluding refineries and other oil and gas industries (LNG, LPG).

REFERENCES

Biro Pusat Statistik. *Indikator Ekonomi*, several issues.

———*Sensus Industri* 1974–1975 and *Sensus Ekonomi* 1986.

———*Statistik Industri Besar dan Sedang*, Vols. I and II.

Government of Indonesia. *The Fourth Five-Year Development Plan*, 1984/85–1988/89, Jakarta, 1984.

———*Financial Report and Government Revenue and Expenditures*, 1987/1988, Jakarta, 1987.

Ministry of Industry. *The Fourth Five Year Development of the Industrial Sector*, 1984/85–1988/89, Jakarta, 1984.

———*The Execution of Linkage Programs of the Industrial Sector*, Jakarta, 1985.

———*Industrial Growth Areas*, Jakarta, 1985.

———*Realization and Export Program of the Industrial Sector*, Jakarta, 1984.

Roepstorff, Torben. "Industrial Development in Indonesia: Performance and Prospects." *Bulletin of Indonesian Economic Studies* April 1985, 37.

SECTION IV

ASIAN NICs AND ASEAN: INVESTMENT PATTERNS/ MANUFACTURING PRODUCTIVITY

AN ECONOMIC ANALYSIS OF U.S. DIRECT INVESTMENT IN MANUFACTURING INDUSTRIES IN SELECTED ASIA/PACIFIC COUNTRIES

Andrew Stern

I. INTRODUCTION

United States investment in the growing economies of East Asia has been increasing dramatically in recent years. Although the more publicized form of such investment has been in the form of portfolio investment, the direct involvment of U.S. firms in the production of goods in the area has also been substantial.

Research in Asian Economic Studies.
Asian Industrialization: Changing Economic Structures,
Volume 1, Part A, pages 289–307.
Copyright © 1988 by JAI Press Inc.
All rights of reproduction in any form reserved.
ISBN: 0-89232-987-4

Data collected by the U.S. Bureau of Economic Analysis in conjunction with its 1982 *Benchmark Survey of U.S. Direct Investment Abroad* shows that 250 U.S.-based multinational corporations (MNCs) reported more than 530 sizable manufacturing affiliates[1] in the countries located in the general area of the South China Sea.[2]

The phenomenon of direct investment in foreign countries has long puzzled economists. That factor price equalization in the case of nontraded goods can be achieved only with factor mobility is self-evident. But the traditional theory of international trade, from its foundations in perfect competition, static comparative advantage, and factor immobility, seems to have little to offer by way of an explanation for foreign direct investment in the production of traded goods. Because of the increasing importance of this kind of direct investment, economists have struggled to find viable theoretical models and the data necessary to validate them. Oligopoly, the product cycle, diversification, ''internationalization,'' and a host of other approaches, including some with a claim to eclecticism, have been invoked in often vain attempts to rescue the pure theorists from their predicament.[3]

In this research, we shall accept the level of direct investment in the manufacturing sector of OAP countries for what it is, and concentrate on explaining its industrial composition. Success in this endeavor would allow us to make plausible conjectures about the future development of U.S. direct investment in the various manufacturing industries.

In pursuing this objective, our next task will be to justify the use of OAP data as a homogenous block. This is followed by a sketch of the average U.S. affiliate operating in the OAP region. A fourth section looks at the share of manufacturing in the total direct investment of the United States in OAP countries. This provides the background for the fifth section, which compares the composition of manufacturing investment between world regions and the United States, between OAP and other world regions, and also within OAP. The sixth section brings out the central thesis of the chapter, namely that wages and incomes provide the best explanation for the present composition of U.S. direct investment in OAP manufacturing. The concluding section extrapolates the findings for a tentative prediction of the future of U.S. manufacturing investment in OAP countries.

II. CLASSIFICATION

Close examination of the data collected by the 1982 *Benchmark Survey* suggests that the level of economic development as evidenced by hourly wage rates and per capita incomes provides the predominant mode of classification for grouping countries and regions. Secondary considerations consist of similarity in economic geography, demographics, and the geographic contiguity of countries within a region. Thus, South Africa is lumped together with Australia and New

Zealand, whereas Turkey, Portugal, and Switzerland are included in one grouping (Europe). Apart from providing the only consistent mode of classification, the wage-rate–income criterion also provides fairly consistent readings on the region's standing along the path of economic development. A clear picture of this last attribute is given by the following tabulation:

Interregional Averages and Ranges of the Hourly Compensation[a] of Workers in Majority Owned Manufacturing Affiliates of U.S. Parents

Region[b]	*High*	*Average*	*Low*
R2		12.17	
R3	13.00	9.44	3.49
R4		9.95	
R5	10.59	8.03	3.64
R6	11.58	3.55	1.78
R7	3.10	2.08	1.34
R8	7.15	6.44	4.12
R9	2.12	1.47	1.04

Source: 1982 Benchmark Survey, 254.

[a] In U.S.$.

[b] For region codes, see the Appendix.

The very narrow range of the OAP (R9) wage rate, although it covers an entire subcontinent and includes at least 10 major countries, provides strong support for the assumption of intraregional homogeneity. Remaining intraregional differences within OAP are mainly locational and administrative. India does not possess a direct outlet on the South China Sea and is thus somewhat more distant from the United States. South Korea and India discourage majority ownership by foreigners of affiliates operated within their borders, and Hong Kong and Singapore are city-states with a natural predilection for trade. These differential features are outweighed by the similarities: OAP countries share geographic proximity with each other, and they possess large and relatively literate populations with low incomes. These considerations would, *inter alia*, justify the classification of Japan as a separate region since it shares OAP's locational and demographic but not its economic characteristics.

III. U.S. DIRECT INVESTMENT IN OAP: A COMPOSITE PORTRAIT

As of the 1982 *Benchmark Survey* of U.S. direct investment abroad, 7.38% of the affiliates of U.S.-based MNCs (worldwide) operated in the OAP region. These affiliates generated 7.06% of all affiliate sales worldwide and controlled 7.53% of all assets. Production of the goods and services sold was achieved by combining 8.18% of all workers employed by U.S. affiliates worldwide with 6.23% of all net property—plant and equipment operated by U.S. affiliates worldwide. Net income generated by this activity in the OAP region represented 12.92% of all affiliate net income, and 10.10% of all foreign income taxes paid by U.S. affiliates in all industries were paid by affiliates operating in OAP countries.

Manufacturing subsidiaries present a somewhat different picture. Although 7.64% of all U.S. manufacturing subsidiaries operated in OAP countries, only 4.15% of sales was generated by these affiliates, using 4.47% of assets. Factors of production were used as follows: 4.15% of all net property—plant and equipment was combined with 8.99% of all workers employed by manufacturing affiliates.[4] Profits amounted to 10.25% of the worldwide total, and taxes paid to OAP governments only 4.40% of all taxes paid by manufacturing subsidiaries of U.S. MNCs worldwide. The role of technology transfer might be inferred from the receipts by U.S. MNCs of royalties and license fees from their foreign affiliates. OAP contributions in this category amounted to only 2.19% of the total of such receipts.

Manufacturing affiliates operating in OAP countries thus reveal some striking differences from those operating in other sectors of the economy. Manufacturing appears to be a highly profitable sector that produces technologically unsophisticated goods using low cost, labor-intensive methods in manufacturing entities that are relatively small if judged by assets and sales. Host OAP countries also seem to favor this sector by imposing relatively low taxes on its income.[5]

IV. THE COMPOSITION OF DIRECT INVESTMENT

We next turn to the composition of U.S. direct investment in OAP countries. Our research strategy is constrained by the nature and availability of the data, which is obtained exclusively from the 1982 *Benchmark Survey*. U.S. direct investment is spread over many regions, countries, economic sectors and individual industries. We shall therefore begin by testing the hypothesis of statistical independence between investment and location. In other words, we start from the assumption that the probability of an affiliate being in a particular industry is independent of the probability of it being in a particular location. This assumption permits us to calculate an expected frequency that, on the hypothesis of independece, is equal to the probability of the affiliate being in a particular country times the probability of it being in a particular industry. When the observed frequency is significantly different from the frequency expected on the hypothesis of independence, this suggests that country and industry are jointly distributed, an attribute that signals the need for further examination.

The chi-square (χ^2) test traditionally used to test the hypothesis of independence exploits the additive property of the χ^2 distribution to compare the statistic:

[χ^2 (d.f.) = Σ(observed-expected)^2/expected] with its critical value. The hypothesis of independece is rejected if the calculated χ^2 is greater than the critical value. This test, however, does not directly provide for a test of the deviation of any individual frequency from its expected value. In order to remedy this shortcoming, at least partially, we shall present in the tables that follow the standardized values of the deviates. On the assumption that these standardized values approximate the "*t*" distribution, we shall take as significant any entry that is greater than or equal to $|3|$. To be sure, this criterion is arbitrary, but it may be approximate because of the small sample size.

Three findings of interest emerge from Table 1, which reports the standardized deviates from expected frequencies for affiliates in various economic activities in the eight regions: First, there does not seem to be any systematic similarity or

Table 1. Standardized Deviates = (Obs – Exp)/$\sqrt{\ }$(Exp)
Economic Sector by World Region[a,b]

	ES1	*ES2*	*ES3*	*ES4*	*ES5*	*ES6*	*ES7*
R2	0.9	3.7	0.3	–5.8	–4.2	–2.0	3.1
R3	–3.6	0.5	4.1	–2.6	–1.7	3.3	–3.7
R4	–3.3	2.1	6.3	0.3	–5.4	–1.5	–2.9
R5	–1.6	0.4	2.2	–2.7	–3.1	0.0	3.3
R6	–2.3	–3.7	–8.5	8.4	15.4	–3.5	–0.6
R7	10.8	–2.9	–2.6	0.0	–0.7	–0.3	2.2
R8	7.6	–3.8	–3.6	1.7	–3.0	7.1	2.5
R9	2.4	0.9	0.8	2.0	–4.2	–0.5	–0.5

[a] χ^2 = 1005.532 (42df). See Appendix for row and column headings.

[b] For a better understanding of the economic meaning of the entries in this table, let's use as an example the entry (R9, ES2), which is 0.9. This number provides a standardized measure of the differences between the observed and expected total of firms operating manufacturing affiliates (code ES2) in OAP countries (code R9). The value 0.9 is obtained as follows: The total number of firms in the underlying distribution is 7607 (see p. 48 in the 1982 *Benchmark Survey*). Of these 7607 firms, 2732 are in the manufacturing sector, and of these 7607 firms, 656 operate affiliates (in all economic sectors) in OAP countries. The probability of a given firm being in the manufacturing sector is thus Pr(Es2) = 2732/7607 = 0.3591 and the probability of a firm operating an affiliate in the OAP countries is Pr(R9) = 656/7607 = 0.0862. What we are seeking to determine is the joint probability, Pr(ES2 *and* R9), that is, the probability of a given firm being in manufacturing and in OAP. Now, if these two attributes are statistically independent of each other, then Pr(ES2 and R9) = [Pr(ES2) • Pr.(R9)]. Given Pr(ES2) = 0.3591 and Pr(R9) = 0.0862, it follows that under the hypothesis of independence, Pr(ES2 *and* R9) is [(0.3591) (0.0862)] = 0.0310. Since 0.0310 of 7607 = 235.8, the expected number of firms operating manufacturing affiliates in OAP countries is 235.8 (actually 235 or 236) under the independence hypothesis. The observed number of U.S. parents operating manufacturing affiliates in OAP countries is 250. The standard deviate is therefore (250 – 235.8) /$\sqrt{235.8}$, or 14.2/15.36 = 0.9. Q.E.D.

difference in the composition of activities as between the developed countries (basically the first four regions) and the developing countries (the last four regions) or within the two groups. Second, there does not appear to be any trend in the deviates as one moves through the various levels of economic development. Finally, the OAP row suggests a calm enclave in an otherwise turbulent landscape. Only the finance, real estate, and insurance sector appears to be significantly underinvested, whereas the other sectors, including manufacturing, are statistically undiscernible from their expected size under the hypothesis of independence.

Table 2 looks at the allocation of direct investment within OAP. Here the manufacturing sector shows some substantial deviations from the hypothesis of independece. In particular, India and Taiwan display significant deviations on the positive side, whereas Hong Kong, and to a lesser degree Singapore, seem to favor the wholesale trade sector. In fact, inspection of the first three columns of Table 2 suggests that with the exception of those countries (Indonesia and "other" OAP) where a disproportionately large investment occurs in petroleum affiliates, manufacturing and wholesale trade deviates display opposite signs. In the two aforementioned cases, both manufacturing and wholesale trade are of the same negative sign and are offset by the large and positive petroleum deviate. This country-specific inverse relationship between manufacturing and wholesale trade,

Table 2. Standardized Deviates = (Obs – Exp)/$\sqrt{\ }$(Exp) Economic Sector by OAP Country[a]

	ES1	*ES2*	*ES3*	*ES4*	*ES5*	*ES6*	*ES7*
C11	–3.3	–5.8	6.2	1.3	2.8	3.4	–0.9
C10	–0.7	5.9	–3.7	–1.9	–2.0	–1.4	–1.1
C9	7.0	–1.3	–3.5	–1.4	0.3	–0.5	2.8
C8	–0.1	0.3	0.5	–1.6	–0.2	–0.4	1.1
C7	–1.5	2.1	–1.6	0.5	0.6	–0.5	–1.3
C6	–0.7	–2.2	2.8	0.8	0.3	–0.3	0.1
C5	–1.6	2.2	–3.1	1.9	0.4	–0.6	–0.3
C4	–2.3	3.7	–1.4	0.9	–1.5	–1.8	–1.5
C3	1.3	–0.2	1.3	–1.4	–1.1	0.1	–0.5
C2	5.2	–0.6	–2.7	–0.5	–2.1	0.3	2.6

[a] χ^2 = 372.579 (54 df). See Appendix for row and column headings

particularly in the case of Hong Kong and Singapore, is intuitively plausible, since both city-states are predominant trading centers.

The conclusions emerging from our analysis of Tables 1 and 2 may be summarized as follows: The data at hand do not suggest any systematic pattern for the allocation of direct investment to the production of traded as against nontraded goods among world regions. In the OAP group as a whole, the total of direct investment in manufacturing appears to be consistent with expectations on the hypothesis of independece. Within the group, systematic patterns are evident, but these admit of uncomplicated explanations.

V. THE COMPOSITION OF DIRECT INVESTMENT IN MANUFACTURING

We now turn our attention to the manufacture of tradable goods in an attempt to discover the determinants of their composition. A glance at Table 3 suggests that the search may prove fruitful. Many of the deviates are significant, but this time the traces of a pattern are discernible. For instance, the economically developed regions appear underinvested in the food sector and generally overinvested in the "other manufacturing" sector, which is a typically large sector inspite of its unimpressive title. Another aspect of the pattern can be seen by comparing Canada with OAP. With the exception of machinery (industry 4), the deviates display opposite signs. The level of development is the obvious candidate for the role of explanatory variable in determining the composition of manufacturing investment, and we shall return to this point later.

The within-group homogeneity of the OAP region is given eloquent expression by Table 4. Only 3 of the 70 values in this table are significant by our

Table 3. Standardized Deviates = (Obs −Exp)/$\sqrt{\ }$(Exp) Manufacturing Industry by World Region[a]

	I1	*I2*	*I3*	*I4*	*I5*	*I6*	*I7*
R2	−1.7	−3.8	2.6	−0.4	−1.4	3.0	2.8
R3	−2.8	−3.0	1.1	5.0	−1.5	−1.2	1.9
R4	−1.5	3.5	−0.8	−0.9	−0.2	−1.2	−0.7
R5	0.4	1.4	0.4	0.4	−1.8	0.1	−1.1
R6	4.8	3.3	−1.8	−3.7	−1.7	1.3	−1.9
R7	3.3	1.0	0.3	−3.1	−0.6	−0.7	−0.4
R8	−1.9	0.9	1.0	−1.0	1.8	−1.4	−0.2
R9	0.8	1.7	−3.2	−3.0	9.6	−1.8	−3.3

[a] χ^2 = 339.433 (42 df). See Appendix for row and column headings

Table 4. Standardized Deviates = (Obs −Exp)/$\sqrt{(Exp)}$
Manufacturing Industry by OAP Country[a]

	I1	*I2*	*I3*	*I4*	*I5*	*I6*	*I7*
C11	−1.0	−1.2	0.4	−0.5	0.8	−1.3	2.0
C10	−1.7	1.8	1.4	1.3	−2.4	0.9	−0.3
C9	−0.9	1.7	1.1	−1.1	−1.4	−1.1	0.7
C8	−1.0	−1.2	0.4	−0.5	3.2	−1.3	−0.6
C7	3.0	0.2	−0.4	−2.3	−1.0	−0.1	0.4
C6	−0.9	−2.8	0.1	7.3	0.7	1.0	−1.9
C5	1.6	0.9	−0.7	−2.0	−1.3	0.2	0.7
C4	−1.5	−0.7	−1.4	−0.9	2.7	2.1	−0.5
C3	1.4	−0.3	0.6	−1.6	−0.9	−1.0	1.3
C2	1.3	2.8	−1.3	−1.5	−0.9	−1.0	−1.3

[a] χ^2 = 186.581 (54 df). See Appendix for row and column headings

criterion,[6] and the total χ^2 value barely rejects the hypothesis of independence. It was noted previously that low wages and incomes were a common characteristic of the countries in the OAP region. The reduced dependence between country and industry shown by Table 4 further strengthens the supposition that wages and income are important in explaining interregional differences in industrial composition, since income homogeneity is a prime feature of the classification into regions.

The χ^2 results tabulated thus far have tested, and by and large rejected the hypothesis that location and industry are statistically independent. More useful information might be gleaned by addressing the question of whether industries are jointly distributed with each other across locations, and whether locations are correlated with each other across industries. More precisely, the first question would examine whether regions having more affiliates in industry A would also have more affiliates in industry B. The second question would seek to determine whether country X's having more affiliates in industry A implies that country Y will also have more affiliates in industry A. A negative answer to the first question would suggest that the industrial composition is not the same in the various locations, but a positive answer would not prove the opposite. A negative answer to the second question means that the composition is not the same, whereas a positive answer signifies that it is.

Table 5 reports some of the answers to the second question. The most noteworthy is the first column of the correlation matrix, which measures the correlation of the industry mix in the various regions with that prevailing in the United States (as measured by the proportion of MNCs in each manufacturing industry group). The ascending pattern of the coefficients as one moves up through higher and higher income levels is the most striking feature of the table. The regression of the coefficients on the hourly rate of compensation is

Table 5. Correlations Among World Regions Across Manufacturing Industries (U.S. Parents and Foreign Affiliates)[a,b]

	R1	*R2*	*R3*	*R4*	*R5*	*R6*	*R7*	*R8*
R2	0.9181							
R3	0.8839	0.9387						
R4	0.5353	0.7212	0.8503					
R5	0.6222	0.8010	0.9140	0.9705				
R6	0.5005	0.7334	0.8244	0.9557	0.9600			
R7	0.3203	0.6047	0.6280	0.7964	0.8062	0.9204		
R8	0.6230	0.7315	0.8064	0.9044	0.8412	0.8062	0.6802	
R9	0.3188	0.4007	0.5458	0.7789	0.6455	0.7292	0.6584	0.8205

[a] Critical R at 95% = 0.755. See Appendix for row and column headings.

[b] As an example of the economic meaning of the coefficients in this table let's consider the lower left corner entry, 0.3188. This coefficient measures the correlation between the composition of manufacturing industries in the United States, as measured by the number of parent firms (MNCs) in the various industries and the composition of manufacturing investment in OAP as measured by the number of affiliates from each industry. The coefficient is calculated from the following data:

ID	*I1*	*I2*	*I3*	*I4*	*I5*	*I6*	*I7*
R1	71	166	170	213	149	59	387
R2	59	152	37	44	127	19	100

The formula for the coefficient is

$$r_{R1_I,R2_I} = \frac{\Sigma(R1_I-\overline{R1_I})(R9_I-\overline{R9_I})}{\sqrt{\Sigma(R1_I-\overline{R1_I})^2\,\Sigma(R9_I-\overline{R9_I})^2}}$$

where $\overline{R1_I} = 173.57$ and $\overline{R9_I} = 76.86$.

$$\text{Correlation} = \underset{(0.086)}{0.259} + \underset{(0.011)}{0.050}\ (\text{hourly compensation in \$}) \qquad R^2 = 0.762$$

Both coefficients attain high levels of significance (see S.E. in parentheses). With each added dollar of hourly compensation the industry mix of the manufacturing affiliates operating in a country becomes more similar to that prevailing in the United States by 5% of the perfect correlation.

Table 6 provides an anwwer to the first question on the basis of interregional data. Industries are almost perfectly correlated across regions, the determinant of the correlation matrix being close to zero, but this merely reflects the unequal importance of the various regions, so that an important region, such as Europe, will have more affiliates in each industry then a less important region, such as ANZA. The results in Table 6 do not, therefore, contradict those in Table 5. The latter suggests that although Europe has generally more affiliates than ANZA, and therefore more in each industry, the composition is nevertheless different.

The homogeneity of the OAP region is once more displayed in Table 7. The low correlation between the U.S. manufacturing mix and that of OAP observed in Table 6 is now replicated with each one of the major countries in the group. Not one of the coefficients in the first column of the matrix is significant, whereas the intercorrelation among the countries in the remaining part of the matrix is sometimes quite high. In fact, Singapore seems to be the only country to be very significantly out of line with the remaining OAP. By our interpretation of these coefficients, the findings indicate that while the composition of manufacturing affiliates in OAP countries differs widely from the U.S. MNC mix, the composition is quite similar among the countries making up the OAP group. The correlation matrix in Table 8 is therefore all the more surprising, since it shows

Table 6. Correlations among Manufacturing Industries across World Regions[a]

	I1	*I2*	*I3*	*I4*	*I5*	*I6*
I2	0.9836					
I3	0.9059	0.9475				
I4	0.8708	0.9331	0.9880			
I5	0.9029	0.9414	0.9220	0.9280		
I6	0.9541	0.9585	0.9713	0.9270	0.9005	
I7	0.9190	0.9592	0.9987	0.9878	0.9364	0.9728

[a] Critical R at 95% = 0.707. See Appendix for row and column headings.

Table 7. Correlations Among U.S. and OAP Countries Across Manufacturing Industries[a]

	C1	*C2*	*C3*	*C4*	*C5*	*C6*	*C7*	*C8*	*C9*	*C10*
C2	−0.0846									
C3	0.4717	0.6276								
C4	0.1191	0.4785	0.4478							
C5	0.2245	0.8814	0.9004	0.5027						
C6	0.1337	−0.1530	−0.3318	0.3411	−0.3279					
C7	0.1571	0.8391	0.9192	0.5578	0.9710	−0.2669				
C8	0.1428	0.3135	0.3966	0.9362	0.3402	0.4536	0.4521			
C9	0.3881	0.8425	0.7641	0.4519	0.8733	−0.2206	0.7749	0.3129		
C10	0.3147	0.8207	0.5192	0.3591	0.7235	−0.0531	0.5831	0.1928	0.9394	
C11	0.6727	0.3047	0.7448	0.7688	0.5727	0.1825	0.6089	0.7743	0.5639	0.3740

[a] Critical R at 95% = 0.755. See Appendix for row and column headings.

Table 8. Correlations Among Manufacturing Industries Across OAP Countries[a]

	I1	*I2*	*I3*	*I4*	*I5*	*I6*
I2	0.4456					
I3	0.0174	0.3671				
I4	−0.1954	−0.1891	0.4724			
I5	0.0400	−0.1049	0.0479	0.3339		
I6	0.1873	0.4812	0.2921	0.5010	0.5648	
I7	0.5318	0.4870	0.4339	−0.1832	0.2491	0.3231

[a] Critical R at 95% = 0.632. See Appendix for row and column headings.

almost complete independence between industries within OAP. More than anything else, however, this result may reflect the roughly equal importance accorded to the OAP countries by U.S. multinational corporations.

VI. WAGES, INCOME, AND THE COMPOSITION OF MANUFACTURING SUBSIDIARIES IN OAP

The sensitivity of the composition of manufacturing affiliates to the wage rate having been demonstrated in the previous section, it remains to show just how that composition changes with a change in wage rates. Discussions of direct investment abroad are more likely to perceive the wage rate as an element of the cost of production. The wage rate, however, is also an indicator of per capita income, and as such it provides a measure of the domestic market in the host country. It follows that industries in which foreign investment is oriented toward expanding markets will prosper with rising incomes, on the assumption that the growth of sales more than compensates for the higher costs of production. Other industries, however, see the low wage as a temporary means to reduce the unit costs of production. For these industries, rising wages and incomes merely mean that the advantages afforded by a market imperfection are being eliminated. For most industries, both effects are important, and it becomes difficult to predict which effect will prevail over time. Because the results displayed in Table 3 provided a strong hint that the hourly wage may correlate significantly with the deviates from independence in each industry group, regressions on the hourly compensation rate were run for each one of the seven industry groups. The results, reported in Table 9, confirm that wage changes have a differential effect

Table 9. Wage Rate Differences Across Regions and the Composition of U.S. Direct Investment in Manufacturing Abroad.

Industry	*a*	*b*	R^2	*F*	*Significance*
I1	3.562 (1.424)	-0.510 (0.188)	0.552	7.393	0.035
I2	3.052 (1.777)	-0.365 (0.234)	0.289	2.437	0.170
I3	-2.249 (1.007)	0.331 (0.133)	0.714	6.242	0.047
I4	-3.940 (1.635)	0.467 (0.215)	0.440	4.709	0.073
I5	4.024 (2.558)	-0.527 (0.337)	0.290	2.445	0.169
I6	-1.350 (1.183)	0.168 (0.156)	0.162	1.157	0.323
I7	-2.920 (0.975)	0.385 (0.128)	0.600	9.005	0.024

Notes: Dependent variable: standard deviates from Table 3. Independent variable: average hourly wage rate from p. 291.
Standard errors are given in parenthesis.

Actual and Predicted Values of the Standardized Deviate for Manufacturing Industries in the OAP Region

Deviate	*I1*	*I2*	*I3*	*I4*	*I5*	*I6*	*I7*
Actual	0.8	1.7	-3.2	-3.0	9.6	-1.8	-3.3
Predicted	2.8	2.5	-1.8	-3.3	3.2	-1.1	-2.4

Equation: standard deviate: $a + b$ (Average hourly wage). $R^2 = 0.677$. Significance = 0.023.

on different industries. Products with low income elasticities, such as food, react badly to wage increases. The group, ''other'' manufactures, however, displays, high income elasticities. Here the rise in wages will be more than offset by the expanding market for the great variety of nonessential products included in this group. Somewhat surprising is the equation for electric and electronic products. In the case of OAP, this is currently by far the largest manufacturing industry, and employs almost half of all the workers associated with U.S. manufacturing affiliates in the OAP region. The bulk of the activity is in the component area, where a labor-intensive intermediate step in the production process is performed in OAP-located plants before the component is shipped back to the United States for final assembly. Yet the wage coefficient, though it displays the "right" sign, is not statistically significant. It is likely, however, that this is the result of the aggregation in the data. In higher income countries, the "electric and electronic equipment" industry is more involved in the production of household appliances and other amenities rather then components. This shift in emphasis helps the industry maintain its share of direct investment.

When assessed against the background of data inadequacies and the smallness of the sample, wage rates perform surprisingly well as predictors of the composition of manufacturing investment. The bottom part of Table 9 displays both the actual deviates replicated from Table 3 for the OAP group and the deviates predicted by the equations in Table 9. The fit, already good, could probably be improved by using industry-specific compensation rates rather than the regional averages the tabulation in Section II, p. 251.

VII. CONCLUSIONS, PREDICTIONS, AND VALIDATION

The results gathered in this chapter seem to support Linder's[7] approach to the industrial composition of direct foreign investment. As wages and incomes rose in the host country, the industrial composition of U.S. direct investment (at least in the traded goods sector) increasingly approximates the U.S. mix. It was not the intent of the paper, and there is nothing in the results, that would support a responsible prediction of the future size of U.S. direct investment in manufacturing in the OAP region. The results concerning the composition of that investment offer more fertile grounds for speculation, should OAP wages and incomes follow the path of their predecessors on the ladder of economic development. If wages, and therefore per capita incomes, increase, then we should experience a reallocation of direct investment away from the manufacture of food products, chemicals, and electronic components, and toward metals, machinery, transportation equipment, and particularly "other manufactures," which include tobacco, textiles, lumber, paper, printing, rubber, plastic, glass, stone, clay and other nonmetallic products, and instruments.

Our data are from the 1982 *Benchmark Survey*, and it would be interesting to find out whether our predictions are borne out by the experience of the post-1982 years. Unfortunately, the BEA does not plan to conduct its next survey until 1989, and the annual estimates of U.S. direct investment published by that agency do not contain any estimates concerning the number and industry composition of affiliates. As a second best method for validating our findings, we might "backcast" the results to see whether the changes in the composition of U.S. direct investment abroad between 1977 (date of the previous survey) and 1982 are consistent with what our hypothesis leads us to expect on the basis of the changes in wages and incomes since 1977.

To be sure, the number of affiliates responding to the 1977 survey is not comparable with that of the 1982 survey, because the former required all affiliates with assets, sales, or income in excess of $500,000 to report, while the 1982 survey raised that minimum to $3,000,000. In order to render the data more comparable, the BEA has made available a count of all 1977 affiliates with sales of assets of $2,000,000 or more. Comparability is based on the broad assumption adopted by BEA analysts that inflation has been on the order of 50% between the two benchmark years.

Our backcasting exercise suggests that hourly wages of foreign affiliates, when adjusted for the 50% inflation factor, show little change from 1977 levels. This may be due to the worldwide recession experienced in 1982, but in any event it implies that if wage rates have remained unchanged in both absolute and relative magnitude, then we should expect the standardized χ^2 deviates based on the industry composition of the 1977 affiliates count to be substantially similar to their 1982 values. Table 10 shows that real wage rates have remained both

Table 10. Average Hourly Compensation[a] of Production Workers in Majority Owned Affiliates and their U.S. Parents, 1977 and 1982

	1977		*1982*		*1982*[b]	
Region	*Wage*	*Rank*	*Wage*	*Rank*	*Wage*	*Rank*
R1	8.76	1	14.01	1	9.34	1
R2	8.31	2	12.17	2	8.11	2
R3	5.89	4	9.44	4	6.29	4
R4	7.37	3	9.95	3	6.63	3
R5	4.55	5	8.03	5	5.35	5
R6	2.17	7	3.55	7	2.37	7
R7	1.30	8	2.08	8	1.39	8
R8	4.08	6	6.44	6	4.29	6
R9	0.82	9	1.47	9	0.98	9
World (ex. U.S.)	4.92		7.27		4.85	

Sources: Benchmark Survey: 1977, 315 and 394; *1982*, 254 and 261.

[a] In U.S.$.

[b] Adjusted for 50% rate of inflation. The 50% adjustment is, admittedly, somewhat arbitrary. According to the statistics appearing in the 1986 *IFS Yearbook*, U.S. prices (GDP deflator) rose by 54.11% from 1977 to 1982, while "World Prices" (GDP deflators) rose by 80.52% over the same period. The dollar, however, appreciated by 12.71% by the IMF's "effective exchange rate" measure.

absolutely and relatively comparable between 1977 and 1982, whereas Table 11 when compared with Table 3, shows a striking resemblence between the standardized deviates in 1977 and 1982. These results occur, moreover, in spite of a substantial change in the total number of affiliates (even after the inflation adjustment) and an equally significant shift in U.S. direct investment in manufacturing away from its more traditional habitat in Europe and Latin America toward an increased presence in selected Asia/Pacific countries.[8]

Table 11. Standardized Deviates = $(\text{Obs} - \text{Exp})^2/(\text{Exp})$
Manufacturing Industry by World Sector—1977[a]

	I1	*I2*	*I3*	*I4*	*I5*	*I6*	*I7*
R2	−0.8	−5.8	4.2	−1.3	−1.2	1.1	4.4
R3	−3.7	−2.5	0.4	6.1	−1.9	−2.2	2.2
R4	−1.5	3.2	−0.6	−0.3	−0.5	−0.6	−0.9
R5	0.7	1.3	−0.8	0.0	−0.9	1.0	−1.0
R6	5.6	4.2	−2.0	−4.6	−0.5	2.9	−3.8
R7	2.5	0.6	−0.3	−2.3	0.3	−0.8	−0.1
R8	−0.6	2.3	0.0	−0.8	0.9	0.1	−1.8
R9	0.4	2.6	−2.5	−4.1	8.6	−1.3	−2.9

[a] χ^a = 400.706 (42 df). See Appendix for row and column headings.

APPENDIX

Following is a list of abbreviations used in the text tables:

World Regions: Data are number of Affiliates of nonbank parents (see BEA).

R1 United States
R2 Canada
R3 Europe
R4 Japan
R5 Australia, New Zealand, South Africa
R6 Latin America
R7 Other Africa (mainly, Egypt, Libya, Liberia, and Nigeria)
R8 Middle East
R9 Other Asia and Pacific (countries C2 through C11 below)

"*Other Asia and Pacific*" OAP countries: Data source same as above.

C2 Other (mainly Pakistan, the People's Republic of China, and Sri Lanka)
C3 Thailand
C4 Taiwan
C5 South Korea
C6 Singapore
C7 Philippines
C8 Malaysia
C9 Indonesia
C10 India
C11 Hong Kong
C1 United States

Economic Sectors

ES1 Petroleum
ES2 Manufacturing
ES3 Wholesale trade
ES4 Banking
ES5 Finance (except banking), insurance, and real estate
ES6 Services (including hotels, business services, health, legal etc.)
ES7 Other industries (including agriculture, mining, construction, transportation, communications, public utilities and retail trade).

Manufacturing Industries

- I1 Food and kindred products
- I2 Chemicals and allied products
- I3 Primary and fabricated metals
- I4 Machinery, except electrical
- I5 Electric and electronic equipment
- I6 Transportation equipment
- I7 Other manufacturing (including tobacco, textiles, lumber, furniture, paper, printing, rubber products, plastic, glass, stone, clay and other nonmetallic products, instruments and related products, etc.).

ACKNOWLEDGMENTS

The author wishes to thank George R. Kruer, Chief of the International Investment Division, Bureau of Economic Analysis (BEA), U.S. Department of Commerce, and A. Gilbert of the same agency, for providing additional data from the BEA's computer tapes. Thanks are also due to John M. Letiche and Kazuo Sato, and the referee for their helpful comments. Of course, they are absolved from any remaining errors.

NOTES

1. Sales, assets, or income in excess of $3,000,000 each.
2. These include Hong Kong, India, Indonesia, Malaysia, Philippines, Singapore, South Korea, Taiwan, and Thailand. We shall henceforth refer to this area as OAP, which is the abbreviation used by the 1982 *Benchmark Survey* for "Other Asia and Pacific" countries, a reference perhaps to the fact that the group does not include Japan, which is listed as a separate entity.
3. Some excellent surveys are available, especially Caves (1982) and Chen (1983).
4. These workers received 2.19% of the compensation paid manufacturing employees of U.S. affiliates worldwide.
5. Note that this does not get the pure theorists off the hook: OAP countries could just as well have produced the goods themselves and exported them to the U.S. and elsewhere.
6. These values relate to the Philippines (C7), where affiliates in the food sector (I1) significantly exceed the expected number. Nonelectrical machinery (I4) is overrepresented in Singapore (C6), as is electrical equipment (I5) in Malaysia (C8). A common feature of all three cases is that hourly wages in the respective industries and countries are substantially below OAP averages for these industries. See, *Benchmark Survey, 1982* (Table III. F. 19, p. 260).
7. Linder (1961) proposed that countries with similar levels of income are most likely to trade with each other.
8. The total number of manufacturing affiliates fell from 7,803 to 6,999 worldwide but rose from 505 to 538 in the OAP region.

REFERENCES

Caves, Richard E. *Multinational Enterprise and Economic Analysis*. Cambridge: Cambridge University Press, 1982.

Chen, Edward K. Y. *Multinational Corporations, Technology and Employment*. London: Macmillan Press. 1983.

International Monetary Fund (IMF). *International Financial Statistics, Yearbook, 1986*. Washington, D.C., 1986.

Linder, Staffan Burenstam. *An Essay on Trade and Transformation*. Uppsala, Sweden: Almqvist & Wiksell, 1961.

U.S. Department of Commerce, Bureau of Economic Analysis.

U.S. Direct Investment Abroad, 1977. U.S. Government Printing Office, Washington, D.C., 1981.

——— *U.S. Direct Investment Abroad: 1982 Benchmark Survey Data*. U.S. Government Printing Office, Washington, D.C., 1985.

UNITED STATES MULTINATIONALS AND EXPORT-LED GROWTH OF ASIAN DEVELOPING COUNTRIES

Steven A. Y. Lin

I. INTRODUCTION

The market economies of the Asian countries, particularly of Northeast and Southeast Asia, experienced remarkable economic growth during the last two to three decades. An average growth rate of at least 6 or 7% was achieved up to the mid-1980s. Export-led industrialization has been the major policy strategy for this economic success. The successful economic performance of the ASEAN countries, Oceana, and the emergence of the Asian NICs (newly industrializing countries) has increased Asia's share of international trade with the advanced developed countries (ADCs), particularly the United States.

Research in Asian Economic Studies.
Asian Industrialization: Changing Economic Structures,
Volume 1, Part A, pages 309–329.
Copyright © 1988 by JAI Press Inc.
All rights of reproduction in any form reserved.
ISBN: 0-89232-987-4

In 1970, U.S. imports from the Asian countries were 26.44% of its total imports, and U.S. exports to Asia were 26.67% of its total exports. In 1981, U.S. import and export shares with Asia rose to 37.50 and 29.76%, respectively, of its total imports and exports. The percentage for manufacturing trades are even higher (See Table 1).

The majority of the Asian countries traded with both Japan and the United States during the 1980s. Most of the countries traded with Japan more than with the United States. For some countries, their trade with Japan was as much as 15–40% of their total tarde. The linkages are not limited to commodity trade; it also extends to services. All of these linkages have affected the overall growth of Asian countries, and also created intense competition among themselves. The Asian NICs have outcompeted Japan in some commodities, and some other Asian countries are beginning to replace NICs in the trade of labor-intensive commodities.

The economic interdependence between the United States and the Asian countries extends beyond trade. Although Japan has a larger amount of foreign direct investment in the neighboring Asian countries, the United States also has a substantial amount of direct foreign investment in Asia (See Table 2).

With lower labor costs and sometimes lower raw materials costs, the United States found it advantageous to have some of the goods produced in some of these Asian countries, and then export them to other ADCs including the U.S. home market (see Table 3).

With the growing trade restrictions, the East Asian Five (Japan and the Asian NICs) also found it advantageous to have some of the goods produced in other low cost countries, low cost in terms of labor and raw materials, and then shipped the products to other countries, mostly ADCs. Japanese multinationals have their export platforms in Taiwan and South Korea (Grunwald and Flamm, 1985: 6). However, the Japanese firms' output is generally produced for local and regional markets, whereas that of the U.S. firms are generally exported back to the U.S. home market (see Table 3).

Many Asian countries became the sites of offshore production because export processing zones were ideal for such an undertaking. Many host countries believe this will serve as the conduit for transferring technology through ADCs' multinational corporations, contributing to host countries' foreign exchange, creating jobs, and obtaining market access. Some countries are more skeptical. Offshore productions are viewed as footloose, without involving much value added, and possibly perpetuating a low-grade labor force. Because offshore production clusters mostly around export processing zones, some doubts are also expressed as to its strength and extent of linkage to the rest of the economy (Reuber, 1973; Cohen, 1975; Riedel, 1975; Yoshihara, 1978), A priori, the economic impacts of offshore production and related-party exports on host countries have been less than clear.

Table 1. Manufacturing Trades between the United States and Asian Countries, 1977, 1984 (Million U.S.$)

	1977				*1984*			
	Exports	%	*Imports*	%	*Exports*	%	*Imports*	%
World	10,013.6	100	12,320.6	100	217,888	100	341,177.7	100
Asian countries	1,974.9	19.7	3,160.6	25.7	55,412	25.4	185,061	54.2
Japan	876.8		1,575.2		23,575		66,911	
Australia	196.4		99.0		4,793		60,371	
New Zealand	33.6		29.7		708		2,899	
Hong Kong	107.6		242.1		3,062		8,899	
India	64.9		65.3		1,570		2,737	
Indonesia	63.6		291.0		1,216		5,867	
Malaysia	46.7		110.5		1,856		2,825	
Philippines	73.0		89.5		1,766		2,622	
Singapore	97.6		73.5		3,675		4,121	
S. Korea	197.6		243.6		5,983		10,027	
Taiwan	149.8		307.2		5,003		16.088	
Thailand	42.9		29.2		1,113		1,426	
Pakistan	24.4		4.8		1,092		268	

Sources: Compiled from OECD, *Historical Statistics of Foreign Trade*. OECD, Paris, 1982. U.S. Department of Commerce (1986).

Table 2. U.S. Direct Investment Position in Asian Countries, 1977 and 1984 (Yearend, Million U.S.$)

	All industries				*Manufacturing*			
	1977	*%*	*1984*	*%*	*1977*	*%*	*1984*	*%*
All countries	149,848	100	212,994	100	66,033	100	85,253	100
Developed countries	108,225	72.2	157,461	73.9	53,709	81.3	66,403	77.9
Asian countries	16,520	11.0	32,223	15.1	6,435	9.7	10,818	12.7
Japan	4,143		7,920		1,903		3,942	
Australia	5,739		8,674		2,597		3,329	
New Zealand	421		510		127		151	
Other Asian and Pacific Countries	6,217		15,119		1,808		3,396	

Source: Compiled from Scholl (1986).

Table 3. Exports Shipped to the U.S. Majority Own Affiliates (MOA) and Imports Shipped by the U.S. MOA to Parent Companies (Million U.S.$)

	U.S. exports shipped to affiliates			*U.S. imports shipped by affiliates*		
	1977	*1982*	*1984*	*1977*	*1982*	*1984*
All countries	39,472	56,718	66,240	41,525	51,406	62,529
Developed countries	31,523	42,956	53,012	22,089	32,340	42,208
Asian countries	4,297	9,561	10,798	7,279	11,734	14,707
Japan	1,190	2,516	2,890	1,162	3,934	4,124
Australia	1,199	1,954	2,560	D	848	957
New Zealand	94	322	—	189	4	—
Other Asian and Pacific	(D)	4,769	5,348	5,928	6,948	9,626
Hong Kong	359	949		1,927	948	
India	22	55		D	5	
Indonesia	137	395		1,865	2,097	
Malaysia	233	977		D	1,142	
Philippines	275	313		191	305	
Singapore	367	956		735	1,334	
South Korea	160	315		D	292	
Taiwan	179	423		535	737	
Thailand	82	299		D	66	
Other	(D)	87		10	22	

Legend: D – Deleted; * including South Africa
Sources: U.S. Department of Commerce (1981) for 1977. Brereton (1986) for the years 1982 and 1984.

The majority of U.S. manufacturing imports assembled abroad in LDCs are under the U.S. tariff items 806.3 and 807, such as electronic equipment, auto parts, textiles and apparel, and metal fabrication. Also they are imported from foreign affiliates of U.S. firms. Import duty is levied only on the value-added component. This tariff provision encouraged U.S. multinationals and even small firms to take advantage of less expensive semiskilled labor in LDCs and extended related-party trade by setting up production or assembly facilities abroad. A related-party transaction is not necessarily equivalent to 806/807 production flow because it also includes sales between affiliates. The 806/807 item imports have been compared to the related-party imports and to the total U.S. imports in 1978 for selected groups of products for 15 countries (Grunwald and Flamm, 1985). They found a strong correlation among the 806/807 imports, related-party imports, and the total U.S. imports for the selected groups of commodities in 1978 (see Table 4). For example, more than 91% of U.S. imports from Malaysia and 71% from Mexico for the selected commodities were related-party imports.

Table 4. The Related-Party Imports and U.S. 806/807 Imports as Percentage of Total Imports, 1978

Country	*806/807 imports*	*Related-party imports*
Mexico	65.3	71.3
Malaysia	85.5	91.4
Singapore	46.6	74.1
Taiwan	12.3	20.8
Hong Kong	10.1	17.2
Korea	10.2	24.3
Philippines	36.3	37.6
Brazil	19.0	43.0
Columbia	17.9	23.3
Fifteen countries	16.2	56.7
All countries	13.7	52.2

Source: Grunwald and Flamm (1985: 22–23).

To assess the conflicting effects of the related-party export production on a host country's economic growth and industrialization is near impossible. This is mainly due to the scarcity of theoretical and methodological antecedents and data collection. Some of the noted drawbacks of measurement not withstanding, this study estimates the effects of U.S. multinationals' related-party export production on 12 Asian countries, in particular (Japan, South Korea, Taiwan, Hong Kong, Singapore, The Philippines, Malaysia, Indonesia, Thailand, India, Australia, and New Zealand), and for an extended sample of 21 semiindustrialized countries in general. The analytical framework employed is the extended version (Lin, 1987; Lin and Parada, 1985; Feder, 1982) of the production function-type model. The expansion of the related-party export production by U.S. multinationals and the externality and technology transfers induced by it are included with capital and labor in an aggregate cross-sectional equation to explain intercountry differences in the rate of economic growth for those countries during the period 1970–1981.

The empirical study is then extended to cover the relationship between economic growth, manufacturing export performance, and technology transfers for these countries. The main focus is on the average experience of the sampled

Asian countries, although the analysis is mostly based on individual country data instead of regional averages. Policy implications are also drawn.

II. THE MODEL

Following the model specifications made in Lin (1987), we shall consider an open economy that has two distinct production sectors: the related-party production sector and the non-related-party sector. The non-related-party sector produces Q_N units of output with K_N units of capital, L_N units of labor, and is influenced by the levels of the output of the related-party export production, Q_R. This specification follows the similar formulations made by Keesing (1967, 1979) and Feder (1982). The related-party export production is hypothesized to generate positive externalities (on the other sector) due to their introduction of better production techniques, more efficient and competitive management practices, better trained labor, and imported resources.

The related-party export sector produces Q_R units of output with K_R units of capital, L_R units of labor, and S_R units of specific factor. Superior technology or management skills transferred to this related-party export production sector from abroad are embodied in this specific factor.

This production function for each of the two sectors, can be formulated as:

$$Q_N = N(K_N, L_N, Q_R) \quad (1)$$

$$Q_R = R(K_R, L_R, S_R) \quad (2)$$

By definition the gross domestic product (Y) is the sum of Q_N and Q_R:

$$Y = Q_N + Q_R \quad (3)$$

In addition,

$$L = L_N + L_R \quad (4)$$

$$K = K_N + K_R$$

and thus,

$$I = I_N + I_R \quad (5)$$

where investment $I \equiv dK$, I_N, $\equiv dK_N$, and $I_R \equiv dK_R$, by definition.

Totally differentiating Eqs. (1) and (2), and utilizing the relations (3) through (5) a growth equation can be derived to assess the impact on economic growth of gross domestic investment, labor force growth, related-party export expansion and its spillover effects, and net inflows of technology. Feder (1982) derived such a growth equation without explicitly incorporating the impact of technology transfers and the growth equation was derived under a different context. In the following, Feder's (1982) growth equation will be restated in our framework and will explicitly incorporate technology transfers. By utilizing the simplifying assumptions listed below in (6) and (7), a growth equation can be derived, which is presented in (8).

The simplifying assumption, (6), assumes that the related export production sector is more productive than the non-related-party export production sector for the reasons alluded to earlier. The productivity differential between the two sectors is written as

$$R_K/N_K = R_L/N_L = 1 + \delta \tag{6}$$

where $R_K(\equiv \partial Q_R/\partial K_R)$ and $R_L(\equiv \partial Q_R/\partial L_R)$.

The productivity differential parameter, δ is a positive constant. R_K and R_L are, respectively, the marginal productivity of capital and labor in the related-party export production. N_K and N_L are similarly defined for the non-related-party export production.

Feder's (1982) other simplifying assumptions were

$$N_K = \alpha \quad \text{and} \quad N_L = \beta(Y/L) \tag{7}$$

That is, the marginal productivity of capital and labor in the other sector production is a constant α and a constant function of per capita gross domestic product (Y/L), respectively.

The resulting growth equations, after utilizing the simplifying assumptions (6) and (7), can be written as

$$\dot{Y}/Y = \alpha(I/Y) + \beta(\dot{L}/L) + (N_R + \delta/1+\delta)Q_R/Y + (1-\delta/1+\delta)R_S S_R/Y \tag{8}$$

where $\dot{Y} \equiv dY$, $\dot{L} \equiv dL$, $S_R \equiv d\dot{S}_R$, $N_R \equiv \partial Q_N/\partial Q_R$, and $Q_R \equiv dQ_R \cdot R_S$ is

the marginal contribution of the special factor used in the related-party export production (i.e., $\partial Q_R/\partial S_R$).

To simply Eq. (8) further, certain additional assumptions are needed. If Q_R is assumed to be weakly separable from K_N and L_N, and S_R is weakly separable from K_R and L_R, due to either Q_R and S_R's affect on Q_N and Q_R, respectively, with constant elasticities or imprecision in measurement of Q_R and S_R, then Eqs. (1) and (2) can be rewritten as

$$Q_N = N(K_N, L_N, Q_R) = Q_R^{\Theta} \cdot g\,(K_N, L_N) \tag{9}$$

and

$$Q_R = R(K_R, L_R, S_R) = S_R^{\gamma} \cdot f\,(K_R, L_R) \tag{10}$$

Where Θ and γ are the constant elasticitics of Q_N and Q_R with respect to Q_R and S_R.

The marginal contribution of specific factor S_R on the related-party export production is

$$\begin{aligned}\partial Q_R/\partial S_R = R_S &= \gamma S_R^{\gamma-1} \bullet f(K_R, L_R) \\ &= \gamma(Q_R/S_R) = \gamma[(Q_R/Y)/(S_R/Y)] \end{aligned} \tag{11}$$

The marginal contribution of related-party export production (Q_R) on domestic production (Q_N) is

$$\partial Q_N/\partial Q_R = N_R = \Theta Q_R^{\Theta-1} \bullet g(K_N, L_N) = \Theta/Q_R/Y - \Theta \tag{12}$$

Substitution of R_S and N_R of Eqs. (11) and (12) into Eq. (6) would result in the following equation:

$$\begin{aligned}\dot{Y}/Y &= \alpha(I/Y) + \beta(\dot{L}/L) + [(\Theta/Q_R/Y - \Theta) + \delta/1+\delta](Q_R/Y) + \\ &\quad (1 - \delta/1+\delta)\,\gamma[(Q_R/Y)/(S_R/Y)(\dot{S}_R/Y)] \\ &= \overset{(+)}{\alpha}(I/Y) + \overset{(+)}{\beta}(\dot{L}/L) + \overset{(+)}{\Theta}(\dot{Q}_R/Q_R) \\ &\quad + (\delta/1 + \overset{(+)}{\delta - \Theta})(\dot{Q}_R/Q_R)(Q_R/Y) \\ &\quad + (\gamma/\overset{(+)}{1} + \delta)(Q_R/Y)(\dot{S}_R/S_R)\end{aligned} \tag{13}$$

Equation (13) is our grand model for empirical analysis. It embodies the framework of the conventional growth equation, Feder's (1982) extension, and our incorporation of technological transfers. The signs on top of each coefficient are our hypothesized signs.

This grand model enables us to assess the impact on economic growth of gross domestic investment, growth of labor force, expansion of related-party export production ($\dot{Q}_R/Q_R$), net inflows of technology ($\dot{Q}_R/Y$) ($\dot{S}_R/S_R$), and the spillover effects of related-party export productions ($\dot{Q}_R/Q_R$) (Q_R/Y), separately. One would expect, theoretically, a positive impact of each of the above listed variables on a country's economic growth.

III. THE GROWTH EQUATION SPECIFICATIONS

Three separate regression equations can be derived from the grand equation (13) following three different subspecifications:

$$\text{(a) when } \delta/(1+\delta) = \Theta \quad \text{and} \quad \gamma = 0$$

(i.e., the related-party export productions do not generate externality and its productivity is not influenced by the net inflows of technology), Eq. (13) in natural log-linear form can then be written as

$$\ln(\dot{Y}/Y) = \ln A + \alpha \ln(I/Y) + \beta \ln(\dot{L}/L) + \Theta \ln(\dot{Q}_R/Q_R). \quad (14)$$

(b) When $\delta/(1+\delta) \neq \Theta$ and $\gamma = 0$ (i.e., net inflows of technology do not contribute to productivity of the related-party export productions), Eq. (13) can then be written as

$$\ln(\dot{Y}/Y) = \ln A + \alpha \ln(I/Y) + \beta \ln(\dot{L}/L) + \Theta \ln(\dot{Q}_R/Q_R) + [\delta/(1+\delta)-\Theta] \ln(\dot{Q}_R/Q_R)(Q_R/Y). \quad (15)$$

(c) when $\delta/(1+\delta) \neq \Theta$ and $\gamma \neq 0$, Eq. (13) can be rewritten as

$$\ln(\dot{Y}/Y) = \ln A + \alpha \ln(I/Y) + \beta \ln(\dot{L}/L) + \Theta \ln(\dot{Q}_R/Q_R) + [\delta/(1+\delta) - \Theta] \ln(\dot{Q}_R/Q_R)(Q_R/Y) + \delta/(1+\delta) \ln(Q_R/Y)(\dot{S}_R/S_R). \quad (16)$$

The subspecification (a), and the accompanying regression equation, is essentially the formulation employed by Michalopoulas and Jay (1973), Balassa (1978), and Tyler (1981) in their studies of the impacts of export expansion on economic growth. Subspecification (b), and the accompanying regression equation, is essentially that of Keesing's (1967, 1979) and Feder's (1982) formulations in studying export expansion and its spillover effects on economic growth. Technology transfer is introduced explicitly in subspecification (c) as an additional explanatory variable. This resulting regression is also the grand Eq. (13).

IV. EMPIRICAL ANALYSIS

Twelve Asian countries (Japan, S. Korea, Taiwan, Hong Kong, Singapore, the Philippines, Malaysia, Indonesia, Thailand, India, Australia, and New Zealand) were selected for our empirical study for the period 1970 through 1981. The 12 countries were chosen for their geographical locations, size of the economies, and volume of trade with the united States.

The natural log-linear regression Eqs. (14), (15), and (16) are estimated with the ordinary least-squares method. A list of the variables involved and their data sources are described in the Appendix. Each of the estimated regression coefficients is interpreted as the growth elasticity with respect to each of the corresponding explanatory variables. The estimation results are presented in Table 5.

Table 5. Related-Party Exports to the United States and Its Spillover Effects in 12 Asian Countries

Variable	*Parameter*	*Model (a)*	*Model (b)*	*Model (c)*	*Sample mean-First entry before log transformation, Second entry after Log transformation*
$\ln(I/Y)$	γ	0.1520	0.0261	-0.1806^{**}	0.2676
		(1.1551)	(0.2670)	(−1.8994)	−1.3438
$\ln(\dot{L}/L)$	β	0.2631^{***}	0.5423^{***}	0.4515^{***}	0.0201
		(2.7046)	(7.0966)	(6.4025)	−3.9646
$\ln(\dot{Q}_R/Q_R)$	Θ	0.4247^{***}	0.1323^{***}	0.2468^{***}	0.1475
		(7.5755)	(2.6746)	(5.0686)	−2.1182
$\ln(\dot{Q}_R/Q_R)$ (Q_R/Y)	$\delta/[(1+\delta)-\Theta]$		0.0481^{***}	0.0314^{***}	0.0018
			(10.8185)	(6.3938)	−12.0533
ln TECH	$\gamma/(1+\delta)$			0.1167^{**}	0.0012
				(5.8063)	−7.3443
Intercept		-0.7279^{*}	0.1696	0.4307	1.0000
		(−1.7201)	(0.5238)	(1.4616)	
$(\dot{Y}/Y)$					0.0622
					−2.8749
R^2		0.5337	0.7468	0.7965	

Notes: t values are in parentheses. Significant at 1% level ***. Significant at 5% level **. Significant at 10% level *.
$\delta = 0.3854$ and $\gamma = 0.1617$.

Single equation aggregate analysis of economic growth across countries, like ours, may incur simultaneous equation bias. The bias may arise due to possible codetermination of dependent and explanatory variables (Hagen and Hawrylyshyn, 1969; Chenery et al., 1980). In addition, the estimated parameters are the average values for the countries under study, assuming that the production functions for these countries are identical and they have similar nonoptimal allocation of resources, if any (Feder, 1982).

A. Related-Party Export Expansion to the U.S., Its Externalities and Growth Elasticities

Based on model specification (a), Eq. (14), the growth elasticity for the explanatory available $\ln(I/Y)$ (the share of gross domestic investment in GDP) is positive, but is statistically insignifiant (see Table 5). It implies that the contribution to economic growth of capital in the other sector (the non-related-party export production sector) is positive, but is relatively less significant. The parameter, β, which is associated with the growth of the labor force, $\ln(\dot{L}/L)$, is statistically highly significant at the 1% level. The parameter, Θ, the growth elasticity of the related-party export expansions $\ln(\dot{Q}_R/Q_R)$, is also statistically highly significant at the 1% level. Any 1% increase in the rate of expansion of related-party export productions, without shifting resources from the other sector, increases approximately 0.42% of the representative country's rate of growth of GDP. Three explanatory variables together in model (a) explain more than 53% of the variance of the rates of GDP growth.

In model specification (b), Eq. (15), an additional explanatory variable, $\ln(\dot{Q}_R/Q_R)$ (Q_R/Y) (the spillover effect of related-party export expansion) is introduced. The growth elasticity of this variable is positive and statistically highly significant at the 1% level. Previous empirical studies indicated that there was no concensus concerning the spillover effects of export-platform production and/or related-party export production on the rest of the host economy. On the one hand, some doubts were expressed as to its extent and strength of linkage to the rest of the economy (Yoshihara, 1978). On the other hand, several case studies on export-platform production observed significant backward linkages (Schive, 1981; Schive and Majumdar, 1981; Lim and Pang, 1982). The result of this empirical study indicates that significant spillover effects were generated by the related-party export production. The positive spillover effects, such as backward and forward linkages, might have been generated by firms engaged in related-party export production through demonstrative effects or inflows of technology.

The growth elasticity of the related-party export expansion, Θ, is also positive and statistically significant at the 1% level. Given this estimated Θ value and the regression coefficient $[\delta/(1+\delta) - \delta]$, which is associated with the explanatory variable $\ln(\dot{Q}_R/Q_R)Q_R/Y)$, the productivity differential parameter, δ, between the related-party production sector and the other sector can be computed. The computed δ value here is 0.22. The positive δ value indicates that the productivity of the related-party export production sector is more productive than the other sector.

The growth elasticity of labor force expansion, β, is also highly significant statistically at the 1% level. This result reflects the labor-intensive nature of the related-party export production and the significance of the contributions of the labor force expansion to economic growth through relatively lower wage rates due to abundant labor supply.

Four explanatory variables together in model (b) explain more than 74% of the growth variations in GDP of the representative country. Compared to model (a), the additional explanatory variable $\ln(\dot{Q}_R/Q_R)(Q_R/Y)$ introduced in model (b) increases the explanatory power of the growth equation substantially.

In model specification (c), Eq. (16), yet another explanatory variable, TECH, is introduced in addition to those explanatory variables that are already included in model (b). The growth elasticities of the explanatory variables $\ln(\dot{Q}_R/Q_R)$ and $\ln(\dot{Q}_R/Q_R)(Q_R/Y)$ are again found to be positive and statistically highly significant at the 1% level. The growth elasticity is 0.25. It indicates that a 1% increase in the rate of growth of related-party export production stimulates approximately a 0.25% increase in the rate of growth of GDP. The computed δ value is 0.3854. It indicates that the productivity for the related-party export production sector is higher than the other sector. The positive and statistically significant regression coefficient for the variable $\ln(\dot{Q}_R/Q_R)(Q_R/Y)$ indicates that the former sector generates positive spillover effects for the latter due to linkages and demonstration effects or technology transfers.

The regression coefficient $[\delta/1+\delta]$ for the ln(TECH) variable is also highly significant statistically. It can be inferred from this observation that γ (i.e., the constant elasticity of Q_R with respect to S_R) is also statistically significant under model specification (c), for δ is statistically significant. The positive and statistically significant $\gamma(\gamma = 0.1617)$ indicates that the transfer of specific factor S_R (e.g., management skill, technology, etc.) through related-party export production does contribute to the host countries' economic growth.

The growth elasticity of labor force expansion, β, is again highly significant statistically at the 1% level. Its magnitude is the largest among all of the five explanatory variables.

The regression coefficient for $\ln(I/Y)$ (the share of gross domestic investment in GDP) is negative and statistically significant at the 5% level. The negative sign is unexpected, theoretically, and it renders the interpretation difficult. However, the regression coefficients for $\ln(I/Y)$ are positive, although statistically insignificant, in models (a) and (b). In view of these empirical observations, contribution to economic growth of the capital in the non-related-party export production sector is deemed to be much less significant than the labor force and related-party export expansions.

When the sample size is extended to cover 21 semiindustrialized countries (dropping Japan, Australia, and New Zealand from the 12-country sample, and then adding Argentina, Brazil, Chile, Columbia, Ecuador, Greece, Mexico, Peru, Portugal, S. Africa, Spain, and Venezuela), the estimated parameters are all positive and significant statistically, including the parameter for $\ln(I/Y)$, using model (c). The parameter α for $\ln(I/Y)$ and $[\delta/(1+\delta)-\Theta]$ for $\ln(\dot{Q}_R/Q_R)(Q_R/Y)$ are statistically significant at the 10% level. The rest of the parameters are highly significant at the 1% level. Magnitudes of the growth elasticities for all of the explanatory variables are larger than that for $\ln(I/Y)$, except the spillover variable.

The growth elasticity for related-party export expansion is consistently positive and highly significant statistically in all of the models estimated (models a, b, and c). Likewise, the growth elasticities for the spillover effects generated by related-party export production, technology inflows, and labor force expansion are all positive and highly significant statistically. The magnitude of the growth elasticities is largest for labor force expansion, followed by the related-party export expansion. A more abundant labor force and the relatively lower wage rates of these countries made them more competitive and attractive for assembly production. In turn, the labor force expansion contributed significantly to their economic growth.

B. Manufacturing Exports to the U.S., Its Externalities and Growth Elasticities

The theoretical framework and the model specifications presented in the previous sections [particularly Eqs. (14), (15), and (16)] can be employed to analyze the impact on economic growth of manufacturing exports from the 12 Asian countries to the United States. To this end, we can substitute the manufacturing export expansion in place of the related-party export expansion in Eqs. (14), (15), and (16). The resulting equations can be written as Eqs. (17), (18), and (19), respectively:

$$\ln(\dot{Y}/Y) = \ln A' + \alpha' \ln(I/Y) + \beta' \ln(\dot{L}/L) + \Theta' \ln(\dot{Q}_X/Q_X) \tag{17}$$

$$\ln(\dot{Y}/Y) = \ln A' + \alpha' \ln(I/Y) + \beta' \ln(\dot{L}/L) + \Theta' \ln(\dot{Q}_X/Q_X) + [\delta'/(1+\delta') - \Theta'] \ln(\dot{Q}_X/Q_X)(Q_X/Y) \tag{18}$$

and

$$\ln(\dot{Y}/Y) = \ln A' + \alpha' \ln(I/Y) + \beta' \ln(\dot{L}/L) + \Theta' \ln(\dot{Q}_X/Q_X) + [\delta'/(1+\delta') - \Theta'] \ln(\dot{Q}_X/Q_X)(Q_X/Y) + [\gamma/(1+\delta)] \ln(Q_X/Y)(\dot{S}_X/S_X) \tag{19}$$

The above listed equations [(17), (18), and (19)] will also be called the model specification (a′), (b′), and (c′). These two sets of labelings will be used interchangeably. The estimation results for models (a′), (b′), and (c′) are presented in Table 6.

In model specification (a′), the parameters for the percentage of gross domestic investment in GDP, labor force expansion, and the manufacturing export expansion to the United States are all positive and highly significant statistically.

The introduction of spillover effects as an additional explanatory variable in model (b′) increased the explanatory power of the growth equation. Although the parameters α' and β' are both statistically insignificant, they both have negative signs, contrary to theoretical expectation. However, the combined impacts of

Table 6. Manufacturing Exports to the United States and Its Spillover Effects on 12 Asian Countries

Variable	*Parameter*	*Model (a′)*	*Model (b′)*	*Model (c′)*	*Sample mean First entry before log transformation, Second entry after log transformation*
$\ln(I/Y)$	α'	0.2434** (1.8592)	−0.1038 (−0.9135)	−0.2153** (−2.0702)	0.2677 −1.3438
$\ln(\dot{L}/L)$	β'	0.3294*** (3.4445)	0.3317*** (4.2745)	0.3073*** (4.3955)	0.0201 −3.9646
$\ln(\dot{Q}_X/Q_X)$	Θ'	0.4198*** (7.0251)	−0.0264 (−0.3716)	0.5165*** (4.5657)	0.1212 −2.2681
$\ln(\dot{Q}_X/Q_X)$ (Q_X/Y)	$\delta'/[(1+\delta')-\Theta']$		0.2705*** (8.5867)	−0.0212 (−0.3676)	0.0477 −3.7370
ln TECH	$\gamma'/(1+\delta')$			0.2176** (5.8165)	0.0012 −7.3443
Intercept		−0.2894 (−0.7046)	−0.7484*** (−2.2178)	0.7446* (1.8731)	
$(\dot{Y}/Y)$					0.0623 −2.8749
R^2		0.5139	0.6824	0.7449	

Notes: t values are in parentheses. *** Significant at 1% level. ** Significant at 5% level. * Significant at 10% level. $\delta' = 0.9814$ and $\gamma' = 0.4312$.

manufacturing export expansion and its spillover effects are positive (i.e., the sum of the growth elasticity Θ' and $[\delta'/(1+\delta') - \Theta']$ is positive).

In model (c′), inflow of technology is introduced as an additional explanatory variable. The growth elasticities for all of the explanatory variables are positive and statistically significant, except for the spillover variable which is negative but insignificant, and the percentage of gross domestic investment in GDP, which is negative and statistically significant.

The empirical results are generally similar to the related-party export expansion presented earlier in Table 5. Again,when the sample size is extended to cover 21 semiindustrialized countries, the estimated growth elasticities are all positive and statistically significant, except for the spillover effect, which is negative but statistically insignificant. The combined effects of manufacturing export expansion and its spillover effect is positive, as expected, and is statistically highly significant.

The growth elasticities for manufacturing export expansion, labor force expansion, and technology inflows are consistently positive and statistically significant (see Table 6). The results are similar to the analysis for related-party export expansions to the United States. By comparison, it has to be noted that the growth elasticity for labor force expansion is larger than the related-party export expansions to the United States (see model C, Table 5), while it is smaller than the manufacturing export expansion to the United States (see model C′, Table 6). This observation is true also for the analysis using the extended sample of 21 semiindustrialized countries. It is understandable that the volume of related-party exports and its rate of expansion are smaller than that of manufacturing exports in almost all of the countries studied. Different magnitudes of the growth elasticities reflect this fact. The growth elasticity for manufacturing export expansion is much larger. It is also understood that the economic growth of most of these countries under study is export-led. The empirical results reconfirm the importance on economic growth of the manufacturing export expansion to the United States and the related-party export expansion. It also reconfirms that the relatively lower wage rates, through labor force expansion, is the Asian countries' attraction and competitive edge.

V. PERSPECTIVE AND CHALLENGE

The empirical analysis clearly indicates that exports played a key role in many Asian countries' economic growth. The United States has been either the number one or number two major trading partner for almost all of these Asian countries for the last couple of decades (Cline, 1984: 24). Flow of trade, aid, and investment from the United States has permitted Japan to grow. In turn, their trade flows with the Asian NICs have boosted these Asian NICs' economies. Too the other Asian countries, such as Thailand, Malaysia, Indonesia, and the Philippines, economies are moving because of the massive amount of technological know-how and capital provided by the United States and the East Asian Five (i.e., Japan and the four NICs). The economic interrelationships are increasing between the East Asian Five and the rest of the Asian countries. The latter countries have become the principal suppliers of raw materials and are becoming more of the promising markets for the Asian Five. These newcomers have begun to replace the Asian NICs as suppliers to ADCs' markets, such as the United States, of products that are of low sophistication technologically, and of high labor intensity. Meanwhile, the Asian NICs replace Japan in supplying goods of moderate sophistication and labor intensity (Cline, 1984, Chapter 1).

The increasing regional economic interrelationships among the Asian countries are a blessing to these countries, particularly the East Asian Five. Facing economic maturation, rising protectionism, and rising raw material and labor costs, the room for export expansion of the East Asian Five to the United States and to the other ADCs is distinctly reduced. The worsening conditions are exacerbated by the recent revaluation of the U.S. dollar and the U.S. Congress' political sentiment toward protectionist legislation.

There will be varied responses to the challenges from each country that is at a different stage of maturation and faces different challenges. Japan, by far the most matured economy among the Asian countries, has fewer technical frontier sectors to be explored, except aerospace and biotechnology. The competition will be tougher than ever. The Asian NICs are in a better position than Japan for being less mature economically and thus having more new industries and products to be produced. They can produce a similar range of product as Japan, except for a few high-tech products. Korea and Taiwan have a wider range of products that they can produce than Hong Kong and Singapore due to the larger sizes of their economies.

They are all adapting to higher energy, raw material, labor, and technology costs by shifting from raw material or energy-intensive product lines into products with more value added and by improving the quality of labor through formal education or on-the-job training. Efforts are also being made to improve management, usages of machinery, and advanced technologies. They are increasing the levels of the local content of the products that they produce. The East Asian Five also found it advantageous to have some of the goods produced in other lower cost countries. Most of them are in Asia and ship their products to the ADCs (Wells, 1981). This may explain why the interrelationships between the East Asian Five and the other Asian countries are increasing. The increasing regional trades among Asian countries may have the potential of compensating the possible declining trade with the United States in the future. Some of these Asian countries have also started setting up factories in the United States to circumvent trade barriers and to gather market information. The number of multinational corporations from NICs is still increasing.

Import substitution and stimulation of domestic demand are also increasingly recognized as essential for economic growth. However, it will be difficult to sustain a desirable growth with these measures. The countercyclical policy of launching major public works and housing construction, at times, can be used to stimulate growth due to slower export expansion.

VI. CONCLUSION

Export-led growth of the Asian countries was fueled by U.S. multinationals' technology transfers, related-party exports to the United States, and the positive externalities induced by the export expansions. Relatively lower wage rates and an abundant semiskilled labor force provided these countries with a competitive edge in both the offshore production exports and manufacturing exports. Manufacturing export to the United States and its expansion are unequivocally the major source of these Asian countries' economic growth.

Increasing energy, raw material, labor, and technology costs, in addition to protectionist measures taken by many ADCs, and the United States alike, distinctly reduce the prospect for continued export-led growth of the Asian countries. Recent devaluation of the U.S. dollar further reduces the wage gap between the United States and the Asian countries. The reduced wage gap and the maturation of some Asian economies added more challenges to these countries that followed the strategy of export-led growth.

There will be varied responses to different challenges facing each of these Asian countries that are at different stages of economic maturation. More countries are shifting to produce products with more value added and are moving toward improved quality of labor, management, and usages of advanced technologies. Firms from the East Asian Five are also increasingly either branching out themselves or setting up their export production platforms in other Asian countries. These countries have become the promising markets for the East Asian Five.

Import substitution and stimulation of domestic demand are increasingly recognized by the Asian countries as essential measures for economic growth. Countercyclical policies, an expanding service industry, and meeting the domestic needs of improving environmental quality and social welfare should also be recognized as important policy goals in addition to their preoccupation with economic growth through export expansion.

APPENDIX: LIST OF VARIABLES AND DATA SOURCES

$(\dot{Y}/Y)$ — Average annual growth rate of GDP (%) at constant factor cost, 1970–1981. *Sources:* World Bank (1983). Taiwan's data is from Statistical Yearbook (1983).

$(\dot{L}/L)$ — Average annual growth rate (%) of population, 1970–1981, as a proxy for growth rate of labor force. *Sources:* World Bank (1983) and UNESCO (1981).

(I/Y) — Percentage of gross domestic investment in gross domestic product; where I = gross domestic investment, current prices in national currency (million), 1970–1981, and Y = gross domestic product, current prices in national currency (million), 1970–1981. *Sources:* World Bank (1983), U.N. (1985), and Taiwan (1983). Argentina's 1981 gross domestic investment is the arithmetic mean of its 1977 through 1979 figures.

$(\dot{Q}_R/Q_R)$ — (Real) Average rate of growth of related-party exports from the Asian countries by affiliates of U.S. multinational corporations to the United States. The average rate is computed as follows:

$$(\dot{Q}_R/Q_R) = e^d - 1,$$

where d is estimated from the equation $\log Q_R = C + dt$ and t = year in digit, 1970 = 1, . . ., 1981 = 12. The Q_R is computed with the following approximation: Q_R = Shipped • Q_X, where Q_X is the real value of manufactured goods exported from each of the Asian countries to the United States (in million U.S.$ deflated by GDP deflator) during 1970–1981, and Shipped is imports from affiliates of U.S. MNCs as a percentage (%) of total import to the United States from the corresponding Asian countries in 1977. *Sources:* U.N., Dept. of International Econ. and Soc. Affairs (1976, 1983, 1984), World Bank (1983), IMF (1984), and U.S. Dept. of Commerce (1983).

$(\dot{Q}_R/Q_R)\ (Q_R/Y)$ — The (real) average rate of growth of related-party exports multiplied by the shares of related-party exports in GDP. *Sources:* Same as $(\dot{Q}_R/Q_R)$ and Y.

TECH — Net direct investment fees and royalties paid by the Asian affiliates to U.S. parent companies (all industries) per dollar of gross domestic product for each (and corresponding) Asian countries, 1977. This is used as a proxy for $(Q_R/Y)(\dot{S}_R/S_R)$ or $(Q_X/Y)(\dot{S}_X/S_X)$. *Sources:* U.S. Dept. of Commerce (1981), World Bank (1983), U.N. (1985), and Taiwan (1983).

$(\dot{Q}_X/Q_X)$ — (Real) Average rate of growth of manufacturing exports from the Asian countries to the United States. *Sources:* Same as $(\dot{Q}_R/Q_R)$.

$(\dot{Q}_X/Q_X)(Q_X/Y)$ The (real) average rate of growth of manufacturing exports multiplied by the shares of manufacturing exports in GDP. *Sources:* Same as $(\dot{Q}_X/Q_X)$ and Y.

REFERENCES

Balassa, Bela. ''Exports and Economic Growth: Further Evidence.'' *Journal of Development Economics 5*(2), 1978, 181–189.

——— ''Exports, Policy Choices, and Economic Growth in Developing Countries after the 1973 Oil Shock.'' *Journal of Development Economics 8*, 1985, 23–35.

Brereton, Barbara F. ''U.S. Multinational Companies: Operations in 1984.'' *Survey of Current Business* September 1986, 27–38.

Chenery, Holis B., Hazel Elkington, and Christopher Sims. *A Uniform Analysis of Development Patterns*. Economic Development Report, No. 148. Cambridge, MA: Harvard University Press, July 1980.

Cline, William R. *Exports of Manufactures from Developing Countries: Performance and Prospects for Market Areas*. Washington, D.C.: The Brookings Institution, 1984.

Cohen, B., *Multinational Firms and Asian Exports*. New Haven, CT: Yale University Press, 1975.

Feder, Gershon. ''On Exports and Economic Growth.'' *Journal of Development Economics 12*, 1982, 59–73.

Grunwald, Joseph and Kennth Flamm. *The Global Factory—Foreign Assembly in International Trade*. Washington, D.C.: The Brookings Institution, 1985.

Hagen, E. Everett and Oli Hawrylyshyn. ''Analysis of World Income and Growth 1955–1965.'' *Economic Development and Cultural Change 18*(1), Part II, October 1969, 1–96.

Keesing, Donald B. ''Outward-Looking Policies and Economic Development.'' *Economic Journal 77*(306), June 1967, 303–320.

——— *Trade Policy for Developing Countries*, 1979.

Lim, Linda Y. C. and Pang End Fong. ''Vertical Linkages and Multinational Enterprises in Developing Countries.'' *World Development 10*, 1982, 585–595.

Lin, Steven A. Y. ''U.S. Multinationals' Intra-Firm Trades and Technology Transfers on LDCs' Growth.'' *Journal of International Economic Integration* Spring 1987, 37–53.

Lin, Steven A. Y. and J. Parada, ''Export-led Growth in the Latin American Countries.'' *The Journal of Economics 11*, 1985, 166–169.

Michalopoulos, C. and Keith Jay. ''Growth of Exports and Income in the Developing World: A Neoclassical View.'' Washington, D.C.: U.S. A.I.D. Discussion Paper, No. 28, 1973.

Reuber, L. *Private Foreign Investment in Development*. Oxford: Clarendon Press, 1973.

Riedel, James. ''Factor Properties, Linkages and the Open Developing Economy.'' *Review of Economics and Statistics 57*(4), November 1975, 487–494.

Schive, Chi. *A Study on the Domestic Purchase of Foreign Direct Investment and Its Relation with the Second Import Substitution Industries*, Taiwan, 1981 (in Chinese).

Schive, Chi and Badal A. Majumdar. *Direct Foreign Investment and Linkage Effects: The Experience of Taiwan*, (mimeo) 1981.

Scholl, Russell B. ''The International Investment Position of the United States in 1985.'' *Survey of Current Business* June 1986, 26–35.

Tyler, William. ''Growth and Export Expansion in Developing Countries: Some Empirical Evidence.'' *Journal of Development Economics 9*(3), 1981, 121–130.

U. S. Department of Commerce. *U.S. Direct Investment Abroad 1977*. Bureau of Economic Analysis, Washington, D.C., April 1981.

——— *U.S. Multinational Companies, U.S. Merchandise Trade, Worldwide Sales and Technology-Related Activities in 1977*. Bureau of Economic Analysis, Washington, D.C., August 1983.

———*United States Trade-Performance in 1985 and Outlook*. International Trade Administration, Washington, D.C., October 1986.

Wells, Louis T. Jr. ''Foreign Investors from the Third Worlds.'' In Krishna Kumar and Maxwell McLeod (eds.) *Multinationals from Developing Countries*, Lexington, MA: D.C. Heath, 1981. 23–51.

The World Bank. *The World Development Report*. New York: Oxford University Press, 1983.

Yoshihara, K. *Japanese Investment in Southeast Asia*. Hawaii: University of Hawaii Press, 1978.

IMPACTS OF FOREIGN JOINT VENTURES ON THE SHAREHOLDER WEALTH OF UNITED STATES CORPORATIONS: THE CASE OF JOINT VENTURES WITH ASIAN COUNTRIES

Insup Lee

I. INTRODUCTION

A joint venture is typically the formation of a new company owned in common by two or more other individuals, corporations, and possibly governmental agencies. The purpose of a joint venture is usually to undertake a project that is

Research in Asian Economic Studies.
Asian Industrialization: Changing Economic Structures,
Volume 1, Part A, pages 331–347.
Copyright © 1988 by JAI Press Inc.
All rights of reproduction in any form reserved.
ISBN: 0-89232-987-4

not suitable for any one party. In joint ventures, each participant provides its resources (expertise and/or capital) to accomplish specific, limited objectives such as developing new products, sharing the cost of exploration, or entering new markets for one or both of the parties' products.

In contrast to corporate mergers and tender offers, joint ventures are controlled by the combined management of the two or more parent companies. This has important implications for the motive for joint ventures vis-à-vis that for corporate mergers. Most merger literature contends that synergy and management displacement are two main motives for mergers. Since any of the original management of the participating entities would not be eliminated under a joint venture, the only relevant motive for joint ventures is operating and/or financial synergy (McConnell and Nantell, 1985).

Another important distinction between a corporate merger and a joint venture is that the latter is more likely to involve international operations. In particular, the international joint ventures have become important devices for applying the resources of developed nations to the needs of less developed countries in the postwar period. In the United States, foreign joint ventures are very common, and the number of such corporate combinations has been significant in the past two decades. This phenomenon may be attributed to two factors. The first is that U.S. federal antitrust legislation has been a major obstacle for potential domestic joint ventures. As a result, more international joint ventures are implemented as an alternative to domestic ones. The second is that international joint ventures are as profitable as domestic ones. Whether the foreign joint venture is indeed superior to domestic alternatives in terms of risk and return is an empirical issue, and will be addressed in this research.

The purpose of this study is to measure empirically the impact that the decision by U.S. corporations to pursue international joint ventures has on shareholder wealth. In particular, this chapter focuses on joint ventures involving U.S. corporations and governments of, or corporations from nine Asian nations including Hong Kong, Indonesia, Japan, South Korea, Malaysia, Singapore, Taiwan, Thailand, and The Philippines over the period beginning January 1968 and ending December 1979. The results from this analysis are compared to those of domestic joint ventures and corporate mergers. Although international joint ventures have been regarded as an important investment alternative in this country, no study has attempted to determine the effects of such ventures on the shareholder return of U.S. corporations.

This chapter will progress as follows. In Section II, the data and sample selection are described. Next, in Section III the empirical methodology is discussed. The results of the empirical investigation into the performance of the U.S. companies involved in joint ventures with the Asian countries are then presented in Section IV. Finally, in Section V a summary and some concluding remarks are presented.

II. DATA AND SAMPLE SELECTION

The initial samples of joint ventures involving U.S. companies and Asian countries was drawn from the ''Joint Venture Roster'' published in *Mergers and Acquisitions*, and the *Wall Street Journal Index* over the period beginning January 1968 and ending December 1979. Over the 12 years 272 international joint ventures were reported. The stock return data for the sample U.S. corporations and market returns come from the CRSP (Center for Research in Security Prices) monthly and index files, respectively. Daily index data, where needed for calculation of particular measures, are extracted from *Standard & Poor's Statistical Services*.[1]

To be included in the final sample, a joint venture must meet the following additional criteria:[2]

1. The U.S. corporation involved in the foreign joint venture was listed on the New York Stock Exchange over the period 84 months prior to the first announcement of the joint venture attempt to 24 months following the announcement.
2. The U.S. corporation in the sample had no other large events in the 48-month period surrounding the joint venture announcement month.
3. The U.S. corporation was classified in a nonregulated industry.
4. The announcement of the joint venture had to be reported in either the *Wall Street Journal Index* or the ''Joint Venture Roster'' of *Mergers and Acquisitions.*

Of the 272 joint ventures reported, 96 satisfied the criteria for inclusion in the final sample.

Table 1 provides summary statistics for the sample. Part A of the table describes the joint ventures by year of initiation over the 12-year period beginning 1968 and ending 1979. The initial sample contains all the joint ventures between U.S. companies and their counterparts from the nine Asian countries, and is inclusive of the final sample. Part A indicates that the joint ventures are approximately normally distributed across the sample period. The number of joint ventures increased through 1973, and then decreased thereafter. The cause of the reduction in the number of joint ventures with the Asian nations after 1973 is not evident.

Part B of the table tabulates the sample by nation involved in joint ventures with U.S. corporations over the sample period. It indicates that Japan with 205 joint ventures has by far the most. South Korea is second with 27 joint ventures. Hong Kong and Indonesia are next with 12 and 11 joint ventures, respectively. The Philippines, Malaysia, Taiwan, Singapore, and Thailand do not appear to be very active partners with U.S. firms in terms of number of joint ventures over the sample period. The tendency for U.S. companies to prefer some nations over

Table 1. Description of the Sample

	Number of initial sample	Number of final sample
A. Joint Venture by Year		
1968	10	4
1969	13	4
1970	22	9
1971	21	6
1972	32	14
1973	45	13
1974	28	10
1975	19	5
1976	32	11
1977	14	5
1978	18	7
1979	18	8
Total	272	96
B. Joint Venture by Nation		
Hong Kong	12	6
Indonesia	11	5
Japan	205	57
Korea	27	16
Malaysia	3	3
Philippines	4	4
Singapore	2	0
Taiwan	6	4
Thailand	2	1
Total	272	96

others as joint venture partners has been consistent throughout the sample period. This phenomenon may be attributed to each host nation's characteristics in terms of availability of resources, risk and return of the project under consideration, and certain regulations and national laws regarding foreign investments.

III. METHODOLOGY

The empirical investigation relates performance measures to the U.S. corporations in the final sample. This study utilizes the ex-post Capital Asset Pricing Model (henceforth, CAPM) to measure the abnormal returns to the sample firms surrounding the joint venture announcement month.[3] The model describes the stochastic process generating securities returns as follows:

$$\tilde{R}_{it} - R_{ft} = \alpha_{it} + \beta_{it} (\tilde{R}_{mt} - R_{ft}) + \tilde{e}_{it} \quad (1)$$

where $\tilde{R}_{it}$ = monthly realized return to firm i in month t,
$\tilde{R}_{mt}$ = monthly realized percentage change of the CRSP value-weighted index with dividends over month t,
R_{ft} = monthly risk-free rate of return over month t,
α_{it} = the intercept term,
β_{it} = "beta" of firm i over month t, the regression coefficient for the independent variable, and
$\tilde{e}_{it}$ = stochastic error term with zero mean, serially uncorrelated, and with constant variance; residual return to firm i over month t due to the occurrence of firm-unique events.

Under the Sharpe–Lintner version of the CAPM, the intercept term (α) is expected to be equal to the equilibrium value of zero, and hence when α is zero the returns are assumed to be generated from a process in equilibrium.

The estimates of parameters α and β for any month t are calculated from Eq. (1) using 60 previous monthly returns of the company's stock, of the value-weighted market portfolio, and of Treasury bills. In particular, the 1-month rate on new issues of the 3-month U.S. Treasury Bill is used as a proxy for the monthly risk-free rate of return. The market return is a monthly rate of return on a value-weighted portfolio of all securities traded on the New York Stock Exchange.[4]

In this study, the estimates of parameters are updated on a monthly basis. This "moving β" approach is applied for the 24 months preceding and following the first public joint venture announcement month.

The abnormal return to firm i over month t is estimated by computing a prediction error term in Eq. (1).

$$\tilde{e}_{it} = \tilde{R}_{it} - R_{ft} - \beta_{it} (\tilde{R}_{mt} - R_{ft}) \quad (2)$$

The average residual (henceforth, *AR*) to the portfolio of sample companies over month t is calculated averaging the error terms of the individual firm's stock.

$$AR_t = \sum_{j=1}^{N_t} \tilde{e}_{it} / N_t \quad (3)$$

where AR_t = average residual or average abnormal return to the portfolio over month t,
$\tilde{e}_{it}$ = stochastic error term; residual or abnormal return to stock i over month t, and
N_t = number of firms in the portfolio over month t.

The cumulative average residual (henceforth, *CAR*) to the portfolio of sample firms from month *K* to month *L* is computed summing the *AR*s during the period.

$$CAR[K,L] = \sum_{t=K}^{L} AR_t \tag{4}$$

where K = first event month in the *CAR* calculation, and
L = last event month through which the *CAR* is computed.

The final sample consists of 96 U.S. firms involved in joint ventures with eight Asian countries (Singapore has no joint venture that satisfied the final sample criteria). As mentioned previously, each sample country may have different characteristics related to the availability of resources, and/or the law and regulations regarding foreign joint ventures. In order to test the impact of such differences on the performance of joint ventures, all the U.S. firms in the final sample are divided into three subsamples: one with firms involved in joint ventures with Japan, one with firms that have a joint venture relationship with South Korea, and one with firms associated with the other six countries, grouped into one subsample primarily due to the limited sample size.

IV. EMPIRICAL RESULTS

Table 2 and Figure 1 present average α, average β, percentage average residuals (AR) and cumulative average residuals (CAR) over the 49-month period for the total sample of 96 companies. The data indicate that the shareholders of these firms, on average, realize small positive abnormal returns of 0.5% over the joint venture announcement month. It also shows that the percentage CAR over the 2-year preannouncement period (month –24 through –1) is 11.819, while the CAR over the 2-year postannouncement period (month 1 through 24) is only 1.853. In particular, the sample firms earn 3.16% over the 3-month period starting in the announcement month. These results for the total sample suggest that, on average, joint ventures with the sample Asian countries result in an upward revaluation of the participating U.S. firms' equity, and that shareholders of these companies realize a small increase in wealth as a result of the joint ventures. Thus, these joint ventures are positive net present value projects. However, the 2-year performance after the announcement month compared to the preannouncement performance is clearly disappointing. One possible explanation for this result is a "time" factor; it may take more than 2 years before the impact of a joint venture is reflected on the participating companies' stock prices.

The third column of Table 2 shows average β for the sample firm over the 49-month period around announcement. The mean value of the average β for the firms in the final sample over the period is 1.17, which is not different from the

Table 2. Average α, Average β, Percentage Average Residuals, and Cumulative Average Residuals for the Total Sample of 96 U.S. Companies Involved in Joint Ventures with Eight Asian Countries

Month	*Average* α	*Average* β	*Average residuals*	*Cumulative avg. residuals*
-24	0.0020	1.1898	1.017	1.017
-23	0.0022	1.1894	0.892	1.909
-22	0.0022	1.1847	0.940	2.849
-21	0.0024	1.1869	0.246	3.095
-20	0.0023	1.1803	0.509	3.604
-19	0.0027	1.1808	-0.833	2.771
-18	0.0025	1.1713	0.254	3.025
-17	0.0023	1.1635	0.631	3.656
-16	0.0023	1.1705	-0.047	3.609
-15	0.0024	1.1745	2.690	6.299
-14	0.0027	1.1732	-0.139	6.160
-13	0.0026	1.1766	0.022	6.182
-12	0.0025	1.1753	2.832	9.014
-11	0.0030	1.1828	0.054	9.068
-10	0.0028	1.1860	0.606	9.674
-9	0.0027	1.1843	0.408	10.082
-8	0.0026	1.1903	0.101	10.183
-7	0.0027	1.1884	-0.698	9.485
-6	0.0027	1.1873	2.093	11.578
-5	0.0031	1.1823	0.496	12.074
-4	0.0031	1.1768	0.811	12.885
-3	0.0034	1.1776	1.354	14.239
-2	0.0036	1.1816	-1.061	13.029
-1	0.0036	1.1803	-1.210	11.819
0	0.0034	1.1735	0.497	12.316
1	0.0036	1.1742	0.733	13.049
2	0.0035	1.1662	1.829	14.878
3	0.0039	1.1645	-0.279	14.599
4	0.0039	1.1653	0.295	14.894
5	0.0039	1.1634	-0.359	14.535
6	0.0040	1.1625	0.673	15.208
7	0.0040	1.1579	-2.385	12.823
8	0.0038	1.1589	-0.195	12.628
9	0.0036	1.1649	0.454	13.082
10	0.0037	1.1629	-1.411	11.671
11	0.0035	1.1631	-0.039	11.632
12	0.0032	1.1595	2.479	14.111
13	0.0038	1.1683	0.065	14.176
14	0.0037	1.1647	0.089	14.265
15	0.0037	1.1732	-0.228	14.037
16	0.0035	1.1664	-0.649	13.388
17	0.0034	1.1671	-0.612	12.776
18	0.0031	1.1677	3.394	16.170
19	0.0038	1.1826	0.133	16.303
20	0.0037	1.1756	0.420	16.723
21	0.0036	1.1793	-1.129	15.594
22	0.0033	1.1766	-2.171	13.423
23	0.0027	1.1708	-0.011	13.412
24	0.0027	1.1628	0.757	14.169

Figure 1. Percentage average residuals (AR) and cumulative average residuals (CAR) for the total sample of 96 U.S. companies involving joint ventures with eight Asian countries relative to the announcement month in the period 1968–1979.

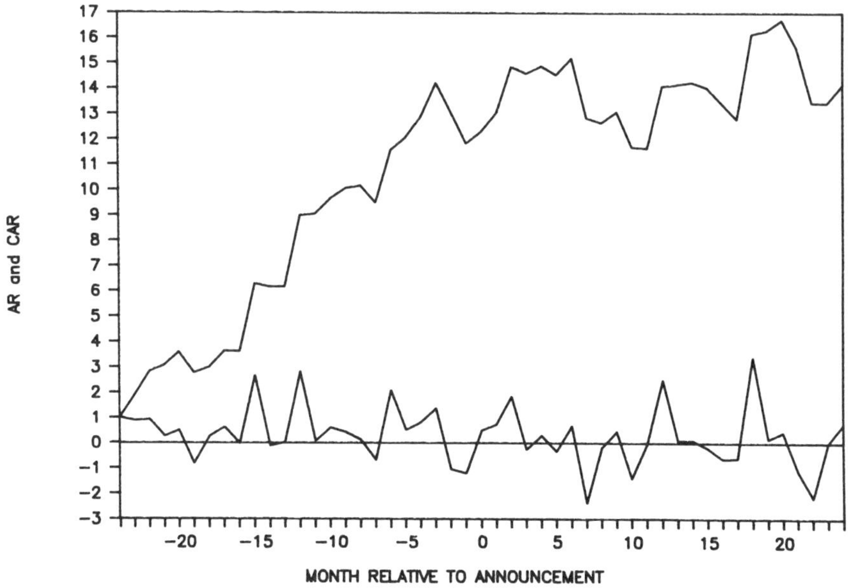

population of publicly traded firms (Brown and Warner, 1980). There appears to be no significant difference in average β across the 49-month period. This suggests that the announcement of joint venture with Asian countries, on average, does not affect the systematic risk of the sample companies' stock.

Table 3 provides the same statistics for the sample of 57 U.S. firms involved in joint ventures with Japan in the period 1968–1979. The AR and CAR series starting in month −24 are plotted in Figure 2. The 24-month CAR from month −24 to −1 for Japan (7.2%) is not as large as that for the total sample (11.82%). Also, the percentage AR over the joint venture announcement month for the Japan sample (0.065) is much lower than that of the total (0.5). However, the 24-month postannouncement CAR (7.94%) for the former is significantly larger than that of the latter (1.853%). This suggests that the shareholders of the U.S. firms involved in joint ventures with Japan, on average, earn significantly higher positive returns from joint ventures than those of U.S. companies involved with other Asian countries in the sample. In addition, this continuous upward revaluation of the shares of the firms in this subsample reflects the stock market's revision of the probability of success from the joint ventures.

Table 3. Average α, Average β, Percentage Average Residuals, and Cumulative Average Residuals for 57 U.S. Companies Involved in Joint Ventures with Japan

Month	*Average* α	*Average* β	*Average residuals*	*Cumulative avg. residuals*
−24	0.0021	1.2529	1.209	1.209
−23	0.0023	1.2584	1.216	2.426
−22	0.0024	1.2485	−0.183	2.243
−21	0.0021	1.2519	0.340	2.583
−20	0.0022	1.2446	0.348	2.931
−19	0.0023	1.2414	−0.945	1.986
−18	0.0020	1.2307	−0.845	1.142
−17	0.0014	1.2259	0.682	1.824
−16	0.0015	1.2383	−0.414	1.409
−15	0.0014	1.2416	3.066	4.475
−14	0.0018	1.2450	−0.390	4.085
−13	0.0018	1.2447	−0.180	3.905
−12	0.0016	1.2437	3.052	6.956
−11	0.0022	1.2520	−0.386	6.570
−10	0.0018	1.2539	0.674	7.244
−9	0.0018	1.2559	0.076	7.321
−8	0.0017	1.2579	−0.826	6.495
−7	0.0017	1.2564	−0.539	5.956
−6	0.0017	1.2536	1.738	7.694
−5	0.0019	1.2441	1.443	9.138
−4	0.0021	1.2381	0.478	9.616
−3	0.0023	1.2399	0.467	10.083
−2	0.0023	1.2472	−0.925	9.158
−1	0.0022	1.2547	−1.960	7.199
0	0.0020	1.2426	0.065	7.264
1	0.0022	1.2415	0.436	7.700
2	0.0020	1.2247	2.040	9.739
3	0.0024	1.2249	−0.150	9.589
4	0.0025	1.2278	0.002	9.591
5	0.0025	1.2203	0.668	10.259
6	0.0027	1.2138	−0.397	9.863
7	0.0025	1.2168	−2.741	7.122
8	0.0024	1.2247	−0.217	6.905
9	0.0023	1.2284	1.830	8.735
10	0.0027	1.2257	−1.755	6.980
11	0.0025	1.2198	−0.911	6.069
12	0.0021	1.2146	3.980	10.049
13	0.0029	1.2216	0.816	10.865
14	0.0030	1.2200	1.405	12.269
15	0.0033	1.2305	0.953	13.222
16	0.0034	1.2294	0.117	13.339
17	0.0036	1.2275	−0.490	12.849
18	0.0032	1.2302	2.858	15.707
19	0.0037	1.2425	0.912	16.619
20	0.0038	1.2377	1.167	17.786
21	0.0039	1.2356	−2.126	15.661
22	0.0034	1.2401	−1.501	14.160
23	0.0029	1.2257	−0.191	13.968
24	0.0027	1.2142	1.232	15.201

Figure 2. Percentage average residuals (AR) and cumulative average residuals (CAR) for the sample of 57 U.S. companies involving joint ventures with Japan relative to the announcement month in the period 1968–1979.

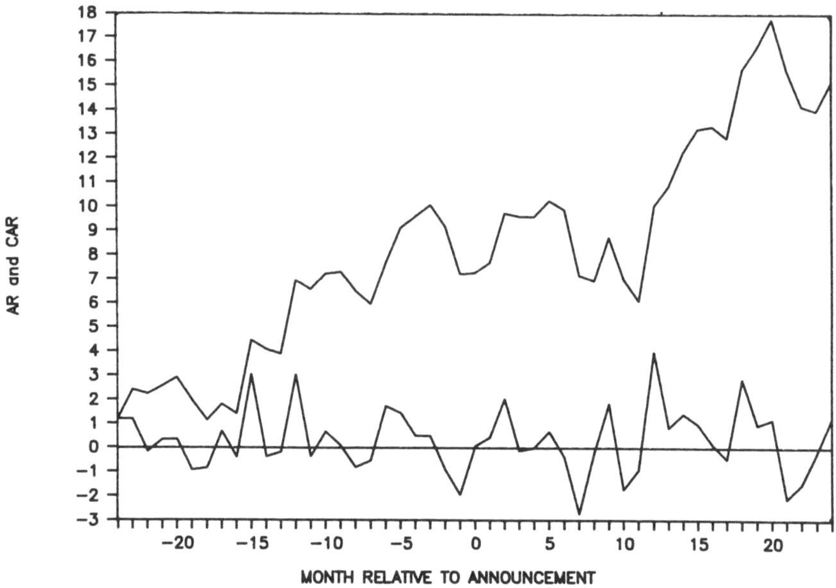

The average β for the Japan sample over the 49-month period ranges from 1.21 to 1.26, and there appears to be no specific change associated with the joint venture announcement. The mean value of the β series is approximately 1.24, which is slightly higher than that of the total sample. This indicates that the U.S. firms involved in joint ventures with Japan are relatively riskier than the average companies in the sample.

Table 4 and Figure 3 present the percentage AR and CAR of the stocks of the 16 U.S. firms that engaged in joint ventures with South Korea over the period 1968–1979. The summary statistics in Table 4 reveal a positive revaluation of the shares of the sample companies on the announcement of the joint venture. The percentage AR over the announcement month for the Korea sample firms (3.44) is much larger than the average (0.05). Also, the percentage CAR over the 2-year preannouncement period (20.13) is almost twice as large as that of the total sample (11.82). These differences in both the CAR series and AR over the preannouncement period and the announcement month between the Korea sample and the Japan or total sample are striking. Two tentative conclusions can be drawn from these results: one is that U.S. firms involved in joint ventures with South Korea had, on average, superior performances before undertaking joint

Table 4. Average α, Average β, Percentage Average Residuals, and Cumulative Average Residuals for 16 U.S. Companies Involved in Joint Ventures with South Korea

Month	*Average* α	*Average* β	*Average residuals*	*Cumulative avg. residuals*
−24	0.0010	1.2085	−0.552	−0.552
−23	0.0013	1.1975	0.765	0.212
−22	0.0013	1.1986	0.742	0.955
−21	0.0012	1.1889	0.459	1.413
−20	0.0013	1.1868	1.247	2.661
−19	0.0019	1.1863	−0.948	1.713
−18	0.0019	1.1886	2.990	4.703
−17	0.0020	1.1716	−0.576	4.127
−16	0.0016	1.1769	−0.038	4.090
−15	0.0018	1.1858	5.851	9.940
−14	0.0030	1.1916	−1.620	8.320
−13	0.0024	1.1895	−0.501	7.819
−12	0.0022	1.1887	3.094	10.913
−11	0.0026	1.1906	0.572	11.484
−10	0.0030	1.1898	0.945	12.430
−9	0.0037	1.1794	3.638	16.068
−8	0.0043	1.1917	1.342	17.410
−7	0.0043	1.1816	2.297	19.707
−6	0.0047	1.1731	2.492	22.199
−5	0.0049	1.1583	0.761	22.960
−4	0.0049	1.1540	0.105	23.065
−3	0.0050	1.1504	0.242	23.308
−2	0.0052	1.1594	−2.104	21.204
−1	0.0050	1.1406	−1.074	20.130
0	0.0049	1.1389	3.440	23.570
1	0.0058	1.1460	0.968	24.538
2	0.0052	1.1426	2.526	27.065
3	0.0060	1.1289	2.253	29.317
4	0.0060	1.1221	1.862	31.179
5	0.0063	1.1241	−1.462	29.718
6	0.0062	1.1232	3.203	32.921
7	0.0070	1.1065	−4.312	28.608
8	0.0061	1.0788	1.089	29.698
9	0.0060	1.0717	0.257	29.955
10	0.0055	1.0659	−3.766	26.189
11	0.0049	1.0830	−1.002	25.188
12	0.0047	1.0771	0.801	25.988
13	0.0048	1.0931	0.663	26.652
14	0.0045	1.0607	−0.747	25.904
15	0.0041	1.0546	−1.659	24.245
16	0.0036	1.0287	−2.109	22.136
17	0.0029	1.0310	−2.248	19.888
18	0.0030	1.0122	5.611	25.499
19	0.0043	1.0429	−0.956	24.543
20	0.0038	1.0242	−0.597	23.946
21	0.0032	1.0340	−0.351	23.594
22	0.0029	1.0127	−2.490	21.104
23	0.0025	1.0213	−0.184	20.920
24	0.0030	1.0189	5.359	26.279

Figure 3. Percentage average residuals (AR) and cumulative average residuals (CAR) for the sample of 16 U.S. companies involving joint ventures with South Korea relative to the announcement month in the period 1968–1979.

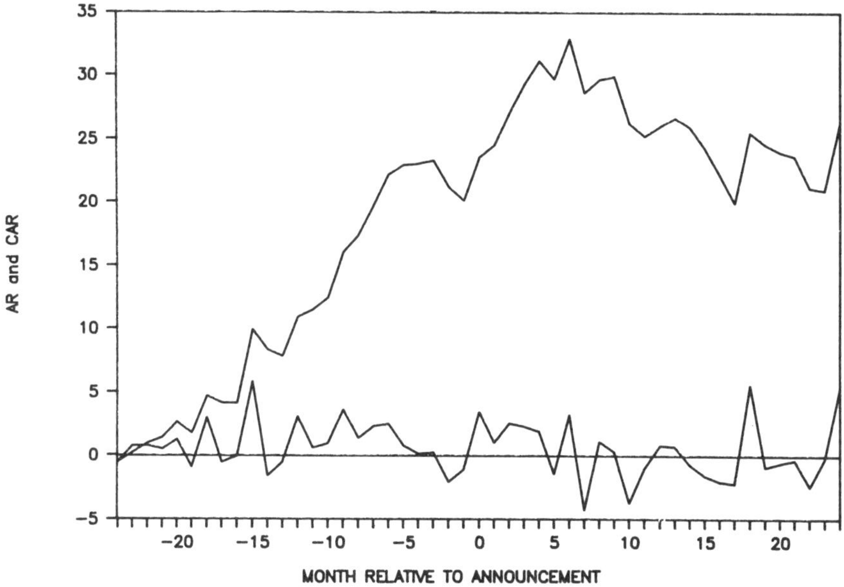

ventures, and the other is that the stock market reacts very favorably to the news of such events. The cause of these results is not evident.

The CAR over the 2-year postannouncement period for the Korea sample (2.7%) is slightly higher than the average (1.85%), but much lower than that of the Japan sample (7.94%). However, the CAR over the 25-month period starting in the announcement month for the Korean sample is 6.15%. This is much higher than that of the total sample (2.35%), and slightly below that of the Japan sample (8%). This implies that the shareholders of the U.S. companies involved in joint ventures with Japan and South Korea realized significant positive abnormal returns from those foreign operations during the period 1968–1979. It must be noted, however, that the postannouncement performance for the Korea sample is not as superior as the preannouncement performance.

The second column of Table 4 provides the average β for the 16 U.S. firms included in the Korea sample. In contrast to previous cases, the average β declines over the 49-month sample period, and the mean value is 1.15. This is slightly lower than that of the total sample (1.17) and of the Japan sample (1.24). These results suggest that the U.S. firms engaged in joint ventures with South Korea are relatively less risky than the average firms in the total sample, and, more importantly, these joint ventures reduce the systematic (market) risk of the sample firms' stocks through international diversification.

Table 5 and Figure 4 report the results for the sample of U.S. firms involved in joint ventures with Hong Kong, Malaysia, Philippines, Indonesia, Taiwan, and Thailand. The primary reason that these six countries are grouped into one subsample is the lack of observations. Each country included in this subsample had too few joint ventures with NYSE listed corporations over the period 1968–1979 (see Table 1). Given the similarity in geographic location, natural resources, and labor force characteristics, it is reasonable to combine these six countries into a single group. It should, however, be noted that Taiwan is more economically advanced in the group of selected six "developing" economies. (The number of joint ventures with Taiwan is only 6 and 4 in the intial and final samples, respectively, see Table 1.)

The summary statistics in Table 5 reveal that the percentage CAR over the 2-year preannouncement period for the sample firms (18.12) is much higher than that for the Japan sample (7.2), but slightly lower than that for the Korea sample (20.13). Thus, U.S. firms included in this sample earned significant positive returns before the announcement month. However, this significant positive

Figure 4. Percentage average residuals (AR) and cumulative average residuals (CAR) for the sample of 23 U.S. companies involving joint ventures with Hong Kong, Malaysia, Taiwan, Thailand, Philippines, and Indonesia relative to the announcement month in the period 1968–1979.

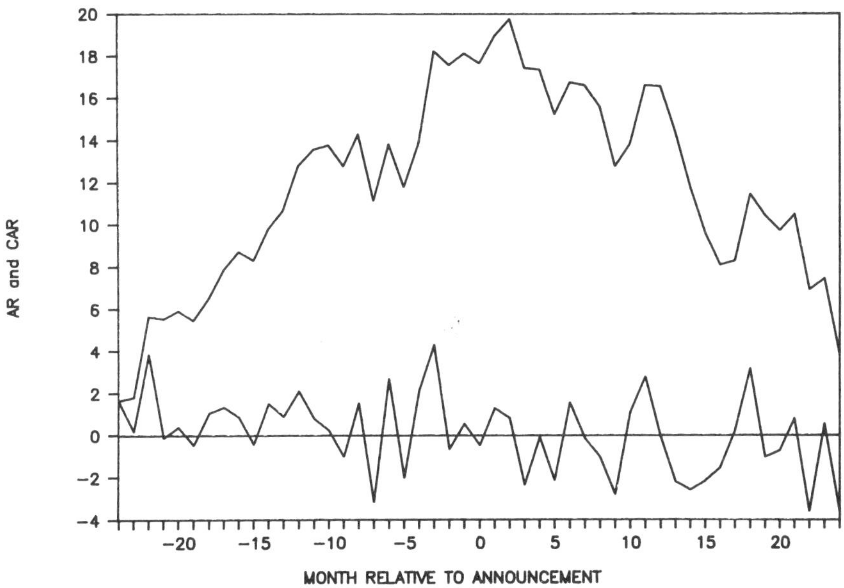

Table 5. Average α, Average β, Percentage Average Residuals, and Cumulative Average Residuals for 23 U.S. Companies Involved in Joint Ventures with Philippines, Indonesia, Malaysia, Taiwan, Thailand, and Hong Kong

Month	*Average* α	*Average* β	*Average residuals*	*Cumulative avg. residuals*
–24	0.0024	1.0205	1.633	1.633
–23	0.0027	1.0127	0.177	1.810
–22	0.0031	1.0168	3.862	5.672
–21	0.0040	1.0243	–0.136	5.536
–20	0.0042	1.0244	0.393	5.929
–19	0.0044	1.0266	–0.475	5.454
–18	0.0042	1.0120	1.075	6.529
–17	0.0046	1.0033	1.345	7.874
–16	0.0049	0.9979	0.858	8.732
–15	0.0053	1.0005	–0.439	8.293
–14	0.0049	0.9826	1.515	9.808
–13	0.0049	0.9988	0.886	10.694
–12	0.0049	0.9964	2.103	12.797
–11	0.0054	1.0060	0.782	13.579
–10	0.0053	1.0150	0.203	13.782
–9	0.0044	1.0125	–1.018	12.764
–8	0.0038	1.0216	1.535	14.299
–7	0.0041	1.0246	–3.176	11.122
–6	0.0038	1.0328	2.696	13.818
–5	0.0047	1.0459	–2.036	11.782
–4	0.0042	1.0408	2.129	13.911
–3	0.0050	1.0421	4.327	18.237
–2	0.0057	1.0345	–0.672	17.566
–1	0.0060	1.0237	0.554	18.120
0	0.0059	1.0265	–0.481	17.638
1	0.0057	1.0270	1.305	18.944
2	0.0060	1.0376	0.820	19.764
3	0.0063	1.0397	–2.358	17.406
4	0.0057	1.0404	–0.067	17.339
5	0.0055	1.0498	–2.136	15.203
6	0.0055	1.0625	1.566	16.769
7	0.0057	1.0475	–0.164	16.605
8	0.0058	1.0515	–1.034	15.570
9	0.0051	1.0722	–2.819	12.752
10	0.0048	1.0748	1.081	13.833
11	0.0050	1.0785	2.790	16.623
12	0.0050	1.0802	–0.073	16.550
13	0.0053	1.0885	–2.211	14.338
14	0.0049	1.1000	–2.592	11.746
15	0.0043	1.1135	–2.158	9.588
16	0.0037	1.1062	–1.533	8.055
17	0.0034	1.1119	0.223	8.277
18	0.0029	1.1208	3.181	11.458
19	0.0039	1.1313	–1.041	10.417
20	0.0032	1.1269	–0.723	9.694
21	0.0032	1.1409	0.799	10.493
22	0.0033	1.1334	–3.611	6.882
23	0.0025	1.1387	0.555	7.438
24	0.0026	1.1355	–3.620	3.818

revaluation over the preannouncement period disappears steadily. The AR for the month of announcement is –0.48%, implying that these sample firms, on average, suffer losses from the joint venture announcement. The CAR over the 2-year postannouncement period is –13.82%. These results are quite different from those of Japan and Korea samples. Thus, the stockholders of the U.S. companies involved with these six nations, on average, suffer a significant wealth loss as a result of these joint ventures.

The Table also reports that the mean value of average β for the sample over the 49-month period is approximately 1.03. This is much lower than the total sample (1.17), Japan sample (1.24), and Korea sample (1.15). Thus, the companies in this subsample are less risky than those involved with Japan and Korea. However, the average β for these companies increases steadily over the 49-month period, which indicates that the risk of these companies' stocks increases. Thus, the joint ventures with these nations do not provide the firms with diversification benefits.

Table 6 summarizes percentage ARs, CARs, the mean value of average β series, and the trend of average β series for the total sample and Japan, South Korea, and other subsamples. Over the 2-year preannouncement period, U.S. firms involved in joint ventures with Asian nations appear to earn large excess returns. In particular, joint ventures with South Korea appear to realize the largest excess returns over this period and the announcement month. However,

Table 6. Percentage Average Residuals, Percentage Cumulative Average Residuals, and Average β for Total Sample and Japan and South Korea, and the Other Subsample in the Period 1968–1979

	Total sample (N=96)	*Japan subsample (N=57)*	*Korea subsample (N=16)*	*Other subsample (N=23)*
CAR [–24, –1]	11.819	7.199	20.130	18.120
AR [0]	0.497	0.065	3.440	–0.481
CAR [0, 24]	2.350	8.002	6.149	–14.302
CAR[1, 24]	1.853	7.937	2.709	–13.820
Mean value of average β series	1.17	1.24	1.15	1.03
Trend of average β series	No change	No change	Decreasing	Increasing

U.S. firms engaged in joint ventures with Japan realize the largest wealth gains over the 2-year postannouncement period, while joint ventures with other nations suffer significant wealth losses during the same period.

V. SUMMARY AND CONCLUSION

This study analyzes the abnormal stock price performance of NYSE firms that engage in joint ventures with selected Asian countries in the period 1968–1979. The evidence presented in this chapter indicates that the stockholders of the total sample of 96 firms, on average, do not earn significant positive abnormal returns on the announcement of joint ventures and through the 2-year postannouncement period. Using daily data, McConnell and Nantell (1985) report that the stockholders of corporations involved in domestic joint ventures earn statistically significant abnormal returns. Although the results from this study and those of domestic joint ventures are not directly comparable, it appears that both Asian and domestic joint ventures are positive net present value projects. Also, the results in this study are consistent with the hypothesis that joint ventures create synergy through the combination of each company's unique resources.

The total sample of 96 corporations is divided into three subsamples. Comparison among the returns to the stockholders of the companies over the 49-month period surrounding the joint venture announcement month in these three subsamples reveals some additional points of interest.

First, the U.S. companies involved in joint ventures with South Korea realize the most significant wealth gain among the subsamples over the 2-year period prior to the announcement month. The companies engaged in joint ventures with Hong Kong, Indonesia, Malaysia, Philippines, Taiwan, and Thailand as a group perform well over the same period, but not as well as those in the Korea sample. The firms involved in joint ventures with Japan have the lowest, yet positive cumulative abnormal returns over the period.

Second, during the announcement month, the stock market reacts more favorably to the news of joint ventures with Korea than with other nations. The news of joint ventures with Japan result in the insignificant positive abnormal returns, whereas the companies engaged in joint ventures with the other six countries actually suffer a significant wealth loss as a result of the joint venture announcement.

Third, the stockholders of the companies involved in joint ventures with Japan earn the most significant positive abnormal returns among the subsamples over 25-month period starting in the announcement month and ending 24 months thereafter. The firms in the Korea sample also realize large gain over the same period. In contrast, the firms engaged in joint ventures with the remaining six countries experience significant wealth loss as a result, of joint venture announcements over the same period. These losses over both the announcement month and the subsequent period can be thought of as an evidence that the capital market forms an unbiased expectation of future unsuccessful joint venture performance.

Finally, for the total sample of 96 firms considered in this study, the joint ventures, on average, do not affect the risk structure of these firms. However, the firms involved in joint ventures with the other six nations experience a small increase in risk, whereas the companies in the Korea sample realize a small reduction in risk as a result of joint ventures. [To what extent statistical findings reported here relative to the ''other'' sample is biased for any arbitrariness in grouping the six Asian nations in a pooled subsample, future research may be able to find an answer.]

NOTES

1. *Standard & Poor's Statistical Service* is an annual publication by Standard & Poor's corporation. In this study, the 1984 edition is used.
2. See Mandelker (1974) for similar sampling criteria.
3. See Lintner (1965) and Sharpe (1964) for more about the Capital Asset Pricing Model.
4. The Center for Research in Security Prices (CRSP) at the University of Chicago has developed a set of monthly stock price tapes and daily stock prices. The monthly tapes contain month-end prices for every stock listed on the New York Stock Exchange. The CRSP value-weighted index is generated by deriving the initial total market value of all stocks listed on the NYSE as the base. Subsequently, a new market value is computed for all stocks in the NYSE index; this is compared to the base value to determine the percentage change.

REFERENCES

Brown, S. J. and J. B. Warner. ''Measuring Security Price Performance.'' *Journal of Financial Economics 8*, 1980, 205–258.

Lintner, J. ''The Valuation of Risk Assets and the Selection of Risky Investments in Stock Portfolios and Capital Assets.'' *Review of Economics and Statistics 47* February 1965, 13–47.

Mandelker, G. ''Risk and Return: The Case of Merging Firms.'' *Journal of Financial Economics 1*, December 1974, 303–335.

McConnell, J. J. and T. J. Nantell. ''Corporate Combinations and Common Stock Returns: The Case of Joint Ventures.'' *Journal of Finance 40*, June 1985, 519–536.

Mergers and Acquisition. McLean, VA: Information for Industry, 1968–1979.

Sharpe, W. ''Capital Asset Price: A Theory of Market Equilibrium under Conditions of Risk.'' *Journal of Finance 19*, September 1964, 425–442.

Standard & Poor's Statistical Service, 1984 Edition. Standard & Poor's Corporation.

Wall Street Journal Index 1968–1979. New York: Dow-Jones, Inc.

A COMPARATIVE STUDY OF MANUFACTURING PRODUCTIVITY AMONG ASEAN COUNTRIES

Richard Hooley

I. INTRODUCTION

Recent years have witnessed an increased awareness of the role of productivity growth in sustained economic progress. This is reflected in the expansion of the productivity literature, which, however, has dealt primarily with the developed countries of the western world. Although there has been some work on industrial productivity in NICs such as Korea and Taiwan, parallel work on LDCs is still at an early stage. This is unfortunate because as Chenery et al. (1976) and Kuznets (1966) repeatedly pointed out, an understanding of the nature and factors underlying changes in productivity is vital to our understanding of growth in per capita income. When undertaken on an industry basis, productivity studies provide a

Research in Asian Economic Studies.
Asian Industrialization: Changing Economic Structures,
Volume 1, Part A, pages 349–359.
Copyright © 1988 by JAI Press Inc.
All rights of reproduction in any form reserved.
ISBN: 0-89232-987-4

wealth of detail on output and inputs over time that is invaluable in making informed judgments regarding the nature of the development process and balanced assessments of the effects of macroeconomic policies.

Initial efforts to measure and analyze productivity performance in ASEAN countries have focused on agriculture. The establishment of the International Rice Research Institute (IRRI) in 1960 was a milestone in this respect. Researchers at the Institute compiled both macro- and microdata on rice productivity trends and performance over an extended period for a number of Asian countries (Barker et al. 1985; Hayami and Ruttan, 1985; Herdt and Wickham, 1978). Although the primary focus of work at IRRI has been on rice, there has also been a spillover toward efforts directed at measuring and analyzing productivity performance of the agricultural sector as a whole. Much less attention has been given to other sectors presumably because agriculture is still considered the dominant industry in these economies. In addition, policymakers often concentrate on productivity improvement in agriculture because of their perception that stability of food (i.e., rice) prices constitutes the vital linchpin between economic progress and political stability.

These widely held perceptions are no longer justified by the facts. As late as 1960, GDP originating in agriculture averaged 32% for the five ASEAN countries (see Table 1), whereas by 1982 the figure had fallen to 19%. Manufacturing in ASEAN countries accounted for only 13% of GDP in 1960, whereas by 1982 the figure had risen to 22%—three percentage points above agriculture. All indicators point to a continuation of these trends for the foreseeable future. It is therefore particularly important to ask what contribution, if any, growth in productivity has made to the expansion of industry.

This study has three objectives. The first is to analyze manufacturing productivity performance of ASEAN countries as a group, starting with a survey of partial productivity measures and moving up to a consideration of total factor productivity indicators. Second, we wish to consider differences of productivity measures among selected countries. Third, to develop hypotheses to explain the trends observed in our time series and cross-country comparisons.

Before analyzing ASEAN productivity growth, it is appropriate to point out that the manufacturing sectors of Southeast Asian countries contain important similarities both in their structure and in the changes that they have undergone in recent years. As Table 1 shows, all of these countries exhibit a high degree of concentration among manufacturing industries. In 1960 three industries among 24 at the three-digit level (food processing, beverages, and tobacco) accounted for an average of 41% of total manufacturing value added. If textiles, apparel, and wood products are added, then six industries accounted for 55% of total value added. The second main point to be made here is that all of these countries have experienced a decline in these "traditional" manufactures, in favor of small machinery and equipment manufacture which is relatively labor-intensive. By 1982, the above-mentioned six industries averaged only 39% of total manufactur-

Table 1. Structure of Southeast Asian Industry (Percentage)

	Indonesia	*Malaysia*	*Philippines*	*Singapore*	*Thailand*	*Average*
Agricultural share of GDP						
1960	54	37	26	4	40	32
1982	25	23	23	1	24	19
Manufacturing share of GDP						
1960	13	9	20	12	13	13
1982	18	19	25	26	20	22
Share in manufacturing VA of selected industries, food, beverage, and tobacco						
1960	51	26	42	26	61	41
1980	34	16	38	5	34	25
Textiles and apparel						
1960	11	2	10	6	4	7
1980	16	7	11	5	10	10
Wood products						
1960	3	14	5	7	6	7
1980	5	10	3	2	2	4
Machinery and equipment						
1960	7	3	8	22	7	9
1980	15	21	11	47	12	21

Source: U.N., *Yearbook of National Income Accounts.*

ing value added, whereas the machinery and equipment group had risen to 21%. The point is that in reviewing the productivity performance in manufacturing for these different countries, we are not dealing with totally dissimilar industries, even when we deal with manufacturing as a whole. The same is true for any particular industry. Consider food processing for example. The major activities are fairly similar across ASEAN states. Sugar milling, rice milling, the processing of edible oils such as coconut and palm oil, and the processing of meat and fish products constitute the main activities of this industry in Malaysia, Thailand, the Philippines, and Indonesia. The presence of these similarities becomes evident when we begin comparing performance among countries.

Our data base for the analysis consists of two parts. First, there are the censuses of manufactures that each of these countries takes annually, except Thailand. The usual variables are covered. Price data for deflation are generally available from government sources, including price data for output of manufactures, consumer price indexes, and indexes appropriate for deflating capital goods. A second body of data consists of estimates of total factor productivity in manufacturing by Hooley (1985) for the Philippines, by Wiboonchutikula (1982) for Thailand, and by Tsao (1982) for Singapore. These three authors engage in considerable refinement of census data and also incorporate additional material on inputs that is often not directly available from the censuses.

II. GROWTH OF MANUFACTURING PRODUCTIVITY, 1970–1980

We begin our analysis by examining trends in some partial productivity measures. We derive these from the industrial census of the various countries. Table 2 shows output per employee for four ASEAN countries in addition to Hong Kong (for comparative purposes). In all of the countries value added per employee was rising with the exception of the Philippines. In Indonesia, Singapore, and Hong Kong the rise was particularly impressive at 9.5, 4.8, and 4.0%, respectively, per year.

A well-known shortcoming of the partial productivity measure (VA/L) is that it ignores the substitution of other factor inputs for labor. In addition, when dealing with the sectoral aggregate of output and inputs, it also is subject to change due to the shift effect within manufacturing either toward or away from more capital-intensive industries. Although our definition of manufacturing excludes petroleum refining, there is still a question as to what extent the rise in (VA/L) is the result of increases in capital per worker (K/L) and to what extent it is due to other factors, presumably linked with the more efficient use of capital and labor.

To answer this question we developed estimates of (VA/L) adjusted for changes in capital per worker. Under the conventional assumptions of constant returns to scale and disembodied technical change, we fit a function of the type $VA = F(K^{\alpha}, L^{(1-\alpha)})A$ where K and L are the inputs and A represents technical change. With a Cobb–Douglas production function it can easily be shown that

$$(VA/L) = A(K/L)^{\alpha} \tag{1}$$

We then computed the value of (K/L) for 1970 for each country and inserted it in the above equation to derive adjusted value added per employee. We then have

$$(VA/L)^{*}_{t} = A_t\ (K/L)^{\alpha}_{70} \tag{2}$$

Table 2. Value Added per Full-Time Employee in Manufacturing,[a] 1970–1980 (Value Added in 1975 Prices)

Year	*Indonesia*	*Malaysia*	*Philippines*	*Singapore*	*Hong Kong*
1970	—	12.3	38.5	12.6	—
1971	—	11.6	41.5	12.7	—
1972	—	10.4	38.9	13.2	—
1973		11.3	35.8	14.8	
1974	557	11.1	34.3	14.0	21.3
1975	643	11.9	26.8	15.0	21.6
1976	682	12.4	19.1	16.0	22.0
1977	770	12.6	19.6	16.7	21.1
1978	875	12.5	27.3	17.1	23.4
1979	801	13.9	26.7	18.0	26.5
1980	960	13.6	25.5	19.9	26.3
1981	1051	14.4	22.3	21.1	28.1
Annual growth rate					
1970–1981	+9.49%[b]	+1.44%	–4.84%	+4.79%	4.0%[b]

Source: Census of Manufactures of the respective countries.

[a] Manufacturing includes all industries in the ISIC classification except petroleum. Data are expressed in 1975 prices as follows: Indonesia, thousand Rupiahs; Malaysia, thousand Ringits; Singapore, thousand Singapore dollars; Philippines, thousand Pesos; and Hong Kong, thousand HK dollars.

[b] 1974–1981.

$(VA/L)^*_t$ is value added per employee for year t given the capital per worker of 1970. When there has been capital deepening $(VA/L)^* < (VA/L)$, and when capital shallowing has taken place $(VA/L)^* > (VA/L)$. Estimates of $(VA/L)^*$ for each country are presented in Table 3 for the same years as covered in Table 2. The results of this adjustment show that value added per worker adjusted for changes in capital per worker is generally far less for ASEAN countries than unadjusted *VA*. Indonesia's 9.5% annual increase in value added per worker is reduced to 1.5%. Malaysia's 2% annual increase becomes –0.4%. Singapore's 4.8% increase in real value added per employee is reduced 1.8%, while for Hong Kong the adjusted value added per worker actually rises by nearly 1% annually. The results are easy to summarize. For Indonesia, and Malaysia, about 85% or more of the increase in manufacturing output per worker was achieved by capital deepening. For Singapore and Hong Kong the comparable figure is lower (between

Table 3. Value Added per Full-Time Employee, Adjusted for Changes in Capital per Worker, All Manufacturing, 1970–1981[a] (Value in 1975 Prices)

Year	*Indonesia*[b]	*Malaysia*	*Philippines*	*Singapore*	*Hong Kong*[c]
1970	—	12.3	38.5	12.6	—
1971	—	11.6	41.5	12.0	—
1972	—	11.1	41.2	11.9	—
1973	—	10.9	39.7	12.0	—
1974	684	10.2	36.4	12.9	20.8
1975	643	10.5	32.5	11.4	20.4
1976	696	10.7	29.2	12.2	20.0
1977	706	10.6	23.9	12.9	18.0
1978	682	10.7	29.4	13.0	19.0
1979	613	11.9	28.4	14.0	21.3
1980	759	—	27.5	14.5	20.9
1981	812	—	27.1	15.3	22.2
Annual growth rate					
	+1.48%	−0.36%	−3.11%	+1.78%	+0.93%

Source: Same as Table 2.

[a] Manufacturing includes all ISIC three-digit industries except petroleum.

[b] (K/L) held constant at 1975 level.

[c] (K/L) held constant at 1974 level.

60 and 80%), indicating that capital deepening was less important in explaining labor productivity gains. Other factors, perhaps connected to organizational improvements and labor quality, were more important. This contrast befits the contrast in resource basis of Singapore and Hong Kong compared with those of Indonesia and Malaysia, particularly during the decade of the 1970s when stepped-up imports of petroleum and other primary products made possible the import of capital on a particularly large scale. In contrast to all these other ASEAN states is the case of the Philippines, which experienced a *decline* in value added per worker that was *entirely* due to factors other than capital per worker. These other factors were so powerful that they more than compensated for an increase in value added per worker equivalent to 1.7% based on the increase in capital per worker. This obviously reflects the macromismanagement and political turmoil that has characterized Philippine economic policies since

the mid-1970s. In addition the Philippines, with its shrinking per capita natural resource base, fell significantly behind its ASEAN neighbors in terms of increases in capital per worker.

It is common practice in productivity studies to estimate the rate of technical change as a residual derived by subtracting the sum of the weighted rates of growth of capital and labor inputs from the rate of growth of value added in constant prices. This method ignores the role of intermediate inputs in production and therefore may bias the results. As Bruno (1978) points out, a value-added specification assumes (1) that the quantities of intermediate input and output move in fixed proportions, (2) that where value added is not double deflated, prices of output and intermediate goods move in fixed proportions, and (3) that intermediate inputs are weakly separable from labor, capital, and time. We have absolutely no basis for making the first assumption. As to prices, given the extent of intervention in the intermediate markets implied by the nature of the tariff systems in many of these countries, and in the complete absence of data for double deflation, a value-added specification is inferior to a gross production specification.

Estimates of total factor productivity (TFP) using a gross production specification have been made for three ASEAN countries, the Philippines, Singapore, and Thailand. The results for the Philippines and Singapore can be compared with our results just discussed above. For neither the Philippines nor Singapore is there any significant growth in total factor productivity (TFP) from 1970 to 1980. Indeed, TFP growth during that period in the Philippines averaged −1.23% per year. That is not as poor a showing as the nearly 5% annual decline in value added per worker shown by our data. However, both studies yield *negative* growth rates for productivity change.

In the case of Singapore, only 11 out of the 28 industries that Tsao studied registered positive TFP change from 1970 to 1979. The remainder exhibit negative rates of TFP growth. The average for all manufacturing is +0.13%, not significantly different from zero. This contrasts with our result of +4.8% annual increase in value added per worker during the same period. A substantial part of the difference (about two-thirds, as explained above) is due to increases in capital per worker. A part of the remaining discrepancy is due to increases in intermediate goods consumption, which grew faster than either labor or real output over the 1970–1979 period. Consumption of intermediate goods is reflected in the gross specification (TFP) but not in our value-added specification. If increases in both capital and intermediate goods consumed are accounted for, the difference between our results based on value added per worker, and the results of previous studies using a gross output specification are fairly small.

We conclude that our results are broadly consistent with those of other investigators. That is to say, real output (and value added) per worker are both growing steadily, but most (and in some cases all) of this growth is accounted for by increases in the traditional, physical inputs of capital and intermediate goods. Increases in the quality of inputs (either labor or capital) still play only a minor role in ASEAN countries.

III. COMPARISONS OF PRODUCTIVITY LEVELS BY INDUSTRY

The results presented thus far deal exclusively with rates of growth of labor productivity for manufacturing as a whole. We turn now to a comparative analysis of levels of productivity performance by industry. We use a value-added specification of the production function with the usual assumptions including separation of input effects. We convert values among countries using the purchasing power parities for output and for capital derived from Kravis, et al. (1982). We estimate value added per employee for each country and then convert these estimates to U.S. dollars using purchasing power parities. The results of this comparison are reported in Table 4.

In 1970, value added per employee was roughly the same for Singapore, Malaysia, and the Philippines. By 1974, however, Singapore had moved ahead of these countries, as well as Hong Kong. Indonesia lagged far behind all other ASEAN countries. By 1980 further changes were taking place. Singapore maintained a distinct lead over Malaysia and Hong Kong. The Philippines fell behind all countries except Indonesia. However, the gap between Indonesia and the other countries (particularly the Philippines) narrowed considerably. If these same trends continue, Indonesian labor productivity in manufacturing should be approximately equal to that in other ASEAN countries by the mid- to late 1980s.

Turning now to individual industries, the same broad trends are evident in the food processing industry as in all manufacturing. Singapore, where labor productivity was once behind Malaysia and the Philippines, is now the leader in the area. The Philippines now trails all other countries except Indonesia due in part to the devastating effects of the decline of the sugar industry. In the beverage industry, however, things are different. Here the Philippines has the highest output per employee by a wide margin, with Hong Kong second. Indonesia is third. This reflects the impact of large, well-organized international corporations. The San Miguel Corp. dominates the beverage industry in the Philippines and in Hong Kong, while the Heineken Corp. plays a major role in the manufacture of beverages in Indonesia. Obviously these large corporations are able to bring modern manufacturing technology and methods of organization to the industry, as well as being able to obtain large capital inputs to the production process.

In the apparel industry, Hong Kong is the undisputed leader. This is so for 1974, the first year for which we have Hong Kong data, as well as in 1980. For the remaining countries (except Indonesia) output per worker is essentially the same—around \$2-1/2 in 1970 compared with \$4–6 in 1980. Indonesia once again has narrowed the gap between it and other ASEAN countries, and by 1980 was nearly at a level equal to that in Malaysia.

Table 4. Production per Employee, All Manufacturing and Selected Industries 1970–1980 (thousands of U.S. Dollars Converted at Intercountry Purchasing Power Parities)

	All Manufacturing (excl. petroleum)	*Food (311)*	*Beverages (313)*	*Apparel (322)*	*Wood products (331)*
Singapore					
1970	3.45	3.92	5.30	2.12	2.62
1974	6.32	8.20	7.59	2.62	3.81
1980	10.20	13.48	18.05	5.96	8.19
Malaysia					
1970	3.55	5.37	6.73	2.28	2.77
1974	5.74	9.85	10.59	3.85	4.28
1980	9.07	13.32	16.83	3.86	6.18
Indonesia					
1970	—	—	—	—	—
1974	1.74	1.91	8.90	1.29	0.97
1980	5.19	4.66	18.48	3.51	6.77
Hong Kong					
1970	—	—	—	—	—
1974	5.49	5.48	12.0	3.48	4.53
1980	9.21	9.64	26.56	7.15	6.49
Philippines					
1970	3.79	5.53	12.23	2.35	1.71
1974	5.40	9.72	16.85	2.62	2.87
1980	8.66	9.70	36.87	5.08	4.97

Sources: Data sources are the same as for Tables 2 and 3.

In wood products, Singapore was clearly the leader in 1980 with output per employee of over $8. Malaysia, Indonesia, and Hong Kong all show somewhat lower labor productivity levels—around $6—whereas in the Philippines the figure is only about $5. Once again, Indonesia appears to be narrowing the gap between itself and other ASEAN countries.

IV. SUMMARY AND CONCLUSION

We began by reviewing data on value added per full-time employee for four Southeast Asian countries and Hong Kong. We found that all but one showed substantial increases in real value added per worker. However, when capital per worker was held constant, the growth in (VA/L) was substantially reduced for all countries. For Singapore and Hong Kong, roughly three-fourths of the growth in real (VA/L) was due to capital augmentation, whereas for Malaysia and Indonesia the fraction was about nine-tenths. The Philippines was the only country that registered a substantial decline in real output per employee.

We also made some comparisons with regard to labor productivity *levels* across the countries for selected years. We did this for the manufacturing sector as a whole and for selected industries at the three-digit level. The results showed that levels of output per worker in Singapore are now about 10–15% higher than in other ASEAN countries, and double those in Indonesia. Second, within Southeast Asia there are shifting disparities. Singapore appears to be slowly increasing its lead over other ASEAN countries. But Indonesia is clearly closing the gap between itself and other ASEAN countries, whereas the Philippines is falling behind.

For several important individual industries including food products, wood products, and apparel, the productivity levels are not that far apart. Indonesia, although still far below Singapore levels, is, nevertheless, closing the gap in foods and wood products. There has also been significant gap closing between Singapore and Hong Kong in all manufacturing and some selected industries. In contrast, the gap between the Philippines and all other Southeast Asian countries is widening (after 1974) at an alarming rate. Hong Kong has continued to hold an impressive lead in apparel manufacture, where (VA/L) remains 20% higher than that of Singapore and almost double that of Indonesia and Malaysia. This, of course, has been a key element to Hong Kong's overall success in pushing up output per worker levels in the manufacturing sector, because apparel remains a dominant industry there.

There are some inferences that can be made from these findings. First, we have found that for the manufacturing sector as a whole, growth of labor productivity is advancing rapidly everywhere except in the Philippines. This growth is heavily capital dependent. When looking at individual industries, we found important examples of industries (e.g., beverages) in which labor productivity is growing much faster than all manufacturing. We infer that there are still a large number of foot-dragging industries in which gains are zero or negative. That appears so for both import substitution economies such as the Philippines and export oriented countries such as Singapore. Government intervention may be one factor here, but there are other candidates. For example, productivity gains in export industries that face an inelastic demand schedule will ''lose'' much of the gains from productivity improvement. Or, it may be that for countries such as

Malaysia and Indonesia, with rich natural resources, the rate of return to increased physical capital formation may be higher than that on research and on human capital formation. Or, it may just appear higher because of the absence of an institutional configuration that makes possible the channeling of the income stream from productivity improvement back to those who undertook them.

The ill effects of government intervention are clearly manifest in the Philippines, where two events occurred after 1975 to drastically reduce real output per worker, however measured. One was the policy of increasing employment in government-controlled and government-affiliated firms. The other was the shortening of the investment horizon by arbitrary and often contradictory interventions in markets that made the rate of return (adjusted for risk) from investment in intermediate inputs less (relative to capital) than otherwise. This multiplied problems of rational management control and caused a shifting along production frontiers that was most dysfunctional for the industrial system, as the results here clearly show.

ACKNOWLEDGMENT

The author acknowledges helpful comments from Romeo Bautista and Anthony M. Tang on an earlier draft of this paper. Responsibility for the final product, however, rests with the author.

REFERENCES

Barker, Randolph, R. Herdt, and B. Rose. *The Rice Economy of Asia*. Washington, D.C. Resources for the Future, 1985.

Bruno, Michael. "Duality, Intermediate Inputs and Value Added." In Melvin Fuss and D. McFadden (eds.) *Production Economics: A Dual Approach to Theory and Application*. Amsterdam: North-Holland, 1978.

Chenery, Hollis, S. Robinson, and M. Syrquin. *Industrialization and Growth: A Comparative Study*. Washington, D.C.: Oxford University Press for The World Bank, 1976.

Hayami, Yujiro and Vernon W. Ruttan. *Agricultural Development: An International Perspective*, 2nd ed. Baltimore, MD: Johns Hopkins University Press, 1985.

Herdt, Robert and T. Wickham. "Exploring the Gap between Potential and Actual Rice Yields in the Philippines." In *Economic Consequences of the New Rice Technology*. Los Banos, Philippines: International Rice Research Institute, 1978.

Hooley, Richard. *Productivity Growth in Philippine Manufacturing: Retrospect and Future Prospects*. Manila: Philippine Institute for Development Studies, 1985.

Kravis, Irving B., Alan Heston, and Robert Summers. *World Product and Income: International Comparisons of Real Gross Product*. Washington, D.C.: Johns Hopkins University Press, 1982.

Kuznets, Simon. *Modern Economic Growth*. New Haven, CT: Yale University Press, 1966.

Tsao, Yuan. "Growth and Productivity in Singapore: A Supply-Side Analysis." Ph.D. Dissertation, Harvard University, 1982.

Wiboonchutikula, Paitoon. "The Total Factor Productivity Growth of the Manufacturing Industries in Thailand. 1963–1967." Ph.D. Dissertation, University of Minnesota, 1982.

J A I P R E S S

Research in Asian Economic Studies

Edited by

M. Dutta

Department of Economics
Rutgers University

Volume 1: Part A: Asian Industrialization: Changing Economic Structures
1988, 359 pp.
ISBN 0-89232-987-4 $63.50
Set ISBN 0-89232-986-6 Set: $127.00

CONTENTS: List of Contributors. Preface. Executive Board. PART I. ASIAN INDUSTRIALIZATION: THE UNITED STATES/JAPAN AND EAST ASIA. The United States and the World Economy: An Asian Perspective, *Leonard Silk, New York Times.* **Industrialization of Japan and Selected East Asian Countries: The Structural Divergence Hypothesis,** *M. Dutta and Daniel Tantum, Rutgers University. The Internalization of United States Service Industries and the Economies in the Asia-Pacific Basin, Chung H. Lee and Seiji Naya, University of Hawaii.* **PART II. ASIAN NICs: KOREA/TAIWAN/HONG KONG. Korea's Economic Strategy: Business, Government, and Economic Development,** *Duk-Choong Kim, Sogang University.* **Korea Approaching a Developed Economy Regime,** *Dong-Se Cha, The ILHAE Institute.* **Taiwan in the 1980s: Policies and Prospects,** *Kuo-shu Liang, Chang Hwa Commercial Bank Ltd.* **Taiwan's Declining Investment Ratio and its Persistent Trade Surplus with the United States,** *Ching-yuan Lin, International Monetary Fund.* **Industrial Evolution and Changes in Trade Environment: A Case Study of Consumer Electronics and Textile/Garment Industries in Hong Kong,** *T.B. Lin and Chyau Tuan, The Chinese University of Hong Kong.* **American Executive's**

Attitudes Toward the Investment Climate in Hong Kong, *Mun Kin-Chok, The Chinese University of Hong Kong.* **Hong-Kong-United States Trade: Its Determinants,** *W.L. Chou and Y.C. Shih, The Chinese University of Hong Kong.* **PART III. ASEAN: THE PHILIPPINES/ INDONESIA. The Characteristics and Role of Small and Medium Industries in the Philippines,** *Jean-Pierre Dumas, Asian Development Bank.* **Industrialization in Indonesia: A Survey,** *Sukanto Reksohadiprodjo, Gadjah Mada University.* **PART IV. ASIAN NIC'S & ASEAN: INVESTMENT PATTERNS/MANUFACTURING PRODUCTIVITY. An Economic Analysis of U.S. Direct Investment in Manufacturing Industries in Selected Asia/ Pacific Countries,** *Andrew Stern, California State University, Long Beach.* **United States Multinationals and Export-Led Growth of Asian Developing Countries,** *Steve A.Y. Lin, Southern Illinois University.* **Impacts of Foreign Joint Ventures on the Shareholder Wealth of United States Corporations: The Case of Joint Ventures with Asian Countries,** *Insup Lee, University of Delaware.* **A Comparative Study of Manufacturing Productivity Among Asean Countries,** *Richard Hooley, University of Pittsburgh.*

Volume 1: Part B: Asian Industrialization: Changing Economic Structures
1988, 377 pp.
ISBN 0-89232-988-2 $63.50
Set ISBN 0-89232-986-6 Set: $127.00

CONTENTS: List of Contributors. Preface. Executive Board. PART I. JAPAN. The Asia-Pacific Arena: Market and Nonmarket Forces, *Kazuo Sato, Rutgers University and Sheng-yann Lii, Virginia Electric and Power Co.* **The Competition Principle in Japanese Companies and Labor Unions: A Premise,** *Ken'ichi Odawara, Sophia University.* **Energy and Trade Policy in Japan and the United States,** *David Jay Green, Hosei University.* **Investment in Human Capital in Pre-Oil Shock Japan,** *M. Anne Hill, Rutgers University.* **Foreign Direct Investment in the United States: A Case Study of the Japanese Investment in Hawaii,** *Richard Y.P. Joun, Department of Planning and Economic Development, Honolulu.* **PART II. CHINA. Infrasturcture in China's**

J A I P R E S S

J A I P R E S S

National Economy: In Retrospect and Prospect, *Li Jingwen and Fang Hanzhong, Chinese Academy of Social Sciences.* **China's Grain Comsumption and Production: Some Observations,** *Chih-Chien Chien, Shanghai Academy of Social Sciences.* **PART III. INDIA. The Tracks of the Managed Exchange Rate of the Indian Rupee with Monetary Shocks and External Disturbances,** *Kanta Marwah and Halldor P. Palsson, Carleton University.* **External Indebtedness of India: The United States As Creditor,** *Pranab Kumar Chatterjee, University of Kalyani.* **PART IV. SELECTED ECONOMIC ISSUES: EAST/SOUTHEAST/SOUTH/CENTRAL ASIA AGRICULTURE. Employment in Pakistan's Agricultural Sector,** *Yasmeen Mohiuddin, The University of the South.* **The Global Co[2] Environmental Problem: Economic Pros and Cons for Asian Cooperation,** *Richard E. Kosobud, Jnanodoy Bhattacharya, University of Illinois, Thomas A. Daly, Argonne National Laboratory, Chandan K. Mukhopadhyay, University of North Bengal, and Zhang Renze, University of Illinois.* **Energy and Income Relationships of the Asian NICs: An Economic Analysis,** *Mei-chu Hsiao, University of Colorado.* **HUMAN CAPITAL AND INTERNATIONAL LABOR MIGRATION. An Economic Analysis of Human Capital Exchanges Between the United States and Pacific Rim Countries,** *john T. Shieh, California State Polytechnic University.* **International Labor Migration, Emigrants' Remittances and Asian Developing Countries: Economic Analysis and Policy Issues,** *M.G. Quibria and M. Thant, Asian Development Bank.* **FINANCING STRATEGY/INTEREST RATE FIRST FAMILY HOME PURCHASE. Strategic Financing and Market Mechanism in the Development of the Textile Industry: Cases of Korea and Thailand,** *Masumi Kishi, Toaki University.* **Interest Rate Determination in Asian Economies: A Multicountry Model,** *Kanhaya L. Gupta, University of Alberta.* **On the First Family Home Purchase in Korea: A Lifecylce Approach,** *Bong Joon Yoon, State University of New York.*

JAI PRESS INC.
55 Old Post Road - No. 2
P.O. Box 1678
Greenwich, Connecticut 06836-1678
Tel: 203-661-7602